Download Disability Listings on Nolo.com

To download the disability listings, go to this book's companion page at:

 www.nolo.com/back-of-book/QSS.html

Checking the companion page is a good way
to stay informed on topics related to this book.

More Resources
from Nolo.com

Legal Forms, Books, & Software
Hundreds of do-it-yourself products—all written in plain English,
approved, and updated by our in-house legal editors.

Legal Articles
Get informed with thousands of free articles on everyday legal
topics. Our articles are accurate, up to date, and reader friendly.

Find a Lawyer
Want to talk to a lawyer? Use Nolo to find a lawyer who can
help you with your case.

NOLO
LAW for ALL

12th Edition

Nolo's Guide to Social Security Disability

Getting & Keeping Your Benefits

David A. Morton III, M.D.

TWELFTH EDITION	MARCH 2024
Editors	BETHANY LAURENCE
	DIANA CHAIKIN
Cover & Book Design	SUSAN PUTNEY
Proofreading	MARTHA C. BENCO
Index	UNGER INDEXING
Printing	SHERIDAN

Names: Morton, David A., 1945- author.

Title: Nolo's guide to social security disability : getting & keeping your benefits / David A. Morton III, M.D.

Other titles: Guide to social security disability

Description: Twelfth edition. | El Segundo, CA : Nolo, 2024. | Includes index.

Identifiers: LCCN 2023024963 | ISBN 9781413331646 (paperback) | ISBN 9781413331653 (ebook)

Subjects: LCSH: Disability insurance--United States--Handbooks, manuals, etc. | Social security--United States--Handbooks, manuals, etc.

Classification: LCC HD7105.25.U6 M675 2024 | DDC 368.38/600973--dc23/eng/20231207

LC record available at https://lccn.loc.gov/2023024963

This book covers only United States law, unless it specifically states otherwise.

Please note

Accurate, plain-English legal information can help you solve many of your own legal problems. But this text is not a substitute for personalized advice from a knowledgeable lawyer. If you want the help of a trained professional—and we'll always point out situations in which we think that's a good idea—consult an attorney licensed to practice in your state.

MH Sub I, LLC dba Nolo, 909 N. Pacific Coast Hwy, 11th Fl, El Segundo, CA 90245

Dedication

To my mother, Mary E. Morton, and to my wife, Mary L. Morton.

Acknowledgments

I would like to thank Nolo founder Ralph "Jake" Warner for seeing the need for a book on Social Security disability that can be read and used by ordinary people. I would also like to thank former Nolo editors Robin Leonard, Steve Elias, and Spencer Sherman for helping to take difficult and complex areas of law and make them accessible to the general public. Thank you also to Nolo editors Ilona Bray, Cathy Caputo, Janet Portman, Bethany Laurence, and Diana Chaikin.

About the Author

David A. Morton has degrees in psychology (B.A.) and medicine (M.D.). For 14 years, he was a consultant for disability determination to the Social Security Administration in Arkansas. He was chief medical consultant for eight years of that time. In that capacity, he hired, trained, supervised, and evaluated the work of medical doctors and clinical psychologists in determining mental disability claims. He also supervised medical disability determinations of physical disorders and personally made determinations of both physical and mental disorders in adults and children in every specialty of disability medicine. Since 1983, Dr. Morton has authored several books on Social Security disability used by attorneys and federal judges.

Table of Contents

Appendixes

Medical Listing Table of Contents

Download the Medical Listings at **www.nolo.com/back-of-book/QSS.html**

Introduction: Your Social Security Disability Companion

This book is about Social Security and Supplemental Security Income (SSI) disability benefits, which are provided through a U.S. government system run by the Social Security Administration (SSA). These disability programs provide cash support for individuals with mental or physical disorders who can't work because of the severity of their conditions. In some cases, dependents can receive benefits as well. This book is useful for anyone who:

- is injured or ill and wants to know if they're eligible for disability benefits
- wants to apply for disability benefits
- wants to appeal a decision denying disability benefits
- is already receiving disability benefits and wants to know how to protect their benefits during periodic reviews of their condition, or
- is helping an adult or child apply for or keep current benefits.

The SSA uses two systems to distribute disability payments:

- Social Security Disability Insurance (SSDI), for workers who have paid into the Social Security trust fund (and for their dependents), and
- Supplemental Security Income (SSI), for disabled individuals with limited incomes and assets.

It's easy to become overwhelmed at the thought of applying for disability benefits. The SSA is one of the world's largest bureaucracies; its regulations, rules, operating policies, and guidelines fill reams of paper. For example, one chapter of the SSA's operating manual is about 20,000 pages long. And much of this information changes over time.

Still, it's very possible to apply for, receive, and keep disability benefits with the help you'll find here. We recognize, however, that people applying for disability benefits are often ill or injured in a way that makes it difficult to accomplish the tasks of daily life, let alone pursue a claim for support from the government. So you may need help beyond this book. We've included an entire chapter on what to do if you need legal assistance (Chapter 15). Also, throughout the book, we've noted situations in which you might need the advice and support of a family member, trusted friend, paid representative, or attorney.

Medical and Legal Questions

When deciding on your disability claim, the SSA considers both legal and medical issues. Social Security officials review your claim to decide whether you're medically and financially entitled to the benefits you request. They also request and review medical opinions on your condition to see if it's severe enough to make you disabled. The SSA considers you disabled only if you're not able to work in your current or most recent job and you don't have the education, experience, or ability to do any other job. For example, a physically disabled 60-year-old nurse might have the ability to work at a desk job in the medical industry and could be denied benefits for that reason. But the same nurse couldn't work as a field laborer picking fruit all day because he wouldn't have the physical ability necessary for the job.

Chapters 1 through 15 lead you through the legal and practical issues of applying for disability payments, appealing if you're denied, and making sure that you retain benefits as long as you need them. For most applicants, it will be useful to read all of these chapters in the order presented. But if you have a particular issue to research (for example, you want to file an appeal), you can start with any chapter and you'll be directed to important information in other parts of the book as needed. Also note that we occasionally give you references to the Social Security portions of the Code of Federal Regulations (C.F.R.) or to the federal laws, the U.S. Code (U.S.C.).

Medical Listings

Information about the requirements and functionally disabling aspects of more than 200 specific medical problems that make individuals eligible for disability payments is available on Nolo's website (free for readers of this book) at:

www.nolo.com/back-of-book/QSS.html
The downloadable files contain descriptions of the medical conditions that are included in the SSA's Listing of Impairments.

Go to Nolo's page and start with the table of contents for these listings—once you find the section that matches or most closely approximates your disability, you'll find all the medical information you need to determine whether your disability meets the requirements to obtain benefits. For example, if you suffer from kidney disease, you will open Part 6 and read through the listings there until you find a disorder that matches or is similar to your illness.

Each section of the Medical Listings begins with a list of medical definitions in plain English related to the disorders discussed in that section. Next, you'll find general background information about the disorders discussed in that section. Finally, each section lists specific medical disorders taken from the official Listing of Impairments that the SSA uses in disability claims. The number before each listing is the official number the SSA uses to identify the disability. Following the numbers is a brief discussion of the meaning of Social Security's criteria and how to interpret each listing.

These Medical Listings contain every listing the SSA has approved for disability claims. We've revised the SSA's wording of the listings to make them more understandable. Rest assured, however, that we haven't made any changes that would compromise their legal meaning.

Also included for each condition are comments about what the SSA calls

How Claims Are Decided

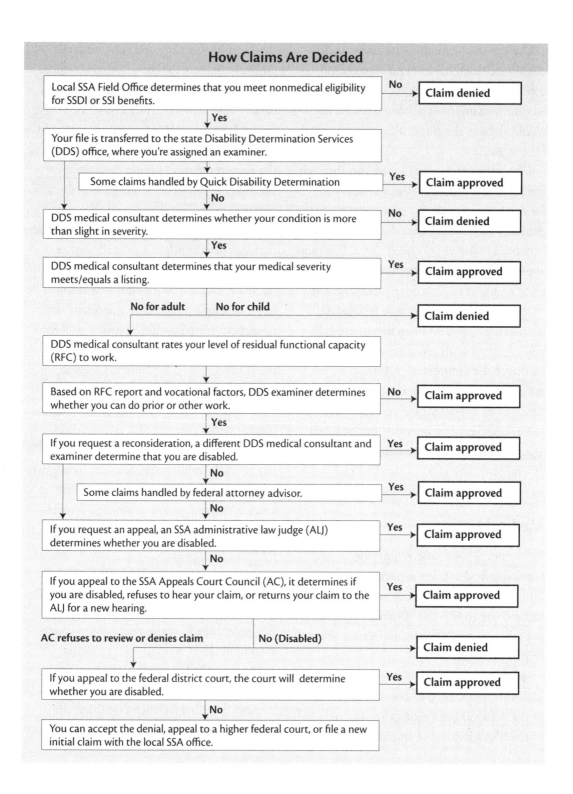

Local SSA Field Office determines that you meet nonmedical eligibility for SSDI or SSI benefits. →**No**→ **Claim denied**

↓ **Yes**

Your file is transferred to the state Disability Determination Services (DDS) office, where you're assigned an examiner.

↓

Some claims handled by Quick Disability Determination →**Yes**→ **Claim approved**

↓ **No**

DDS medical consultant determines whether your condition is more than slight in severity. →**No**→ **Claim denied**

↓ **Yes**

DDS medical consultant determines that your medical severity meets/equals a listing. →**Yes**→ **Claim approved**

No for adult   **No for child** → **Claim denied**

↓

DDS medical consultant rates your level of residual functional capacity (RFC) to work.

↓

Based on RFC report and vocational factors, DDS examiner determines whether you can do prior or other work. →**No**→ **Claim approved**

↓ **Yes**

If you request a reconsideration, a different DDS medical consultant and examiner determine that you are disabled. →**Yes**→ **Claim approved**

↓ **No**

Some claims handled by federal attorney advisor. →**Yes**→ **Claim approved**

↓ **No**

If you request an appeal, an SSA administrative law judge (ALJ) determines whether you are disabled. →**Yes**→ **Claim approved**

↓ **No**

If you appeal to the SSA Appeals Court Council (AC), it determines if you are disabled, refuses to hear your claim, or returns your claim to the ALJ for a new hearing. →**Yes**→ **Claim approved**

AC refuses to review or denies claim   **No (Disabled)** → **Claim denied**

↓

If you appeal to the federal district court, the court will determine whether you are disabled. →**Yes**→ **Claim approved**

↓ **No**

You can accept the denial, appeal to a higher federal court, or file a new initial claim with the local SSA office.

residual functional capacity (RFC). This is a type of rating given to a disability claimant (applicant) who doesn't meet the requirements of a listing. The RFC says what kind of work a claimant could do, even considering their impairments. If no work is available anywhere in the United States that's suitable for someone with the claimant's RFC, the claimant could be approved for disability payments.

Quick Disability Determination (QDD)

The Quick Disability Determination (QDD) process is a quicker disability determination process for those who are obviously disabled (with, for example, metastatic cancer, severe blindness, profound intellectual disability, severe kidney failure requiring dialysis, and the inability to walk—to name a few possibilities). Favorable decisions will be made in such cases within a month after the claim is received by the state Disability Determination Servies (DDS) agency. The average time is about 25 days, but many people get a response on a QDD claim within two weeks. See Chapter 6 for more information about QDD.

CAUTION
Throughout this book, you will see samples of Social Security Administration forms. These samples are to help you fill out the actual forms. But the SSA requires that you obtain the blank forms from a Social Security office in person, by mail, or from the SSA website (www.ssa.gov). Throughout the book, we tell you where to locate the forms you need.

Get Alerts and More Online

If there are important changes to the information in this book, we'll post them online, on a page dedicated to this book: www.nolo.com/back-of-book/QSS.html You'll find the downloadable Medical Listings there as well.

What Is Social Security Disability?

The Social Security Administration (SSA) decides who is eligible for disability payments under rules established in the Social Security Act by Congress. In this chapter, we describe the two main programs for disability payments that the SSA administers. We briefly explain the requirements that any claimant must meet to receive benefits. We also provide tips on how to deal with the SSA bureaucracy and include answers to some of the most frequently asked questions about Social Security disability.

A. Two Different Programs

Once you qualify as disabled under the Social Security Act, the SSA makes disability payments under one of two programs:

- Social Security Disability Insurance (SSDI), for workers who have paid into the Social Security trust fund (and their dependents), or
- Supplemental Security Income (SSI), for disabled individuals with limited incomes and assets.

SSDI claims are also referred to as *Title 2 claims* because they're authorized under Title 2 of the Social Security Act. SSI claims may be referred to as *Title 16 claims* because they're authorized under Title 16 of the Social Security Act. A person applying for disability benefits is called a *claimant*. Some applications are for both Title 2 and Title 16 benefits. These are known as *concurrent claims*.

When the SSA receives your application, it will determine whether you're eligible for disability benefits under SSDI, SSI, or both, even if you haven't specified more than one program on your application. This means that if you apply only for SSDI benefits, Social Security will automatically process your claim for any SSI disability benefits to which you might be entitled. If your SSDI claim is turned down, you don't have to file another claim for possible SSI benefits.

1. Social Security Disability Insurance

SSDI provides payments to workers who have made contributions to the Social Security trust fund through the Social Security tax on their earnings. SSDI is also available to certain dependents of workers. If you're found eligible for SSDI, you might be entitled to retroactive (past due) benefits if you can show that you were disabled before the date of your application. (See Chapter 10 for more details on when benefits begin.)

a. Who Qualifies?

To qualify for SSDI, you must fall into one of the two following categories.

i. You're a disabled insured worker under full retirement age

You can apply for SSDI up to one year before your full retirement age. Full retirement age is gradually changing. Currently, the full retirement age is 66 years for those born between 1943 and 1955. By 2027, full

Comparing SSDI and SSI		
	SSDI (Title 2)	SSI (Title 16)
Must have paid Social Security tax to qualify?	Yes	No
Disability benefits for children?	Only adult children at least 18 years of age and disabled before age 22	Children of any age
Waiting period before benefits begin?	Adults: 5 months Children: none	No
Health insurance comes with disability award?	Yes, Medicare starts 24 months after waiting period.	Yes, Medicaid starts immediately in most states.
Can be presumed disabled before actual approval of benefits?	No	Yes, up to six months before decision. Claimant does not have to return payments if found not disabled.
Retroactive benefits?	Yes, up to 12 months	No
Minimum duration of disability?	12 months	12 months. (Blind claimants are exempt from duration requirement.)
What financial factors may prevent eligibility for benefits?	Substantial gainful activity: Work earning more than $1,550/month ($2,590/month if blind) in 2024	a. Substantial gainful activity b. Having more than $2,000 in countable resources ($3,000 for couples)
Benefits to noncitizens in United States?	Yes	Generally not, but some exceptions
Possible freeze on earnings?	Yes	No
Benefits for past period of disability (*closed period*), even if not currently disabled?	Yes	Yes
Auxiliary benefits to others available on the work earnings of a relative or spouse?	Yes	No
Benefits continued during a period of trial work?	Yes	Yes
Quick reentitlement to benefits if work effort fails after termination of benefits?	Yes	Yes
Benefits outside of United States?	Yes, both U.S. citizens and noncitizens	Generally not for U.S. citizens; never for noncitizens

retirement age will be 67 years for everyone born in 1960 or later. You can find your exact retirement age online at www.ssa.gov/benefits/retirement/planner/ageincrease.html.

To qualify for SSDI benefits, you must have worked both long enough and recently enough. If too much time has elapsed since you last worked and paid Social Security taxes, you might not be eligible. The law requires that you earn a certain number of work credits in a specified time before you can qualify for SSDI. You can earn up to four credits per year, each credit representing three months. The amount of earnings required for a credit increases each year as general wage levels rise. For example, in 2023, one work credit was equivalent to $1,640 in covered earnings. In 2024, the amount is $1,730.

The number of work credits you need to qualify for disability benefits depends on how old you are when you become disabled. Most people need at least 20 credits earned over ten years, ending with the year they become disabled. Younger workers may qualify with fewer credits.

In effect, you count backwards from the year that you became disabled to see whether you have the appropriate number of credits. That means that credits from many years before you became disabled are automatically wiped out, or expire. This can lead to trouble for people who haven't worked for many years before they became

disabled. Their credits might dip below the required amount, and they can lose eligibility for SSDI. The date after which they lose their eligibility is called the *date last insured* (DLI)—an important date, and often a subject of dispute in Social Security disability claims. If you think your DLI is too far in the past to qualify you for SSDI, talk to your local Social Security Field Office to make sure. The SSA will have better detailed earnings records with more specific calculations about the exact date of your DLI, so you might still qualify.

Here are the rules for the number of work credits you need based on your age.

- **Before age 24.** You'll need at least six credits earned in the three-year period ending when your disability started.
- **Age 24 to 31**. The amount of credits you'll need must reflect that you've worked at least half the time between age 21 and the time you become disabled. For example, if you become disabled at age 27, you would need credit for three years of work (12 credits) during the six years between ages 21 and 27.
- **Age 31 or older.** In general, you'll need the number of work credits shown in the chart below. Unless you're blind (see Part 2 of the Medical Listings on Nolo.com for definitions of legal blindness), at least 20 of the credits must have been earned in the ten years immediately before you became disabled.

Age of Disability Onset	Credits needed
31 through 42	20
44	22
46	24
48	26
50	28
52	30
54	32
56	34
58	36
60	38
62 or older	40

TIP

You can find out how many credits you have by contacting your local SSA office or, if you have access to the internet, by looking at your Social Security Statement at www.ssa.gov/mystatement.

ii. You are the family member of an eligible worker

The SSA pays *auxiliary benefits* (also called *dependents benefits*) to people who qualify for SSDI based on a family member's entitlement to Social Security retirement or disability benefits. Auxiliary benefits are based on the earnings record of the insured worker who paid Social Security taxes. If you qualify for auxiliary benefits, you don't necessarily have to be disabled. You also don't need to have the work credits described above.

Spouse's and divorced spouse's benefits. To qualify for auxiliary benefits as a spouse or divorced spouse, one of the following must apply (42 U.S.C. § 402(b), (c), (e), (f); 20 C.F.R. §§ 404.330–349):

- You're at least 62 years old, you've been the spouse of a disabled worker for at least one year, and you aren't entitled to a retirement or disability insurance benefit that is half or more of your spouse's benefit.
- You're the ex-spouse of a disabled worker who is entitled to benefits, you're 62 years old or older, and you were married to the worker for at least ten years.
- You're the ex-spouse of a worker insured under SSDI who has not filed a claim for benefits, you're age 62 or older, your former spouse is age 62 or older, you were married for at least ten years, and you've been divorced for at least two years.
- You're a disabled widow or widower, at least 50 years old but younger than 60, and you're the surviving spouse or ex-spouse of a worker who received Social Security disability or retirement benefits.
- You're the surviving spouse or ex-spouse of a deceased insured worker, and you're at least 60 years old.

- You're the surviving spouse or ex-spouse of a deceased insured worker, and you care for a child of the deceased who either is younger than 16 or has been disabled since before age 22. (These benefits are known as *mother's or father's benefits*.)

Child's benefits. A dependent, unmarried child is entitled to child's insurance benefits on the Social Security record of an insured parent, or deceased parent who was insured at death, if any of the following apply (42 U.S.C. § 402(d); 20 C.F.R. §§ 404.350–369):

- The child is younger than 18.
- The child is age 18 or 19 and a full-time student.
- The child is an adult and has been disabled since before age 22.

(See Chapter 3 for a more detailed discussion of benefits for children.)

Parent's benefits. You might qualify for parent's benefits if you meet all of the following requirements (42 U.S.C. § 402(h); 20 C.F.R. §§ 404.370–374):

- Your child was an insured worker who died.
- You're at least 62 years old.
- You're divorced, widowed, or unmarried and have not married since your child's death.
- You were receiving at least one-half of your support from your child at the time of death.
- You can provide evidence of this support within two years of the death (you may be exempt from providing

evidence if unusual circumstances, such as extended illness, mental or physical incapacity, or language barrier, show that you could not have reasonably known of the two-year rule).

Lump-sum death benefits. A lump-sum death payment of several hundred dollars may be paid to the surviving spouse of an insured worker if the survivor was living in the same household as the deceased at the time of death. You must apply for this benefit within two years of the insured worker's death. (42 U.S.C. § 402(i); 20 C.F.R. §§ 404.390–395.)

b. Citizenship or Residency Requirements

If you qualify for SSDI based on the criteria listed above, you may receive SSDI payments if you are a U.S. citizen or permanent resident, living in the United States or abroad. If you're neither a citizen nor a permanent resident, you still may be entitled to receive SSDI if you can show that you are lawfully present in the United States and meet certain other criteria. (8 U.S.C. § 1611(b)(2).)

If you're a citizen when you apply for SSDI, you'll have to show proof of your citizenship. Acceptable forms of proof include a birth certificate showing that you were born in:

- the United States
- Puerto Rico on or after January 13, 1941
- Guam
- the U.S. Virgin Islands after 1917
- American Samoa

- Swains Island, or
- the Northern Mariana Islands.

Any of the following documents will also satisfy the proof of citizenship requirement:

- Forms N-550 and N-570, *Certificate of Naturalization*, issued by U.S. Citizenship and Immigration Services (USCIS) or its predecessor, the Immigration and Naturalization Service (INS)
- U.S. passport issued by the U.S. State Department
- Form I-197, *U.S. Citizen Identification Card*, issued by USCIS or the INS
- Form FS-240, *Consular Report of Birth Abroad of a Citizen of the U.S.*, issued by the U.S. State Department
- Form FS-545, *Certification of Birth*, issued by a foreign service post
- Forms N-560 and N-561, *Certificate of Citizenship*, issued by USCIS or the INS
- Form DS-1350, *Certificate of Report of Birth*, issued by the U.S. State Department

In some cases, other forms of identification will be valid to establish citizenship, like evidence of membership in certain Indian tribes (such as American Indian Card I-872 for the Kickapoo Indian Tribe). Another example is Northern Mariana Card I-873 (INS card for birth in the Northern Mariana Islands before 1986).

If you're not sure whether your documents are sufficient to establish citizenship, contact your local Social Security Field Office.

If you're a permanent resident or resident alien, you will have to show that you are lawfully in the United States under one of the following conditions:

- you have lawful admission for permanent residence (LPR, or green card status)
- you were admitted as a refugee or were granted conditional entrance as a refugee
- you have asylum status or a pending application for political asylum
- you've been paroled into the United States for at least a year
- you have a withholding of removal from the United States or a pending application for withholding of removal
- you're a member of a class of aliens permitted to remain in the United States for humanitarian or other public policy reasons, or
- you've been battered or subjected to cruelty by a family member while in the United States.

Most foreign workers in the United States are covered under the U.S. Social Security program and can potentially qualify for disability benefits. If you are neither a citizen nor a permanent resident, you still may be covered under SSDI. Federal law generally requires that all workers pay Social Security taxes and, therefore, be covered under SSDI for services performed in the United States. This is true even for workers who aren't resident aliens or employees who work here for short periods.

International Social Security Agreements

The United States has entered into several international Social Security agreements called *totalization agreements*, which have two major purposes. First, they eliminate dual Social Security taxation, which occurs when a citizen or national of one country works in another country and is required to pay Social Security taxes to both countries on the same earnings. Second, the agreements help fill gaps in benefit protection for workers who have divided their careers between the United States and another country. The United States has totalization agreements with Australia, Austria, Belgium, Brazil, Canada, Chile, Czech Republic, Denmark, Finland, France, Germany, Greece, Hungary, Iceland, Ireland, Italy, Japan, Luxembourg, Netherlands, Norway, Poland, Portugal, Slovakia, Slovenia, South Korea, Spain, Sweden, Switzerland, the United Kingdom, and Uruguay. (42 U.S.C. § 433.) (See Chapter 13 for a more complete list and discussion of international agreements.)

There are a few exceptions, however. Some nonimmigrant foreign students and exchange visitors temporarily working in the United States may be exempt from paying Social Security taxes and, therefore, wouldn't qualify for disability benefits under SSDI if they become disabled.

Noncitizen or permanent residents of the United States who are entitled to SSDI might be paid benefits while they reside abroad, depending upon their citizenship status and the countries in which they live. However, with some exceptions, non-residents of the United States (alien beneficiaries) who leave the United States must return to the United States at least every 30 days or for 30 consecutive days during each six-month period to continue drawing benefits.

One exception is made for alien beneficiaries who are on active military duty for the United States. Another exception exists for alien beneficiaries who live in and are citizens of Germany, Greece, Ireland, Israel, Italy, or Japan. The United States has treaty obligations with these nations to continue paying benefits regardless of how long beneficiaries are outside the United States. Citizens of the Netherlands may receive partial benefits. (See Chapter 13 for more information about receiving benefits outside of the United States.)

 CAUTION
Be aware of restricted countries.
There are a few countries where residents can't receive benefits even if they otherwise qualify. These include:

- Azerbaijan
- Belarus
- Cuba
- Kazakhstan
- Kyrgyzstan
- Moldova
- North Korea
- Tajikistan
- Turkmenistan, and
- Uzbekistan.

c. SSDI Payments

If you're eligible for Social Security Disability Insurance (SSDI) benefits, the amount you receive each month will be based on your average lifetime earnings. Your benefit isn't based on how severe your disability is or how much income you have. However, if you're receiving disability payments from other sources, as discussed below, your payment may be reduced.

The SSA recognizes that, if your income has declined between the period when you worked and when you stopped working full time because of your disability, you're usually better off having your earnings "frozen" in order to reflect your higher income before you became disabled. Therefore, the SSA excludes low-income years of earnings resulting from a period of disability from its benefit calculations, unless it's to your financial advantage to include those years. (42 U.S.C. §§ 423(a), 426(b)(f); 20 C.F.R. § 404.320.)

(SSDI payments are discussed in more detail in Chapter 13.)

2. Supplemental Security Income

The SSI program provides payments to adults or children who are disabled and have limited income and resources. If your income and resources are too high, you'll be turned down for SSI benefits no matter how severe your medical disorders are, and regardless of whether you qualify for SSDI.

Figuring out exactly what counts as income and resources under the SSI threshold is complicated. Although the most important points are covered here, only a Social Security representative can accurately determine your income and resources for the purpose of qualifying for SSI.

a. Income Limits

To qualify for SSI, your monthly income—as counted by Social Security—can't exceed the *federal benefit rate* (also known as the SSI Federal Payment Standard). The federal benefit rate is set by law and increases annually as dictated by cost-of-living adjustments. For 2024, the federal benefit rate (FBR) is $943 per month for individuals and $1,415 for couples.

If only one member of a couple is eligible for SSI, both spouses' income is still considered when determining whether the income limit is met (with some deductions allowed). Children younger than 18 who apply for SSI and are living with their parents will have their parents' income considered, also with some deductions allowed.

The federal benefit rate sets both the SSI income limit and the maximum federal SSI payment. However, the maximum federal benefit may be supplemented with an extra payment by every state except Arizona, Arkansas, Mississippi, North Dakota, Tennessee, and West Virginia. (The U.S. territory of the Northern Mariana Islands also doesn't pay an SSI supplement.) In all other states, the allowed SSI income level (and the SSI payments) might be higher than the federal maximums. And in California, Iowa, Massachusetts, and Nevada, the state supplements are higher for blind recipients than for others.

Although the amount of the state supplement varies widely, it can be as much as several hundred dollars or as little as $10. The exact amount of the state supplement depends on your marital status and your living arrangements (such as whether you live alone, in somebody else's home, or in a Medicaid facility).

The SSA doesn't count the following income and benefits when calculating your income level:

- $20 per month of income except wages
- $65 per month of wages and one-half of wages over $65
- food stamps, and
- home energy or housing assistance.

(See Chapter 13 for more detailed information on income limitations.)

b. Resource Limits

In addition to the income limits, in order to qualify for SSI, you can't have more than a certain amount in total resources. Social Security defines a resource as cash or another asset that can be converted to cash and used for your support. If you or your spouse has the right to sell a particular piece of property and keep the proceeds, it will be considered a resource.

Resources are categorized as either *liquid or nonliquid*. Liquid resources include cash and other assets that could be converted to cash within 20 working days. The most common types of liquid resources are savings and checking accounts, stocks, bonds, mutual funds, promissory notes, and certain types of life insurance. Nonliquid resources can't be converted to cash within 20 working days. They include both real estate (land) and personal property. The SSA may consider some resources to be both liquid and nonliquid (such as an automobile or life insurance policy).

Conditional Payments

Even if you don't qualify for SSI benefits due to your resource levels, you might be entitled to conditional payments—in essence, a loan. This happens when you're disabled and your resources are above the SSI resource limits, but they include nonliquid assets that may take months for you to convert into cash in order to use as support. In that situation, the SSA will make conditional payments to you until you sell your nonliquid assets and can support yourself. You still won't be eligible for regular SSI benefits, however, and at the end of the conditional payment period, you must refund to the SSA the amount you received.

ABLE Accounts

The Achieving a Better Life Experience (ABLE) Act allows people with disabilities to create special savings accounts in which funds of up to $100,000 don't count as assets for the purpose of SSI (or Medicaid). In order to qualify for an ABLE account, you must have a disabling condition that began before age 26. The funds in the ABLE account can be spent only on qualified disability-related expenses, which include:

- health care, including assistive technology and personal support services (such as home health aides)
- housing
- transportation
- employment training
- education expenses
- financial management, and
- basic living expenses.

Not all states offer ABLE accounts, but some states' ABLE programs are available to other states' residents.

The SSI resource limits are set by Congress, You won't be eligible for SSI disability payments if your assets exceed:

- $2,000 for a single person, or
- $3,000 for a married couple (even if only one member is eligible for SSI).

If the resources limits seem low to you, you aren't alone—the SSI threshold levels were last updated in the 1980s. But in 2023, a bill called the SSI Savings Penalty Elimination Act (S. 2767) was introduced in the Senate that, if passed, would raise the asset caps to $10,000 for individuals and $20,000 for couples. Those limits would then be indexed to inflation moving forward.

The SSA isn't allowed to count certain assets toward the limit, including the following:

- your home (including adjacent land and related buildings), regardless of how much it's worth, as long as it's owned by you or your spouse and used as your principal residence
- restricted allotted Indian lands
- household goods and personal effects
- one wedding ring and one engagement ring of any value
- necessary health aids, such as a wheelchair or prosthetic device
- one automobile, regardless of value, if used to provide necessary transportation, but if not used for that purpose, then one automobile up to $4,500 in value
- money in an ABLE account, up to $100,000 (see the discussion of ABLE accounts above.)
- grants, scholarships, fellowships, or gifts used to pay tuition, fees, or other necessary educational expenses at an educational institution (including vocational or technical institution) for nine months beginning the month after the month the educational assistance was received
- nonbusiness property needed for support, up to a reasonable value

- life insurance with a face value of $1,500 or less
- burial plots and certain burial funds up to $1,500
- disaster relief
- any housing assistance paid under the U.S. Housing Act, the National Housing Act, or the Housing and Urban Development Act, and
- resources needed to fulfill an approved Plan for Achieving Self-Support (PASS). (See Chapter 13 for more information on PASS.)

c. Citizenship and Residency Requirements

SSI disability payments are usually available only to U.S. citizens. But there are several exceptions in which noncitizens might be eligible, including the scenarios listed below.

- You're a permanent resident (green card holder).
- During the first seven years after you were admitted to the United States, you are legally residing in the United States as a refugee, have been granted asylum, satisfy certain conditions of withheld deportation, have been granted status as a Cuban or Haitian entrant, or (under some conditions) entered as an Amerasian immigrant. (8 U.S.C. § 1612(a)(2)(A)(i)(I–V).)
- You've been battered or subjected to cruelty in the United States by a family member. (See Public Law 104-193, the Personal Responsibility and Work Opportunity Reconciliation Act of

1996, as amended by Public Law 104-208, the Illegal Immigration Reform and Immigrant Responsibility Act of 1996, and Public Law. 105-33, the Balanced Budget Act of 1997.)

In addition, you must meet at least one of the following conditions:

- You're a permanent resident with 40 qualifying quarters of work. (Your spouse's or parent's work also might count for SSI eligibility purposes.)
- You're on active duty or were honorably discharged from the U.S. military, or you're the spouse, unmarried dependent child, or unmarried surviving spouse of a veteran or person on active duty. (8 U.S.C. § 1612(a)(2)(C)(i–iii).)
- You were lawfully residing in the United States and receiving SSI benefits on August 22, 1996. (8 U.S.C. § 1612(a)(2)(E).)
- You were lawfully residing in the United States on August 22, 1996 and you are blind or otherwise became disabled at any time. (8 U.S.C. § 1612(a)(2)(F).)
- You're lawfully residing in the United States and are a Native American born in Canada. (8 U.S.C. § 1612(a)(2)(G).)

 SEE AN EXPERT

Exceptions to the residency require-ments often involve complex legal issues. If you think an exception might apply to you, your best bet would be to consult an attorney, preferably one knowledgeable in the areas of immigration and Social Security.

d. Receiving Benefits When Outside of the United States

SSI payments are generally only available to people residing in the 50 states, the District of Columbia, or the Northern Mariana Islands. If you're receiving SSI disability benefits and you leave the United States for 30 days or more, Social Security will stop your payments. For example, if you receive SSI disability benefits and move to Mexico or Puerto Rico, you will lose those benefits. There are a few exceptions for some U.S. citizen children and students:

- A blind or disabled child may be eligible for SSI benefits while outside the United States if the child is a U.S. citizen, lives with a parent who is a member of the U.S. Armed Forces assigned to permanent duty outside the United States, and was eligible to receive SSI benefits in the month before the parent reported for duty abroad.
- A student of any age may be eligible for SSI benefits while temporarily outside the United States for the purpose of engaging in studies not available in the U.S., sponsored by an educational institution in the U.S., and designed to enhance the student's ability to engage in gainful employment. The student must have been eligible to receive SSI benefits in the month preceding their first full month abroad.

B. Defining Disability

Social Security's definition of disability for adults means being unable to engage in any substantial gainful activity (SGA) (in other words, full-time work) because of a *medically determinable* physical or mental impairment. The disabling impairment must last for a continuous period of at least 12 months or be expected to result in death.

For children, the definition is slightly different. As with disabled adults, disabled children must have a medically determinable physical or mental impairment that lasts for a continuous period of at least a year or is expected to result in death. But children don't need to show that they can't work to be considered disabled. Instead, they need to show that their impairment causes *marked* and severe functional limitations.

Let's break these concepts down further.

1. Inability to Engage in Substantial Gainful Activity

Substantial gainful activity (SGA) is what Social Security considers full-time work. If you earn more than a certain amount of money (the SGA threshold), then Social Security won't consider you disabled. In 2024, the SGA amount for nonblind people is $1,550 per month. For blind people, the 2024 amount is $2,590 per month.

The SGA amount changes every year. If you ever need to find out the SGA income limit for a given year, simply call a local SSA office or check the SSA's website. (See Section C, below.)

Even if you have a severe medical impairment, you won't qualify for SSDI or SSI if you earn more than the SGA level. It doesn't matter if you earn the entire SGA amount in one week and can't work for the rest of the month—Social Security can't find you disabled.

If you worked recently, either before or after applying for disability, in some circumstances, Social Security might consider part or all of your work to be what's called an *unsuccessful work attempt*. You must be able to show that your medical condition became worse so that you could no longer work or that special help you required to do your job was no longer available.

For example, say you held a job for several months but had to stop working again because of your medical problems. If you don't have a medical reason why you stopped working, your earnings won't count as an unsuccessful work attempt.

Keep in mind that SGA refers only to money you obtain from working, not money you obtain from other sources (such as investments or gifts).

2. Medically Determinable Impairment

A medically determinable physical or mental impairment is any illness, disorder, or condition that results from abnormalities in the structure or function of the body or brain and that can be proven by medically acceptable techniques. The Social Security Act requires that a physical or mental impairment be established by medical evidence consisting of signs (objective findings by a medical provider), symptoms (subjective complaints by you), and laboratory findings or clinical diagnostic techniques.

In other words, the SSA must be able to determine that you have something wrong with you, either physically or mentally.

To help make such a determination, the SSA can ask to examine your treating doctor's records and your hospital records, order X-rays or other tests as needed, and have you examined by a consulting doctor. Subjective symptoms (such as pain) are important, but aren't enough to get you benefits by themselves. They must be linked to some physical or mental problem. Any statements you make about your symptoms have to be supported by medical evidence showing that your physical or mental condition could reasonably cause the symptoms you say you have.

 MEDICAL LISTINGS
Remember: The Medical Listings are on Nolo's website. (See Appendix D for the link.) Parts 1 through 14 contain the Listing of Impairments, which includes helpful details about the kinds of diagnostic techniques and laboratory results the SSA looks for to determine whether your impairment is disabling.

Pain and Other Symptoms

Your pain and symptoms are important parts of your disability claim. SSA staff frequently hand out forms that allow you to describe your pain and symptoms in your own words. For example, you might be asked to say where you have pain, what it feels like, what activities cause it or make it worse, and how long it lasts. In addition, you might be asked what medications you are taking and what side effects they may be causing. In fact, you should be asked these questions at some point during the claims process because federal law requires that the SSA consider your allegations of pain and other symptoms in reaching a decision. (Pain and other symptoms are discussed more fully in Chapter 5.)

3. Duration of Disability

The SSA doesn't pay disability benefits for temporary conditions. You'll need to show that your impairment has lasted (or will last) for at least 12 continuous months or will result in your death. The 12-month duration requirement doesn't mean that you must have been severely ill for a year before applying for benefits, just that you don't expect to recover for at least one year. For example, most bone fractures heal in several months, and therefore are unlikely to meet the duration requirement. But if you have a complex fracture that needs several surgeries and lengthy physical therapy to repair,

Social Security may expect you to take longer than 12 months to heal.

For some very severe impairments, the SSA can make an immediate disability determination. For example, if your spinal cord were to be crushed in an automobile accident, it would be highly unlikely that you'd be able to walk again. The SSA doesn't need to wait to see if you get better before approving your claim (assuming you otherwise qualify).

When it comes to determining whether an impairment is likely to result in death, the SSA provides little guidance. Some cancer prognoses include a median life expectancy of 36 months. (See Part 13 of the Medical Listings on Nolo's website for more on cancer listings.) The SSA sometimes uses median life expectancies when determining whether noncancer disabilities might result in death. These estimates can be difficult to make and require medical knowledge.

Many people apply for disability after acute injuries or impairments without knowing how long symptoms from these conditions are going to last. Even if you're not sure when (if ever) your disorder will improve, consider applying for benefits, especially if you're 50 years of age or older. Older people don't need to be as severely impaired as people younger than 50 do for the SSA to award them benefits.

You can ask your doctor how long you can expect your impairment to last, but ultimately it will be up to the SSA to decide whether you meet the minimum duration requirement of 12 months. In some cases, the SSA might think your impairment will last long enough, even if your doctor doesn't.

There is one exception to the durational requirement: SSI claims based on blindness don't need to show that they're expected to last for 12 months.

C. Contacting the Social Security Administration

The SSA maintains over 1,200 local offices across the country where you can apply for Social Security and SSI benefits.

You can also:

- check on your earnings record
- enroll in health insurance
- receive assistance in applying for food stamps
- get information about your rights and obligations under the law, and
- obtain forms you need to apply for or maintain benefits or appeal SSA decisions.

There is no charge for these services. Employees of the SSA are public servants paid by your tax dollars. They are obligated to be helpful and courteous. If you encounter someone who is not helpful and courteous, ask to talk to a supervisor.

Supervisors are usually very interested in working out any problems, but if you feel you've been treated really badly, you can contact your local U.S. congressperson or senator. The SSA is very sensitive to public

relations, and it's in the agency's best interest to resolve any complaints that have merit.

Local Social Security offices (Field Offices) exist in every state. They're typically open between 9:00 a.m. and 4:00 p.m., Monday through Friday, although some of the smaller field offices may be closed on Wednesday afternoons. If you live far away from the city or town where your nearest field office is located, you might be able to meet a Social Security staff member at a "contact station" closer to you. In some cases, a Social Security representative might even be able to make a personal visit to your home.

The head of the entire agency is known as the Commissioner of Social Security. The commissioner's office, many administrative offices, and appellate operations are located in Baltimore. The SSA discourages visits to these central offices regarding individual claims because service can be better provided by local offices.

If you're denied SSDI or SSI, you can appeal that decision. (Appealing is discussed in Chapter 12.) The Office of Hearings Operations (OHO), formerly known as the Office of Disability Adjudication and Review, administers the entire hearings and appeals program for the SSA. Administrative law judges, located in major cities throughout the United States and its territories, hold hearings and issue decisions when a claimant appeals a determination. The Appeals Council, located in Falls Church, Virginia, can review hearing decisions.

You can reach a live service representative by calling the SSA hotline at 800-772-1213, Monday through Friday (except holidays), from 8:00 a.m. to 7:00 p.m. If you are deaf or hard of hearing, TTY service representatives are available during the same hours at 800-325-0778. All calls are confidential. If you call after hours, you can obtain prerecorded information on a variety of topics.

SSA representatives can direct you to the Social Security office nearest you, as well as answer numerous other questions. Once you have contacted your SSA field office, you'll deal with a local representative rather than using the national hotline.

The SSA's phone lines are busiest early in the week and early in the month. If your business can wait, call at other times. You can help speed up the process by having the following items handy when you call:

- your Social Security number
- a list of questions you want to ask
- any recent correspondence you received from the SSA, and
- a pencil and paper to write down information and answers to your questions. Always write down the date you called.

On the internet, you can find information about Social Security at www.ssa.gov.

D. Frequently Asked Questions About Social Security Disability

Following are some frequently asked questions about SSDI and SSI.

1. How Is the Disability Determination Made?

The SSA disability evaluation is a five-step evaluation process. For adults, this process requires step-by-step review of your current work activity, the severity of your impairment, your remaining physical and mental abilities, your past work, and your age, education, and work experience.

For children applying for SSI, the process requires sequential review of the child's current work activity (if any), the severity of the impairment, and an assessment of whether the impairment results in marked and severe functional limitations.

The sequential evaluation process is discussed in Chapter 7.

2. When Do Disability Benefits Start?

SSDI payments can't be made until five months after the onset date (beginning) of disability. SSDI claimants might be entitled to retroactive (past) benefits if the SSA determines that they were disabled before their application date. But cash benefit payments can't be paid retroactively to cover more than 12 months before the application date, even if your disability began well before that date.

There are some exceptions to the five-month waiting period requirement. These exceptions—along with more detailed information about the disability onset date—can be found in Chapter 10.

Under SSI, disability payments may begin as early as the first day of the month after an individual files an application, but no earlier. If your claim isn't approved until months after you apply, you'll be entitled to back payments to that date. In addition, under the SSI program, you may be found *presumptively disabled* and receive cash payments for up to six months while the formal disability determination is made. The presumptive payments are designed to allow needy claimants to meet their basic living expenses during the time it takes to process the application. Claimants who receive presumptive disability payments but end up having their application denied aren't required to refund the payments. (Presumptive disability is covered in Chapter 4.)

3. What If I Disagree With the Determination?

If you disagree with the SSA's initial disability determination, you can appeal the decision. The first appeal of a disability denial is called a *reconsideration*, which is a review of your case by a Disability Determination Services (DDS) team that wasn't involved in the original determination.

If your case is denied at the reconsideration stage, you can request a hearing before an administrative law judge. If you receive an unfavorable decision from a judge and wish to continue pursuing the case, you can request a review by the Appeals Council, and if you're denied review by the Appeals Council, you can file a civil lawsuit in federal district court. (Appeals are covered in Chapter 12.)

4. Can I Receive Disability Benefits or Payments While Getting Medicare or Medicaid Coverage?

Yes. Medicaid and Medicare are our country's two major government-run health insurance programs. Generally, people on SSI and other people with low incomes qualify for Medicaid, while Medicare coverage is earned by working in jobs covered by Social Security, in jobs covered by the Railroad Retirement Act, or for the federal government. Many people qualify for both. In most states, you don't have to do anything additional in order to obtain Medicare or Medicaid coverage once you qualify for disability—the federal government will send you any forms you need to fill out. This isn't true for Medicaid in all states, however. (See "SSI and Medicaid," below.)

SSDI and Medicare. SSDI recipients qualify for Medicare coverage. However, the coverage doesn't start for two years from the date of entitlement to disability benefits—and that means two years starting after the initial five-month waiting period. Therefore, you might be left without medical insurance coverage for several years if you don't have some other type of coverage or can't qualify for SSI Medicaid coverage.

There are three exceptions to the two-year rule:

- If you have end-stage renal disease with kidney failure and you require dialysis or a kidney transplant, Medicare coverage can begin the third month after the month in which dialysis began.
- If you're terminally ill with a life expectancy of six months or less and receive hospice care, Medicare coverage can begin immediately.
- If you have amyotrophic lateral sclerosis (ALS, or Lou Gehrig's disease), you can qualify for Medicare as soon as you begin collecting disability benefits.

If you receive Medicare and have a low income and few resources, your state may pay your Medicare premiums and (in some cases) other out-of-pocket Medicare expenses such as deductibles and coinsurance. Contact your state's department of social and health services, search for "Medicare Savings Programs" on www.medicare.gov, or read Nolo's book *Social Security, Medicare & Government Pensions* to learn more.

SSI and Medicaid. Most states allow SSI recipients to qualify automatically for Medicaid coverage. In states where SSI recipients automatically qualify, Medicaid coverage starts immediately. In a few states, eligibility for Medicaid isn't automatic when you receive SSI—you'll need to apply for Medicaid separately. Your local SSA office can tell you if you need to file a separate application for Medicaid. Or

you can call your state's medical assistance office for help applying. Call the Centers for Medicare and Medicaid Services at 800-633-4227 to get the telephone number of your state medical assistance office.

5. Can I Work and Still Receive Disability Benefits

Social Security allows people to test their ability to work without losing their rights to cash benefits and Medicare or Medicaid through certain work incentive programs. The rules are different for SSDI and SSI beneficiaries, but both can receive:

- ongoing cash benefits while working
- help with medical bills
- help with work expenses, or
- vocational training.

For more information about work incentives, see Chapter 13, Section D.

6. How Can I Receive Vocational Training Services?

The SSA sometimes refers disability claimants to a state vocational rehabilitation agency. Vocational services may be medical or nonmedical and can include counseling, learning new employment skills, training in the use of prostheses, and job placement. Medical evidence from your treating doctor is very important in determining whether vocational rehabilitation services would benefit you. (Vocational rehabilitation is discussed more in Chapter 9.)

7. Do I Have to Be Disabled for a Year Before I Can Get Benefits?

You don't have to wait a year after the onset of the disability before you can get benefits. You can file any time you think you've become disabled. But the SSA has to agree that you'll be disabled for at least 12 months in order for you to receive benefits. If you have a problem that's disabling but unlikely to last 12 months—like an uncomplicated broken bone—you can apply for benefits, but you're unlikely to receive them.

8. Is There a Time Limit on How Long I Can Receive Social Security Disability Benefits?

No. You will continue to receive disability benefits for long as your condition keeps you from working. But your case will be reviewed periodically to see if your condition has improved and whether you're still eligible for benefits (see Chapter 14).

Social Security disability benefits automatically change to retirement benefits when you reach full retirement age. You can't receive both retirement and disability benefits at the same time. If you're receiving early retirement benefits, you can still apply for disability, but if you're approved, your retirement benefits won't restart until your full retirement age.

9. If I Reapply for Benefits After Going Off Disability Because My Back Had Gotten Better, Will My Wait Be as Long as It Was the First Time?

Maybe not. It depends on what the new medical reports say and whether additional evidence is required. Workers who become disabled a second time within five years after their benefits stop can have their checks start again, beginning with the first full month of disability, if the new claim is approved. (For SSDI, the five-month waiting period can be waived.)

10. My Brother Is Receiving SSDI Benefits. Is His Daughter by a Woman to Whom He Has Never Been Married Entitled to Some Benefits as Well?

Yes. Even though your brother was not married to the child's mother, Social Security pays benefits to all of his children. Each child is entitled to equal benefits.

Applying for Disability Benefits

This chapter explains how to apply for disability benefits.

A. Preparing to Apply

You can play an active and important role in ensuring that your claim is processed accurately and quickly. The best advice is to keep thorough records that document the symptoms of your illness or injury and how it affects your daily activities before you apply. Then, provide this information to the Social Security Administration (SSA) when you file your claim.

1. Document Your Symptoms Early and Often

Use a calendar to jot down brief notes about how you feel each day. Record any of your usual activities that you could not do. Be specific. Remember to include any psychological (emotional or mental) difficulties.

2. Help Your Doctor Help You

Not all doctors are aware of the kind of information the SSA needs to document a disability. Ask your doctor to track the course of your symptoms in detail over time and to keep a thorough record of any evidence of fatigue, depression, forgetfulness, dizziness, and other hard-to-document symptoms. Note that the SSA will accept medical opinions as to your limitations only from doctors who are *acceptable medical sources*. (Acceptable medical sources are covered in Chapter 5.)

If you don't have a doctor, the SSA will have you examined at its expense, but it's better to establish a relationship with a doctor before you file your claim, if you can.

3. Record How Your Condition Affected You on the Job

If you were working but lost your job because of your illness or injury, make notes that describe what it is about your condition that forced you to stop working.

B. Applying for Disability Benefits

You can apply for disability benefits at a local Field Office. You don't have to call or make an appointment to visit a Field Office, but you probably should. Otherwise, you might have to wait a long time or come back another day. You can also apply for benefits online or over the phone. See "Applying Online" and "Applying Over the Phone," below, for details.

If you apply at an SSA office, when you arrive, tell the desk or counter clerk that you want to apply for disability benefits. You'll be scheduled to meet an interviewer, who will inform you of your rights and responsibilities, assist you in completing your application, and obtain information from you that the agency needs to determine your eligibility for benefits.

Note the name of the specific person assigned to help you in case you need to contact someone later for help. Bring reading materials with you. You may have a bit of a wait before you see the interviewer.

TIP

The Social Security Administration has a helpful website filled with useful information and up-to-date rules and regulations for disability claimants at www.ssa.gov. Another useful website, www.disabilitysecrets.com, is one of Nolo's partners.

Applying Over the Phone

If you prefer, you can call the SSA at 800-772-1213 to file an application. This is especially convenient if you live some distance from the nearest Field Office (you can find the location of the nearest SSA facility by calling the 800 number listed above). If you need help, a family member, caseworker, or other representative can contact the SSA for you. You don't have to give that person power of attorney—the authority to sign legal documents and make legal decisions for you—to help you obtain an application form and file a claim.

If you can't go to the Social Security office because of poor health, or if there is no Social Security office nearby, you can get full information and application forms by making an appointment for a telephone interview. Even if you can't get to the Field Office to file an application (due to illness, lack of transportation, or another reason), an SSA representative can do the interview over the telephone.

You can speed up the processing of your claim by being as prepared as possible before contacting the SSA Field Office. Remember that the SSA is a huge and complex bureaucracy that needs a lot of information about you. If you do some basic preparation, the whole process can proceed smoothly. But you don't have to wait until you have every conceivable detail ready for review before you contact the Field Office.

You are responsible for submitting the necessary evidence to support your claim of disability (see Chapter 5). The Social Security office will assist you by telling you what evidence is required to establish your claim and how you can obtain that evidence. If you can't get the necessary evidence, the Social Security office will offer special assistance, based upon your needs, to make sure your claim gets the full consideration it deserves.

Never assume that the claims representative can read your mind. If you have a special problem regarding your application, mention it. SSA claims representatives are instructed to help you if they can reasonably solve a problem that is related to your application.

For example, if a claimant can't read or write, the claims representative will assist in completing the forms. In addition, the Social Security Field Office will provide an interpreter if you need language translation. The SSA uses whatever qualified interpreters or interpreter services are most appropriate to the situation and are most reliable and readily available.

Applying Online

You can apply for SSDI benefits online at www.ssa.gov. Before you fill out the online application, use the "Benefit Eligibility Screening Tool" (BEST) at https://ssabest. benefits.gov. This tool helps you identify all the different Social Security programs for which you may be eligible, and you should use it before you start the application process. The SSA's website also has a number of useful links to planners, calculators, and additional information about the disability program.

When you're ready to apply, go to www. socialsecurity.gov/applyfordisability to get started. The SSA will guide you through the three-step process, in which you'll:

- review the Adult Disability Starter Kit, which answers common questions about applying for benefits and includes a worksheet to help you gather the information you'll need
- fill out the online application for Social Security benefits, and

- fill out the online Adult Disability Report.

One of the nice things about an online application is that you can work at your own speed. If you don't have some needed information, for example, you can stop your application and return to it later where you stopped. The SSA will issue a confirmation number you can use to access your application at a later time. Make sure you write it down. Your application is confidential.

If you decide you need help applying online or simply decide to apply in a different way, it's no problem. The SSA displays contact telephone numbers right on the application page. Representatives are available Monday through Friday. For many people, however, an online application is a very attractive alternative to going to a Social Security Field Office in person or applying over the telephone.

Furthermore, the SSA maintains cooperative relationships with many groups and organizations that provide assistance with the application process. Each Social Security office keeps a list of public and private organizations in the community and the types of services (such as help filling out an application or legal representation at a hearing) they provide. If you ask, you can immediately be referred to an agency providing the needed services.

1. Your Application

If you're applying for adult disability offline, the SSA will send you Form SSA-3368-BK, *Disability Report—Adult*, to begin the process. We include a sample filled-in form below, starting at page 3 (the first two pages contain instructions on how to complete the form and don't have any fields for you to fill out). If you're applying for a child, you'll receive Form SSA-3820-BK, *Disability*

Report—Child. (See Chapter 3 for a sample of that form.)

When you arrive at the Social Security Field Office for an interview, the official will ask you many questions. Your answers will be put on either Form SSA-16-BK, *Application for Disability Insurance Benefits*, or Form SSA-8000-BK, *Application for Supplemental Security Income (SSI.)*

Take a look at the appropriate samples below before you head out to the Social Security office or have your interview. That way you can gather as much information and paperwork as possible in advance. Don't worry if you can't answer every question or find all documents—the claims representative or interviewer will help you. Keep in mind that if you don't have key information with you at the time of your interview (see below), you might have to get it and send it in to the SSA office. This could delay the processing of your application. You should also be aware that various Social Security forms for filing online, such as the SSA-3368-BK adult application form, will look different than the paper forms. However, the information required is the same.

CAUTION

You must use forms provided by the SSA. You can obtain them at your local SSA Field Office or by calling the SSA hotline at 800-772-1213, Monday through Friday (except holidays), from 8:00 a.m. to 7:00 p.m. If you're deaf or hard of hearing, TTY service representatives are available at the same times at 800-325-0778. You

can also download many necessary forms from the Social Security Administration website at www.ssa.gov.

2. What the SSA Needs to Process Your Claim

The SSA needs several types of information to process your disability claim.

a. Social Security Number and Birth Certificate

If you're applying for SSDI, the SSA needs your Social Security number and birth certificate (or other proof of your age). You'll also need to provide the Social Security numbers and birth certificates for any family members, such as a disabled adult child, who are applying for benefits on your earnings record.

If you submit an original record of some kind, the SSA will return it to you after making a copy. If you can't or don't want to submit an original record, you can offer a copy, if it's properly certified. You can obtain a properly certified copy from any of the following:

- the official custodian of the record
- an SSA employee authorized to certify copies, who can certify that the copy is an exact reproduction of an original
- a U.S. consular officer or employee of the State Department authorized to certify evidence received outside the United States, or
- an employee of a state agency or state welfare office authorized to certify copies of original records in the agency's or office's files.

Form SSA-3368-BK, *Disability Report—Adult* (Page 3)

DISABILITY REPORT ADULT	For SSA Use Only- Do not write in this box. Related SSN Number Holder

Anyone who makes or causes to be made a false statement or representation of material fact for use in determining a payment under the Social Security Act, or knowingly conceals or fails to disclose an event with an intent to affect an initial or continued right to payment, commits a crime punishable under Federal law by fine, imprisonment, or both, and may be subject to administrative sanctions.

If you are filling out this report for someone else, please provide information about him or her. When a question refers to "you" or "your," it refers to the person who is applying for disability benefits.

SECTION 1 - INFORMATION ABOUT THE DISABLED PERSON

1.A. Name (First, Middle Initial, Last)
William I. Hamilton

1.B. Social Security Number
999-99-9999

1.C. Mailing Address (Street or PO Box) Include apartment number or unit (if applicable).
P.O. Box 24007

City	State/Province	ZIP/Postal Code	Country (If not USA)
Chicago	IL	60681	

1.D. Email Address
WIH@yahoo.com

1.E. Daytime Phone Number, including area code, and the IDD and country codes if you live outside the USA   Phone number 515-123-4567

☐ Check this box if you do not have a phone or a number where we can leave a message.

1.F. Alternate Phone Number - another number where we may reach you, if any.
Alternate phone number 515-123-4568

1.G. Can you speak and understand English?   ☒ Yes   ☐ No

If no, what language do you prefer?

If you cannot speak and understand English, we will provide an interpreter, free of charge.

1.H. Can you read and understand English?   ☒ Yes   ☐ No

1.I. Can you write more than your name in English?   ☒ Yes   ☐ No

1.J. Have you used any other names on your medical or educational records? Examples are maiden name, other married name, or nickname.   ☐ Yes   ☒ No

If yes, please list them here:

SECTION 2 - CONTACTS

Give the name of someone (**other than your doctors**) we can contact who knows about your medical conditions, and can help you with your claim.

2.A. Name (First, Middle Initial, Last)
Mildred Payne

2.B. Relationship to you
Cousin

2.C. Daytime Phone Number (as described in **1.E.** above)
515-123-6789

2.D. Mailing Address (Street or PO Box) Include apartment number or unit if applicable.
456 Center Street, #112

City	State/Province	ZIP/Postal Code	Country (If not USA)
Chicago	IL	60692	

2.E. Can this person speak and understand English?   ☒ Yes   ☐ No
If no, what language is preferred?

Form SSA-3368-BK, *Disability Report—Adult* (Page 4)

SECTION 2 - CONTACTS (continued)

2.F. Who is completing this report?

☒ The person who is applying for disability. (Go to Section 3 - Medical Conditions)

☐ The person listed in **2.A.** (Go to Section 3 - Medical Conditions)

☐ Someone else (Complete the rest of Section 2 below)

2.G. Name (First, Middle Initial, Last)

2.H. Relationship to Person Applying

2.I. Daytime Phone Number

2.J. Mailing Address (Street or PO Box) Include apartment number or unit if applicable.

City	State/Province	ZIP/Postal Code	Country (If not USA)

SECTION 3 - MEDICAL CONDITIONS

3.A. List all of the physical or mental conditions (including emotional or learning problems) that limit your ability to work. If you have cancer, please include the stage and type. List each condition separately.

1. Arthritis right shoulder
2. Liver problems (cirrhosis)
3. Cataracts
4. Nervous
5. Back pain

If you need more space, go to Section 11- Remarks on the last page

3.B. What is your height without shoes?   5 feet   10 inches   OR   _____ centimeters (if outside USA)

3.C. What is your weight without shoes?   176 pounds   OR   _____ kilograms (if outside USA)

3.D. Do your conditions cause you pain or other symptoms?   ☒ Yes   ☐ No

SECTION 4 - WORK ACTIVITY

4.A. Are you currently working?

☐ No, I have never worked (Go to question **4.B.** below)

☒ No, I have stopped working (Go to question **4.C.** below)

☐ Yes, I am currently working (Go to question **4.F.** on page 5)

IF YOU HAVE NEVER WORKED:

4.B. When do you believe your conditions(s) became severe enough to keep you from working (even though you have never worked)? (month/day/year) _____ (Go to Section 5 on page 5)

IF YOU HAVE STOPPED WORKING:

4.C. When did you stop working? (month/day/year) 10/12/2023 _____

Why did you stop working?

☒ Because of my condition(s).

☐ Because of other reasons. Please explain why you stopped working (for example: laid off, early retirement, seasonal work ended, business closed). _____

Even though you stopped working for other reasons, when do you believe your conditions(s) became severe enough to keep you from working? (month/day/year) _____

4.D. Did your condition(s) cause you to make changes in your work activity? (for example: job duties, hours, or rate of pay)

☐ No (Go to Section 5 - Education and Training on page 5)

☒ Yes, When did you make changes? (month/day/year) 5/15/2023 _____

Form SSA-3368-BK, *Disability Report—Adult* (Page 5)

SECTION 4 - WORK ACTIVITY (continued)

4.E. Since the date in 4.D. above, have you had gross earnings greater than $1,180 in any month? Do not count sick leave, vacation, or disability pay. (We may contact you for more information.)

☐ No (Go to Section 5) ☒ Yes (Go to Section 5)

IF YOU ARE CURRENTLY WORKING:

4.F. Has your condition(s) caused you to make changes in your work activity? (for example: job duties or hours)

☐ No When did your condition(s) first start bothering you? (month/day/year) _____

☐ Yes When did you make changes? (month/day/year) _____

4.G. Since your condition(s) first bothered you, have you had gross earnings greater than $1,180 in any month? Do not count sick leave, vacation, or disability pay. (We may contact you for more information.)

☐ No ☐ Yes

SECTION 5 - EDUCATION AND TRAINING

5.A. Check the highest grade of school completed. (Select 12, if you have education equivalent to high school from another country.)

														College:			
0	1	2	3	4	5	6	7	8	9	10	11	12	GED	1	2	3	4 or more
☐	☐	☐	☐	☐	☐	☐	☐	☐	☐	☐	☐	☒	☐	☐	☐	☐	☐

Date completed: 06 / 1992
MM YYYY

Name of school: Lakeside High

City: Denver State/Province: CO Country (if not USA) _____

5.B. Did you receive special education, such as through an Individualized Education Plan (IEP) or equivalent education?

☐ Yes ☒ No (Go to **5.C.**)

Dates from: ___ / ___ to ___ / ___
MM YYYY MM YYYY

Check the last grade you received special education.

Pre K	K	1	2	3	4	5	6	7	8	9	10	11	12
☐	☐	☐	☐	☐	☐	☐	☐	☐	☐	☐	☐	☐	☐

Reason(s) for IEP or equivalent education: _____

The school where you last received special education:

☐ Same as **5.A.**

☐ If different from **5.A.**, complete below.

Name of school: _____

City: _____ State/Province: _____ Country (if not USA) _____

Form SSA-3368-BK, *Disability Report—Adult* (Page 6)

SECTION 5 - EDUCATION AND TRAINING (continued)

5.C. Have you completed any type of specialized job training, trade, or vocational school?

        ☒ Yes   ☐ No

If "Yes," what type? Electrician helper   Date completed: $\frac{07}{\text{MM}}$ / $\frac{1995}{\text{YYYY}}$

5.D. What written language do you use every day in most situations (at home, work, school, in community, etc.)?

English

5.E. In the language you identified in **5.D.**, can you **read** a simple message, such as a shopping list or short and simple notes?   ☒ Yes   ☐ No

5.F. In the language you identified in **5.D.**, can you **write** a simple message, such as a shopping list or short and simple notes?   ☒ Yes   ☐ No

If you need to list other educations or training use Section 11 - Remarks on the last page.

SECTION 6 - JOB HISTORY

6.A. List the jobs (up to 5) that you have had in the 15 years before you became unable to work because of your physical or mental conditions. List your most recent job first.

☐ Check here and go to Section 7 - Medicines on page 8 if you did not work at all in the 15 years before you became unable to work.

Job Title	Type of Business	Dates Worked		Hours Per Day	Days Per Week	Rate of Pay	
		From MM/YY	To MM/YY			Amount	Frequency
1. Electrician Helper	Utility	09/95	10/22	8	6	$25	Hour
2.							
3.							
4.							
5.							

Check the box below that applies to you.

☒ I had **only one job** in the last 15 years before I became unable to work. Answer the question below.

☐ I had **more than one job** in the last 15 years before I became unable to work. Do not answer the question on this page; go to Section 7 - Medicines on page 8. (We may contact you for more information.)

Form SSA-3368-BK, *Disability Report—Adult* (Page 7)

SECTION 6 - JOB HISTORY (continued)

Do not complete this page if you had **more than one job** in the last 15 years before you became unable to work.

6.B. Describe this job. What did you do all day?
Numerous duties, including assisting in installation and repair of electric power equipment, underground cable and related activities

(If you need more space, use Section 11 - Remarks on the last page.)

6.C. In this job, did you:

Use machines, tools or equipment?	☒ Yes	☐ No
Use technical knowledge or skills?	☒ Yes	☐ No
Do any writing, complete reports, or perform any duties like this?	☐ Yes	☒ No

6.D. In this job, how many hours each day did you do each of the tasks listed:

Task	Hours	Task	Hours	Task	Hours
Walk	6-8	Stoop *(Bend down & forward at waist.)*	3	Handle large objects	6-8
Stand	6-8	Kneel *(Bend legs to rest on knees.)*	2-3	Write, type, or handle small objects	6-8
Sit	0-1	Crouch *(Bend legs & back down & forward.)*	2-3	Reach	6-8
Climb	3	Crawl *(Move on hands & knees.)*	1-2		

6.E. Lifting and carrying (*Explain in the box below, what you lifted, how far you carried it, and how often you did this in your job.*)
Heavy machine parts, electrical cable, worked with heavy equipment like transformers, rigged scaffolding & hoists. Carried heavy objects 50-100 feet most of day

6.F. Check heaviest weight lifted:
☐ Less than 10 lbs.   ☐ 10 lbs.   ☐ 20 lbs.   ☐ 50 lbs.   ☒ 100 lbs. or more   ☐ Other

6.G. Check weight **frequently** lifted: *(by frequently, we mean from 1/3 to 2/3 of the workday.)*
☐ Less than 10 lbs.   ☐ 10 lbs.   ☒ 25 lbs.   ☐ 50 lbs. or more   ☐ Other

6.H. Did you supervise other people in this job?   ☐ Yes (Complete items below)   ☒ No (if No, go to **6.I.**)

How many people did you supervise? _____

Did you hire and fire employees?   ☐ Yes   ☐ No

What part of your time did you spend supervising people? _____

6.I. Were you a lead worker?   ☐ Yes   ☒ No

Form SSA-3368-BK, *Disability Report—Adult* (Page 8)

Form **SSA-3368-BK** (11-2020) UF   Page 8 of 15

SECTION 7 - MEDICINES

7. Are you taking any medicines (prescription or non-prescription)?

   ☒ Yes, (Give the information requested below. You may need to look at your medicine containers.)

   ☐ No, (Go to Section 8 - Medical Treatment)

Name of Medicine	If prescribed, give name of doctor	Reason for medicine
Aldactone	Dr. Simmons	Remove excess fluid in abdomen
Xanax	Dr. Hill	Nervousness
Ibuprofen	Dr. Bates	Back pain

If you need to list other medicines, go to Section 11 - Remarks on the last page.

SECTION 8 - MEDICAL TREATMENT

Have you seen a doctor or other health care professional or received treatment at a hospital or clinic, or **do you have a future appointment scheduled**?

8.A. For any **physical** condition(s)?   ☒ Yes   ☐ No

Dr. Bates, June 22, 2024, for back pain.
Dr. Simmons, July 12, 2024, for liver problem

8.B. For any **mental** condition(s) **(including emotional or learning problems)**?   ☒ Yes   ☐ No

Dr. Hill, August 13, 2024, about my anxieties.

If you answered "No" to both 8.A. and 8.B., go to Section 9 - Other Medical Information on page 14.

Form SSA-3368-BK, *Disability Report—Adult* (Page 9)

SECTION 8 - MEDICAL TREATMENT (continued)

Tell us who may have medical records about any of your **physical and/or mental** condition(s) (including emotional or learning problems). This includes doctors' offices, hospitals **(including emergency room visits)**, clinics, and other health care facilities. Tell us about your next appointment, if you have one scheduled.

8.C. Name of Facility or Office	Name of healthcare professional who treated you
Midwest Orthopedics	David Bates, M.D.

ALL OF THE QUESTIONS ON THIS PAGE REFER TO THE HEALTH CARE PROVIDER ABOVE.

Phone	Patient ID# (if known)
312-555-1234	None

Mailing Address
2325 Front Street

City	State/Province	ZIP/Postal Code	Country (if not USA)
Chicago	IL	unknown	

Dates of Treatment

1. Office, Clinic, or Outpatient visits	2. Emergency Room visits List the most recent date first	3. Overnight hospital stays List the most recent date first	
First Visit May 2021	A.	A. Date in	Date out
Last Visit November 2021	B.	B. Date in	Date out
Next scheduled appointment (if any) June 20, 2024	C.	C. Date in	Date out

What medical conditions were treated or evaluated?
Back pain due to arthritis and degenerated disks in spine. Arthritis in shoulder.

What treatment did you receive for the above conditions? (Do not describe medicines or tests in this box.)
Ibuprofen, physical therapy, advice not to do any more heavy lifting or frequent bending.

Tell us about any tests the provider performed or sent you to, or has scheduled you to take. Please give the dates for past and future tests. If you need to list more tests, use Section 11 - Remarks on the last page.

☐ Check this box if no test by this provider or at this facility.

Kind of Test	Dates of Tests	Kind of Test	Dates of Tests
☐ EKG (heart test)		☐ EEG (brain wave test)	
☐ Treadmill (exercise test)		☐ HIV Test	
☐ Cardiac Catheterization		☐ Blood Test (not HIV)	
☐ Biopsy (list body part)		☒ X-Ray (list body part) Back, shoulder	November 2023
☐ Hearing Test		☐ MRI/CT Scan (list body part)	
☐ Speech/Language Test			
☐ Vision Test		☐ Other (please describe)	
☐ Breathing Test			

If you do not have any more doctors or hospitals to describe, go to Section 9 on page 14.

Form SSA-3368-BK, *Disability Report—Adult* (Page 10)

SECTION 8 - MEDICAL TREATMENT (continued)

Tell us who may have medical records about any of your **physical and/or mental** condition(s) (including emotional or learning problems). This includes doctors' offices, hospitals **(including emergency room visits)**, clinics, and other health care facilities. Tell us about your next appointment, if you have one scheduled.

8.D. Name of Facility or Office	Name of healthcare professional who treated you
The Gastroenterology Clinic	John Simmons, M.D.

ALL OF THE QUESTIONS ON THIS PAGE REFER TO THE HEALTH CARE PROVIDER ABOVE.

Phone	Patient ID# (if known)
312-555-9999	512488

Mailing Address
17 Outer Loop Drive

City	State/Province	ZIP/Postal Code	Country (if not USA)
Chicago	IL	60686	

Dates of Treatment

1. Office, Clinic, or Outpatient visits	2. Emergency Room visits List the most recent date first	3. Overnight hospital stays List the most recent date first	
First Visit January 2021	A.	A. Date in January 12, 2021	Date out January 21, 2021
Last Visit December 2022	B.	B. Date in	Date out
Next scheduled appointment (if any)	C.	C. Date in	Date out

What medical conditions were treated or evaluated?

Abdominal problems - liver cirrhosis
Shunt to drain abdominal fluid. I don't remember surgeon's name.

What treatment did you receive for the above conditions? (Do not describe medicines or tests in this box.)

Diuretic to remove excess fluid in abdomen; advice to stop drinking; advice about nutrition.

Tell us about any tests the provider performed or sent you to, or has scheduled you to take. Please give the dates for past and future tests. If you need to list more tests, use Section 11 - Remarks on the last page.

☐ Check this box if no test by this provider or at this facility.

Kind of Test	Dates of Tests	Kind of Test	Dates of Tests
☒ EKG (heart test)	Jan. 2021	☐ EEG (brain wave test)	
☐ Treadmill (exercise test)		☐ HIV Test	
☐ Cardiac Catheterization		☒ Blood Test (not HIV)	Jan. 2021
☒ Biopsy (list body part) Liver	Jan. 2021	☒ X-Ray (list body part) Chest	Jan. 2021
☐ Hearing Test		☒ MRI/CT Scan (list body part) Abdomen	Jan. 2021
☐ Speech/Language Test			
☐ Vision Test		☐ Other (please describe)	
☐ Breathing Test			

If you do not have any more doctors or hospitals to describe, go to Section 9 on page 14.

Form SSA-3368-BK, *Disability Report—Adult* (Page 11)

SECTION 8 - MEDICAL TREATMENT (continued)

Tell us who may have medical records about any of your **physical and/or mental** condition(s) (including emotional or learning problems). This includes doctors' offices, hospitals **(including emergency room visits)**, clinics, and other health care facilities. Tell us about your next appointment, if you have one scheduled.

8.E. Name of Facility or Office	Name of healthcare professional who treated you
Mental Health Associates, Inc.	Henry Hill, M.D.

ALL OF THE QUESTIONS ON THIS PAGE REFER TO THE HEALTH CARE PROVIDER ABOVE.

Phone	Patient ID# (if known)
312-555-6789	

Mailing Address
4800 State Building, Ste. 43

City	State/Province	ZIP/Postal Code	Country (if not USA)
Chicago	IL	60686	

Dates of Treatment

1. Office, Clinic, or Outpatient visits	2. Emergency Room visits List the most recent date first	3. Overnight hospital stays List the most recent date first	
First Visit June 2021	A.	A. Date in	Date out
Last Visit December 2022	B.	B. Date in	Date out
Next scheduled appointment (if any)	C.	C. Date in	Date out

What medical conditions were treated or evaluated?
Anxieties

What treatment did you receive for the above conditions? (Do not describe medicines or tests in this box.)
Talk about how to handle nervousness. Take anxiety pills--Xanax.

Tell us about any tests the provider performed or sent you to, or has scheduled you to take. Please give the dates for past and future tests. If you need to list more tests, use Section 11 - Remarks on the last page.
☐ Check this box if no test by this provider or at this facility.

Kind of Test	Dates of Tests	Kind of Test	Dates of Tests
☐ EKG (heart test)		☐ EEG (brain wave test)	
☐ Treadmill (exercise test)		☐ HIV Test	
☐ Cardiac Catheterization		☐ Blood Test (not HIV)	
☐ Biopsy (list body part)		☐ X-Ray (list body part)	
☐ Hearing Test		☐ MRI/CT Scan (list body part)	
☐ Speech/Language Test			
☐ Vision Test		☒ Other (please describe)	2021
☐ Breathing Test		Mental tests	

If you do not have any more doctors or hospitals to describe, go to Section 9 on page 14.

Form SSA-3368-BK, *Disability Report—Adult* (Page 12)

SECTION 8 - MEDICAL TREATMENT (continued)

Tell us who may have medical records about any of your **physical and/or mental** condition(s) (including emotional or learning problems). This includes doctors' offices, hospitals **(including emergency room visits)**, clinics, and other health care facilities. Tell us about your next appointment, if you have one scheduled.

8.F. Name of Facility or Office	Name of healthcare professional who treated you

ALL OF THE QUESTIONS ON THIS PAGE REFER TO THE HEALTH CARE PROVIDER ABOVE.

Phone	Patient ID# (if known)

Mailing Address

City	State/Province	ZIP/Postal Code	Country (if not USA)

Dates of Treatment

1. Office, Clinic, or Outpatient visits	2. Emergency Room visits List the most recent date first	3. Overnight hospital stays List the most recent date first	
First Visit	A.	A. Date in	Date out
Last Visit	B.	B. Date in	Date out
Next scheduled appointment (if any)	C.	C. Date in	Date out

What medical conditions were treated or evaluated?

What treatment did you receive for the above conditions? (Do not describe medicines or tests in this box.)

Tell us about any tests the provider performed or sent you to, or has scheduled you to take. Please give the dates for past and future tests. If you need to list more tests, use Section 11 - Remarks on the last page.

☐ Check this box if no test by this provider or at this facility.

Kind of Test	Dates of Tests	Kind of Test	Dates of Tests
☐ EKG (heart test)		☐ EEG (brain wave test)	
☐ Treadmill (exercise test)		☐ HIV Test	
☐ Cardiac Catheterization		☐ Blood Test (not HIV)	
☐ Biopsy (list body part)		☐ X-Ray (list body part)	
☐ Hearing Test		☐ MRI/CT Scan (list body part)	
☐ Speech/Language Test			
☐ Vision Test		☐ Other (please describe)	
☐ Breathing Test			

If you do not have any more doctors or hospitals to describe, go to Section 9 on page 14.

Form SSA-3368-BK, *Disability Report—Adult* (Page 13)

SECTION 8 - MEDICAL TREATMENT (continued)

Tell us who may have medical records about any of your **physical and/or mental** condition(s) (including emotional or learning problems). This includes doctors' offices, hospitals **(including emergency room visits)**, clinics, and other health care facilities. Tell us about your next appointment, if you have one scheduled.

8.G. Name of Facility or Office	Name of healthcare professional who treated you

ALL OF THE QUESTIONS ON THIS PAGE REFER TO THE HEALTH CARE PROVIDER ABOVE.

Phone	Patient ID# (if known)

Mailing Address

City	State/Province	ZIP/Postal Code	Country (if not USA)

Dates of Treatment

1. Office, Clinic, or Outpatient visits	2. Emergency Room visits List the most recent date first	3. Overnight hospital stays List the most recent date first	
First Visit	A.	A. Date in	Date out
Last Visit	B.	B. Date in	Date out
Next scheduled appointment (if any)	C.	C. Date in	Date out

What medical conditions were treated or evaluated?

What treatment did you receive for the above conditions? (Do not describe medicines or tests in this box.)

Tell us about any tests the provider performed or sent you to, or has scheduled you to take. Please give the dates for past and future tests. If you need to list more tests, use Section 11 - Remarks on the last page.

☐ Check this box if no test by this provider or at this facility.

Kind of Test	Dates of Tests	Kind of Test	Dates of Tests
☐ EKG (heart test)		☐ EEG (brain wave test)	
☐ Treadmill (exercise test)		☐ HIV Test	
☐ Cardiac Catheterization		☐ Blood Test (not HIV)	
☐ Biopsy (list body part)		☐ X-Ray (list body part)	
☐ Hearing Test		☐ MRI/CT Scan (list body part)	
☐ Speech/Language Test			
☐ Vision Test		☐ Other (please describe)	
☐ Breathing Test			

If you do not have any more doctors or hospitals to describe, go to Section 9 on page 14.

Form SSA-3368-BK, *Disability Report—Adult* (Page 14)

SECTION 9 - OTHER MEDICAL INFORMATION

9. Does **anyone else** have medical information about your physical and/or mental condition(s) (including emotional and learning problems), or are you scheduled to see anyone else? (This may include places such as workers' compensation, vocational rehabilitation, insurance companies who have paid you disability benefits, prisons, attorneys, social service agencies and welfare.)

☐ Yes (Please complete the information below)

☒ No (If you are receiving Supplemental Security Income (SSI) and have been asked to complete this report, go to Section 10 - Vocational Rehabilitation; if not, go to Section 11 - Remarks on the last page.)

Name of Organization	Phone Number

Mailing Address

City	State/Province	ZIP/Postal Code	Country (if not USA)

Name of Contact Person	Claim or ID number (if any)

Date of First Contact	Date of Last Contact	Date of Next Contact (if any)

Reasons for Contacts

If you need to list other people or organizations use Section 11 - Remarks on the last page and give the same detailed information as above for each one you list.

COMPLETE THIS SECTION ONLY IF YOU ARE ALREADY RECEIVING SSI.

SECTION 10 - VOCATIONAL REHABILITATION, EMPLOYMENT, OR OTHER SUPPORT SERVICES

10.A. Have you participated, or are you participating in:

- An individual work plan with an employment network under the Ticket to Work Program;
- An individualized plan for employment with a vocational rehabilitation agency or any other organization;
- A Plan to Achieve Self-Support (PASS);
- Any Individualized Education Program (IEP) through a school (if a student age 18-21); or
- Any program providing vocational rehabilitation, employment services, or other support services to help you go to work?

☐ Yes (Complete the following information)   ☐ No (Go to Section 11 - Remarks)

10.B. Name of Organization or School

Name of Counselor, Instructor, or Job Coach	Phone Number

Mailing Address

City	State/Province	ZIP/Postal Code	Country (if not USA)

10.C. When did you start participating in the plan or program?

Form SSA-3368-BK, *Disability Report—Adult* (Page 15)

Form **SSA-3368-BK** (11-2020) UF   Page 15 of 15

SECTION 10 - VOCATIONAL REHABILITATION, EMPLOYMENT, OR OTHER SUPPORT SERVICES (continued)

10.D. Are you still participating in the plan or program?

☐ Yes, I am scheduled to complete the plan or program on: _____

☐ **No,** I completed the plan or program on: _____

☐ **No,** I stopped participating in the plan or program before completing it because:

_____

10.E. List the types of service, tests, or evaluations that you received (for example: intelligence or psychological testing, vision or hearing test, physical exam, work evaluation, or classes.

If you need to list another plan or program use Section 11 - Remarks and give the same detailed information as above.

SECTION 11 - REMARKS

Please write any additional information you did not give in earlier parts of this report. If you did not have enough space in the sections of this report to write the requested information, please use this space to tell us the additional information requested in those sections. Be sure to show the section to which you are referring.

Although Dr. Bates originally gave me pain medicine for my back and shoulder, it had to be stopped, because it worsened my liver problem. So I have little relief of my back and shoulder pain. I can't bend over because of fluid in my abdomen and back pain. Lifting over 10 lbs. hurts my back and shoulder, and I can't reach overhead with my right arm any more. I feel weak all the time and cannot do much even around the house: mostly, I sit in a chair and read or watch TV. I try to help with some of the housework but get tired in a few minutes. My wife now takes care of the car and all the shopping. Sometimes, my daughter comes over and helps.

All of our savings are about gone. I lost my health insurance when I could no longer work, so my wife lost hers too. I can't afford to get treatment for my cataracts, and my vision is getting worse.

My psychiatrist, Dr. Hill, says that my nervousness will improve if my financial situation gets better. I'd like to learn some other type of work, if I can get help for my medical problems. But I just can't do the heavy work I did before.

Date Report Completed (MM/DD/YYYY) Oct 11, 2023

Form SSA-16, *Application for Disability Insurance Benefits* (Page 1)

Form **SSA-16** (06-2022) UF
Discontinue prior editions
Social Security Administration

Page 1 of 7
OMB No. 0960-0618

APPLICATION FOR DISABILITY INSURANCE BENEFITS

(Do not write in this space)

I apply for a period of disability and/or all insurance benefits for which I am eligible under Title II and Part A of Title XVIII of the Social Security Act, as presently amended.

1.	**PRINT your name**	FIRST NAME, MIDDLE INITIAL, LAST NAME John D. Doe
2.	Enter your Social Security Number	123-45-6789
3.	Check (X) whether you are	☐ Female ☒ Male

Answer question 4 if English is not your preferred language. Otherwise, go to item 5.

4.	Enter the language you prefer to: speak	write

5.	(a) Enter your date of birth	6/14/85
	(b) Enter name of city and state or foreign country where you were born.	Los Angeles, CA

6.	(a) Are you a U.S. citizen?	☒ Yes (If "Yes," go to item 7)	☐ No (If "No," answer (b))
	(b) Are you an alien lawfully present in the U.S.?	☐ Yes (If "Yes," answer (c))	☐ No (If "No," go to item 7)
	(c) When were you lawfully admitted to the U.S.?		

7.	(a) Enter your name at birth if different from item (1)		
	(b) Have you used any other names?	☐ Yes (If "Yes," answer (c))	☒ No (If "No," go to item 8)
	(c) Other name(s) used.		

8.	(a) Have you used any other Social Security number(s)?	☐ Yes (If "Yes," answer (b))	☒ No (If "No" go to item 9)
	(b) Enter Social Security number(s) used.		

9.	When do you believe your condition(s) became severe enough to keep you from working (even if you have never worked)?	Feb., 2024	
10.	Did you or your spouse (or prior spouse) work in the railroad industry for 5 years or more?	☐ Yes	☒ No
11.	(a) Do you have Social Security credits (for example, based on work or residence) under another country's Social Security System?	☐ Yes (If "Yes," answer (b))	☒ No (If "No," go to item 12)
	(b) List the country(ies):		
12.	(a) Are you entitled to, or do you expect to be entitled to, a pension or annuity (or a lump sum in place of a pension or annuity) based on your work after 1956 not covered by Social Security?	☐ Yes (If "Yes," answer (b) and (c))	☒ No (If "No," go to item 13)
	(b) ☐ I became entitled, or expect to become entitled, beginning MONTH		YEAR
	(c) ☐ I became eligible, or expect to become eligible, beginning MONTH		YEAR
	I AGREE TO PROMPTLY NOTIFY the Social Security Administration if I become entitled to a pension or annuity based on my employment not covered by Social Security, or if such pension or annuity stops.		

Form SSA-16, *Application for Disability Insurance Benefits* (Page 2)

Form **SSA-16** (06-2022) UF   Page 2 of 7

13.

(a) Have you ever been married?   ☒ Yes   ☐ No
(If "Yes," answer (b))   (If "No," go to item 14)

(b) Give the following information about your current marriage. If not currently married, write "None." _____ (If "None," go on to item 13(c))

Spouse's name (including maiden name)	When (Month, day, year)	Where (Name of City and State)
Jane J. Doe (maiden Jane J. Rubio)	4/5/2005	Los Angeles, CA

Marriage performed by:	Spouse's date of birth (or age)	Spouse's Social Security Number (If none or unknown, so indicate)
☒ Clergyman or public official		
☐ Other (Explain in Remarks)	9/5/1982	111-22-3333

(c) Enter information about any other marriage if you:

- Had a marriage that lasted at least 10 years; or
- Had a marriage that ended due to the death of your spouse, regardless of duration; or
- Were divorced, remarried the same individual within the year immediately following the year of the divorce, and the combined period of marriage totaled 10 years or more. If none, write "None." _____ Go on to item 13 (d) if you have a child(ren) who is under age 16 or disabled or handicapped (age 16 or over and disability began before age 22) and you are divorced from the child's other parent who is now deceased and the marriage lasted less than 10 years.

Spouse's name (including maiden name)	When (Month, day, year)	Where (Name of City and State)

How marriage ended	When (Month, day, year)	Where (Name of City and State)

Marriage performed by:	Spouse's date of birth (or age)	Date of spouse's death	Spouse's Social Security Number (If none or unknown, so indicate)
☐ Clergyman or public official			
☐ Other (Explain in Remarks)			

(d) Enter information about any marriage if you:

- Have a child(ren) who is under age 16 or disabled or handicapped (age 16 or over and disability began before age 22); and
- Were married for less than 10 years to the child's mother or father, who is now deceased; and
- The marriage ended in divorce

     If none, write "None." _____

Spouse's name (including maiden name)	When (Month, day, year)	Where (Name of City and State)

Date of divorce (Month, day, year)	Where (Name of City and State)

Marriage performed by:	Spouse's date of birth (or age)	Date of spouse's death	Spouse's Social Security Number (If none or unknown, so indicate)
☐ Clergyman or public official			
☐ Other (Explain in Remarks)			

Use the "REMARKS" space on page 5 for marriage continuation or explanation.

---

14. If your claim for disability benefits is approved, your children (including adopted children, and stepchildren) or dependent grandchildren (including stepgrandchildren) may be eligible for benefits based on your earnings record.

List below: FULL NAME OF ALL such children who are now or were in the past 12 months UNMARRIED and:

- UNDER AGE 18
- AGE 18 TO 19 AND ATTENDING ELEMENTARY OR SECONDARY SCHOOL FULL-TIME
- DISABLED OR HANDICAPPED (age 18 or over and disability began before age 22)

Form SSA-16, *Application for Disability Insurance Benefits* (Page 3)

Form **SSA-16** (06-2022) UF	Page 3 of 7

15.	(a) Did you have wages or self-employment income covered under Social Security in all years from 1978 through last year?	☒ Yes ☐ No
		(If "Yes," go to item 16) (If "No," answer (b))
	(b) List the years from 1978 through last year in which you did not have wages or self-employment income covered under Social Security.	

16. Enter below the names and addresses of all the persons, companies, or Government agencies for whom you have worked this year and last year. IF NONE, WRITE "NONE" BELOW AND GO TO ITEM 17.

NAME AND ADDRESS OF EMPLOYER (If you had more than one employer, please list them in order beginning with your last (most recent) employer)	Work Began		Work Ended (If still working show "Not Ended")	
	MONTH	YEAR	MONTH	YEAR
Bay Area Shipping Containers 12310 Front St., San Francisco, CA	August	2004	July	2006
Acme Security Services 1984 Ashley Ave., San Francisco, CA	Sept	2006	Nov.	2011
Jewel's Food Services 400 W. 19th St., Los Angeles, CA	Feb.	2012	Sept.	2020

(If you need more space, use "Remarks".)

17. Complete item 17 even if you were an employee.

(a) Were you self-employed this year or last year?	☒ Yes ☐ No	
	(If "Yes," answer (b)) (If "No," go to item 18)	

(b) Check the year (or years) you were self-employed	In what type of trade/business were you self-employed? (For example, storekeeper, farmer, physician)	Were your net earnings from the trade or business $400 or more? (Check "Yes" or "No")
☒ This year	Landscaping	
☒ Last year	Landscaping	☒ Yes ☐ No

18.	(a) How much were your total earnings last year? Count both wage and self-employment income. (If none, write "None.")	Amount $ 32,500
	(b) How much have you earned so far this year? (If none, write "None.")	Amount $ 12,500
19.	(a) Are you still unable to work because of your illnesses, injuries, or conditions?	☒ Yes ☐ No
		(If "Yes," go to item 20) (If "No," answer (b))
	(b) Enter the date you became able to work.	MONTH, DAY, YEAR
20.	Are your illnesses, injuries, or conditions related to your work in any way?	☒ Yes ☐ No
21.	Are you blind or do you have low vision even with glasses or contacts?	☐ Yes ☒ No

Form SSA-16, *Application for Disability Insurance Benefits* (Page 4)

Form **SSA-16** (06-2022) UF

Page 4 of 7

22.	(a) Have you filed, or do you intend to file, for any other public disability benefits (including workers' compensation, Black Lung benefits and SSI)?	☒ Yes (If "Yes," answer (b))	☐ No (If "No," to item 23)

(b) The other public disability benefit(s) you have filed (or intend to file) for is (Check as many as apply):

☐ Veterans Administration Benefits   ☐ Welfare

☒ Supplemental Security Income   ☐ Other (If "Other," complete a Workers' Compensation/Public Disability Benefit Questionnaire)

23.	(a) Did you receive any money from an employer(s) on or after the date in item 9 when you became unable to work because of your illnesses, injuries, or conditions? If "Yes", give the amounts and explain in "Remarks".	☐ Yes ☒ No Amount $ _____
	(b) Do you expect to receive any additional money from an employer, such as sick pay, vacation pay, other special pay? If "Yes," please give amounts and explain in "Remarks".	☐ Yes ☒ No Amount $ _____
24.	Do you, or did you, have a child under age 3 (your own or your spouse's) living with you in one or more calendar years when you had no earnings?	☐ Yes ☒ No
25.	Do you have a dependent parent who was receiving at least one-half support from you when you became unable to work because of your disability? If "Yes," enter the parent's name and address and Social Security number, if known, in "Remarks".	☐ Yes ☒ No
26.	If you were unable to work before age 22 because of an illness, injury or condition, do you have a parent (including adoptive or stepparent) or grandparent who is receiving social security retirement or disability benefits or who is deceased? If yes, enter the name(s) and Social Security number, if known, in "Remarks" (if unknown, check "Unknown").	☐ Yes ☒ No ☐ Unknown

Form SSA-16, *Application for Disability Insurance Benefits* (Page 5)

Form **SSA-16** (06-2022) UF   Page 5 of 7

REMARKS (You may use this space for any explanation. If you need more space, attach a separate sheet.)

I have developed high blood pressure, back pain, and arthritis in my hands and knees. I request my treating doctor be asked about my medical problems before a decision is made on my claim.

Also, I request a licensed medical doctor or osteopathic physician make the determination about the severity of my disorders whether I am disabled. I want to be informed before the SSA makes any denial determination, if a doctor has not reviewed my claim or if the SSA has not contacted my treating doctor for an opinion. I feel I have a right to have my medical record reviewed by a real doctor, not merely a disability examiner, and that my treating doctor's opinion be considered.

I declare under penalty of perjury that I have examined all the information on this form, and on any accompanying statements or forms, and it is true and correct to the best of my knowledge. I understand that anyone who knowingly gives a false statement about a material fact in this information, or causes someone else to do so, commits a crime and may be subject to a fine or imprisonment.

SIGNATURE OF APPLICANT	Date (Month, Day, Year) March 15, 2024
Signature (First name, middle initial, last name) (Write in ink) *John D. Doe*	Telephone Number(s) at which you may be contacted during the day. (Include the area code) 320-555-1111

DIRECT DEPOSIT PAYMENT INFORMATION (FINANCIAL INSTITUTION)

Routing Transit Number	Account Number		
111111111111	22222222222	[X] Checking [ ] Savings	[X] Enroll in Direct Express [ ] Direct Deposit Refused

Applicant's Mailing Address *(Number and street, Apt No., P.O. Box, or Rural Route) (Enter Residence Address in "Remarks," if different.)*

P.O. Box 24840

City and State Los Angeles, CA	ZIP Code 90028	County *(if any)* in which you now live Los Angeles

Witnesses are required ONLY if this application has been signed by mark (X) above. If signed by mark (X), two witnesses to the signing who know the applicant must sign below, giving their full addresses. Also, print the applicant's name in Signature block.

1. Signature of Witness	2. Signature of Witness
Address *(Number and street, City, State and ZIP Code)*	Address *(Number and street, City, State and ZIP Code)*

Form SSA-8000-BK, *Application for Supplemental Security Income (SSI)* (Page 1)

Form **SSA-8000-BK** (05-2021) UF
Discontinue Prior Editions
Social Security Administration

Page 1 of 24
OMB No. 0960-0229

APPLICATION FOR SUPPLEMENTAL SECURITY INCOME (SSI)

Note: Social Security Administration staff or others who help people apply for SSI will fill out this form for you.	**Do Not Write in This Space** **DATE STAMP**

I am/We are applying for Supplemental Security Income and any federally administered state supplementation under Title XVI of the Social Security Act, for benefits under the other programs administered by the Social Security Administration, and where applicable, for medical assistance under Title XIX of the Social Security Act.

Filing Date (MM/DD/YYYY)

☐ Receipt   ☐ Protective

☐ SNAP-SSA/APP   ☐ SNAP-Referred

Preferred Language
Written: Spoken:

TYPE OF CLAIM ☒ Individual   ☐ Individual with Ineligible Spouse   ☐ Couple   ☐ Child   ☐ Child with Parents

PART 1 - BASIC ELIGIBILITY - Answer the questions below beginning with the first moment of the filing date month.

1.	(a) First Name, Middle Initial, Last Name	Sex	Birthdate (MM/DD/YYYY)	Social Security Number
	Susan L. Clark	☐ Male ☒ Female	07/15/1974	234-56-7890

(b) Did you ever use any other names (including maiden name) or any other Social Security Numbers?	☐ YES Go to (c)	☒ NO Go to (d)

(c) Other Name(s)	Other Social Security Number(s) used

(d) If you are also filing for Social Security Benefits, go to #2; otherwise complete the following:

Parent 1's Name(s)	Parent 2's Name(s)
Parent 1's Other Name(s) (Including Name at Birth)	Parent 2's Other Name(s) (Including Name at Birth)
	Go to #2

2. Applicant's Mailing Address (Number & Street, Apt. No., P.O. Box, Rural Route)

100 West 95th Street

City and State (U.S.)/State/Province/Region (Foreign)	ZIP Code/Postal Code	County/Country
Los Angeles, CA	90055	LA

3. Claimant's Residence Address (If different from applicant's mailing address)

City and State (U.S.)/State/Province/Region (Foreign)	ZIP Code/Postal Code	County/Country

4. **DIRECT DEPOSIT PAYMENT INFORMATION (FINANCIAL INSTITUTION)**

Routing Transit Number	Account Number		
12044182	000-111111	☒ Checking	☒ Enroll in Direct Express
		☐ Savings	☐ Direct Deposit Refused

Form SSA-8000-BK, *Application for Supplemental Security Income (SSI) (Page 2)*

Form **SSA-8000-BK** (05-2021) UF		Page 2 of 24

5.

(a) Are you married?	☒ YES Go to (b)	☐ NO Go to #6

(b) Date of marriage: (MM/DD/YYYY)

6/30/2005

(c) Spouse's Name (First, middle initial, last)	Birthdate (MM/DD/YYYY)	Social Security Number
Paul A. Clark	04/30/1971	234-56-6891

(d) Did your spouse ever use any other names (including maiden name) or Social Security Numbers?	☐YES Go to (e)	☒ NO Go to (f)
(e) Other Name(s)	Other Social Security Number(s) Used	

(f) Are you and your spouse living together?	☒ YES Go to #6	☐ NO Go to (g)

(g) Date you began living apart :   (MM/DD/YYYY)

(h) Address of spouse or name of someone who knows where spouse is. (Complete only if spouse is age 65, blind or disabled.)

6.

(a) Have you had any other marriages?	**You**		**Your Spouse, if filing**	
If never married, check this box ☐	☒ YES Go to (b)	☐ NO Go to 6(c)	☐ YES Go to (b)	☐ NO Go to 6(c)

(b) Give the following information about your prior marriages. If there was more than one prior marriage, show the remaining information in Remarks. Go to #7.

	YOU	YOUR SPOUSE
FORMER SPOUSE'S NAME (including maiden name)	Mike Glenn	
BIRTHDATE (MM/DD/YYYY)	05/16/1960	
SOCIAL SECURITY NUMBER	Unknown	
DATE OF MARRIAGE (MM/DD/YYYY)	12/20/1997	
DATE MARRIAGE ENDED (MM/DD/YYYY)	03/18/1999	
HOW MARRIAGE ENDED	Divorce	

(c) Are you and another person living together in the same household and presenting to others or the community as a married couple?

☐　YES   If YES, provide the date holding out began _____ , then go to (d)*

☒　NO   Go to #7

(d) Other person's Name (First, middle initial, last)	Other person's Social Security Number

*Use SSA-4178 to develop the holding out relationship.

Form SSA-8000-BK, *Application for Supplemental Security Income (SSI)* (Page 3)

| Form **SSA-8000-BK** (05-2021) UF | | | Page 3 of 24 |

7. If you are filing for yourself, go to (a); if you are filing for a child, go to (e).

	You		Your Spouse	
(a) Are you unable to work because of illnesses, injuries or conditions?	☒ YES Go to (b)	☐ NO Go to #8	☐ YES Go to (b)	☐ NO Go to #8
(b) Enter the date you became unable to work.	(MM/DD/YYYY) 06/01/2019		(MM/DD/YYYY)	

	You		Your Spouse	
(c) Are you blind or do you have low vision even with glasses or contacts?	☐ YES Go to (d)	☒ NO Go to (d)	☐ YES Go to (d)	☐ NO Go to (d)

(d) If you were unable to work because of illnesses, injuries, or conditions before you were age 22, do you have a parent who is age 62 or older, unable to work because of illnesses, injuries or conditions, or deceased?

☐ YES   Parent's Name: _____

            Social Security Number: _____

            Address: _____

            _____

            _____

            Parent's Name: _____

            Social Security Number: _____

            Address: _____

            _____

            _____

☒ NO   Go to #8

(e) When did the child become disabled?   (MM/DD/YYYY)

                                                       Go to (f)

| (f) Is the child blind or do they have low vision even with glasses or contacts? | ☐ YES
Go to (g) | ☐ NO
Go to (g) |

(g) Does the child have a parent(s) who is age 62 or older, unable to work because of illness, injuries, or conditions, or deceased?

☐ YES   Parent's Name: _____

            Social Security Number: _____

            Address: _____

            _____

            _____

            Parent's Name: _____

            Social Security Number: _____

            Address: _____

            _____

            _____

☐ NO   Go to #8

8.

Birthplace	City	State	Country (if other than the U.S.)
You	Chicago	Illinois	
Your Spouse, if filing			Go to #9

Form SSA-8000-BK, *Application for Supplemental Security Income (SSI)* (Page 4)

Form **SSA-8000-BK** (05-2021) UF

		You		Your Spouse, if filing	
9.	Are you a United States citizen by birth?	☒ YES Go to #15	☐ NO Go to #10	☐ YES Go to #15	☐ NO Go to #10
10.	Are you a naturalized United States citizen?	☐ YES Go to #15	☐ NO Go to #11	☐ YES Go to #15	☐ NO Go to #11
11.	(a) Are you an American Indian born outside the United States?	☐ YES Go to (b)	☐ NO Go to (c)	☐ YES Go to (b)	☐ NO Go to (c)

(b) Check the block that shows your American Indian status.

You	Your Spouse, if filing
☐ American Indian born in Canada Go to #15	☐ American Indian born in Canada Go to #15
☐ Member of a Federally recognized Indian Tribe; Name of Tribe Go to #15	☐ Member of a Federally recognized Indian Tribe; Name of Tribe Go to #15
☐ Other American Indian Explain in Remarks, then Go to (c)	☐ Other American Indian Explain in Remarks, then Go to (c)

(c) Check the block below that shows your current immigration status

You	Your Spouse, if filing
☐ Amerasian Immigrant Go to #12	☐ Amerasian Immigrant Go to #12
☐ Asylee Date status granted: Go to #14	☐ Asylee Date status granted: Go to #14
☐ Conditional Entrant Date status granted: Go to #14	☐ Conditional Entrant Date status granted: Go to #14
☐ Cuban/Haitian Entrant Go to #14	☐ Cuban/Haitian Entrant Go to #14
☐ Deportation/Removal Withheld Date: Go to #14	☐ Deportation/Removal Withheld Date: Go to #14
☐ Lawful Permanent Resident Go to #12	☐ Lawful Permanent Resident Go to #12
☐ Parolee for One Year Go to #14	☐ Parolee for One Year Go to #14
☐ Refugee Date of entry: Go to #14	☐ Refugee Date of entry: Go to #14
☐ Unknown/Other Explain in Remarks, then Go to (d)	☐ Unknown/Other Explain in Remarks, then Go to (d)

(d) If you have status or have applied for status as the spouse, child, or parent of a child of a US citizen or lawfully admitted permanent resident alien, Go to #13; otherwise Go to #15.

12.	If you are lawfully admitted for permanent residence:		
		You (MM/DD/YYYY)	**Your Spouse** (MM/DD/YYYY)
	(a) Date of Admission		
	(b) Was your entry into the United States sponsored by any person or promoted by an institution or group?	☐ YES Go to (c) ☐ NO Go to (d)	☐ YES Go to (c) ☐ NO Go to (d)

(c) Give the following information about the person, institution, or group, then Go to (d):

Name

Address

Telephone Number

Form SSA-8000-BK, *Application for Supplemental Security Income (SSI)* (Page 5)

Form **SSA-8000-BK** (05-2021) UF   Page 5 of 24

12.		You	Your Spouse, if filing
	(d) What was your immigration status, if any, before adjustment to lawful permanent resident?	Status:	Status:
		(MM/DD/YYYY) From: To:	(MM/DD/YYYY) From: To: Go to (e)
	(e) If filing as an adult, did your parents ever work in the United States before you were age 18?	**You** ☐ YES Go to (f) ☐ NO Go to #14	**Your Spouse, if filing** ☐ YES Go to (f) ☐ NO Go to #14
	(f) Name and Social Security Number of parent(s) who worked.		
	Name		Social Security Number
	Name		Social Security Number

13.		You		Your Spouse, if filing	
	(a) Have you, your child or your parent, been subjected to battery or extreme cruelty while in the United States?	☐YES Go to (b)	☐NO Go to #15	☐YES Go to (b)	☐NO Go to #15
	(b) Have you, your child, or your parent filed a petition with the Department of Homeland Security for a change in immigration status because of being subjected to battery or extreme cruelty?	☐YES Go to #14	☐NO Go to #15	☐YES Go to #14	☐NO Go to #15
14.	Are you, your spouse, or parent an active duty member or a veteran of the armed forces of the United States?	☐YES Explain in #60(b), then Go to #15	☐NO Go to #15	☐YES Explain in #60(b), then Go to #15	☐NO Go to #15
15.	(a) When did you first make your home in the United States?	(MM/DD/YYYY) 07/15/1974 (birth)		(MM/DD/YYYY)	
	(b) Have you lived outside of the United States since then?	☐YES Go to (c)	☒NO Go to #16	☐YES Go to (c)	☐NO Go to #16
	(c) Give the dates of residence outside the United States.	(MM/DD/YYYY) From: To:		(MM/DD/YYYY) From: To:	
16.	(a) Have you been outside the United States (the 50 states, District of Columbia and Northern Mariana Islands) 30 consecutive days prior to the filing date?	☐YES Go to (b)	☒NO Go to #17	☐YES Go to (b)	☐NO Go to #17
	(b) Give the date (MM/DD/YYYY) you left the United States and the date you returned to the United States.	Date Left: Date Returned:		Date Left: Date Returned:	

IF YOU ARE FILING ON BEHALF OF YOUR CHILD, GO TO #17.
IF YOU ARE MARRIED AND YOUR SPOUSE IS NOT FILING FOR SUPPLEMENTAL SECURITY INCOME AND YOU LIVED TOGETHER AT ANY TIME SINCE THE FIRST MOMENT OF THE FILING DATE MONTH, GO TO #17; OTHERWISE GO TO #18.

Form SSA-8000-BK, *Application for Supplemental Security Income (SSI)* (Page 6)

Form **SSA-8000-BK** (05-2021) UF			Page 6 of 24

17.	(a) Is your spouse/parent the sponsor of an alien who is eligible for supplemental security income?	☐ YES Go to (b)	☒ NO Go to #18
	(b) Eligible Alien's Name	Eligible Alien's Social Security Number Go to #18	

18.		**You**		**Your Spouse, if filing**	
	(a) Do you have any unsatisfied felony warrants for your arrest?	☐ YES Go to (b)	☒ NO Go to #19	☐ YES Go to (b)	☐ NO Go to #19
	(b) In which State or Country was this warrant issued?	Name of State/Country Go to (c)		Name of State/Country Go to (c)	
	(c) Was the warrant satisfied?	**You** ☐ YES Go to (d)	☐ NO Go to #19	**Your Spouse, if filing** ☐ YES Go to (d)	☐ NO Go to #19
	(d) Date warrant satisfied	(MM/DD/YYYY)		(MM/DD/YYYY)	

PART 2 - LIVING ARRANGEMENTS - The questions in this section refer to the signature date.

19.	Check the block which best describes your present living situation:		
	☒ Household	Since (MM/DD/YYYY) 09/01/2005	Go to #24
	☐ Non-Institutional Care	Since (MM/DD/YYYY)	Go to #22
	☐ Institution	Since (MM/DD/YYYY)	Go to #20
	☐ Transient or homeless	Since (MM/DD/YYYY)	Go to #37

INSTITUTION

20.	Check the block that identifies the type of institution where you currently reside, then Go to #21:	
	☐ School	☐ Rehabilitation Center
	☐ Hospital	☐ Jail
	☐ Rest or Retirement Home	☐ Other (Specify)
	☐ Nursing Home	

21.	Give the following information about the INSTITUTION:
	(a) Name of institution:
	(b) Date of admission:
	(c) Date you expect to be released from this institution: Go to #37

NON-INSTITUTIONAL CARE

22.	Check the block that best describes your current residence, then Go to #23:		
	☐ Foster Home	☐ Group Home	☐ Other (Specify)

Form SSA-8000-BK, *Application for Supplemental Security Income (SSI)* (Page 7)

Form **SSA-8000-BK** (05-2021) UF   Page 7 of 24

23. Give the following information about your Non-institutional Care:

(a) Name of facility where you live:

(b) Name of placing agency

Address

Telephone Number

(c) Does this agency pay for your room and board?

☐ YES   Go to #37

☐ NO   If NO, who pays?

Go to #37

HOUSEHOLD ARRANGEMENTS

24. Check the block that describes your current residence, then Go to #25:

☐	House	☐	Mobile Home
☒	Apartment	☐	Houseboat
☐	Room (private home)	☐	Other (Specify)
☐	Room (commercial establishment)		

25. Do you live alone or only with your spouse?   ☒ YES Go to #27   ☐ NO Go to #26

26. (a) Give the following information about everyone who lives with you:

Name	Relationship	Public Assistance		Sex		Birthdate	Blind or Disabled		If Under 22				Social Security Number
									Married		Student		
		YES	NO	M	F	MM/DD/YYYY	YES	NO	YES	NO	YES	NO	
		☐	☐	☐	☐		☐	☐	☐	☐	☐	☐	
		☐	☐	☐	☐		☐	☐	☐	☐	☐	☐	
		☐	☐	☐	☐		☐	☐	☐	☐	☐	☐	
		☐	☐	☐	☐		☐	☐	☐	☐	☐	☐	
		☐	☐	☐	☐		☐	☐	☐	☐	☐	☐	
		☐	☐	☐	☐		☐	☐	☐	☐	☐	☐	

If anyone listed is under age 22 and not married, Go to (b); otherwise, Go to #27.

Form SSA-8000-BK, *Application for Supplemental Security Income (SSI)* (Page 8)

26.	(b) Does anyone listed in 26(a) who is under age 18, OR between ages 18-22 and a student, receive income?	☐ YES Go to (c)	☒ NO Go to #27

(c) Child Receiving Income	Source and Type	Monthly Amount
		$
		$
		$
		$
		$
		$

27.	(a) Do you (or does anyone who lives with you) own or rent the place where you live?	☐ YES Go to #28	☒ NO Go to (b)

(b) Name of person who owns or rents the place where you live

  Donald Kemp

Address

  114 Temple St, Lost Angeles, CA

Telephone Number   1-310-555-4444

(c) If you live alone or only with your spouse, and do not own or rent, Go to #37; otherwise, Go to #31.

28.			
	(a) Are you (or your living with spouse) buying or do you own the place where you live?	☐ YES Go to (c)	☒ NO If you are a child living with your parent(s) Go to (b); otherwise Go to #29
	(b) Are your parent(s) buying or do they own the place where you live?	☐ YES Go to (c)	☐ NO Go to #29

(c) What is the amount and frequency of the mortgage payment?

  Amount: $

  Frequency of Payment:

                                                                          Go to (d)

(d) If you are a child living only with your parents, or only with your parents and their other children who are subject to deeming, or with others in a public assistance household, or living alone or with your spouse, Go to #37; otherwise Go to #31.

Form SSA-8000-BK, *Application for Supplemental Security Income (SSI)* (Page 9)

Form **SSA-8000-BK** (05-2021) UF   Page 9 of 24

29.			
(a) Do you (or your living with spouse) have rental liability for the place where you live?	☐ YES Go to (d)		☐ NO If you are a child living with your parent(s) Go to (b); otherwise Go to (c)
(b) Does your parent(s) have rental liability?	☐ YES Go to (d)		☐ NO Go to (c)

(c) Does anyone who lives with you have rental liability for the place where you live?

☐ YES Give name of person with rental liability: _____ Go to #30

☐ NO Give name of person with home ownership: _____ Go to #31

(d) What is the amount and frequency of the rent payment?

    Amount: $

    Frequency of Payment: Go to #30

30.			
(a) Are you (or anyone who lives with you) the parent or child of the landlord or the landlord's spouse?	☐ YES Go to (b)		☐ NO Go to (c)

(b) Name of person related to landlord or landlord's spouse

Relationship

    Name and address of landlord (include telephone number and area code, if known):

(c) If you are a child living only with your parents, or only with your parents and their other children who are subject to deeming, or with others in a public assistance household, or living alone or with your spouse, Go to #37.

31.			
(a) Does anyone living with you contribute to the household expenses? (NOTE: See list of household expenses in #36)	☐ YES Go to (b)	☐ NO	Go to #32
(b) Amount others contribute: $			Go to #32

32.			
(a) Do you eat all your meals out?	☐ YES Go to #33		☐ NO Go to (b)
(b) Do you buy all your food separately from other household members:	☐ YES Go to #33		☐ NO Go to #33

33.			
Do you contribute to household expenses?			
☐ YES Average Monthly Amount: $_____ Go to #34			☐ NO Go to #34

34.			
(a) Do you have a loan agreement with anyone to repay the value of your share of the household expenses?	☐ YES Go to (b)		☐ NO Go to #34(d)

(b) Give the name, address and telephone number of the person with whom you have a loan agreement :

(c) Will the amount of this loan cover your share of the household expenses?	☐ YES Go to #37		☐ NO Go to (d)

(d) **If you contribute** toward household expenses and you answered "NO" to both 32(a) & (b), Go To #35. If you answered "YES" to either 32(a) or 32(b), Go to #36.

If you do not contribute toward household expenses, go to #37.

Form SSA-8000-BK, *Application for Supplemental Security Income (SSI)* (Page 10)

35. (a) Is part or all of the amount in #33 just for food?

☐ YES Give Amount: $ _____   Go to (b)   ☐ NO Go to (b)

(b) Is part or all of the amount in #33 just for shelter?

☐ YES Give Amount: $ _____   Go to #36   ☐ NO Go to #36

36. What is the average monthly amount of the following household expenses:
(Show average over the past 12 months unless you have been residing at your present address less than 12 months. If so, show average for the months you have resided at your present address.)

CASH EXPENSES	AVERAGE MONTHLY AMOUNT
Food (complete only if #32(a) & (b) are answered NO)	$
Mortgage or Rent	$
Property Insurance (if required by mortgage lender)	$
Real Property Taxes	$
Electricity	$
Heating Fuel	$
Gas	$
Sewer	$
Garbage Removal	$
Water	$
TOTAL	$ 0.00 Go to #37

37. (a) Does anyone who does NOT LIVE with you pay for, or provide you or your household (if applicable), any of your food or shelter items?

☐ YES Name of Provider (Person or Agency) John Ford

     List of Items Food

     Monthly Value: $ 200

☐ NO   Go to (b)

(b) Does anyone who does NOT LIVE with you give you, or your household (if applicable), money to pay for any of your or your household's food or shelter items?

☐ YES Name of Provider (Person or Agency) Betty Clark

     List of Items Electricity

     Monthly Value: $ 100

☐ NO   Go to #38

38.

(a) Has the information given in #19-37 been the same since the first moment of the filing date month?	☒ YES Go to (b)	☐ NO Explain in Remarks, then Go to (b)
(b) Do you expect any of this information to change?	☐ YES Explain in Remarks, then Go to #39	☒ NO Go to #39

Form SSA-8000-BK, *Application for Supplemental Security Income (SSI)* (Page 11)

PART 3 - RESOURCES - The questions in this section pertain to the first moment of the filing date month.

39.

	You		**Your Spouse, if filing**	
(a) Do you own or does your name appear, either alone or with other people on any trust?	☐ YES	☒ NO	☐ YES	☐ NO
	Go to (b)	Go to #40	Go to (b)	Go to #40

(b) If you answered "YES" to (a), give the following information:

Title of the Trust	Funding type, i.e., self-funded or third party funded alleged	Date established (MM/DD/YYYY)	Total alleged value	Specific assets contained within the trust, i.e., vehicles, homes, bank accounts, etc.

40.

	You		**Your Spouse**	
(a) Do you own, or does your name appear (alone or with any other person's name) on the title of any vehicles (auto, truck, motorcycle, camper, boat, etc.)?	☒ YES	☐ NO	☒ YES	☐ NO
	Go to (b)	Go to #41	Go to (b)	Go to #41

(b) Owner's Name	Description (Year, Make & Model)	Used For	Current Market Value	Amount Owed
Paul Clark	1997 Ford	Personal	$ 200	$
			$	$
			$	$
			$	$

41.

	You		**Your Spouse**	
(a) Do you own, or does your name appear (alone or with any other person's name) on any land, houses, buildings, real property, property in foreign country, equipment, mineral rights, items in a safe deposit box, assets set aside for emergencies or heirs, or any other property of any kind that has not been shown anywhere else on the application	☐ YES	☒ NO	☐ YES	☒ NO
	Go to (b)	Go to #42	Go to (b)	Go to #42

(b) Describe the property (including size, address, and how it is used). If the property is not used now, when was it last used? Do you plan to use the property in the future?

Item #1

Item #2

Owner's Name	Estimated Current Market Value	Owed on Item
	$	$
	$	$
	$	$
	$	$

Form SSA-8000-BK, *Application for Supplemental Security Income (SSI)* (Page 12)

Form **SSA-8000-BK** (05-2021) UF   Page 12 of 24

42. (a) Do you own, or does your name appear on (either alone or with any other person's name) any of the following items?	You		Your Spouse	
	YES	NO	YES	NO
Cash at home, with you, or anywhere else	☐	☒	☐	☒
Financial Institution Accounts	☐	☒	☐	☒
Achieving a Better Life Experience (ABLE)	☐	☒	☐	☒
Checking	☐	☒	☐	☒
Savings	☐	☒	☐	☒
Credit Union	☐	☒	☐	☒
Christmas Club	☐	☒	☐	☒
Time Deposits/Certificates of Deposit	☐	☒	☐	☒
Individual Indian Money Account	☐	☒	☐	☒
Other (Including IRAs and Keough Accounts)	☐	☒	☐	☒

(b) If all the items in #42(a) are answered "NO", Go to #42(c). For any "YES" answer, give the following information:

Owner's Name	Name of Item	Value	Name & Address of Bank or Other Organization	Identifying Number
		$		
		$		
		$		
		$		

(c) Do you give us permission to obtain any financial records from any financial institution?	You		Your Spouse, if filing	
	☒ YES Go to #43	☐ NO Go to #43	☐ YES Go to #43	☐ NO Go to #43

43. (a) Do you own or does your name appear on any of the following items:	You		Your Spouse	
	YES	NO	YES	NO
Stocks or Mutual Funds	☐	☒	☐	☒
Bonds (Including U.S. Savings Bonds)	☐	☒	☐	☒
Promissory Notes	☐	☒	☐	☒
Other items that can be turned into cash	☐	☒	☐	☒

Form SSA-8000-BK, *Application for Supplemental Security Income (SSI)* (Page 13)

Form **SSA-8000-BK** (05-2021) UF

43. (b) If all the items in #43(a) are answered "NO", Go to #44. For any "YES" answer, give the following information:

Owner's Name	Name of Item	Value	Name & Address of Bank or Other Organization	Identifying Number
		$		
		$		
		$		
		$		

44. (a) Do you own or are you buying any life insurance policies?

	You	Your Spouse
	☐ YES Go to (b) ☒ NO Go to #45	☐ YES Go to (b) ☒ NO Go to #45

(b) Owner's Name	Name of Insured	Name & Address of Insurance Company	Policy Number
Policy (#1)			
Policy (#2)			
Policy (#3)			

	Face Value	Cash Surrender Value	Date of Purchase	Dividends		Accumulations	
				YES	NO	YES	NO
Policy (#1)				☐	☐	☐	☐
Policy (#2)				☐	☐	☐	☐
Policy (#3)				☐	☐	☐	☐

(c) Loans Against Policy?

☐ YES   Policy Number: _____

Amount: $ _____

☐ NO

Go to #45

45. (a) Have you or your spouse acquired any assets since the first moment of the filing date month?   ☐ YES Go to (b)   ☒ NO Go to (c)

(b) Explain:

Form SSA-8000-BK, *Application for Supplemental Security Income (SSI)* (Page 14)

45. (c) Has there been any increase or decrease in the value of you or your spouse's resources since the first moment of the filing date month?   ☐ YES Go to (d)   ☒ NO Go to #46

(d) Explain:

46.

(a) Do you (either alone or jointly with any other person) own any:	You		Your Spouse	
	YES	NO	YES	NO
Life estates or ownership interest in an unprobated estate?	☐	☐	☐	☐
Items acquired or held for their value as an investment?	☐	☐	☐	☐

(b) Give the following information for any "Yes" answer in #46(a); otherwise, Go to #47.

Owner's Name	Name of Item	Value	Amount Owed	Name & Address of Bank or Other Organization
		$	$	
		$	$	
		$	$	
		$	$	

47.

(a) Do you have any assets set aside for burial expenses such as burial contracts, trusts, agreements, or anything else you intend for your burial expenses? Include any items mentioned in #39, #41-45, and #49.	You		Your Spouse	
	☐ YES Go to (b)	☒ NO Go to #48	☐ YES Go to (b)	☒ NO Go to #48

(b) DESCRIPTION (Where appropriate, give name & address of organization and account/ policy number.)	Value	When Set Aside (MM/DD/YYYY)	Owner's Name
Item (#1)	$		
Item (#2)	$		

For Whose Burial	Is Item Irrevocable?		Will Interest Earned or Appreciation in Value Remain in the Burial Fund?	
Item (#1)	☐ YES	☐ NO	☐ YES Go to #48	☐ NO Explain in (c)
Item (#2)	☐ YES	☐ NO	☐ YES Go to #48	☐ NO Explain in (c)

(c) Explanation

Form SSA-8000-BK, *Application for Supplemental Security Income (SSI)* (Page 15)

Form **SSA-8000-BK** (05-2021) UF

48.			You	Your Spouse
	(a) Do you own any cemetery lots, crypts, caskets, vaults, urns, mausoleums, or other repositories for burial or any headstones or markers?		☐ YES ☒ NO Go to (b) Go to #49	☐ YES ☒ NO Go to (b) Go to #49

(b) Owner's Name	Description	For Whose Burial	Relationship to You or Your Spouse	Current Market Value
				$
				$
				$ Go to #49

49.		You	Your Spouse
	(a) Have you or your spouse sold, transferred title, disposed of or given away, any money or other property, (including money or property in foreign countries), since the first moment of the filing date month or within the 36 months prior to the filing date month?	☐ YES ☒ NO Go to (b)	☐ YES ☒ NO Go to (b)
	(b) If you co-owned any money or property with another person(s), did you or any co-owner sell, transfer, or give away any co-owned money or property within the 36 months prior to the filing date month?	☐ YES ☒ NO	☐ YES ☒ NO

IF YOU ANSWERED "YES" TO (a) OR (b), GO TO (c). IF "NO" TO BOTH, GO TO #50.

(c) Owner's/Co-Owner's Name	Description of Property	Date of Disposal
Item (#1)		
Item (#2)		
Item (#3)		

Name and Address of Purchaser or Recipient	Relationship to Owner	Value of Property and/or Amount of Cash Gift
Item (#1)		
Item (#2)		
Item (#3)		

Sales Price or Other Consideration	Are Other Consideration or Proceeds Expected? Explain.	Do You Still Own Part of the Property?
Item (#1)		☐ YES ☐ NO
Item (#2)		☐ YES ☐ NO
Item (#3)		☐ YES ☐ NO

	Sold on Open Market?	Given Away?	Traded for Goods/ Services?
Item (#1)	☐ YES ☐ NO	☐ YES ☐ NO	☐ YES ☐ NO
Item (#2)	☐ YES ☐ NO	☐ YES ☐ NO	☐ YES ☐ NO
Item (#3)	☐ YES ☐ NO	☐ YES ☐ NO	☐ YES ☐ NO

Form SSA-8000-BK, *Application for Supplemental Security Income (SSI) (Page 16)*

Form **SSA-8000-BK** (05-2021) UF   Page 16 of 24

PART 4 - INCOME

50.	(a) Since the first moment of the filing date month, have you (or your spouse) received or do you (or your spouse) expect to receive income in the next 14 months from any of the following sources?	You		Your Spouse	
		YES	NO	YES	NO
	State or Local Assistance Based on Need	☐	☒	☐	☒
	Refugee Cash Assistance	☐	☒	☐	☒
	Temporary Assistance for Needy Families	☐	☒	☐	☒
	General Assistance from the Bureau of Indian Affairs	☐	☒	☐	☒
	Disaster Relief	☐	☒	☐	☒
	Veteran Benefits Based on Need (Paid Directly or Indirectly as a Dependent)	☐	☒	☐	☒
	Veteran Payments Not Based on Need (Paid Directly or Indirectly as a Dependent)	☐	☒	☐	☒
	Other Income Based on Need	☐	☒	☐	☒
	Social Security	☐	☒	☐	☒
	Black Lung	☐	☒	☐	☒
	Railroad Retirement Board Benefits	☐	☒	☐	☒
	Office of Personnel Management (Civil Service)	☐	☒	☐	☒
	Pension (Foreign Military, State, Local, Private, Union, Retirement or Disability)	☐	☒	☐	☒
	Military Special Pay or Allowance	☐	☒	☐	☒
	Unemployment Compensation	☐	☒	☐	☒
	Workers' Compensation	☐	☒	☐	☒
	State Disability	☐	☒	☐	☒
	Insurance or Annuity Payments	☐	☒	☐	☒
	Dividends/Royalties	☐	☒	☐	☒
	Rental/Lease Income Not from a Trade or Business	☐	☒	☐	☒
	Alimony	☐	☒	☐	☒
	Child Support	☐	☒	☐	☒
	Other Bureau of Indian Affairs Income	☐	☒	☐	☒
	Gambling/Lottery Winnings	☐	☒	☐	☒
	Other Income or Support	☐	☒	☐	☒

Form SSA-8000-BK, *Application for Supplemental Security Income (SSI)* (Page 17)

Form **SSA-8000-BK** (05-2021) UF						Page 17 of 24

50. (b) Give the following information for any block checked YES in #50(a); otherwise, Go to #51

Person Receiving Income	Type of Income	Amount Received	Frequency of Payment	Date Expected or Received	Source (Name, Address of Person, Bank, Organization, or Company)	Identifying Number
		$				
		$				
		$				

IF YOU EVER RECEIVED SSI BEFORE, GO TO #51; OTHERWISE GO TO #52.

	You	Your Spouse
51. Are any overpayments being collected from benefits you receive from the Social Security Administration, Railroad Retirement Board, Office of Personnel Management, Veterans' Affairs, Military Pensions, Military Special Pay Allowances, Black Lung, Workers' Compensation, or State Disability or Unemployment Benefits?	☐ YES ☒ NO Explain in Go to #52 Remarks, then Go to #52	☐ YES ☒ NO Explain in Go to #52 Remarks, then Go to #52
52. Since the first moment of the filing date month, have you received or do you expect to receive any meals or other gifts which are not cash?	☐ YES ☒ NO Explain in Go to #53 Remarks, then Go to #53	☐ YES ☒ NO Explain in Go to #53 Remarks, then Go to #53
53. (a) Have you (or your spouse) received wages or sick pay since the first moment of the filing date month through the current month?	☐ YES ☒ NO Go to (b) Go to (e)	☐ YES ☒ NO Go to (b) Go to (e)

(b) Name and Address of Employer (include telephone number and area code, if known)

You

Go to (c)

Your Spouse

Go to (c)

(c)	Date last worked (MM/DD/YYYY)	Date last paid (MM/DD/YYYY)	Date next paid (MM/DD/YYYY)
You			
Your Spouse			

	Your Amount	Your Spouse's Amount
(d) Total monthly wages received (before any deductions)	$	$

	You	Your Spouse
(e) Do you (or your spouse) expect to receive any wages in the next 14 months?	☐ YES ☒ NO Go to (f) Go to #54	☐ YES ☒ NO Go to (f) Go to #54

Form SSA-8000-BK, *Application for Supplemental Security Income (SSI) (Page 18)*

Form **SSA-8000-BK** (05-2021) UF

53. (f) Name and address of employer if different from #53(b) (include telephone number, if known)

You

Your Spouse

(g) Give the following information:

Rate of Pay	Amount Worked Per Pay Period	How Often Paid	Pay Day or Date Paid	Date Last Paid (MM/DD/YYYY)
You				
Your Spouse				

	You		Your Spouse	
(h) Do you expect any change in wage information provided in #53(g)	☐ YES Go to (i)	☐ NO Go to #54	☐ YES Go to (i)	☐ NO Go to #54

(i) Explain Change:

You

Your Spouse

54. (a) Have you been self-employed at any time since the beginning of the taxable year in which the filing date month occurs or do you expect to be self-employed in the current taxable year?

	You		Your Spouse	
	☐ YES Go to (b)	☒ NO Go to #55	☐ YES Go to (b)	☒ NO Go to #55

(b) Give the following information; then Go to #55

Date(s) Self-Employed	Type of Business	Last Year's: Gross Income	Last Year's: Net Profit	Last Year's: Net Loss
		$	$	$
Date(s) Self-Employed	Type of Business	This Year's: Gross Income	This Year's: Net Profit	This Year's: Net Loss
		$	$	$

55. If you or your spouse are blind or disabled, do you have any special expenses that you paid which are necessary for you to work?

	You		Your Spouse	
	☐ YES Explain in Remarks, then Go to #56	☒ NO Go to #56	☐ YES Explain in Remarks, then Go to #56	☒ NO Go to #56

Form SSA-8000-BK, *Application for Supplemental Security Income (SSI)* (Page 19)

Form **SSA-8000-BK** (05-2021) UF   Page 19 of 24

56.	(a) Does your spouse/parent who lives with you have to pay court-ordered support?	☐ YES Go to (b)	☒ NO Go to NOTE

(b) Give amount and frequency of court-ordered support payment.

    Amount: $

    Frequency of Payment:

Go to (c)

(c) Give the following information about the person who receives these payments:

    Name:

    Address:

NOTE: IF YOU ARE FILING AS A CHILD AND YOU ARE EMPLOYED OR AGE 18 - 22 (WHETHER EMPLOYED OR NOT), GO TO #57; OTHERWISE, GO TO #58.

57.	(a) Have you attended school regularly since the filing date month?	☐ YES Go to (d)	☐ NO Go to (b)
	(b) Have you been out of school for more than 4 calendar months?	☐ YES Go to (c)	☐ NO Go to (c)
	(c) Do you plan to attend school regularly during the next 4 months?	☐ YES Explain absence in Remarks and Go to (d)	☐ NO Go to #58

(d) Name of School	Name of School Contact	Dates of Attendance		Course of Study
		From	To	
	Phone Number	Hours Attending or Planning to Attend		

PART 5 - POTENTIAL ELIGIBILITY FOR SUPPLEMENTAL NUTRITION ASSISTANCE PROGRAM (SNAP)/MEDICAL ASSISTANCE/OTHER BENEFITS

58.		You		Your Spouse, if filing	
	(a) Are you currently receiving SNAP benefits (formerly food stamps)?	☐ YES Go to (b)	☒ NO Go to (c)	☐ YES Go to (b)	☐ NO Go to (c)
	(b) Have you received a recertification notice within the past 30 days?	☐ YES Go to (e)	☒ NO Go to #59	☐ YES Go to (e)	☐ NO Go to #59
	(c) Have you filed for SNAP in the last 60 days?	☐ YES Go to (d)	☒ NO Go to (e)	☐ YES Go to (d)	☐ NO Go to (e)
	(d) Have you received an unfavorable decision?	☐ YES Go to (e)	☒ NO Go to #59	☐ YES Go to (e)	☐ NO Go to #59
	(e) If everyone in the household receives or is applying for SSI, Go to (f); otherwise Go to #59.				
	(f) May I take your SNAP application today?	☐ YES Go to #59	☒ NO Explain in (g)	☐ YES Go to #59	☐ NO Explain in (g)
	(g) Explanation:				

Form SSA-8000-BK, *Application for Supplemental Security Income (SSI)* (Page 20)

Form **SSA-8000-BK** (05-2021) UF   Page 20 of 24

59.	You may be eligible for Medicaid. However, you must help your State identify other sources that pay for medical care. Also, you must give information to help the State get medical support for any child(ren) who is your legal responsibility. This includes information to help the State determine who a child's parent is. If you want Medicaid, you must agree to allow your State to seek payments from sources, such as insurance companies, that are available to pay for your medical care. This includes payments for medical care for you or any person who receives Medicaid and is your legal responsibility. The State cannot provide you Medicaid if you do not agree to this Medicaid requirement. If you need further information, you may contact your Medicaid Agency.

IN STATES WITH AUTOMATIC ASSIGNMENT OF RIGHTS LAWS, Go to (b).

	You		Your Spouse, if filing	
(a) Do you agree to assign your rights (or the rights of anyone for whom you can legally assign rights) to payments for medical support and other medical care to the State Medicaid agency?	☒ YES Go to (b)	☐ NO Go to #60	☐ YES Go to (b)	☐ NO Go to #60
(b) Do you, your spouse, parent or stepparent have any private, group, or governmental health insurance that pays the cost of your medical care? (Do not include Medicare or Medicaid.)	☐ YES Go to (c)	☒ NO Go to (c)	☐ YES Go to (c)	☐ NO Go to (c)
(c) Do you have any unpaid medical expenses for the 3 months prior to the filing date month?	☒ YES Go to #60	☐ NO Go to #60	☐ YES Go to #60	☐ NO Go to #60

60.

	You					
(a) Have you ever worked under the U.S. Social Security System?	☐ YES Go to (b)			☒ NO Go to (b)		

(b) Have you, your spouse, or a former spouse (or parent if you are filing as a child) ever:	You		Your Spouse/ Parent		Filed for Benefits	
	YES	NO	YES	NO	YES	NO
Worked for a railroad	☐	☒	☐	☒	☐	☒
Been in military service	☐	☒	☐	☒	☐	☒
Worked for the Federal Government	☐	☒	☐	☒	☐	☒
Worked for a State or Local Government	☐	☒	☐	☒	☐	☒
Worked for an employer with a pension plan	☐	☒	☐	☒	☐	☒
Belonged to union with a pension plan	☐	☒	☐	☒	☐	☒
Worked under a Social Security system or pension plan of a country other than the United States?	☐	☒	☐	☒	☐	☒

(c) Explain and include dates for any "Yes" answer given in #14 or #60(a); otherwise Go to #61.

You

Your Spouse, if filing/Your Parent, if filing as a child:

PART 6 - MISCELLANEOUS - (Answer #61 ONLY IF YOU ARE APPLYING ON BEHALF OF SOMEONE ELSE: OTHERWISE GO TO #62.

61.	(a) Name of Person/Agency Requesting Benefits.	Relationship to Claimant	Your Social Security Number (or EIN)
	(b) If SSA determines that the claimant needs help managing benefits, do you wish to be selected representative payee?	☐ YES	☐ NO (Explain in Remarks)
	(c) Have you ever served as a representative payee for a Social Security beneficiary or SSI claimant?	☐ YES	☐ NO Go to #62

There is one exception to the requirement that you submit an original record to prove your age: You can give the SSA an uncertified photocopy of a birth registration notification where it's the practice of the local birth registrar to issue them in this way.

The agency's preferred proof is a birth certificate or hospital birth record that was recorded before age five, or a religious record (such as a baptism record) that shows your date of birth and was recorded before age five. If you can't obtain any of these, the SSA will ask for other convincing evidence of your date of birth or age at a certain time. Possible evidence includes the following (20 C.F.R. § 404.701–716):

- original family Bible or family record
- school records
- census records
- statement signed by a physician or midwife present at your birth
- insurance policies
- marriage record
- passport
- employment record
- delayed birth certificate, or
- immigration or naturalization record.

The SSA needs proof of your age unless your eligibility for disability or your benefit amount doesn't depend on how old you are (like with SSI).

b. Medical Records

The SSA will need several kinds of medical records, including the following:

- information from your doctors, therapists, hospitals, clinics, and caseworkers
- laboratory and test results
- names, addresses, phone numbers, and fax numbers of your doctors, clinics, and hospitals, and
- names of all medications you take.

You might not have your medical records when you first apply for benefits. That's okay—Disability Determination Services (DDS), the agency that processes the medical portion of your application, will send a request to your medical providers for your records. (See Section E, below.) Waiting for medical records is one of the biggest causes of delays in the disability process. The more medical records you can turn over to the SSA with your application, the faster a decision on your claim is likely to be made. Also, if you claim that your disability began many years before you filed for benefits, the SSA has to obtain those old medical records, which can further delay your claim.

The SSA won't send your disability application forms (such as SSA-16 or SSA-8000-BK) to your treating doctors. In fact, the SSA specifically asks that you don't send your paperwork to your doctor. This is good advice, because your form might get lost or be delayed for months in a doctor's office. You're responsible for completing your application forms, not your doctors. Instead, the SSA will request specific medical information it wants directly from your doctors without your needing to do anything other than identify the doctors. If you want to get involved, call your doctor's office and make sure your doctor responds to the SSA's request for information and sends in a complete and accurate report.

CAUTION
Ask your doctors to send you a copy of the documents they send the SSA. This is extremely important. Review each one carefully. If your doctor is missing treatment records or misstates your symptoms or abilities, let your doctor know so they can fix the error and start keeping better records.

c. Employment Information

You'll need to inform the SSA of the names of your employers and your job duties for the last 15 years. If you can't remember, write "unknown" in the space where the information is required, but don't leave it blank. (The SSA might think that you haven't worked at all instead of not remembering where you worked.)

You'll also be asked if your medical disorder affected your attendance at work or the hours you could work, and whether your employer had to give you special help so you could do your job. Adding this information can help you because, if Social Security concludes that you're disabled, it might help the agency find that your disability started at an earlier date—resulting in a larger amount of disability benefits. In some instances, knowing that a former employer gave you help might even

be critical in determining whether you are disabled.

Specific information about your work history can be extremely important. You'll need to give your job title, type of business, dates worked, days per week, and rate of pay. Again, if you can't remember, state that in the appropriate spaces. Do not leave parts of the form blank. Where you can remember, you'll be asked to describe your basic job duties, such as:

- the machines, tools, and equipment you used and the operations performed
- the technical knowledge or skills involved in your work
- the type of writing you did and the nature of any reports, and
- the number of people you supervised and the extent of your supervision.

You'll be asked to describe the type and frequency of physical activity you did at work, including walking, standing, sitting, and bending. In addition, the SSA wants to know about how much lifting and carrying you did on the job.

You don't have to answer all questions about your work at the time you apply for disability benefits, but the information will have to be given to the SSA at some time before the agency makes a disability determination. If you leave out any information, you'll hear from the SSA or DDS. If you don't understand a question, contact an SSA representative at the Field Office or the disability examiner who has been assigned your claim once it leaves the Field Office.

d. Activities of Daily Living

The claims representative or interviewer may give you forms asking detailed questions about your activities of daily living, called *ADLs*. You'll fill out your ADLs on Form SSA-3373, *Function Report—Adult*. This form asks specific questions about what you do during a typical day to give the SSA an idea of how your impairments affect your daily life. ADLs are important in all kinds of disabilities, especially mental disorders. Questions typically deal with your ability to do household chores, cook, shop, visit friends, attend social activities, and attend to finances.

If you don't answer the questions about your ADLs when you apply, DDS will send you forms requesting the information. (DDS is discussed in more depth in Section B6, below.) Some people just put "none" in answer to all questions about what they do during a typical day. These answers are considered uncooperative and won't help your claim, because everyone does something. Even sitting in a chair all day watching TV is an activity. Try to explain how your mental or physical impairments are related to what you can or can't do during the day.

Don't rely on your doctor to answer these questions. Few doctors actually know what their patients do during the day. If you want your doctors to have this information, discuss your daily activities with them. The SSA is more likely to find you disabled if your doctor can verify the limitations you reported in your ADLs.

e. School Records

If you're applying for disability on behalf of a child, you'll need to provide school records regarding the child's disability. (This is explained in more detail in Chapter 3.)

f. Income and Asset Information

To qualify for SSI, your income and assets can't exceed a certain limit. You'll need records—such as bank statements, rent receipts, and car registrations—to prove that your earnings and savings are below the SSI eligibility thresholds.

In addition, the SSA will want a copy of your most recent W-2 form (if you're employed by someone else), or your tax return (if you're self-employed.) The agency needs this information is to help determine your income and assets.

3. Field Office Observations

If you don't apply over the phone, the Field Office representative will observe you while you complete your application form. The representative will note how you perform reading, writing, answering, hearing, sitting, understanding, using your hands, breathing, seeing, walking, and anything else that might relate to your claim. You won't be given any medical tests at the Field Office, and the person who takes your application isn't a doctor. But the representative will write down these observations.

The SSA reviewers will pay attention to these observations, which don't determine the outcome of your claim but are considered with the other data in your file. If the Field Office representative stated that you had no difficulty walking while the medical information says you do, then the observation would be disregarded. But usually, field officers bring things to the attention of the evaluator that otherwise might be missed. For example, a Field Office representative can note if you need special assistance in completing your application because of apparent mental illness or illiteracy. Somebody who is unable to read or write has fewer work opportunities, which can be important in the final decision on whether to award benefits.

4. Onset of Your Disability

On your disability application, you'll have to state the date you became disabled. This is called the *alleged onset date* (AOD). (See Chapter 10 for more on the onset date.)

If you're applying for SSDI, you set the date of your AOD. But the SSA doesn't have to use your AOD as your onset date. The agency won't allow you to receive benefits for any time when you were engaged in substantial gainful activity and earning too much money to qualify for SSDI. So the SSA gives you an *established onset date*, which can be different from the AOD that you put in your application. Your established onset date is influenced by both nonmedical eligibility factors (see the next section) and the date the SSA considered you unable to do substantial gainful work.

If you're applying for SSI only, your alleged onset date doesn't matter. That is because SSI benefits are never awarded for earlier than the first day of the month after you file for disability.

5. Nonmedical Eligibility Requirements

Having a medical disorder that prevents you from working is only one factor in determining your eligibility to receive disability benefits. First, you'll need to establish that you're covered under SSDI or that you're qualified for SSI benefits because of low income and resources. You must satisfy the nonmedical eligibility requirements before the SSA will even consider your medical disorder. Determining whether you satisfy the nonmedical requirements of the SSDI or SSI programs is the job of the Field Office. Nonmedical criteria include your age, work history, marital status, income, and other factors.

Age, education, and work experience can also be important later in your claim. (These are called *vocational factors* and are discussed in Chapter 9.)

6. Processing Your Application (or Claim)

DDS—Disability Determination Services—is the state agency that decides whether your medical disorder is severe enough to qualify you for benefits. Your file is sent to DDS once the SSA Field Office determines that you meet the nonmedical eligibility requirements based on the information in your application and your interview with an SSA representative. Several states with large populations have more than one DDS office, but most states have only one. (Your local SSA Field Office can give you the contact information for DDS that will handle your claim.)

Although Field Offices deal with all kinds of Social Security issues, DDS is concerned only with determining your medical eligibility for disability benefits. While DDS is federally funded, DDS employees and consultants are hired by your state, not by the SSA.

Once DDS receives your file, representatives there collect more information about your claim—particularly medical information—and decide whether you're

eligible for disability benefits. DDS sends requests to your treating doctors and hospitals for your medical records, based on the information you provide. DDS might also obtain additional nonmedical information, such as detailed data about your work activities or skills.

If DDS needs more information, a claims examiner will contact you by telephone or in writing. It's crucial that DDS be able to get in touch with you in order to obtain full and accurate information about your health and, in some cases, to ask that you undergo medical examinations or laboratory tests at the SSA's expense. If DDS can't get a hold of you, you risk having your entire application denied before the evidence is fully considered. The types of evidence DDS might need are discussed in Chapter 5, and the role of DDS in determining your disability claim is discussed more fully in Chapter 6.

 CAUTION
It's not the job of the Social Security Field Office to make a medical determination about you. This is the responsibility of DDS. If you meet the nonmedical eligibility requirements, the SSA Field Office must forward your application to DDS. Social Security representatives at Field Offices and contact stations are not doctors and shouldn't give you an opinion regarding whether you're medically disabled.

C. The Role of Health Care Professionals

Health care professionals play an important role in the disability determination process and participate in the process in a variety of ways. These professionals include:

- *treating sources*, who provide medical evidence and opinions on behalf of their patients
- *consultative examiners*, who perform necessary examinations or tests at the SSA's request
- *medical consultants*, who review claims at DDS, and
- *medical experts*, who testify at administrative hearings.

1. Treating Sources

A treating source is the physician, nurse practitioner, physician's assistant, psychologist, or other acceptable medical source who has treated or evaluated you and has had an ongoing treatment relationship with you. (Acceptable medical sources are discussed in Chapter 5.)

Your treating source is usually the best source of medical evidence about the nature and severity of your condition. If DDS or the SSA needs additional examinations or tests to process your claim, your treating source is usually the preferred person to perform the examination or test.

The treating source is neither asked nor expected to decide if you're disabled. But the SSA may ask your treating source to provide a statement about how your health problems have an impact on your ability to do work-related physical or mental activities.

2. Consultative Examination Sources

If your treating sources don't provide sufficient medical evidence for DDS to make a disability determination, the agency might request that you go to a consultative examination (CE). Consultative examinations or tests are performed by physicians, psychologists, or other health professionals, such as audiologists and speech therapists. All consultative examiners must be currently licensed in your state and have the training and experience to perform the type of examination or test requested.

If the SSA requests that you attend a CE, you won't have to pay for it. The SSA will bear the cost of the exam and the agency might, in some cases, provide transportation for you to attend.

If you're denied benefits and then appeal, the SSA can ask DDS to administer the tests or examinations if it needs more information.

Medical professionals who serve as consultative examiners must have a good understanding of the SSA's disability programs and the type of evidence required

Life-Threatening Situations

If you have had a consultative examination and the examining doctor detects something that might be life threatening, DDS must send a copy of the examination medical report to your treating doctor, if it appears your treating doctor might be unaware of the problem. A DDS doctor might also have an examiner call or write to you stating that there is a potentially serious problem you should have evaluated. In all cases, DDS will include in your file any action it took regarding life-threatening situations.

In general, any doctor who examines you should inform you of any serious impairments. But this might not happen if the doctor assumes DDS will tell you, or if you're no longer around when the doctor gets the results of some test. For example, say DDS has you undergo a chest X-ray. By the time the report is done, but before the doctor can tell you about a suspicious and possibly cancerous tumor, you have left the hospital. A DDS medical consultant who sees the X-ray report should ask the examiner to send a copy of the report to your treating doctor, provided you consented to the release. DDS medical consultants who receive information of a life-threatening condition must exercise medical judgment regarding the urgency of the situation and method of informing you.

to make a disability determination. DDS is responsible for oversight of its CE program.

DDS advises these medical professionals of their responsibilities and obligations regarding confidentiality, as well as the administrative requirements for scheduling examinations and tests and issuing a report. (Consultative examinations are discussed more fully in Chapter 5.)

3. Medical Consultants

The medical consultants who review claims for disability benefits on behalf of DDS or the SSA include licensed medical doctors of virtually all specialties and psychologists with a Ph.D. The work is performed in a DDS office, an SSA regional office, or the SSA's central office. Medical consultants do strictly paper reviews of your medical records—the consultant usually has no contact with you. (Medical consultants are discussed in more detail in Chapter 6.)

4. Medical Experts

If you appeal your claim after being denied benefits twice, an administrative law judge (ALJ) in the Office of Hearings Operations (OHO) will hear your case. To help them in their work, ALJs sometimes request expert testimony on complex medical issues from medical experts (MEs). Unlike medical consultants, MEs have no official authority regarding whether you should be allowed benefits. They only testify in hearings.

Each hearing office maintains a list of MEs who are called to testify as expert witnesses at hearings. The SSA pays MEs a fee for their services. (Medical experts don't work in state or federal agencies.) They never examine disability claimants in person, though they may review your medical records. (Appeals and medical experts are covered in Chapter 12.)

D. How Other Disability Payments May Affect Social Security Benefits

Workers' compensation benefits or benefits you receive from another public disability program affect the amount of Social Security disability benefits you receive.

1. Workers' Compensation and Public Disability

Workers' compensation payments are made to a worker because of a job-related injury or illness, or to the workers' dependents if the worker dies from a work-related injury or illness. "Workers' comp," as it's commonly called, might be paid by a government workers' compensation agency, an employer, or an insurance company on behalf of employers. In most states, employers are required to participate in workers' compensation insurance programs.

No state has a workers' comp program that covers all jobs, but many of the state programs cover most jobs. Some states cover only work that's considered dangerous, while others cover only companies with a minimum number of employees. Coverage varies for agricultural workers and domestic workers (meaning people who work in private homes doing work such as cleaning, babysitting, and cooking). All laws include some or all diseases attributable to the worker's occupation. Most states exclude coverage for injuries due to the employee's intoxication, willful misconduct, or gross negligence.

Other public disability payments that may affect your Social Security benefits are those paid under a federal, state, or local government plan that covers conditions that aren't job related. Examples include civil service disability benefits, military disability benefits, state temporary disability benefits (available in six states), and state or local government retirement benefits based on disability.

 SEE AN EXPERT

Workers' compensation and public disability benefit cases can be legally complex and vary among states, especially when combined with Social Security disability benefits. If you might be eligible for benefits under multiple programs, consider using the services of an attorney experienced in how Social Security disability interacts with other programs to make sure you obtain all the benefits you're entitled to.

a. How Much Your Disability Benefits May Be Reduced

Your Social Security disability benefits will be reduced so that the combined amount of your Social Security benefits plus your workers' compensation and public disability payment doesn't exceed 80% of your average current earnings. But the SSA should deduct legal, medical (including future medical expenses paid by workers' compensation), and rehabilitation expenses from a workers' compensation award before reducing your Social Security disability benefit.

To calculate your SSDI disability benefit, first the SSA will calculate your *average current earnings*. (All earnings covered by Social Security, including amounts above the maximum taxable by Social Security, can be used when figuring average current earnings.)

Average current earnings are the highest of the following:

- the average monthly earnings the SSA used to figure your Social Security disability benefit
- your average monthly earnings from any work you did that's covered by Social Security during the five highest years in a row after 1950, or
- your average monthly earnings from work during the year you became disabled, or in the highest year of earnings you had during the five-year period just before you became disabled.

The SSA uses your average earnings and a complex formula to calculate your disability benefit. Then your monthly disability benefit, including any benefits payable to your family members, is added to your workers' compensation or other public disability payment. If this sum exceeds 80% of your average current earnings, the excess amount is deducted from your Social Security benefit. But the amount of the combined benefits will never be less than the total Social Security benefits before they were reduced. The reduction will last until the month you reach age 65 or the month your workers' compensation and/or other public disability payment stops, whichever comes first.

Some states offset (reduce) their workers' compensation benefits to account for SSDI, rather than the other way around. Social Security won't reduce an SSDI payment when the state is already offsetting its workers' compensation payment.

b. Reporting Other Benefits to the SSA

You must notify the SSA if any of the following occurs:

- The amount of your workers' compensation or public disability payment changes. This may affect the amount of your Social Security benefits.
- Your workers' compensation or public disability payment ends. If your workers' compensation or public disability payment stops, your Social Security benefit may increase.

- You receive a lump-sum disability payment. If you get a lump-sum workers' compensation or other disability payment to settle your claim, your Social Security benefits may be reduced.

2. Railroad Retirement Act and Social Security Disability

The Railroad Retirement Act sets up a system of benefits for railroad employees and their dependents and survivors. The Railroad Retirement Act works with the Social Security Act to provide disability benefits—as well as retirement, survivors, and dependents benefits—to people who've worked in the railroad industry.

An important distinction is made between railroad workers who have worked less than ten years and those who have worked ten years or more. The Social Security Act typically covers wage compensation for people who've worked less than ten years of work in the railroad industry before becoming disabled.

The wages of people who've worked for a railroad for ten years or more generally are covered under the Railroad Retirement Act. The distinction has primary importance when you seek survivors benefits based on the death of the insured railroad worker, and so the details aren't covered here. But

if it might apply to you, be aware of the distinction and ask your local SSA office for more information.

3. Federal Employee Benefits

If you're receiving both SSDI and disability retirement benefits under the Federal Employee Employment System (FERS), your benefits may be reduced. Your FERS annuity benefit will be reduced by 100% of your Social Security benefit during the first 12 months. After 12 months, your FERS annuity will be decreased by 60% of your SSDI benefit. So, although your SSDI won't be decreased, your FERS benefit may be reduced.

If you're in the FERS, your SSDI benefits are generally not affected if you're receiving a FERS retirement pension. But if you worked as a FERS employee before 1983, when Social Security taxes were not with-held from your federal employment income, your SSDI benefits could be affected—if you had less than 30 years of employment or you qualify for a Government Pension Offset (GPO) as a spouse.

FERS benefits and Social Security disability benefits can involve complex issues. You may want to consult with your local SSA office or a financial adviser experienced in this area of law about how these benefits interact.

4. Black Lung Benefits and Social Security Disability

Black lung benefits are payments to coal miners—and their survivors—who become disabled from a lung disease known as *pneumoconiosis* from breathing fine dust-like particles of coal while working in the mines. The Federal Coal Mine Health and Safety Act of 1969 assigned initial responsibility for processing black lung benefit claims to the SSA. The Department of Labor (DOL) assumed eventual responsibility.

For many years, the SSA handled some aspects of the black lung program for the DOL, such as taking initial applications and deciding black lung benefit appeals. However, as of March 30, 2012, the SSA no longer has any responsibility or involvement in the black lung program. If you want to apply for black lung benefits, appeal a denial of benefits, or have any questions about that program, you will need to contact the DOL.

5. Long-Term Disability Insurance Benefits

If you receive long-term disability (LTD) insurance benefits through your employer, the LTD insurance company is allowed to offset your SSDI benefit against your LTD payment. In other words, the insurance company can subtract the amount of your Social Security benefit from your LTD benefit. As a result, most long-term disability policies will require you to file for Social Security disability benefits.

6. What Payments Don't Affect Your Social Security Disability Benefits?

The SSA doesn't count certain types of payments in considering whether to reduce your disability check. These include:

- Veterans Administration (VA) benefits
- Supplemental Security Income (SSI) payments, and
- private pensions.

E. Availability and Disclosure of Confidential Records

Several laws and regulations govern access to, and disclosure of, confidential information and official records entrusted to the SSA, DDS, and other nonfederal entities or individuals.

1. Your Medical Records

Under the Privacy Act, you or your authorized representative has the right to examine federal government records pertaining to you. (Public Law 93-579; 5 U.S.C. § 552a; 20 C.F.R. §§ 401.30–200.) Your *authorized representative* is someone you appoint in writing to pursue your rights under the

Social Security Act. You can name any responsible person, including a lawyer, a disability advocate, or a family member, as your authorized representative.

This right means that you can request to see the medical and other evidence used to evaluate your application for SSDI or SSI benefits. Make this request in writing to the SSA Field Office handling your claim (see below for more details on the SSA procedure for releasing records). Medical records include:

- records kept by physicians or other health professionals
- records derived from reports by physicians or other health professionals
- medical evaluations and determinations on Social Security forms, including rationales and diagnoses, and
- records created by laypeople relevant to your claim (such as statements by witnesses who saw epileptic seizures or signs of mental impairment).

This law concerns your own requests to see your medical records. You can't directly access your child's medical records. Instead, you must name a physician or another health professional (excluding family members) to receive the records as a *designated representative*.

The SSA will release your records to you as long as the SSA doesn't think they will have an adverse effect on you. According to the SSA, an adverse effect is likely to occur

if direct access by an individual to their medical records is expected to:

- disrupt a doctor-patient relationship
- interfere with the patient's medical management, or
- negatively affect the patient in some other way.

Here are some of the SSA's own examples of when an adverse effect is and isn't likely to occur.

EXAMPLE 1: Devi has been diagnosed as diabetic. Devi's medical record shows that she has a good prognosis with treatment involving medication, diet, weight control, and exercise. An adverse effect is not likely, and the SSA is likely to release Devi's records to her directly.

EXAMPLE 2: Klaus has a severe mental health disorder, and his doctor has noted that Klaus struggles with aggressive behavior tendencies. Because the doctor's candid remarks about Klaus might provoke him to threaten the doctor or the doctor's staff, the SSA is likely to find that there would be an adverse effect of releasing the records directly to Klaus. Instead, the agency is likely to designate a representative to receive the records.

EXAMPLE 3: Kaitlyn has a severe heart impairment. The doctor has noted in the medical record that Kaitlyn's knowing the severity of her condition could cause complications. An adverse effect is possible, and the SSA might not release the records to Kaitlyn.

There is one exception, however. Direct disclosure of medical information can be made to you, upon request, in any case in which you have requested a hearing or a review by the Appeals Council.

The person at the SSA deciding whether you should see your medical records doesn't have to be a doctor. Nondoctors in SSA Field Offices can make that determination, or they can refer your file to doctors working for the SSA. If the SSA thinks that releasing your medical records will have an adverse effect on you, you won't be told. The SSA policy instruction specifically states: "Do not tell an individual that direct access of a medical record is likely to have an adverse effect on him/her."

Instead, you will be told that Privacy Act regulations require that you designate a representative to receive your records. Not many people are aware of this policy, probably because few people ask to see their medical records.

Your representative, however, doesn't have the authority to withhold any part of your medical records. After an initial discussion with you about the records, your representative must provide them to you promptly if you ask to see them. Details regarding your right to access to your records can be found at 20 C.F.R. Part 404, § 401.55.

Sample Letter When SSA Wants a Designated Representative

Dear [*claimant*]:

You asked for copies of medical records we used in your [*type of*] claim. We reviewed the records. We decided that we must give them to someone you choose who will review and discuss the information with you. Because this is medical information, we prefer you choose a doctor or a health worker.

Please give us the name and address of the person you want to receive your medical records. You may use the office address shown above to send us this information.

If you have any questions, you may call, write, or visit any Social Security office. If you call or visit our office, please have this letter with you and ask for [*name of SSA representative*]. The telephone number is [*xxx-xxx-xxxx*].

If you receive a letter like the one above, the SSA thinks that your seeing your records will have an adverse effect on you. If you don't follow through by naming a designated representative, the SSA will send you a form letter like the one below.

Sample Letter If You Don't Give a Designated Representative

Dear [_claimant_]:

We are writing to you about your request for copies of medical records we used in your [_type of_] claim.

As we told you earlier, we require that you choose someone to receive your records. This person will review the information and discuss it with you. Because this is medical information, you may wish to choose a doctor or a health worker to review your records.

Since you have not yet chosen someone, we want to give you some suggestions about groups that might be able to help. We have found that the following groups are often willing to help people by reviewing their records:

- local social services
- local public health services
- legal aid societies, and
- other public agencies.

When you give us the name and address of the person you want to review your medical records, we will make sure they get the records. You may use the office address shown above to send us this information.

If you have any questions, you may call, write, or visit any Social Security office. If you call or visit our office, please have this letter with you and ask for [_name of SSA representative_]. The telephone number is [_xxx-xxx-xxxx_].

If you still don't name a representative, the SSA will mail your file to the SSA's central Office of Disability in Baltimore. If this happens, you'll have to wait months for a response to any further requests for your file. To avoid waiting longer than you need to, make sure you respond in a timely manner to the SSA's request for a designated representative.

2. Consultative Examination Records

If the SSA requires that you attend a consultative examination (CE), you must give permission for the agency to get medical records from your treating doctor for the CE doctor to review. (The consultative examiner needs to see some of your treating doctor's notes in order to have a better sense of your health history during the exam.)

After your consultative exam, the SSA can't release the results of the exam to your treating doctor without your consent, but it's generally to your benefit to have CE records sent to your treating doctor. That's because a CE doctor might have information your treating doctor doesn't have.

However, the SSA doesn't have to share the results of your consultative exam with you, except in life-threatening situations (as discussed in Section C, above). Most disability applicants don't ask CE doctors for personal copies of their examinations or tests. If they do, the examiner must contact DDS for permission to release the information.

3. Disclosure With Consent

Most disclosures by the SSA require your consent. Your consent must be in writing, be signed by you or your authorized representative, be dated, and specify what information you want disclosed. The SSA or DDS must obtain your consent to:

- contact your treating sources for information necessary to review your claim
- release your records (particularly your medical records) to the SSA, and
- disclose information about you to any third party, such as physicians and medical institutions—with the exception of parties permitted disclosure without your consent. (See Section E4, below.)

In most situations, any consent statement you sign will include a revocation clause, allowing you to take back your consent, or else it will be valid for only a specified time.

4. Disclosure Without Consent

Under the U.S. Privacy Act, the SSA can disclose your records without your consent for certain purposes. The SSA must keep a record of all such disclosures. Acceptable reasons for disclosure without consent include the following:

- sharing information within an SSA agency on a need-to-know basis
- complying with the Freedom of Information Act (FOIA)
- routine uses (purposes compatible with the reason the information was collected, such as disability determination)
- assisting the Census Bureau in planning or carrying out a census, survey, or related activity
- research and statistical purposes
- transferring records to the National Archives of the United States when their historical or other value warrant their continued preservation
- cooperating with another government agency's civil or criminal law enforcement activity
- helping someone whose health and safety are affected by compelling circumstances (after notice of disclosure is sent to you)
- informing the House of Representatives or the Senate, to the extent necessary, on a matter within its jurisdiction
- cooperating with the Comptroller General while performing duties of the General Accounting Office, or
- a court order.

More specific examples of disclosures that are covered under the above list include information disclosed to the following people and governmental agencies:

- your representative payee (the person designated to receive your payments) or authorized representative to pursue a Social Security claim or to manage payments
- your designated representative

- the IRS if needed to conduct an audit, collect Social Security taxes, or investigate a tax crime
- the Department of Justice or U.S. Postal Service for law enforcement purposes, or
- members and staff of the legislative or executive branches, if they need non–tax return (and usually non-medical) information in order to answer inquiries from you or your authorized representative.

Finally, if the SSA sends your records to someone without your consent, the SSA doesn't have to inform you of that action.

5. Penalties for Violating Disclosure Laws

Your privacy rights are protected by a variety of federal statutes.

Social Security Act. Under the Social Security Act, the following violations are punishable as misdemeanors by a fine of up to $1,000 and/or a year in prison:

- disclosure by an SSA employee of tax return information, files, records, reports, or other SSA papers or documents, except as permitted by regulation or federal law, or
- misrepresentation by an individual who purports to be an employee or agent of the United States, with the intent to elicit information regarding another person's date of birth, employment, wages, or benefits.

Freedom of Information Act (FOIA). The FOIA provides that agency officials found to have arbitrarily and capriciously withheld disclosable records may be subject to disciplinary action recommended by the Special Counsel to the Merit Systems Protection Board.

Privacy Act. You can sue the SSA in a U.S. District Court for various reasons, including:

- refusing to amend your Social Security record
- refusing to let you (or another person chosen by you) view your record and obtain a copy of it
- failing to disclose that you dispute information in your record, or
- failing to accurately maintain your record.

If the court determines that the SSA acted intentionally or willfully, it may assess against the United States the attorneys' fees, other litigation costs, and actual damages you sustain. The court can award you at least $1,000 in damages in such cases.

The SSA might be found guilty of a misdemeanor, mostly due to the willful disclosure of information in violation of the Policy Act. You can't normally bring criminal actions against an SSA employee unless you convince the Justice Department that the employee willfully and knowingly disclosed information. If they're convinced, the agency might prosecute.

Finally, an SSA employee may be subject to disciplinary action for knowing and willful violations of the Policy Act.

Internal Revenue Code (IRC). Under the code, a federal employee who discloses information found on a federal tax return may be found guilty of a felony and fined $5,000 and/or sentenced to five years in prison. Furthermore, you can sue the IRS and any person who knowingly or negligently discloses federal tax returns or return information.

Alcohol and Drug Abuse Patient Records. Any person who violates the Drug Abuse and Treatment Act or the Comprehensive Alcohol Abuse and Alcoholism Prevention, Treatment, and Rehabilitation Act by disclosing such information may be fined as much as $500 for a first offense and as much as $5,000 for each subsequent offense.

6. Reporting Possible Violations

If you suspect an SSA employee has violated one of the above laws, report the incident to the employee's supervisor or call the SSA's Office of the Inspector General (OIG) Hotline at 800-269-0271; TTY 866-501-2101. You can also write to the SSA on the internet at www.socialsecurity.gov/oig. Click "Fraud," then "Report Fraud."

F. Fraud and Other Crimes

Both SSA and DDS employees are looking for fraud—for example, allegations of disability that aren't consistent with other information and indications that an individual may have been coached.

The SSA says fraud has occurred when someone, with the intent to wrongfully obtain a benefit, right, or credit, knowingly makes a false statement, causes a false statement to be made, willfully attempts to conceal a material fact, or fails to disclose a material fact. (§§ 208 and 1632 of the Social Security Act.)

Claimants have been known to claim that they have impairments they don't have. Most of the time, this is innocent—perhaps they self-diagnosed after reading about their symptoms. But sometimes it isn't, like when a person says they have a serious illness while their medical records show no such evidence. Some doctors can aid fraudulent claims as well—they might know they're giving a diagnosis to the SSA that isn't supported by current medical knowledge.

The SSA rarely goes after treating doctors or claimants for fraud—the agency needs the goodwill of both the public and medical professionals, and it's difficult to prove intentional lies. But the SSA doesn't ignore fraud. Examiners ignore statements they know are false when making disability determinations.

The SSA may identify fraud anywhere in the claims process. If the SSA finds fraud after determining that a person is eligible for benefits, the SSA can reopen the file and redo the determination (at any time), ignoring the false information.

It is a crime to do any of the following:

- furnish false information in connection with your Social Security records or to obtain someone else's records
- use an SSN obtained through false information
- use someone else's SSN
- disclose or force the disclosure of or use an SSN in violation of U.S. law
- forge or falsify SSA documents
- conspire over a false claim
- knowingly buy, sell, or alter an SSN card, or
- process an SSN card or counterfeit an SSN card.

Civil penalties can also be imposed for fraud. Amendments made to the Social Security Protection Act of 2004 impose civil penalties of up to $5,000 per occurrence for not notifying the SSA of changed circumstances that affect eligibility or benefit amounts. These penalties apply when a person or organization knew (or should have known) that a fact was withheld that could affect eligibility for benefits, and that the failure to come forward was misleading. For example, penalties would apply if somebody who has a joint bank account with a beneficiary continues to receive the beneficiary's Social Security checks after the beneficiary's death, or if a person receives benefits under one SSN while working under another SSN.

Civil penalties can also apply for engaging in the following activities:

- claiming that your services are endorsed by the SSA, including the misleading use of SSA symbols or emblems
- selling services to the public that are available for no cost from the SSA, unless clearly disclosing that fact
- converting a beneficiary's benefit to a third party, or
- marketing products or services using certain prohibited words (such as "Death Benefits Update," "Federal Benefit Information," "Funeral Expenses," or "Final Supplemental Program").

You should be aware of these rules because they are meant to protect the public, including Social Security disability beneficiaries.

Disability Benefits for Children

A bout 1,000,000 children receive disability benefits from the Social Security Administration (SSA). This chapter is for the parents and caregivers of children (generally considered to be people under the age of 18) with disabilities, as well as for the parents and caregivers of dependent adults who've been disabled since childhood.

Although some of this information appears in other chapters, we bring it together here to provide one place for important information needed by parents and caregivers of disabled children.

The person who handles the benefits on behalf of a child is called, in Social Security lingo, the *representative payee*. The representative payee must be willing and able to be responsible for managing the child's benefits. Practically speaking, this means the representative payee is typically the child's parents.

CAUTION

The representative payee is not the same as the authorized representative. An authorized representative is any person, including an attorney, named in writing by the disability applicant (*claimant*), to act in place of the claimant in pursuing his or her rights under the Social Security Act. If you hire an attorney to help with your child's disability claim, the lawyer won't be managing your child's benefits if you win the case.

You can use the information in this chapter to understand the kinds of Social Security Disability Insurance (SSDI) and Supplemental Security Income (SSI) available to an eligible child and to learn how the SSA evaluates disability claims for children.

A. Three Benefit Programs for Children

There are three ways a child might be eligible for SSDI or SSI benefits.

1. SSDI Auxiliary Benefits for Children Under 18

Although this is a book about disability benefits, children without disabilities might be eligible for Social Security dependents' or survivors benefits—what the agency calls *auxiliary benefits or dependents benefits*. Children can be eligible for auxiliary benefits if they're dependent on someone (usually, but not always, a parent) who receives disability benefits, or if they're the surviving children of someone who died while receiving benefits.

Social Security dependents benefits are available to unmarried children younger than 18 based on the work record of a parent who collects Social Security or disability benefits. Social Security survivors benefits are also available to children younger than 18 based on the work record of a deceased parent who was entitled to

Social Security disability benefits. *On the (work) record* means that the child's benefits are paid based on the earnings record of someone else—the insured worker who paid enough Social Security taxes to qualify for SSDI benefits. Parent means biological parent, adoptive parent, or stepparent.

Child dependents and survivors benefits are called auxiliary (meaning providing additional help) benefits because they're meant to ease the financial burden of the disabled worker. The theory behind auxiliary benefits is that a disabled parent or the surviving spouse of a deceased disabled worker needs more money to take care of dependent children, because they can't get that extra help from their job or their spouse.

A child found to be eligible for dependents benefits can receive them until they turn 18—or 19 if enrolled as a full-time student in high school. Full-time students will receive a form from the SSA at the beginning and end of each school year asking whether they're still in school. The SSA can stop the benefits if the student (or living parent) doesn't send back a completed form.

If the child turns 19 during a school term, the SSA can continue their benefits for up to two months, in order to allow the student to complete the term. Before turning 19, a student may receive benefits during a vacation period of four months or less if the student plans to go back to school full time at the end of the vacation.

If the student leaves school, reduces their enrollment from full time to part time, or changes schools, the student or parent must notify the SSA immediately. The SSA also needs to know if the student is paid by an employer for attending school. A student over 18 who stops attending school generally can receive benefits again upon returning to school full time before age 19, but they'll need to contact the SSA and reapply for benefits.

If you have a stepchild who receives benefits on your earnings record, and you divorce your stepchild's parent, the stepchild's benefit will end the month following the month the divorce becomes final. (This is not the case with biological or legally adopted children.) You must notify the SSA as soon as the divorce becomes final.

2. SSDI Benefits for Adults Disabled Since Childhood

Social Security dependents or survivors benefits normally end when a child reaches age 18, or age 19 if the child is a full-time student. But children who are disabled can continue to receive benefits if both of the following requirements are met:

- The disability began before age 22.
- The recipient is the child of someone receiving Social Security retirement or disability benefits, or of someone who was insured for Social Security retirement or disability benefits but is now deceased.

Someone who qualifies under these rules is said by the SSA to be an *adult child*, or an *adult disabled since childhood*. Although many recipients of these benefits are in their 20s and 30s, the benefit is considered a child's benefit because of the eligibility rules.

Sometimes, a person doesn't become eligible for a disabled child's benefit until well into adulthood.

> **EXAMPLE:** John retires and starts collecting Social Security retirement benefits at age 62. He has a 38-year-old son, Ben, who has had cerebral palsy since birth. Ben couldn't collect Social Security benefits before John retired because John was still working and not collecting benefits. When John retired, however, Ben started collecting a disabled adult child's benefit based on John's Social Security record. If, instead, Ben had become disabled when he was 23 or older, he would have to rely on his own earnings record to collect SSDI (or he could try to qualify for SSI).

3. SSI Benefits for Children

SSI is a program that pays monthly benefits to elderly and disabled people with low incomes and limited assets. Children under the age of 18 can qualify for SSI if they meet the SSA's definition of disability (see Section C, below) and if their income and assets—or, more likely, the income and assets of their parents—fall within the eligibility requirements.

The income and asset limits vary from state to state, and were discussed in Chapter 1. Check with your local Social Security office to find out the SSI eligibility levels in your state. You can call 800-772-1213 from 8:00 a.m. to 7:00 p.m. Monday through Friday (local time) to find the location of an SSA office near you, or go to www.ssa.gov/locator.

The SSA considers a child who has turned 18 to be an adult, and eligibility for SSI for people 18 and older is no longer determined under the rules for children. For example, a parent's income and assets aren't relevant in deciding if their adult son or daughter is eligible to receive SSI.

Instead, the child's own income and resources are used to determine eligibility for SSI. This means that children who weren't eligible as minors because their parents' income and assets were too high might become eligible when they turn 18—assuming their income and assets are below the SSI earnings and assets threshold.

Note that if, at age 18, the young adult still receives food and shelter paid for by their parents, the SSA considers these to be *in-kind income*, which will result in a lower disability benefit payment.

When a child SSI beneficiary reaches age 18, they'll be evaluated under adult disability criteria (during what's called a *redetermination*). The SSA will send a written notice to the child's parents before the child's 18th birthday. If the child isn't medically eligible for disability benefits any longer, the benefits usually end. But in some special circumstances, the benefits can continue temporarily. When this happens, the benefits are referred to as *301 Payments*.

In order to qualify for 301 payments, the beneficiary must participate in vocational rehabilitation or an educational program that started before the month in which disability would have stopped under the SSA's rules, and the SSA must determine that continued participation in the program is likely to result in the beneficiary no longer needing disability benefits.

Some specific examples given by the SSA of acceptable programs are:

- an Individualized Education Program (IEP) for a youth who is between ages 18 and 21
- a vocational rehabilitation agency using an individualized plan for employment
- support services using an individualized written employment plan
- a written service plan with a school under Section 504 of the Rehabilitation Act
- an approved Plan to Achieve Self-Support (PASS). (See Chapter 13 for more on PASS.)

Other approved special education programs or similar services might also qualify. If you have questions about whether a specific program qualifies, contact your local Social Security office.

Section 301 payments will continue until the beneficiary stops participating in one

of the qualifying programs or finishes the program, or the SSA determines that even if the person continues in the program, they're likely to resume disability benefits.

More details can be found at www.ssa. gov/pubs/EN-05-11005.pdf.

B. Applying for SSDI or SSI Benefits

You can apply for SSDI or SSI benefits for your child by calling or visiting your local SSA office. Bring the child's Social Security card—or at least the number—and birth certificate with you. If you are applying for SSI for your child, you also will need to provide records that show your income and your assets, as well as those of the child.

You will be sent or given SSA-3820-BK, *Disability Report—Child*, to fill out. We provide a sample form here. Look at the form to see what information you will need to gather to fill it out.

 CAUTION
You must use forms provided by the SSA. You can obtain them at your local SSA Field Office or by calling the SSA hotline at 800-772-1213, Monday through Friday (except holidays), from 8:00 a.m. to 7:00 p.m. If you're deaf or hard of hearing, TTY service representatives are available at the same times at 800-325-0778. You can also download many necessary forms from the SSA website at www.ssa.gov.

Form SSA-3820-BK, *Disability Report—Child* (Page 3)

Form **SSA-3820-BK** (05-2021) UF
Discontinue Prior Editions
Social Security Administration

Page 3 of 14
OMB No. 0960-0160

Disability Report - Child

Section 1 - Information About the Child

A. Child's Name *(First, Middle Initial, Last)*

Penny A. Reeves

B. Child's Social Security Number

123-45-6789

C. Your Name *(If agency, provide name of agency and contact person)*

Marilyn Reeves

Your Mailing Address *(Number and Street, Apt. No. (if any), P.O. Box, or Rural Route)*

43-1 West Markam Street

City	State	ZIP Code
Oklahoma City	OK	73999

Your Email Address (Optional)   PAReeves@yahoo.com

D. Your Daytime Phone Number   *(If you do not have a phone number where we can reach you, give us a daytime number where we can leave a message for you.)*

405   555-1111

Area Code   Number   [X] Your Number   [ ] Message Number   [ ] None

E. What is your relationship to the child?   Parent/Mother

F. Can you speak and understand English? [X] Yes [ ] No   If "No," what is your preferred language? _____

NOTE: If you cannot speak and understand English, we will provide you an interpreter, free of charge. **If you cannot speak and understand English**, is there someone we may contact who speaks and understands English and will give you messages?

[ ] Yes *(Enter name, address, phone number, relationship)*   [ ] No

Name: _____   Relationship to Child: _____

Address: _____

(Number, Street, Apt. No. (if any), P.O. Box, or Rural Route)

City	State	ZIP	Daytime Phone	Area Code	Number

Can you **read and understand English**? [X] Yes [ ] No

G. Does the child live with you?   [X] Yes [ ] No   If "No," with whom does the child live?

Name: _____   Relationship to Child: _____

Address: _____

(Number, Street, Apt. No. (if any), P.O. Box, or Rural Route)

City	State	ZIP	Daytime Phone	Area Code	Number

Can this person **speak and understand English**?   [ ] Yes [ ] No

If "No," what is this person's preferred language? _____

Can this person **read and understand English**?   [ ] Yes [ ] No

Form SSA-3820-BK, *Disability Report—Child* (Page 4)

Form **SSA-3820-BK** (05-2021) UF

Section 1 - Information About the Child

H. Can the child speak and understand English? ☒ Yes ☐ No

    If "No," what languages can the child speak? _____

    If the child understands any other languages, list them here: _____

I. What is the child's height *(without shoes)*? 56 in.

    What is the child's weight *(without shoes)*? 80 lbs.

J. Does the child have a **medical assistance** card? ☐ Yes ☒ No

    If "Yes," show the **number** here: _____

Section 2 - Contact Information

A. Does the child have a legal guardian or custodian other than you?

    ☐ Yes *(Enter name, address, phone number, relationship)* ☒ No

Name: _____

Address: _____

        (Number, Street, Apt. No. (if any), P.O. Box, or Rural Route)

City _____ State _____ ZIP _____

Daytime Phone Number _____ _____

        Area Code   *Number*

Relationship to Child: _____

    Can this person **speak and understand English**? ☐ Yes ☐ No

      If "No," what is this person's preferred language? _____

    Can this person **read and understand English**? ☐ Yes ☐ No

B. Is there another adult who helps care for the child and can help us get information about the child if necessary?

    ☒ Yes *(Enter name, address, phone number, relationship)* ☐ No

Name of Contact: Betty Slocum

Address: 300 West Pine Street

        (Number, Street, Apt. No. (if any), P.O. Box, or Rural Route)

    Oklahoma City   OK   555-1789

City _____ State _____ ZIP _____

Daytime Phone Number: 405   555-1789

               Area Code   *Number*

Relationship to Child: _____

    Can this person **speak and understand English**? ☒ Yes ☐ No

      If "No," what is this person's preferred language? _____

    Can this person **read and understand English**? ☒ Yes ☐ No

Form SSA-3820-BK, *Disability Report—Child* (Page 5)

Section 3 - The Child's Illnesses, Injuries or Conditions and How They Affect Him/Her

A. What are the child's disabling **illnesses, injuries, or conditions?**

Intellectual disability

Heart disease from birth

B. When did the child become disabled?   4-14-2009

                                                 MM/DD/YYYY

C. Do the child's illnesses, injuries or conditions cause **pain** or other symptoms?   ☒ Yes ☐ No

Section 4 - Information About the Child's Medical Records

A. Has the child been seen by a **doctor/hospital/clinic** or anyone else for the illnesses, injuries or conditions?

☒ Yes ☐ No

B. Has the child been seen by a **doctor/hospital/clinic** or anyone else for emotional or mental problems?

☒ Yes ☐ No

Form SSA-3820-BK, *Disability Report—Child* (Page 6)

Section 4 - Information About the Child's Medical Records

Tell us who may have medical records or other information
about the child's illnesses, injuries or conditions.

C. List **each Doctor/HMO/Therapist/Other**. Include the child's **next appointment**.

1. Name

   Dr. Jessica Cook, psychologist (Ph.D.)

	Dates
Street Address 1001 Polk Street	First Visit November 2009

City Oklahoma City	State OK	ZIP 73888	Last Visit January 2016
Phone 405 555-1234 *Area Code* *Number*	Patient ID # (if known)		Next Appointment January 2017

   Reasons for visits

   Penny's intellectual disability

   What treatment was received?

   Testing (IQ and others); advice about Penny's behavior and limitations

2. Name

   Dr. John Barrow

	Dates
Street Address 95 Capitol Avenue	First Visit May 18, 2009

City Oklahoma City	State OK	ZIP 73887	Last Visit July 2016
Phone 405 555-3333 *Area Code* *Number*	Patient ID # (if known)		Next Appointment July 2017

   Reasons for visits

   Evaluation of Penny's heart problem

   What treatment was received?

   Heart surgery to repair defects present at birth

Form SSA-3820-BK, *Disability Report—Child* (Page 7)

Section 4 - Information About the Child's Medical Records

Doctor/HMO/Therapist/Other

3. Name			Dates
Peggy Hall, M.D.			
Street Address			First Visit
975 Fairview Drive			June 2009
City	State	ZIP	Last Visit
Oklahoma City	OK	73888	October 2015
Phone		Patient ID # (if known)	Next Appointment
Area Code Number			October 2016

Reasons for visits

Regular medical check-ups. Dr. Hall is Penny's pediatrician.

What treatment was received?

For Penny's heart condition, consulting with Dr. Barrow

If you need more space, use Section 10.

D. List each **Hospital/Clinic**. Include the child's **next appointment**.

1. Hospital/Clinic	Type of Visit	Dates	
Name	[X] **Inpatient Stays**	Date In	Date Out
Children's Hospital	(Stayed at least overnight)	April 2009	June 2009
Street Address	[X] **Outpatient Visits**		
183 Popular Avenue	(Sent home same day)		
City Oklahoma City	[ ] **Emergency Room Visits**	Date First Visit	Date Last Visit
State OK ZIP		Sept 2009	Sept 2009
Phone		Dates of Visits	
Area Code Number		Once 2009	

Next appointment	The child's hospital/clinic number
None	Unknown

Reasons for visits

Penny's heart had an irregular rhythm and she was short of breath

What treatment did the child receive?

Oxygen and drugs to make her heart rhythm regular.

What doctors does the child see at this hospital/clinic on a regular basis?

Mostly Dr. Hall, but sometimes other doctors have substituted.

Form SSA-3820-BK, *Disability Report—Child* (Page 8)

Section 4 - Information About the Child's Medical Records

Hospital/Clinic

2.	Hospital/Clinic	Type of Visit		Dates	
	Name	☐ **Inpatient Stays** *(Stayed at least overnight)*		Date In	Date Out
	Street Address	☐ **Outpatient Visits** *(Sent home same day)*			
	City	☐ **Emergency Room Visits**		Date First Visit	Date Last Visit
	State / ZIP				
	Phone / *Area Code* / *Number*			Dates of Visits	

Next **appointment**

The child's hospital/clinic number

Reasons for visits

What **treatment** did the child receive?

What **doctors** does the child see at this hospital/clinic on a regular basis?

If you need more space, use Section 10.

E. Does **anyone else have medical records or information** about the child's illnesses, injuries or conditions (foster parents, social workers, counselors, tutors, school nurses, detention centers, attorneys, insurance companies, and/or Worker's Compensation), or is the child scheduled to see anyone else?

☐ Yes (If "Yes," complete information below.)   ☒ No

Name			Dates
Address			First Visit
City	State	ZIP	Last Seen
Phone / *Area Code* / *Number*			Next Appointment
Claim Number *(if any)*			
Reasons for Visits			

If you need more space, use Section 10.

Form SSA-3820-BK, *Disability Report—Child* (Page 9)

Section 5 - Medications

Does the child currently take any **medications** for illnesses, injuries or conditions? ☒ Yes ☐ No

If "Yes," tell us the following: *(Look at the child's medicine containers, if necessary)*

Name of Medicine	If Prescribed, Give Name of Doctor	Reason for Medicine	Side Effects The Child Has
Propranol	Dr. Hall	Irregular heart	feels tired, sleepy

If you need more space, use Section 10.

Section 6 - Tests

Has the child had, or will he/she have, any **medical tests** for illnesses, injuries, or conditions?

☐ Yes ☐ No   If "Yes," tell us the following *(give approximate dates, if necessary)*

Kind of Test	When Was/Will Tests Be Done (Month, Day, Year)	Where Done (Name of Facility)	Who Sent The Child For This Test
EKG (Heart Test)	2009, 2011, other dates	Hospital and office	Dr. Hall
Treadmill (Exercise Test)	None		
Cardiac Catheterization	01/01/2009	Children's Hospital	Dr. Barrow
Biopsy - Name of body part	None		
Speech/Language	Currently	Fair Park School	School
Hearing Test	Yes, forgot date	Dr. Hall's office	Dr. Hall
Vision Test	Yes, forgot date	Dr. Hall's Office	Dr. Hall
IQ Testing	01/01/2013	Dr. Cook's office	Dr. Cook
EEG (Brain Wave Test)	01/01/2009	Children's Hospital	Dr. Hall
HIV Test	None		
Blood Test (Not HIV)	Blood count, liver, other	Children't Hospital	Dr.Hall
Breathing Test	No		
X-Ray - Name of body part	No		
MRI/CAT Scan - Name of body part Heart	MRI 2009, 2012	Children's Hospital	Dr. Barrow

If the child has had other tests, list them in Section 10.

Form SSA-3820-BK, *Disability Report—Child* (Page 10)

Section 7 - Additional Information

A. Has the child been **tested or examined** by any of the following?

Headstart (Title V)	☐ Yes	☒ No
Public or Community Health Department	☐ Yes	☒ No
Child Welfare or Social Service Agency or WIC	☐ Yes	☒ No
Early Intervention Services	☐ Yes	☒ No
Program for Children with Special Health Care Needs	☐ Yes	☒ No
Mental Health/Developmental Disabilities Center	☒ Yes	☐ No

B. Has the child received Vocational Rehabilitation or other employment support services to help him or her go to work?

☐ Yes ☒ No

If you answered "Yes" to any of the above A. or B., please complete C. below:

C.   1. Name of Agency   Community Mental Health Center

     Address   1001 Polk Street

     (Number, Street, Apt. No. (if any), P.O. Box, or Rural Route)

Oklahoma City	OK	93888
City	State	ZIP

     Phone Number   405   555-6666

                Area Code   *Number*

     Type of Test IQ test   When Done   01/01/2013

     Type of Test   When Done

     File or Record Number   don't know

   2. Name of Agency

     Address

     (Number, Street, Apt. No. (if any), P.O. Box, or Rural Route)

City	State	ZIP

     Phone Number

                Area Code   *Number*

     Type of Test   When Done

     Type of Test   When Done

     File or Record Number

If the child has had other tests, list them in Section 10.

Form SSA-3820-BK, *Disability Report—Child* (Page 11)

Section 8 - Education

A. Is this child currently enrolled in any school?   ☒ Yes, grade: 1st   ☐ No (too young)

         ☐ No, other reason (complete B)

B. Other reason the child is not enrolled in school:

C. List the name of the school the child is **currently attending** and give dates attended. If the child is no longer in school, list the name of the last school attended and give dates attended.

Name of School Peabody Elementary

Address 2500 Pine Street

(Number, Street, Apt. No. (if any), P.O. Box, or Rural Route)

Oklahoma City	Polk	OK	93777
City	County	State	ZIP

Phone Number   405   555-7777

      Area Code   Number

Dates Attended 8/2014 - Current

Teacher's Name Ms. Harrison

Has the child been tested for behavioral or learning problems? ☒ Yes ☐ No
If "Yes", complete the following:

Type of Test IQ   When Done 01/01/2015

Type of Test McCarthy Scale Children Abilities   When Done 01/01/2016

Is the child in special education?   ☒ Yes ☐ No
If "Yes", and different from above, give:

Name of Special Education Teacher Ms. Ramirez

Is the child in speech/language therapy?   ☒ Yes ☐ No
If "Yes", and different from above, give:

Name of Speech/Language Therapist Mr. Johnson

Form SSA-3820-BK, *Disability Report—Child* (Page 12)

Section 8 - Education

D. List the names of all other schools **attended in the last 12 months** and give dates attended.

Name of School See above.

Address

(Number, Street, Apt. No. (if any), P.O. Box, or Rural Route)

City   County   State   ZIP

Phone Number

       Area Code   *Number*

Dates Attended

Teacher's Name

Was the child tested for behavioral or learning problems? ☐ Yes ☐ No
If "Yes", complete the following:

Type of Test   When Done

Type of Test   When Done

Was the child in special education? ☐ Yes ☐ No
If "Yes", and different from above, give:

Name of Special Education Teacher

Was the child in speech/language therapy? ☐ Yes ☐ No
If "Yes", and different from above, give:

Name of Speech/Language Therapist

If the child has had other tests, list them in Section 10.

E. Is the child attending Daycare/Preschool? ☐ Yes ☐ No
If "Yes", complete the following:

Name of Daycare/Preschool/Caregiver

Address

(Number, Street, Apt. No. (if any), P.O. Box, or Rural Route)

City   County   State   ZIP

Phone Number

       Area Code   *Number*

Dates Attended

Teacher's/Caregiver's Name

Form SSA-3820-BK, *Disability Report—Child* (Page 13)

Section 9 - Work History

A. Has the child ever worked (including sheltered work)? ☐ Yes ☒ No
   If "Yes", complete the following:

   Dates Worked _____

   Name of Employer _____

   Address _____
                (Number, Street, Apt. No. (if any), P.O. Box, or Rural Route)

   _____
   City   County   State   ZIP

   Phone Number _____ _____
                   Area Code   *Number*

   Name of Supervisor _____

B. List job title, and briefly describe the work and any problems the child may have had doing the job.

_____
_____
_____
_____
_____
_____
_____
_____
_____

Section 10 - Date and Remarks

Please give the date you filled out this disability report.

1/11/2023
_____
Date (MM/DD/YYYY)

Use this section for any additional information about your child.

Penny tires easily and is frustrated by not being able to learn as fast as other children. Her teachers say she is falling further and further behind in her school work. Dr. Hall says Penny's heart is becoming more irregular and increasing in size. She says Penny needs more tests in the hospital and might even need surgery again, but we can't afford the costs. Penny's doctors and teachers say they will provide any information requested. Please contact me, Penny's other, if there is any problem obtaining Penny's medical or school records. Also, I request Penny's medical information be evaluated by a real doctor to determine her disability also that Penny's treating doctors' opinions be considered.

If a child meets the initial nonmedical eligibility requirements, their file is forwarded to a state agency called Disability Determination Services (DDS). There, a disability evaluation team—made up of a claims examiner and a medical consultant—reviews the child's case to decide if the SSA's definition of disability has been met. (See Chapter 6 for more on DDS agencies, examiners, and medical consultants.)

The doctors at DDS need thorough and detailed medical records to help them decide if your child is disabled. You can speed up the process by providing your child's medical records to the SSA, or helping the SSA get them. When you fill out the application for your child, you'll be asked to provide names, addresses, and telephone numbers of all the doctors, hospitals, clinics, and specialists your child has visited. Be as thorough as you can. If you have them, provide the dates of visits to doctors and hospitals, insurance policy numbers, and any other information that will help the SSA get your child's medical records as soon as possible.

If your child is under age 18 and applying for SSI, you'll be asked to describe how your child's disability limits their ability to function like other children their age. Be ready to let DDS know the names of teachers, day care providers, and family members who can give information about how your child's day-to-day activities are affected by their impairments. If you can get any school records, bring them along.

In many communities, the SSA has made special arrangements with medical providers, social services agencies, and schools to help it get the information it needs to process your child's claim. Most DDSs have Professional Relations Officers who work directly with these organizations. But don't rely solely on these officers to get the information. You need to be an active participant in your child's quest for benefits.

C. Disability Evaluation

SKIP AHEAD
The first section below applies only to children applying for SSI. As mentioned above, children under 18 can't receive SSDI benefits unless they qualify for dependents benefits from an eligible parent. Most minor children will need to apply for disability under the SSI program.

1. Disability in Children for SSI

Unlike adult disability evaluations, the SSA (understandably) doesn't consider whether a child's medical impairment has an impact on their ability to work. Instead, the SSA considers a child disabled when the child has a medical impairment that causes *marked and severe* functional limitations. So rather than proving your child can't work, you'll need to show that your child has very significant difficulties with day-to-day activities.

Gathering the evidence to prove that your child is disabled works much in the same way that it does for adult disability applications. You must submit all of the child's medical records to the SSA, or the SSA will obtain them from the child's doctor. Then they are forwarded to DDS. If the available records are not thorough enough for the DDS team to decide if your child qualifies as disabled, you may be asked to have your child undergo a *consultative examination* (CE), paid for by the SSA.

a. Marked and Severe

Marked and severe is a legal standard in the Social Security Act. It applies to the disabling conditions that either satisfy a specific medical requirement listing in the SSA's Listing of Impairments or result in equivalent functional limitations. (The listings are discussed in Section C2, below, and are laid out in detail in the Medical Listings that are downloadable from Nolo's website.)

Marked and severe is meant to emphasize the intent of Congress to grant disability benefits only to children with the worst medical conditions. When used by the SSA, marked and severe indicates that a child's impairments are disabling enough to qualify under a specific listing in the Listing of Impairments.

Some listings mention only the level of medical severity required, rather than the level of functional severity, because they presume that extreme functional limitations result from the medical disorder. For example, if a child has been diagnosed with acute leukemia, the SSA will find that the child meets the listing. The agency can grant the child benefits without needing to consider the child's functional limitations.

Defining Marked and Severe

Marked means more than moderate and less than extreme. The listings authorize the SSA to grant benefits when a child's condition causes marked limitations in two areas of functioning or extreme limitations in one area of functioning. The exact areas of functioning depend on the type of impairment. For example, children with nervous system disorders can struggle with walking and using their hands to pick up small objects, such as crayons. Mental disorders can cause difficulty with memory, maintaining social relationships, and focusing in class. Functional limitations are considered in light of what is age appropriate. The SSA requires that its doctors use medical judgment in making these decisions.

Severe means a condition that is more than mild or slight. Conditions that don't have any meaningful impact on functioning (such as needing glasses) are called not severe or nonsevere by the SSA. Keep in mind that the common meaning of severe implies a medical condition worse than moderate, but the SSA requires only worse than mild or slight. (See Chapter 7 for a more detailed explanation of a severe condition.)

MEDICAL LISTINGS

For more information: The Medical Listings, with full commentary, are available for download on Nolo's website (see Appendix D for the link). Parts 1 through 14 contain the listings, which detail the information (usually specific results from medical tests or imaging) that the SSA needs to determine whether a disability applicant meets the requirements to obtain benefits.

b. Child Listing of Impairments

A DDS medical consultant initially checks to see whether the child's medical condition is on the Listing of Impairments found in the Social Security regulations, or whether the child has an impairment of equivalent severity. The listings say what sort of symptoms, signs, or laboratory findings show that a physical or mental condition is severe enough to disable a child. For example, the listings specify exactly what symptoms are needed for your child to qualify for disability due to an autism spectrum disorder. If your child's condition is one of the listed impairments (or considered equivalent to the listed impairments), your child is considered disabled for SSI purposes.

When determining whether your child's condition is disabling under the Listing of Impairments, the medical consultant reviews evidence from treating doctors and other health professionals, as well as your child's teachers, counselors, therapists, and social workers. All of these people have knowledge of how your child functions day to day and how your child has functioned over time. (Parts 1 through 14 of the Medical Listings can be found on Nolo's website. See Appendix D for the link.)

c. Special Rules for Children With Very Severe Disabilities

The disability evaluation process generally takes several months. But the SSA includes special provisions for people, including children, whose condition is so severe that the agency presumes they're disabled. In these cases, the presumptively disabled child begins to receive SSI benefits immediately and keeps receiving them for up to six months while the formal disability evaluation is being made. (The child must still meet the other nonmedical eligibility requirements for SSI.) These payments are called *presumptive disability payments*. (See Chapter 4 for more details.)

Is Your Child in Special Education?

Your child won't be automatically found disabled for SSI purposes based solely on the fact that they're enrolled in special education classes. At the same time, just because your child is mainstreamed doesn't automatically mean that they won't be found disabled. DDS looks at the entirety of how your child is doing in school compared with other children their age.

If the SSA makes these payments and later decides that the child's disability is not severe enough to qualify for SSI benefits, the money doesn't have to be paid back.

d. Special Rules for Children With HIV Infection

Children with HIV who are applying for disability need to submit an additional form completed by a medical professional. This form is called SSA-4815, *Medical Report on Child With Allegation of Human Immunodeficiency Virus (HIV) Infection.* The form asks your child's doctor to list the complications and manifestations of their HIV diagnosis, as well as evidence of their immune suppression (CD4 count) and growth failure. (See Part 14 of the Medical Listings for more detailed discussion of children with HIV and AIDS.)

2. Disability in Adult Children for SSDI

A child older than 18 who is applying for SSDI disability for the first time (or who was already awarded SSI as a minor but turned 18) will be evaluated using the adult disability criteria. Social Security calls adults who are applying for SSDI benefits based on their parents' work record adult children, because while they may be disabled according to adult medical criteria, they'll be awarded benefits as the child of an insured worker. (You become insured for SSDI benefits by having paid enough into the Social Security program by way of payroll taxes.)

In order to qualify for disability as an adult, a person must have a physical or mental impairment that is expected to keep them from doing any substantial work for at least a year, or is expected to result in death. Generally, if the claimant holds a job that pays $1,550 or more per month (in 2024), the work is considered substantial, and will disqualify the claimant from getting disability benefits. (See Chapter 1, Section B, for more on defining disability.)

The SSA will review the claimant's medical records and compare their conditions to a list of impairments that are considered to be severe enough to prevent working for a year or more. The types of conditions that are included in the adult listing of impairments is very similar to those in the childhood listing of impairments, but the medical documentation required to prove disability can differ. Claimants who aren't working and have a condition that meets or equals the requirements of a listed impairment are considered disabled for Social Security purposes.

If the SSA doesn't think the claimant's condition fits the requirements of a listed impairment, then the agency assesses the claimant's current ability to perform the type of work they've done in the past—if any. Young adults usually don't have a past work history, so DDS will consider their ability to do any kind of suitable work. Claimants who aren't able to do any substantial work will then qualify for SSDI benefits. (For more information on this issue, see Chapter 7.)

D. Continuing Disability Reviews for SSI Children

Once a child is found disabled by the SSA, the law requires that the SSA periodically do a *continuing disability review* (CDR) to determine whether a child younger than age 18 is still disabled. The CDR must be done on the following schedule:

- at least every three years for recipients under 18 whose conditions are likely to improve
- not later than 12 months after birth for babies whose disability is based on low birth weight, and
- sometime during the year they turned 18, if the person received benefits for at least one month before turning age 18 (after turning 18, the eligibility will be based on the adult criteria).

Continuing disability reviews for SSI recipients younger than 18 whose conditions are not likely to improve are done at the SSA's discretion. Despite legal requirements, the SSA frequently stops doing CDRs when the agency is short of money. This means that actual intervals for CDRs may be longer than described above.

One thing you must show during a CDR is that the child is and has been receiving treatment that is considered medically necessary for the disabling condition. The only time the SSA doesn't require this evidence is when the agency determines that it would be inappropriate or unnecessary (for example,

the child is blind and there's no treatment that could help). If the SSA requests this evidence and you refuse to provide it, the SSA will suspend payment of benefits to you and select another representative payee if that would be in the best interest of the child. If the child is old enough, the SSA might pay the child directly.

Representative Payees

Generally, if the child is younger than 18, the SSA will make payments only to a representative payee. Under certain circumstances, however, the SSA will make direct payments to a beneficiary under age 18 who shows the ability to manage such benefits. Examples of these circumstances are:

- The child beneficiary is also a parent who filed an application on their own (or filed for their child) and has experience in handling their own finances.
- The child is capable of using the benefits to provide for their needs, and no qualified payee is available. (The SSA determines whether the child is capable.)
- The child is within seven months of reaching age 18 and is filing an initial claim for benefits.

(CDRs are discussed further in Chapter 14.)

E. Other Health Care Concerns

Federal law recognizes that disabled children need more than simply monthly cash benefits for their health care. Some types of health care assistance available to disabled children are summarized below and are directed especially toward helping children who receive SSI.

1. Medicaid

Medicaid is a health care program for people with low incomes and limited assets. In most states, children who receive SSI also qualify for Medicaid. In many states, Medicaid comes automatically with SSI eligibility. In other states, you must sign up for it. And in some states, children can qualify for Medicaid coverage even if they don't qualify for SSI. Check with your local Social Security office or your state or county social services office for more information.

2. Children With Special Health Care Needs

If the SSA determines that a child is disabled and eligible for SSI, the SSA refers the child for health care services under the Children with Special Health Care Needs (CSHCN) provision of the Social Security Act. CSHCN services are generally administered through state-run health agencies, and most provide specialized services through arrangements with clinics, private offices, hospital-based outpatient and inpatient treatment centers, or community agencies.

Depending on your state, the CSHCN program might be called the Children's Special Health Services, Children's Medical Services, Handicapped Children's Program, or something else. Even if your child isn't eligible for SSI, you might be able to obtain some kind of health service for your child through a CSHCN program. Contact a local health department office, social services office, or hospital to find out how to contact your CSHCN program.

3. Children in Certain Medical Care Facilities

Living in a public institution might affect whether a disability claimant is eligible for SSI or the amount they can receive if they're awarded benefits. That's because residents of public institutions generally aren't eligible for SSI. For SSI purposes, a public institution is one operated by or controlled by a federal, state, or local government agency, and housing 17 or more residents.

There are exceptions to this rule. If a child lives for an entire month in a public institution or private medical care facility where more than 50% of the costs are covered by private insurance, Medicaid, or a combination of the two, the child may be eligible for a $30 monthly SSI payment. (20 C.F.R. § 416.211 (b)(1)(i)(ii).) This exception also applies if a child spends part of a month in a public institution and part in a private medical facility where more than 50% of the costs are covered by private insurance, Medicaid, or a combination of the two. (Examples of medical facilities include hospitals, skilled nursing facilities, and intermediate care facilities. However, any medical facility can qualify.) There's no limitation on the SSI payment if the child is in a private facility and doesn't receive or expect to receive more than 50% of the cost of the child's care from private insurance or Medicaid. (Program Operations Manual System (POMS) SI 00520.001.)

> EXAMPLE: Matthew, a disabled child, was born at Tall Oaks Multi-Care Center on October 4. He remained in the hospital until January 5, when he was released to live with his parents at home. Private health insurance paid for more than 50% of the cost of Matthew's care for the months of October and November. For December and January, more than 50% of the cost of his care was paid for by a combination of private insurance and Medicaid. Matthew is eligible for the $30 per month benefit.

Because of the complexity of laws involving SSI for children living in institutions, call your local Social Security Field Office if your disabled child who receives SSI is going to be in a facility. In fact, the SSA requires that you report if your child is admitted or discharged from a medical facility or another institution. (See Chapter 13 for details.)

4. Medicare

Medicare is a federal health insurance program for people 65 or older and for those who have received two years of SSDI benefits. Because children don't qualify for SSDI benefits on their own (remember that if they receive SSDI at a younger age, they're receiving dependents benefits based on their parents' work record) until they turn 18, the earliest a child can qualify for Medicare coverage is 20 years of age. The only exception is for children with chronic renal disease who need a kidney transplant or maintenance dialysis. Those children will be eligible for Medicare only if a parent receives SSDI or has worked enough to be insured by Social Security.

Getting Benefits During the Application Process (SSI)

Presumptive disability payments are made to a person who is *initially applying* for SSI benefits and whose medical condition is such that there's a strong likelihood the person will be found eligible for disability payments. The person must meet all nonmedical factors of eligibility, such as having low income and few assets. If you're an SSDI claimant—a worker who has paid Social Security taxes—you aren't entitled to presumptive disability. If you apply simultaneously for SSI and SSDI, any presumptive disability you might qualify for will be based on the SSI claim only.

SKIP AHEAD

If you are applying only for SSDI benefits, you do not need to read this chapter. You may proceed to Chapter 5.

If the SSA agrees that you're presumptively disabled, you may receive payments for up to six months while your application for disability benefits is pending. Payments begin in the month in which the SSA made the presumptive disability finding. If, after six months of presumptive disability payments, the SSA hasn't made a formal determination on your disability application, the presumptive disability payments end until this formal determination is made.

People applying for SSI based on a disability are commonly awarded presumptive disability cash payments. It never hurts to request them. If you're granted presumptive disability, you can also receive free health care under Medicaid earlier than would otherwise be possible. But being granted presumptive disability doesn't necessarily mean that the SSA will make a favorable final determination on your disability application. And if the SSA denies your request for benefits before you have received a full six months of presumptive disability benefits, you won't receive the remaining balance.

You won't have to pay back any of the presumptive disability payments you were given before your claim was denied, except in some unusual situations (20 C.F.R. § 416.537(b)1):

- The SSA later determines that you didn't qualify under the nonmedical eligibility requirements—this exception primarily targets those people who commit fraud to obtain benefits.
- The SSA made an error in computing your monthly presumptive disability payment—in this situation, you need only repay the amount of money that went over the amount you were supposed to receive. Even in this situation, the SSA can waive the requirement that you repay the money if both of the following are true:
  - You were not at fault.

- Repayment would defeat the purpose of the SSI law, would be unfair, or would interfere with administration of SSI law due to the small amount of money involved.

Note: The sponsor of an immigrant who is denied disability may be responsible for repaying the immigrant's presumptive disability payments. (20 C.F.R. § 416.550.)

Emergency Payments

In cases of extreme hardship, the law permits a one-time emergency cash advance payment to people who appear to qualify for presumptive disability through SSI. (42 U.S.C. § 1383(a)(4)(A); 20 C.F.R. § 416.520.) Extreme hardship means that without the payment, you risk an immediate threat to your health or safety, such as the lack of food, clothing, shelter, or medical care.

This advance payment is not extra benefit money. The SSA eventually gets the money back by deducting it from your presumptive disability checks, usually spread out over a period of six months.

If you think you need an emergency advance payment, tell the Social Security Field Office when you are applying for SSI benefits. If you are eligible, you will receive an emergency payment, which will take seven to ten days to process. The amount of the payment for one person cannot exceed $943 (the federal benefit rate in 2024), plus any applicable state supplementary amount.

Emergency Versus Immediate Payments

Do not confuse emergency payments with *immediate payments*. The SSA will issue immediate payments through a Field Office in critical cases within 24 hours. (You must already be receiving SSI or SSDI payments to collect an immediate payment, so immediate payments don't apply to presumptive disability.)

Immediate payments can be made to both SSI and SSDI claimants who qualify. To qualify, you must have a financial emergency or present a potential public relations problem for the SSA. Critical cases are those involving delayed or interrupted benefit payments. Examples might include the loss of a benefit check in the mail or a natural disaster like a hurricane or tornado wiping out parts of a town and interfering with normal benefit check delivery to a number of people.

For immediate payments, the maximum amount payable for either SSI or SSDI is $999. The exact amounts vary and must be calculated by the SSA Field Office.

A. Applying for Presumptive Disability

You apply for presumptive disability at your local SSA Field Office when you apply for SSI. The SSA Field Office can grant presumptive disability at that time if you have any of a limited number of impairments (see Section B, below). Most applications, however, are forwarded to the state Disability Determination Services (DDS) without an award of presumptive disability. But DDS also has wide discretion to grant presumptive disability. So even if your condition isn't listed below, once your file is forwarded to DDS, be sure to ask the examiner handling your claim about presumptive disability (see Section C, below).

B. Impairments Qualifying for Presumptive Disability by Field Office

An SSA Field Office representative has the power to grant you six months of presumptive disability payments when you apply for benefits, if there is a reasonable basis for believing that you have a disabling impairment. Of course, Field Office representatives are not doctors, but they can award presumptive disability to claimants who are obviously disabled. This is one way the SSA is trying to speed up providing low-income disabled people with financial assistance.

The Field Office may grant presumptive disability in three ways: based on the representative's observations, based on the claimant's statements, or after requesting confirmation from another source. The sections below cover each method.

1. Observation

Under federal regulations, the Field Office representative can award presumptive disability upon seeing that a claimant has one of the following disabling conditions:

- amputation of two limbs, or
- amputation of a leg at the hip.

2. Statement by the Claimant or Guardian

The Field Office representative can award presumptive disability payments based on the word of the claimant (or, if the claimant is a child, the claimant's parent or guardian) that certain disabling impairments exist. The disabling impairments must be very severe, because the Field Office personnel aren't doctors and are screening only for obvious cases. Note that the actual medical severity needed to ultimately qualify for disability benefits based on one of these disorders may be less than what is required to receive presumptive disability payments. The disabling impairments are as follows:

- total blindness
- total deafness

- bed confinement or immobility without a wheelchair, walker, or crutches due to a long-standing condition—such as a chronic condition that is not likely to improve with further treatment and has been present for a year or more
- a stroke more than three months in the past with continued marked difficulty in walking or using a hand or an arm—*marked* means more than moderate (but less than extreme), and doesn't require an inability to walk or total paralysis in an arm
- cerebral palsy, muscular dystrophy, or muscle atrophy along with marked difficulty in walking without using braces, in speaking, or in coordination of the hands or arms
- Down syndrome characterized by intellectual disability, abnormal development of the skull, short arms and legs, and hands and feet that tend to be broad and flat, and
- severe intellectual disability in someone who is at least seven years of age (*severe* means the person depends on others for meeting personal care needs and in doing other routine daily activities).

Saying that you (or the claimant, in case of a child) are disabled isn't enough. A statement by you or a child claimant's parent or guardian that the claimant is disabled won't establish presumptive disability if the SSA Field Office representative believes the allegation may be false, based on personal observation. For example, if a claimant alleges total blindness but the Field Office representative sees her reading a book, the SSA won't grant presumptive disability at the time of the application.

3. Disorders Requiring Confirmation From Another Source

With certain impairments, the Field Office may need to confirm the claimant's allegation before granting presumptive disability. This situation arises when the alleged impairment is not observable by the Field Office representative or when the representative's observations are inconsistent with the claimant's statements. These are some of the conditions that can qualify for presumptive disability but require confirmation:

- symptomatic human immunodeficiency virus (HIV) infection
- terminal illness (a physician must confirm by telephone or in a signed statement that an individual has a terminal illness with a life expectancy of six months or less, or a physician or hospice official, such as a hospice coordinator, staff nurse, social worker, or medical records custodian, must confirm that an individual is receiving hospice services because of a terminal illness)
- a child six months or younger with a birth weight below 1,200 grams (2 pounds, 10 ounces)

- a child 12 months or younger whose birth weight was as listed in the following chart:

Gestational Age (in Weeks)	Weight at Birth
37–40	under 2,000 grams (4 pounds, 6 ounces)
36	1,875 grams or less (4 pounds, 2 ounces)
35	1,700 grams or less (3 pounds, 12 ounces)
34	1,500 grams or less (3 pounds, 5 ounces)
33	1,325 grams or less (2 pounds, 15 ounces)

- a spinal cord injury producing an inability to move without the use of a walker or bilateral handheld assistive device for more than two weeks (with confirmation of such status from an appropriate medical professional)
- end-stage renal disease (ESRD) requiring chronic dialysis (Form CMS-2728-U3, *End Stage Renal Disease Medical Evidence Report: Medicare Entitlement and/or Patient Registration*, must be filled out), and
- amyotrophic lateral sclerosis (ALS), also known as Lou Gehrig's disease.

To confirm allegations for presumptive disability (except for HIV infection—see "Special Confirmation Needed With HIV Infection," below), the Field Office representative must do all of the following:

- Record the information given by the claimant on a Report of Contact form, which is placed in the claimant's file.
- Explain the presumptive disability procedures to the claimant, and the need to contact a source to verify the allegation (claimant's statement) in order to make a presumptive disability finding.
- Ask the claimant or guardian for the name and telephone number of a reliable source who can verify the allegation. An appropriate source might include school personnel, a social services agency worker, a doctor, a member of the clergy, or another member of the community who knows of the condition based on frequent contacts or a long-term association with the claimant.
- Contact an appropriate source to determine if the claimant meets the presumptive disability criterion.
- Record the information obtained from the source on the Report of Contact form in the claimant's file.
- Inform the claimant.

Special Confirmation Needed With HIV Infection

If a claimant alleges HIV infection, including AIDS, the Field Office must send the claimant's treating doctor a form requesting information about the severity of the infection. The medical severity required for presumptive disability is like that described in the Listing of Impairments that deals with HIV infection. (See Part 14 of the Medical Listings.)

C. Qualifying for Presumptive Disability Through DDS

Once the SSA determines that you're legally entitled to presumptive disability benefits, it leaves the initial determination of medical eligibility for SSI benefits to a state agency called Disability Determination Services, or DDS.

If you don't win presumptive benefits during the initial application process at the SSA Field Office, you can try again when your case is forwarded to DDS for the SSI disability determination. (A DDS representative has much wider discretion in granting presumptive disability than a Field Office representative.) The presumptive

disability determinations that DDS can make fall into three general categories.

1. High Potential for Presumptive Disability

The DDS is most likely to grant presumptive disability for the following disabilities:

- severe intellectual disability
- cancer
- central nervous system diseases resulting in paralysis or difficulty in walking or using hands and arms
- irreversible kidney disease, and
- symptomatic HIV infection.

2. Caution in Granting Presumptive Disability

DDS uses caution in granting presumptive disability in the following disabilities because of the difficulty in predicting the severity or duration of the impairment:

- diabetes
- epilepsy
- high blood pressure
- heart disease caused by high blood pressure
- peptic ulcer
- cirrhosis of the liver, and
- bone fractures.

3. Low Potential for Presumptive Disability

DDS rarely authorizes presumptive disability payments for the following disorders:

- mental impairments (with the exceptions of severe intellectual disability or where there is convincing evidence of prolonged severe psychosis or chronic brain syndrome)

- breathing disorders, because medical tests of breathing ability are crucial to a determination of disability for most respiratory impairments, and

- back conditions, except in cases involving traumatic injury to the spinal cord (in which case, an award of presumptive disability benefits is more likely).

Proving You're Disabled

All claimants who file a disability claim for SSDI or SSI are responsible for providing medical evidence to the Social Security Administration (SSA) showing that they have at least one severe impairment that might make them eligible for disability benefits. You don't have to physically provide medical reports to the SSA—although you can, to help expedite a decision. If you give your permission, the SSA will request your reports from medical sources (such as physicians or psychologists) that have treated or evaluated you.

Once you've established that you have an impairment, the SSA considers both medical and nonmedical evidence to assess the severity of your impairment. In order to do this, the SSA requests copies of medical evidence from hospitals, clinics, or other health facilities where you've been treated (if the SSA doesn't already have those records).

A. Acceptable Medical Sources

When considering both the existence and severity of your impairment, the SSA evaluates reports from all medical providers who have treated you. These providers are called your *treating sources.* They can include doctors, nurse practitioners, physician's assistants, chiropractors, naturopaths, and other alternative providers. But the SSA trusts medical opinions and information from some providers more than others. The SSA calls these providers *acceptable medical sources.* Reports from these sources enhance the credibility of your disability claim.

EXAMPLE: You apply for disability benefits, but your only treating source for your back pain is your chiropractor. Any information provided to the SSA by that chiropractor, no matter how detailed, is not sufficient for the SSA to make a disability determination. You will be sent to an acceptable medical source, such as a physician, for an examination of your back complaints.

Only the following types of health care providers are considered acceptable medical sources:

- **Licensed physicians.** Licensed physicians hold an M.D. degree with a valid license to practice medicine in the states in which they practice. (Licensed physicians include psychiatrists, mental health professionals who are medical doctors.) Chiropractic, homeopathic, naturopathic, and other alternative providers do not qualify.
- **Licensed doctors of osteopathy.** Licensed doctors of osteopathy hold a D.O. degree with a valid license in the states in which they practice.
- **Licensed or certified psychologists.** A licensed or certified psychologist holds a doctoral degree (Ph.D.) in psychology. For the purpose of establishing severe intellectual disability or learning disabilities, a licensed or certified psychologist includes a school psychologist or another licensed or

certified individual with a different title who performs the function of a school psychologist in a school setting. Psychologists must be licensed in the state in which they practice.

- **Licensed optometrists.** An optometrist holds an O.D. degree. The SSA will recognize medical evidence from optometrists as acceptable and sufficient for diagnostic purposes (establishing the presence of visual disorders only), and for measuring visual acuity and visual fields. An exception: Optometrists in the U.S. Virgin Islands can only measure visual acuity and visual fields, not provide a diagnosis. Optometrists must be validly licensed in the states in which they practice. Medical doctors (M.D.s) or doctors of osteopathy (D.O.s) who specialize in the treatment of eye diseases are called *ophthalmologists*, and shouldn't be confused with optometrists.

- **Licensed podiatrists.** Licensed podiatrists hold a D.P.M. degree and are validly licensed in the states in which they practice. Podiatrists are an acceptable medical source only to establish impairments of the foot (or foot and ankle, depending on the laws of the state in which they practice).

- **Speech-language pathologists.** Qualified speech-language pathologists are fully certified by the state education agency in the state in which they practice, are licensed by the state professional licensing board, or hold a Certificate of Clinical Competence from the American Speech-Language-Hearing Association. A speech-language pathologist is an acceptable medical source only to establish speech or language impairments.

- **Licensed audiologists** are accepted for impairments of hearing loss, auditory processing disorders, and balance disorders, within the licensed scope of their practice, which can vary state by state.

- **Licensed advanced practice registered nurses (APRNs),** advanced registered nurse practitioners (ARNPs), or other advanced practice nurses with a different title are acceptable medical sources within their licensed scope of practice, as determined by their state's laws.

- **Licensed physician assistants (PAs),** are accepted within their licensed scope of practice, under the laws of their state.

B. Medical Evidence From Treating Sources

Many disability claims are decided on the basis of medical evidence from treating sources (your doctors), so long as they're acceptable medical sources. For example, the doctor who treats you for high blood pressure is often the best medical source of information for how serious your heart condition is. SSA regulations, in some situations, place special emphasis on evidence from your treating doctors because they're likely to provide the most detailed and long-term picture of your impairment. They may also bring a perspective to the medical evidence that can't be obtained from the medical findings alone (such as examination reports or hospital discharge records).

1. All Relevant Medical Records

The SSA requires you or your lawyer to submit *all* records that relate to your disability claim (20 C.F.R.§§ 404.1512, 416.912). By relate, the SSA means anything that has a logical or causal connection to your medical condition, whether it's favorable or unfavorable to your claim.

Since the SSA is required by law to consider the totality of your impairments—even those that you didn't include on your application—the agency needs to see all of the available medical records. For example, if you had back surgery following a work injury and opened up a worker's compensation claim, the SSA wants to see both the surgical records and the worker's compensation claim records. If you have a mental impairment and physical impairment, both are relevant and should be mentioned on the application. You, your doctor, or your lawyer should submit all of the relevant records for any medical treatment you've received, both physically and mentally.

If you have a mental impairment that interferes with your ability to obtain accurate records, or you're homeless and face barriers to accessing your records, the disability examiner who works for the state Disability Determination Services (DDS) agency can help. Relevant nonmedical records must also be submitted, such as information about your education, vocational skills, and employment.

When lawyers or other representatives are representing applicants, they aren't free to choose what information to submit. They can't, for example, withhold evidence that they think might be unfavorable to a claim. For instance, you or your representative can't submit some evidence from a medical event or hospitalization but hold back certain pieces that might appear unfavorable. Say you were hospitalized for a possible heart attack, but your cardiac scan was normal. That information must be included with the other evidence from your hospitalization.

Communication between you and your representative, however, is privileged information and doesn't have to be given to the SSA. Furthermore, any investigation your representative makes into the merits of your claim is protected information, including discussions between your representative and your doctor regarding the severity of your disorders or your lawyer's personal opinion about your disability. Also note that you (or your representative) aren't required to request an opinion from any doctor about the severity of your medical condition. But if you do ask your doctor for a *treating source opinion* on the severity of your condition, then you must submit the response to the SSA.

2. Timely, Accurate, and Sufficient Medical Records

Timely, accurate, and sufficient records from your treating doctors can greatly reduce or eliminate the need for the SSA to obtain additional medical evidence, which means you can get a faster determination on your disability claim. Timely, accurate, and sufficient means the following:

- **Timely** records are recent enough to be relevant to your current medical condition. How recent is a matter of medical judgment, depending on the disorder. A condition that is rapidly changing requires more up-to-date information than one that is slowly progressing or has been unchanged for years. Generally, the SSA wants to see updated records for the past six months. (That doesn't mean older records aren't important—they absolutely are. Records dating back for many years are crucial to establish when your disability began.)
- **Accurate** records correctly describe your condition according to the standards of acceptable medical sources. To use a common example, a chiropractor may describe subluxation (slippage) of your spine on X-rays, but this will not be considered accurate if an acceptable medical source (see Section A, above) reports normal X-rays. Also, acceptable medical sources must report their information accurately. For instance, a treating medical doctor's records that say you can't walk one block because of chest pain will be rejected if specific exercise testing shows that you can do much more exercise.
- **Sufficient** medical records contain enough accurate information from acceptable medical sources to allow the SSA to make an independent medical judgment regarding the nature and severity of your medical condition. For example, having a diagnosis of cancer isn't sufficient on its own to establish disability. The SSA will want to know: Did a biopsy prove the cancer's presence? What kind? Where in the body? When did symptoms appear? What did a physical examination show? What did X-rays and other imaging tests show? What did blood tests show? Did you have surgery? Did it remove all of the cancer? Did you have chemotherapy? What side effects did you suffer, if any? Did you have radiation therapy? What were the results?

It isn't enough for your doctor to start keeping detailed records only when you apply for disability.

EXAMPLE: You were sick for six months before you applied for disability and were unable to work during that time. You might be eligible for a retroactive award of benefits for the six months you couldn't work and before you applied for disability. But if your doctor doesn't have detailed medical records for the entire period he has been seeing you, you might not be able to prove you were unable to work during those six months.

There is no way for your doctor to believably recreate detailed medical records from memory. If your doctor does remember something not in the written records, the SSA will evaluate such statements on a case-by-case basis. For example, if your doctor remembers that you've always had pain in the joints of your hands, that's more believable than remembering that you had ten degrees of motion in the second joint of your left little finger three years ago. In all instances, however, the SSA knows that memory is not as reliable as written records.

3. Thorough Medical Records

The medical records of a treating doctor are of critical importance to a disability claim, and they should be as comprehensive as possible. Luckily, doctors usually write things down about their patients and their treatment—and patients expect their doctors to remember them and their conditions. But not all doctors record complaints, diagnoses, and treatments with the same detail. A doctor can see as many as 30 or 40 patients a day. Even if your doctor sees only 20 people in a day, your doctor may have seen, evaluated, and treated as many as 400 patients from the time of your first visit to your next one a month later. You might not even see the same doctor on each visit, depending on your health care provider.

Medical consultants working for the SSA and DDS review thousands of doctors' notes when evaluating a disability claim. The quality of these records varies greatly. Some are typed, mention all of the patient's complaints, show the results of examinations, note what treatment was given, state the response to treatment, and mention future plans. But many records are unreadable or don't contain enough information to determine disability.

EXAMPLE: Many people apply for disability benefits based on arthritis. When a disability examiner reviews the records provided by a treating doctor, often the file contains a few scribbles that the patient has joint pains and arthritis, and further notes that some form of treatment has been given. Many medical records contain no description of diseased joints, no range-of-motion test results, and no X-rays. (The SSA spends extensive time and money each year obtaining data from joint examinations, X-rays, and other lab tests.)

The SSA can't read medical records that are scribbled and illegible, nor can they evaluate medical records that lack significant information about your condition. But if your files are incomplete, it's not necessarily because of malice or incompetence on the part of your doctor. Doctors don't routinely document their files for disability purposes. Their records are for them to help treat their patients. On the other hand, the SSA often does see treating doctor records that are of quite poor quality, for either treatment or disability determination purposes.

> **EXAMPLE:** To qualify for disability based on epilepsy, you must have had a certain number of seizures during a specified time period. But physicians—even neurologists who specialize in treating epileptics—don't often record the number of seizures patients have had between visits (even though they should, in the event that adjustments of medication might be needed due to increased seizures). Nor do physicians usually describe seizures in detail in their records, though they'll note the type of seizures involved and drugs given. The SSA needs this information to help evaluate the severity of epilepsy, but it's often missing from a treating doctor's file.

You need to make sure the records your doctor keeps on your health are thorough enough to prove your case to the SSA. If they aren't, you should ask your doctor to add to the information they contain.

4. The Weight of Your Treating Doctor's Opinion

For disability applications filed before March 27, 2017, federal regulations required the SSA to accept a treating doctor's assessment unless the SSA's own decision maker (such as a DDS medical consultant or administrative law judge on appeal cases) could give a reasonable explanation for rejecting it. This was informally known as the Treating Source Rule. Specific information about your condition from your treating doctor was supposed to be given greater weight than the opinion of other doctors who might have seen you only once—such as a doctor who examined you for DDS

But, as of March 27, 2017, this policy favoring the opinion of your treating doctor is no longer in effect. Instead, the current rule about medical evidence says that the most persuasive medical opinion will be given the most weight. The key factors that will be considered in evaluating the persuasiveness of an opinion are supportability and consistency.

The first factor, supportability, means that a medical opinion should be backed up by medical tests, such as X-rays or blood tests, other signs, and a doctor's clinical notes. The second factor, consistency, refers to whether the medical opinion makes sense within the context of the other evidence in the file (for instance, the applicant's statements and other doctors' opinions).

If there are opinions from two or more doctors (for instance, the treating doctor and a consultative examiner) that are equally well-supported by the evidence and consistent with the applicant's file, then Social Security will consider the length of the patient's relationship with the doctor and whether the doctor is a specialist. However, the doctors' familiarity with Social Security rules and with the applicant's disability file will also be considered, and this factor tends to be in favor of Social Security's consultative doctors.

The rule change often has little practical effect for several reasons. At the initial application level, medical consultants have never blindly followed treating doctor opinions anyway—the SSA regulations said that medical consultants and claims examiners didn't have to give weight to a treating doctor's opinion if it was inconsistent with other evidence in the file or if it wasn't supported by medically acceptable diagnostic techniques. Medical consultants have always weighed all of the evidence in a file, including different opinions from different treating doctors, to make a well-informed decision. The SSA's own studies have found that the most important determining factor in disability cases is the analysis of the evidence as a whole, not reliance on any one person's opinion. The totality of the medical evidence is what's most important.

For example, if your doctor says you can't lift more than ten pounds because of arthritis in your hands, the opinion has little weight without other evidence of how arthritis limits your activities. If your doctor says you can't lift more than ten pounds because of arthritis, describes your physical abnormalities, and provides X-ray reports showing the arthritis, their opinion will have more weight. The SSA will still make its own determination of your physical abilities, using all of the evidence in the file, based on federal regulations.

Note that the SSA can refuse to consider medical evidence from treating sources, including acceptable medical sources, in some circumstances, under Section 223(d)(5)(C)(i) of the Social Security Act. This can happen if your treating source has ever been convicted of a felony, excluded from a federal health care program, or found to have submitted false evidence.

Some exceptions to these rules are allowed, however. If the evidence is a laboratory test that seems reliable, or if the treatment evidence was obtained before the treating source was convicted of a felony or excluded from a federal health care program, the SSA may be required to consider the evidence.

5. Treating Source Statements and Medical Assessments About Your Ability to Function

If your treating doctor gives a medical opinion about your ability to function, the SSA must consider that opinion. These opinions are called *treating source statements*. It's useful for you to have such statements from your treating doctor (or doctors), provided they're backed up by objective evidence. The SSA will weigh such opinions in the context of all the medical evidence, but your doctors' opinions will have no effect unless the SSA thinks they are reasonable. As discussed above, the SSA no longer gives special weight to your treating doctors' opinions, but it's still worthwhile to have a supportive doctor's opinion. For one, if you have doctors who are very familiar with your case, they can point out medical problems and limitations that the SSA might otherwise overlook.

6. Obtaining and Reviewing Records From Your Treating Doctor

Many doctors consider medical records to be their property, even though the records state your health history. In rare instances, doctors might be reluctant to give you copies of your medical records. Laws vary across the country on a doctor's obligation to hand over your medical records. The best approach is to ask politely for them. For most people, a call to the doctor's office explaining that you're applying for disability is sufficient.

If your treating doctor is hesitant to let you have copies of your records, don't just say, "Thanks a lot," and hang up. Explain again that you need to see your records for your disability claim, and ask why you can't have a copy. If you're dealing with resistant office personnel who simply say it is an office policy, ask to speak with the doctor. If you get the runaround on talking

to the doctor, write a letter explaining why you want your records. Write "personal and confidential" on the envelope to make sure the doctor gets the letter.

If your doctor still refuses to let you have a copy of your file, won't answer your questions regarding your medical conditions, treats you poorly, or generally has little time for you, then you should consider finding a new treating doctor. An uncooperative doctor probably won't cooperate with the SSA on your behalf anyway. The SSA can't force a doctor or hospital to turn over medical records, and it's not unusual for the SSA to wait months to receive medical records from treating doctors. If you're really determined to get records from an uncooperative doctor, you might need the services of an attorney who might be able to make the doctor to turn over your records. Fortunately, most doctors will give you a copy of your records simply for the asking.

Be sure to review the records when you get them and make sure that all information contained in them is correct.

7. Obtaining and Reviewing Records From Hospitals and Medical Centers

Like most treating doctors, most hospitals and medical centers will let you have copies of your records without any problem. Just call the hospital and say you want a copy of your medical records. You don't have to ask your doctor's permission.

Releasing Records for Mental Disorders

Psychiatrists and psychologists are more likely to release medical records to the SSA than to patients. Some won't even release records to the SSA. These records may contain comments about a claimant's mental disorder that could harm the doctor-patient relationship or the claimant's relationship with other people.

One simple way to avoid this problem is to talk with your treating professional about writing a summary of their findings on your mental condition only as it relates to your disability claim.

This summary should contain detailed comments about the kind of information the SSA wants in evaluating a mental disorder (see Part 12 of the Medical Listings on Nolo's website), while omitting personal information irrelevant to the disability determination. In fact, this might be the preferable solution if your psychologist or psychiatrist has voluminous records on you.

Before writing a summary, your treating professional should review the listing requirements of your disability in the SSA Listing of Impairments to see what the SSA is looking for. A summary or letter that does not address the requirements of a medical listing will do little or no good to your claim.

Note that some hospitals charge substantial copy fees to former patients—as high as a dollar a page! It isn't reasonable to have to pay such a high fee when copying costs only a few cents per page. If a hospital can provide copies of records to the SSA for a small fee, there's no reason they should charge a private citizen a large fee. Tell the hospital you know they make records available to the SSA for a small fee.

Many states also limit how much providers can charge for providing copies of medical records. Check your state's regulations to see if there's a fee cap on obtaining your records. Some states have a medical records fee cap only if you're applying for disability, so let your provider know that you're requesting records in support of a disability application. Mention your state's statute pertaining to medical records fee caps if you get any pushback from the records department.

If the hospital still refuses, you can call the facility's social services department and ask for help. You can also look for free legal aid clinics in your area that may be able to negotiate on your behalf. Of course, you can also wait until the hospital sends the records to the SSA and then review them when they are in your file. But hospitals are often slow in sending files to the SSA.

It's very important for you to review hospital records being used to determine your eligibility for disability. Some of the information may be incorrect. For example, when treating hospitalized patients, it's common for doctors to focus on the immediate reason the patient was admitted to the hospital and ignore other problems. A doctor examining a patient for a heart problem may report that all other areas of the body are normal, even if they haven't done a complete physical examination.

Such practices aren't uncommon, even with patients the doctor has never seen before. This can lead to errors and conflicts in your medical records. Doctors often do this to save time while satisfying hospital rules that require complete exams of hospitalized patients.

When reviewing your records, ask yourself: Did the doctor really examine all parts of your body they reported as normal? Did the surgeon who did your abdominal surgery really look in your eyes, ears, nose, and throat? Did they really check your reflexes and your skin sensation? Examine your joints for arthritis? If you were hospitalized for a heart attack, did the cardiologist look at anything but your heart and lungs before dictating an "otherwise normal" physical examination into hospital records?

Doctors tend to concentrate on their areas of specialty, but when they report normal for the other areas they didn't examine, it can be a real problem for you when attempting to establish disability. If you find that this has happened in your case, make sure that you call or write to the SSA and tell them that various parts of your body were not actually examined and aren't normal. In these instances, the SSA should arrange for an independent consultative examination.

8. Evidence the SSA Needs From Treating Sources

In general, here is the basic evidence the SSA needs:

- your medical history
- clinical findings, including the results of physical or mental status examinations
- laboratory findings, such as the results of blood pressure tests or X-rays
- your doctor's diagnosis of your condition
- your doctor's prescribed treatment, as well as your response to that treatment and your doctor's prognosis—that is, the prospect for your recovery from a medical condition, and
- your doctor's opinion about what you can do despite your impairments, based on the medical findings. This statement should describe your ability to perform

work-related activities, such as sitting, standing, walking, lifting, carrying, handling objects, hearing, speaking, and traveling. In cases involving mental impairments, the statement should describe your ability to understand, carry out, and remember instructions, and to respond appropriately to supervision, coworkers, and work pressures. For a child, the statement should describe the child's ability to function effectively in an age-appropriate manner. (If you're legally blind (vision worse than 20/200 best corrected in both eyes or visual fields of 20 degrees or less), your doctor need not describe your ability to perform the above activities.)

Keep in mind that your claim could be denied—no matter how much information your doctor provides—if you don't fit the criteria for disability or if you're found ineligible based on nonmedical reasons. If you're denied benefits, the SSA will tell you the reasons for denial. (See Chapter 12 for more on appealing a denial.)

9. If Your Records Provide Insufficient or Unhelpful Evidence

Once you see your medical records, you may be concerned that they aren't sufficient for Social Security purposes. Don't necessarily blame your doctor. The files of many treating doctors are incomplete from the point of view of the SSA, but contain a perfectly reasonable amount of information

to treat their patients. Furthermore, your medical file might omit certain symptoms or conditions, simply because you forgot to tell your doctor about them.

Doctors are often bogged down with paperwork. Insurance companies, workers' compensation programs, employers, government agencies, lawyers, patients, and other physicians all request written information from doctors. Few doctors enjoy tasks that take them away from seeing patients.

In addition, your doctor may never have thought about the kind of evidence the SSA needs. Let your doctor know that to support your claim of disability, the SSA requires specific medical evidence about your impairments and how your impairment affects your day-to-day functioning, not merely a letter stating that you're disabled. If your doctor sends the SSA a brief letter and no other medical information, you'll be required to attend an examination paid for by the SSA.

If your doctor wants to send a letter to the SSA, emphasize that it must contain extensive detail about your impairment and how it affects your ability to function— including your ability to walk, breathe, or use your hands and arms. It might be helpful if your doctor fills out an RFC form to detail your abilities and limitations (see Chapter 8 for more information). Don't assume that your doctor knows all of your impairments and how they limit your daily activities. Make sure you tell your doctor the details of your limitations.

Some doctors are willing to simply write that you're "permanently and totally disabled," even if you don't have that much wrong with you. They want to please their patients. But federal law requires that your SSA file contain actual objective evidence showing how your impairments limit your ability to function.

Your doctor doesn't have to become an expert in job performance. Your doctor may be inclined to write the SSA saying that you cannot work at all. Although this may be well intentioned, your doctor isn't a vocational counselor. The SSA has vocational specialists who determine what kinds of jobs can be done by people with various impairments. Many people are capable of some kind of work, even though their doctors think the medical evidence shows that they're disabled. Many people who qualify for disability benefits do so because of both nonmedical (age, education, and work experience) and medical factors. The SSA, not your doctor, ultimately determines whether you're disabled—that is, if you can or cannot work given your particular impairments.

Nevertheless, your doctor can have a positive influence on the outcome of your claim for disability by providing ample medical information about your impairments. It will help your case enormously if your doctor provides detailed evidence of your physical or mental medical disorders and how they limit your functioning.

MEDICAL LISTINGS
The Medical Listings on Nolo's website (see Appendix D for the link) provide details on what constitutes a disability for the purposes of SSDI and SSI. If your doctor needs help determining what kind of evidence the SSA will need, the information included in the Medical Listings can help. In addition, Section D, below, includes information related to symptoms.

C. The Role of Consultative Examinations in Disability Determination

If the evidence provided by your treating doctor and other medical sources isn't adequate to determine whether you're disabled, the SSA may seek additional medical information by paying for you to visit a doctor for a *consultative examination* (CE).

1. When Are Consultative Examinations Used?

A significant percentage of disability claims involve the use of CEs. The SSA spends many millions of dollars on CEs every year. The SSA must order a large number of CEs for several reasons:

- Many claimants don't have treating doctors.
- Medical records from treating doctors may be too old.
- Claimants have complaints they have never mentioned to their treating doctors.

- Some treating doctors refuse to provide records.
- Some treating doctors' records aren't useful for disability determination.

2. Who Performs Consultative Examinations?

The SSA prefers that your treating physician administer the CE, provided that they're qualified, willing, and able. But most of the time, an independent doctor, called a *consultative examiner*, will perform the CE.

3. When an Independent Doctor Performs the Consultative Examination

If your treating doctor refuses to administer the CE, the SSA will arrange it with an independent doctor.

Even if your doctor agrees to administer your CE, the SSA can send you to a different CE doctor if any of the following is true:

- Your doctor doesn't have the equipment to provide the specific data needed.
- Your doctor doesn't want to perform the CE because they don't want to strain the doctor-patient relationship.
- Conflicts or inconsistencies in your medical file won't be resolved by using your doctor.
- You prefer that someone other than your doctor administer the CE and you have a good reason for wanting it—for example, you don't want to compromise your relationship with your doctor.

- The SSA has prior experience with your doctor and doesn't think that they'll conduct a proper CE. This might happen, for example, if DDS knows from past experience that your treating doctor does a poor job in conducting CEs. Some treating doctors do adequate CEs, but are so slow sending the results to DDS that a case can be held up unnecessarily for many months.

Consultative Examiners Versus Medical Consultants

Doctors who do CEs for the SSA are not the same as DDS medical consultants. This can be confusing, because CE doctors may also work as medical consultants for DDS. When they are performing work for DDS, they are called *DDS medical consultants*.

Here's the difference: A CE doctor examines a claimant and sends a report to the SSA with an opinion on what a claimant can do, given the claimant's medical condition. CEs don't necessarily have the training or authority to make a medical disability determination.

On the other hand, DDS medical consultants don't actually examine claimants, but do have the authority to make disability determinations based on the special training by the SSA/DDS that they must undergo before being allowed to make decisions (as well as the ongoing training they receive).

4. Who Serves as Independent Consultative Examiners?

All consultative examiners used by the SSA are acceptable medical sources (see Section A, above) in private practice. For example, the SSA may have your hearing tested by an audiologist. (An audiologist's report may be all that's needed in some cases. However, the SSA will always want to know what disorder is causing a hearing loss, and that may require examination by an ear, nose, and throat (ENT) doctor, if such an exam isn't already in the claimant's file.) On the other hand, the SSA will never send you to a chiropractor, naturopath, herbalist, or other alternative healer for an examination.

5. Who Pays for the Consultative Examination?

The SSA pays for all CEs and reports— even if your own treating doctor administers the CE.

6. Contents of a CE Report

A complete CE is one in which the doctor conducts all the elements of a standard examination required for the applicable medical condition. If you undergo a complete CE, the doctor's report should include the following information:

- your chief complaints
- a detailed history of the chief complaints

- details of important findings, based on your history, examination, and laboratory tests (such as blood tests and X-rays), as related to your main complaints. This should include any positive findings (abnormalities such as swollen joints for physical disorders or the presence of delusions in mental disorders), as well as abnormalities that could have but didn't show up during your exam (negative findings). Any abnormalities found during a physical exam or with laboratory testing should also be reported, even if you didn't know about them or complain of them.
- the results of laboratory and other tests (such as X-rays or blood tests) performed according to the Listing of Impairments. (See Chapter 7 and Parts 1 through 14 of the Medical Listings on Nolo's website.)
- the diagnosis and prognosis for your impairments, and
- a statement about what you can do despite your impairment. This is the same kind of information that the SSA requests from your treating doctor, except that your treating doctor's opinion generally carries more weight than an independent doctor's.

Consultative examination doctors can't decide whether you qualify for disability or not. Their assessments can be useful, but usually don't carry the weight of your treating doctor's medical assessments supported by evidence.

Many CEs aren't comprehensive physical or mental examinations but are specific tests, such as breathing tests or X-rays. For example, many claimants who complain of shortness of breath caused by lung disorders are sent for breathing tests only, because their treating doctor (or a prior CE) already provided the necessary physical examination data. And because meeting a listed impairment usually requires specific test results, many claimants are sent for only the type of test needed to determine whether they meet the listing. (See Chapter 7 for a discussion of disability listings.) X-rays are another kind of CE frequently performed without a full examination.

A CE doctor who administers only a specific test isn't expected to provide an opinion regarding what you can do given your impairments.

7. Your Protections in a Consultative Examination

It's the SSA's responsibility to make sure that consultative examiners provide professional and reasonable care. Examining rooms should be clean and adequately equipped, and you should be treated with courtesy. DDS is supposed to ask you questions about your CE—how long you had to wait, whether you were treated with courtesy, how long the examination took, and whether it seemed complete. If you

have a complaint about your CE experience and haven't been asked about it by DDS, call the professional relations department at your state's DDS to voice your concern. You can find the number here: www.ssa.gov/disability/professionals/procontacts.htm

The SSA tries to screen out doctors who violate adequate standards for a CE or who provide incomplete or repeatedly inaccurate reports. Doctors may take shortcuts with a CE because the SSA doesn't pay much for them and doctors are often in a hurry. A nurse can record a part of your history, as long as the doctor reads what the nurse wrote and reviews the important parts with you. But no one other than a doctor (or another acceptable medical source, like a nurse practitioner or advanced practice nurse) should examine you.

The SSA provides CE doctors with detailed instructions regarding the requirements for an adequate and complete examination. These standards are generally accepted by the medical profession as needed for the competent examination of any patient in the specialty concerned.

EXAMPLE: You're sent to an arthritis specialist (rheumatologist) because you complained of joint and back pains. The doctor has a nurse take your history and spends ten minutes with you, looking briefly at some of your joints. The doctor does not test how well the joints move or how well you can walk. This inadequate exam will be unacceptable to the SSA.

8. If the Consultative Examination Is Inadequate

If you didn't receive an adequate consultative examination—particularly if the doctor did not examine you about your complaint—contact the DDS examiner who arranged it. Call, but also send your complaint in writing so that it can be added to your SSA file.

If you've appealed a disability denial and are at the hearing level, complain to the administrative law judge. Tell the judge about the inadequate examination and ask to be sent to someone who will examine you properly. If your complaint isn't taken seriously, write to the DDS professional relations department and the DDS director. If that doesn't work, call the SSA's hotline (800-772-1213) and ask for assistance.

D. Evidence of Symptoms

The SSA will investigate many areas of your life and the effect of symptoms—such as pain, shortness of breath, or fatigue—on your ability to function.

1. Evidence Related to Symptoms

Evidence of your symptoms will include the following kinds of information provided by your treating doctor and other sources:

- everything you do during a typical day. Of particular importance is how these *activities of daily living*—called ADLs in SSA lingo—are affected by your pain and other symptoms.
- where you have pain or other symptoms, how long the symptoms last, how often the symptoms occur, and how strong the symptoms are
- what activities or other factors are known to cause (*precipitate*) or worsen (*exacerbate*) your symptoms
- whether any medication you're taking is prescribed or purchased over the counter, how much you're taking, whether the medication works to ease your symptoms, and what kind of side effects you have (if any). Medications include herbal or other alternative medicine remedies. Be sure to let your treating doctor know if you're taking anything that wasn't prescribed.
- other treatments, such as hydrotherapy, music therapy, relaxation therapy, biofeedback, hypnosis, massage, physical therapy, transcutaneous electrical nerve stimulators, and meditation
- any measures you use or have used to relieve pain or other symptoms (such as elevating your legs or using a back cushion) that provide the SSA with insight into the nature and severity of your condition, and
- other factors concerning your functional limitations not covered above.

TIP

Using cannabis to treat yourself could raise issues related to substance use. If you use recreational or medicinal marijuana to ease symptoms of pain or anxiety, the SSA will want to know. Cannabis use is legal in many states, and while the SSA is a federal agency, the agency treats drug and alcohol usage similarly when determining whether it's *material* to a finding of disability. (Drug and alcohol abuse problems are discussed in Chapter 11, Section F.)

2. The SSA Evaluation of Symptoms

The SSA makes its disability determinations based on how your individual symptoms limit you (and only you). For example, most people don't have headaches that are so constant and severe that they can't work. But some people do have intense, frequent migraine headaches that last hours (or even days) at a time and which don't respond to treatment by doctors. It's rare to have headaches this severe, but if you do have them, the SSA can decide that they occur often enough and are severe enough to warrant disability benefits in your individual case. In the case of a disorder like headaches, where a physical examination shows very little abnormality, it's critical that your treating doctor have good records about the severity, duration, and frequency of the headaches. These records will provide credibility to your allegation that the headaches are disabling.

Just because you say you have certain symptoms, you won't automatically be granted disability. Although the SSA must consider your individual symptoms, the agency isn't obligated to believe that you have the symptoms you say you have or to believe that they are as severe as you say they are. Remember, an acceptable medical source must provide objective evidence that reasonably supports the severity of the symptoms you allege.

What you do regarding your symptoms is much more important than what you say. If you have back pain and have frequently seen doctors in an attempt to improve the pain, this indicates that you do have severe back pain. But your statement about severe pain becomes less believable when you haven't seen a doctor. And if you've seen an acceptable medical source, then that doctor's evaluation and treatment are very important.

EXAMPLE 1: You have back pain. Despite having multiple back surgeries to address what your doctor believes to be the cause of the problem, your pain has continued. Your doctor has given you corticosteroid injections to help block the pain, and you've used a TENS electrical stimulator unit. You're also on a fairly high dose of pain medicine. When you say that you're highly restricted in what you can do because of pain, the SSA should give considerable weight to your statements.

EXAMPLE 2: You have back pain, but you've never had surgery, have no abnormalities on physical examination, and have normal X-rays of your back. When you say you can't do anything because of back pain, the SSA is not likely to believe you.

Almost everybody who applies for disability has complaints of symptoms such as pain, weakness, fatigue, or nervousness. Any DDS or SSA medical consultant or administrative law judge who doesn't ask about your symptoms or who doesn't take them into account is in violation of federal regulations.

3. The SSA Evaluation of Pain

Pain and other symptoms often go to the heart of the restrictions on your activities of daily living. As explained in Chapter 2, you must complete forms describing what you do during an average day and what you cannot do.

In back pain cases, it's important to measure how long you can sit and stand in one continuous period. Inability to sit or stand very long can be very critical to the outcome of your claim, if the SSA believes in the duration and intensity of your symptoms. If your doctor writes the SSA about your back pain, make sure the report remarks on your ability to lift, bend, and stoop. Your doctor should also state an opinion as to how long you can stand and

sit in one continuous period, as well as the total time you can sit and stand during a typical eight-hour workday.

4. If Physical Evidence Does Not Support Your Claim of Pain

If you allege that you have severe restrictions from pain, but no doctor (whether your own or a CE doctor) can find any reasonable physical basis for it, the SSA is likely to consider the possibility that you have a mental disorder of some kind.

EXAMPLE: You apply for disability, and the evidence indicates there is very little wrong with you physically. But you say you must use crutches to walk, or even use a wheelchair, and have been living that way for some time. The SSA might wonder if you have a mental disorder, and the agency is likely to ask you to go to a mental examination by a clinical psychologist or psychiatrist.

In obvious cases of malingering (pretending to have an illness), the SSA would not request a mental examination. An example of malingering would be if a claimant borrows a wheelchair or crutches just to attend a CE, and is then seen by the doctor walking normally to a car after the exam. Most CE doctors can tell when there is no medical reason for a wheelchair, crutches, or walker. In other words, attempted fraud when no condition exists is not likely to be successful. But claimants who have significant impairments may sometimes successfully exaggerate the severity of their conditions. Such dishonesty is difficult to detect, but can be exposed when the SSA obtains treating doctor records showing that the claimant's symptoms aren't as severe.

E. Other Evidence

Information from sources other than your treating physician and any consultative examiner might help show the extent to which your impairments affect your ability to function. These sources can include public and private social welfare agencies, teachers, day care providers, social workers, relatives, clergy, friends, employers, and other practitioners such as physical therapists, audiologists, chiropractors, and naturopaths.

If you want evidence from these types of sources, ask them to write a letter to be put in your file for DDS to review. You may also mail in the records of any practitioner yourself or give them to the SSA Field Office representative when you file your claim.

However, if the evidence contradicts the evidence of acceptable medical sources described in Section A above or doesn't consist of evidence generally acceptable to the medical community, the evidence will be given little weight in evaluating your claim.

F. Expedited Determinations

In response to complaints about how slowly disability claims are processed, the SSA developed two programs for exceptionally serious or advanced illnesses—the Compassionate Allowances and Terminal Illness programs.

1. Compassionate Allowances Cases

The SSA provides expedited processing for medical conditions that are listed in the Compassionate Allowances List (CAL). Compassionate allowance cases don't involve any special criteria for qualifying for disability benefits. Rather, CAL cases involve such severe impairments that they would always satisfy one of the SSA's disability listings.

CAL cases are selected for fast processing through DDS based solely on the allegations of a claimant or the parent of a child claimant. If the allegations fit the SSA's predictive model that the claim will result in an approval with minimal objective information necessary (such as a positive biopsy for esophageal cancer), the claim will qualify for CAL treatment.

The evidence DDS needs is truly minimal—sometimes just enough information to establish the correct diagnosis is sufficient. The type of information you need to provide for a CAL case depends on the nature of your condition. For example, most CAL cases involve cancer. If you have leukemia or another form of cancer, the most important thing to submit is the biopsy report. Along with a hospital discharge summary or letter from your doctor, that would be sufficient evidence for the SSA to approve your claim under the CAL.

Hospitals or treating doctors sometimes take weeks (or even months) to respond to a DDS request for basic medical records. You can speed up processing of your claim by submitting basic medical information along with your application, or by sending it to the disability examiner at DDS yourself.

Because minimal objective information is required, these cases can be allowed in much less time than it typically takes a claim to be approved. This is the compassion component of the program—the SSA gives these cases priority, so that a CAL case is decided in a matter of days rather than months. In that sense, these cases are similar to Quick Disability Determination (QDD) cases (see Chapter 6). Unlike a QDD claim, however, a medical consultant is needed to medically assess and sign a CAL case before approval or denial.

The CAL list is updated regularly. As of the time of publication, the complete list of CAL impairments is as follows:

- 1p36 Deletion Syndrome
- Acute Leukemia
- Adrenal Cancer—with distant metastases or inoperable, unresectable, or recurrent
- Adult NonHodgkin Lymphoma

- Adult Onset Huntington Disease
- Aicardi-Goutières Syndrome
- Alexander Disease (ALX)—Neonatal and Infantile
- Allan-Herndon-Dudley
- Alobar Holoprosencephaly
- Alpers Disease
- Alpha Mannosidosis—Type II and III
- ALS/Parkinsonism Dementia Complex
- Alström Syndrome
- Alveolar Soft Part Sarcoma
- Amegakaryocytic Thrombocytopenia
- Amyotrophic Lateral Sclerosis (ALS)
- Anaplastic Adrenal Cancer—Adult with distant metastases or inoperable, unresectable, or recurrent
- Anaplastic Ependymoma
- Angelman Syndrome
- Angioimmunoblastic T-Cell Lymphoma
- Angiosarcoma
- Aortic Atresia
- Aplastic Anemia
- Astrocytoma—Grades III and IV
- Ataxia Telangiectasia
- Atypical Teratoid/Rhabdoid Tumor
- Batten Disease
- Beta Thalassemia Major
- Bilateral Optic Atrophy—Infantile
- Bilateral Retinoblastoma
- Bladder Cancer—with distant metastases or inoperable or unresectable
- Blastic Plasmacytoid Dendritic Cell Neoplasm
- Breast Cancer—with distant metastases or inoperable or unresectable
- Calciphylaxis

- CACH—Vanishing White Matter Disease, Infantile and Childhood Onset Forms
- Canavan Disease (CD)
- Carcinoma of Unknown Primary Site
- Cardiac Amyloidosis—AL Type
- Caudal Regression Syndrome—Types III and IV
- CDKL5 Deficiency Disorder
- Cerebro-Oculo-Facio-Skeletal (COFS) Syndrome
- Cerebrotendinous Xanthomatosis
- Charlevoix-Saguenay Spastic Ataxia (ARSACS)
- Cholangiocarcinoma
- Child Lymphoblastic Lymphoma
- Child Lymphoma
- Child Neuroblastoma—with distant metastases or recurrent
- Chondrosarcoma—with multimodal therapy
- Choroid Plexus Carcinoma
- Chronic Idiopathic Intestinal Pseudo-Obstruction
- Chronic Myelogenous Leukemia (CML)—Blast Phase
- CIC-Rearranged Sarcoma
- Coffin-Lowry Syndrome
- Congenital Lymphedema
- Congenital Myotonic Dystrophy
- Congenital Zika Syndrome
- Cornelia de Lange Syndrome—Classic Form
- Corticobasal Degeneration
- Creutzfeldt-Jakob Disease (CJD)—Adult
- Cri du Chat Syndrome
- Degos Disease—Systemic
- DeSanctis-Cacchione Syndrome
- Desmoplastic Mesothelioma
- Desmoplastic Small Round Cell Tumors
- Dravet Syndrome
- Duchenne Muscular Dystrophy—Adult
- Early-Onset Alzheimer's Disease
- Edwards Syndrome (Trisomy 18)
- Eisenmenger Syndrome
- Endometrial Stromal Sarcoma
- Endomyocardial Fibrosis
- Ependymoblastoma (Child Brain Cancer)
- Erdheim-Chester Disease
- Esophageal Cancer
- Esthesioneuroblastoma
- Ewing Sarcoma
- Farber Disease (FD)—Infantile
- Fatal Familial Insomnia
- Fibrodysplasia Ossificans Progressiva
- Fibrolamellar Cancer
- Follicular Dendritic Cell Sarcoma—metastatic or recurrent
- FOXG1 Syndrome
- Friedreich's Ataxia (FRDA)
- Frontotemporal Dementia (FTD), Picks Disease—Type A—Adult
- Fryns Syndrome
- Fucosidosis—Type 1
- Fukuyama Congenital Muscular Dystrophy
- Fulminant Giant Cell Myocarditis
- Galactosialidosis—Early and Late Infantile Types
- Gallbladder Cancer

- Gaucher Disease (GD)—Type 2
- Gerstmann-Sträussler-Scheinker Disease
- Giant Axonal Neuropathy
- Glioblastoma Multiforme (Brain Cancer)
- Glioma Grades III and IV
- Glutaric Acidemia—Type II
- Head and Neck Cancers—with distant metastasis or inoperable or unresectable
- Heart Transplant Graft Failure
- Heart Transplant Wait List—1A/1B
- Hemophagocytic Lymphohistiocytosis (HLH)—Familial Type
- Hepatoblastoma
- Hepatopulmonary Syndrome
- Hepatorenal Syndrome
- Histiocytosis Syndrome
- Hoyeraal-Hreidarsson Syndrome
- Hutchinson-Gilford Progeria Syndrome
- Hydranencephaly
- Hypocomplementemic Urticarial Vasculitis Syndrome
- Hypophosphatasia Perinatal (Lethal) and Infantile Onset Types
- Hypoplastic Left Heart Syndrome
- I Cell Disease
- Idiopathic Pulmonary Fibrosis
- Intracranial Hemangiopericytoma
- Infantile Free Sialic Acid Storage Disease
- Infantile Neuroaxonal Dystrophy (INAD)
- Infantile Neuronal Ceroid Lipofuscinoses
- Inflammatory Breast Cancer (IBC)
- Intracranial Hemangiopericytoma
- Jervell and Lange-Nielsen Syndrome
- Joubert Syndrome
- Junctional Epidermolysis Bullosa—Lethal Type
- Juvenile Onset Huntington Disease
- Kidney Cancer—inoperable or unresectable
- Kleefstra Syndrome
- Krabbe Disease (KD)—Infantile
- Kufs Disease—Types A and B
- Large Intestine Cancer—with distant metastasis or inoperable, unresectable, or recurrent
- Late Infantile Neuronal Ceroid Lipofuscinoses
- Leber Congenital Amaurosis
- Leigh's Disease
- Leiomyosarcoma
- Leptomeningeal Carcinomatosis
- Lesch-Nyhan Syndrome (LNS)
- Lewy Body Dementia
- Liposarcoma—metastatic or recurrent
- Lissencephaly
- Liver Cancer
- Lowe Syndrome
- Lymphomatoid Granulomatosis—Grade III
- Malignant Brain Stem Gliomas—Childhood
- Malignant Ectomesenchymoma
- Malignant Gastrointestinal Stromal Tumor
- Malignant Germ Cell Tumor
- Malignant Multiple Sclerosis
- Malignant Renal Rhabdoid Tumor
- Mantle Cell Lymphoma (MCL)

- Maple Syrup Urine Disease
- Marshall-Smith Syndrome
- Mastocytosis—Type IV
- MECP2 Duplication Syndrome
- Medulloblastoma—with metastases
- Megacystis Microcolon Intestinal Hypoperistalsis Syndrome
- Megalencephaly Capillary Malformation Syndrome
- Menkes Disease—Classic or Infantile Onset Form
- Merkel Cell Carcinoma—with metastases
- Merosin-Deficient Congenital Muscular Dystrophy
- Metachromatic Leukodystrophy (MLD)—Late Infantile
- Metastatic Endometrial Adenocarcinoma
- Microvillus Inclusion Disease—Child
- Mitral Valve Atresia
- Mixed Dementias
- Mowat-Wilson Syndrome
- MPS I, formerly known as Hurler Syndrome
- MPS II, formerly known as Hunter Syndrome
- MPS III, formerly known as Sanfilippo Syndrome
- Mucosal Malignant Melanoma
- Multicentric Castleman Disease
- Multiple System Atrophy
- Myelodysplastic Syndrome With Excess Blasts
- Myoclonic Epilepsy With Ragged Red Fibers Syndrome

- Neonatal Adrenoleukodystrophy
- Nephrogenic Systemic Fibrosis
- Neurodegeneration With Brain Iron Accumulation—Types 1 and 2
- NFU1 Mitochondrial Disease
- Nicolaides-Baraitser Syndrome
- Niemann-Pick Disease (NPD)—Type A
- Niemann-Pick Disease—Type C
- Nonketotic Hyperglycinemia
- Non-Small Cell Lung Cancer
- NUT Carcinoma
- Obliterative Bronchiolitis
- Ohtahara Syndrome
- Oligodendroglioma Brain Tumor—Grade III
- Ornithine Transcarbamylase (OTC) Deficiency
- Orthochromatic Leukodystrophy with Pigmented Glia
- Osteogenesis Imperfecta (OI)—Type II
- Osteosarcoma, formerly known as Bone Cancer—with distant metastases or inoperable or unresectable
- Ovarian Cancer—with distant metastases or inoperable or unresectable
- Pallister-Killian Syndrome
- Pancreatic Cancer
- Paraneoplastic Cerebellar Degeneration
- Paraneoplastic Pemphigus
- Patau Syndrome (Trisomy 13)
- Pearson Syndrome
- Pelizaeus-Merzbacher Disease—Classic Form
- Pelizaeus-Merzbacher Disease—Connatal Form

- Pericardial Mesothelioma
- Peripheral Nerve Cancer—metastatic or recurrent
- Peritoneal Mesothelioma
- Peritoneal Mucinous Carcinomatosis
- Perry Syndrome
- Pfeiffer Syndrome—Types II and III
- Phelan-McDermid Syndrome
- Pineoblastoma—Childhood
- Pitt-Hopkins Syndrome
- Pleural Mesothelioma
- Pompe Disease—Infantile
- Pontocerebellar Hypoplasia
- Posterior Cortical Atrophy
- Primary Central Nervous System Lymphoma
- Primary Effusion Lymphoma
- Primary Omental Cancer
- Primary Peritoneal Cancer
- Primary Progressive Aphasia
- Progressive Bulbar Palsy
- Progressive Multifocal Leukoencephalopathy
- Progressive Supranuclear Palsy
- Prostate Cancer—Hormone Refractory Disease—or with visceral metastases
- Pulmonary Atresia
- Pulmonary Kaposi Sarcoma
- Refractory Hodgkin Lymphoma
- Renal Amyloidosis—AL Type
- Renpenning Syndrome
- Retinopathy of Prematurity—Stage V
- Rett (RTT) Syndrome
- Revesz Syndrome

- Rhabdomyosarcoma
- Rhizomelic Chondrodysplasia Punctata
- Richter Syndrome
- Roberts Syndrome
- Rubenstein-Taybi Syndrome
- Salivary Cancers
- Sandhoff Disease
- Sarcomatoid Carcinoma of the Lung—Stages II–IV
- Sarcomatoid Mesothelioma
- Schindler Disease—Type 1
- SCN8A-Related Epilepsy with Encephalopathy
- Seckel Syndrome
- Secondary Adenocarcinoma of the Brain
- Severe Combined Immunodeficiency—Childhood
- Single Ventricle
- Sinonasal Cancer
- Sjögren-Larsson Syndrome
- Skin Malignant Melanoma With Metastases
- Small Cell Cancer (Large Intestine, Prostate, or Thymus)
- Small Cell Cancer of the Female Genital Tract
- Small Cell Lung Cancer
- Small Intestine Cancer—with distant metastases or inoperable, unresectable, or recurrent
- Smith-Lemli-Opitz Syndrome
- Soft Tissue Sarcoma—with distant metastases or recurrent

- Spinal Muscular Atrophy (SMA)—Types 0 and 1
- Spinal Nerve Root Cancer—metastatic or recurrent
- Spinocerebellar Ataxia
- Stiff Person Syndrome
- Stomach Cancer—with distant metastases or inoperable, unresectable, or recurrent
- Subacute Sclerosing Panencephalitis
- Superficial Siderosis of the Central Nervous System
- SYNGAP1-related NSID
- Tabes Dorsalis
- Tay-Sachs Disease—Infantile Type
- Taybi-Linder Syndrome
- Tetrasomy 18p
- Thanatophoric Dysplasia—Type 1
- Thyroid Cancer
- Transplant Coronary Artery Vasculopathy
- Tricuspid Atresia
- Trisomy 9
- Ullrich Congenital Muscular Dystrophy
- Ureter Cancer—with distant metastases or inoperable, unresectable, or recurrent
- Usher Syndrome—Type I
- Ventricular Assist Device Recipient—Left, Right, or Biventricular
- Walker-Warburg Syndrome
- Wolf-Hirschhorn Syndrome
- Wolman Disease
- X-Linked Lymphoproliferative Disease
- X-Linked Myotubular Myopathy
- Xeroderma Pigmentosum
- Zellweger Syndrome

Compassionate Allowances apply to both SSDI and SSI claims. The five-month waiting period for SSDI claims is not waived by having a Compassionate Allowance. An exception is for amyotrophic lateral sclerosis (ALS), which has no waiting period for either the monthly cash benefit or Medicare, effective July 23, 2020 (based on the ALS Act, Public Law 117-3).

2. Terminal Illness Cases

The SSA also expedites disability decisions for applicants with terminal illnesses through its TERI program. Terminal illness cases are those that are expected to result in death. DDS is expected to handle these cases quickly and with sensitivity to the claimant's condition.

The SSA and DDS are alerted to possible TERI cases by any of the following situations:

- An allegation (e.g., from the claimant, a friend, family member, doctor, or other medical source) is made that the illness is terminal.
- An allegation or diagnosis is made of amyotrophic lateral sclerosis (ALS), commonly known as Lou Gehrig's disease.
- An allegation or diagnosis is made of acquired immune deficiency syndrome or acquired immunodeficiency syndrome (AIDS).

- The claimant is receiving inpatient hospice care or is receiving home hospice care; e.g., in-home counseling or nursing care.

Some examples of TERI cases include, but aren't limited to, the following:

- chronic dependence on a cardio-pulmonary life-sustaining device
- claimants awaiting a heart, heart/lung, lung, liver, or bone marrow transplant (excludes kidney and corneal transplants)
- chronic pulmonary or heart failure requiring continuous home oxygen and an inability to care for personal needs
- any malignant neoplasm (cancer) that is:
  - metastatic (has spread)
  - defined as stage IV
  - persistent or recurrent following initial therapy, or
  - inoperable or unresectable
- an allegation or diagnosis of:
  - cancer of the esophagus
  - cancer of the liver
  - cancer of the pancreas
  - cancer of the gallbladder
  - mesothelioma
  - small cell or oat-cell lung cancer
  - cancer of the brain, or
  - acute myelogenous leukemia (AML) or acute lymphocytic leukemia (ALL)
- comatose for 30 days or more, or
- newborn with a lethal genetic or congenital defect.

If your claim fits the CAL list or you think it may be a TERI case, you should tell SSA that when you first apply for benefits. That way, it will be expedited from the very start.

Note that QDD (see Chapter 6) and CAL cases (see above) don't necessarily imply terminal illness, although they sometimes involve such a prognosis. Like a CAL case, a medical consultant is required to make a TERI determination, and some CAL cases are also TERI cases.

If an SSA Field Office classifies a claim as a TERI claim, DDS has the authority to remove that classification if DDS finds that the medical evidence doesn't justify it. Unfortunately, the SSA's operating guidelines don't require the DDS to use a medical consultant to remove TERI status. Of course, if the issue is merely something like a typographical error—such as entering "ALS" instead of an intended "ACL" (anterior cruciate ligament) tear—it makes sense that a doctor isn't required to remove a TERI classification because the error doesn't require medical knowledge. However, the SSA uses an example where an examiner could remove the TERI classification when the examiner belives that "the claimant's neoplastic disease (cancer) is responding to multimodal therapy." One would think that only a medical doctor would be qualified to determine whether a patient's cancer has improved, but the SSA doesn't require a doctor to make this decision.

3. Wounded Warriors

The SSA processes military casualty/ wounded warrior (MC/WW) cases under expedited procedures similar to those of TERI cases, but doesn't classify them as TERI unless there's an indication of a terminal illness. If you're a wounded veteran or active-duty servicemember who became disabled while on active duty, you should let the SSA know you have MC/WW status because wounded warrior cases are evaluated more quickly than most. The SSA's processing of claims involving military or former military personnel can be complex; for example, military wages alone may not determine whether a servicemember is doing substantial gainful activity, because servicemembers usually continue to receive full military pay even if they're too sick or injured to work.

If you're an MC/WW veteran or service- member applying for Social Security disability, you should take copies of all Department of Defense (DOD) Forms DD 214 to the Field Office where you apply for disability. DDS needs all the information possible to determine the onset date of your disability and any possible closed periods of disability.

If you apply for disability online, you should still make sure these forms reach your disability examiner once you find out how to contact them. But you shouldn't delay applying for disability to obtain these documents from DOD. The Field Office can forward them to your disability examiner later if you don't do it directly yourself. Since these forms contain dates of active duty and other useful information in disability adjudication, it's in your best interest to make sure they are submitted. The SSA has more information for wounded warriors on its website, including a brochure called "Disability Benefits for Wounded Warriors."

CHAPTER

6

Who Decides Your Claim?

After the Social Security Administration (SSA) Field Office finds that you meet the nonmedical eligibility requirements for disability benefits, your file is sent to the state agency responsible for making a decision on your application. This agency is known as Disability Determination Services, or DDS. Your file will contain your application, the few administrative documents you completed at the SSA Field Office, and copies of any medical records or other relevant papers you provided to the SSA when you applied.

A. DDS Basics

DDS offices are run by each state, but they're federally funded and must follow the federal laws and regulations. Each DDS has a computer system connected to the SSA federal computers in Baltimore and to the local SSA Field Offices. These computers allow DDS and the SSA to quickly communicate.

1. Types of Claims Handled by DDS

DDS handles several types of disability claims, including:

- a new application, called an initial claim
- a *reconsideration* claim, if you're turned down
- a second initial claim—in fact, you can file as many initial claims as you want, and

- *continuing disability reviews* (CDRs), in which DDS periodically reviews the files of disability recipients to see if their health has improved.

2. Contacting Your DDS

Your DDS will have a toll-free telephone number you can use from anywhere in your state. If you don't have this number, check the government section of your phone book, call the SSA Field Office where you made your application, call the general number for the SSA, 800-772-1213, or check the SSA website at www.ssa.gov.

3. When the Outcome of a Claim Is Uncertain

If you apply for disability when you're acutely sick or hurt and the outcome of your treatment isn't clear, DDS might *diary* your claim. This means that DDS will hold your file to see how your illness or injury progresses. DDS will wait to determine if you will have an ongoing or permanent disability. For example, heart impairment claims often require diaries because claimants apply for disability soon after they've had a heart attack or heart surgery, and the outcome of their treatment is unknown.

Other claimants who might need a diary include people who apply soon after incurring multiple serious fractures in an automobile wreck or soon after incurring a brain injury. Diaries usually last up to three months but can sometimes last as many as six months.

B. DDS Claims Examiners

When DDS receives your file, it assigns a disability claims examiner to your case. The claims examiner's job is to obtain the medical records listed on your application, maintain contact with you, and do other administrative work as necessary (discussed below). Claims examiners are your point of contact with DDS.

There are various types of claims examiners: those who handle initial claims, those who do reconsideration claims, those in the quality-assurance department who review the work of other examiners, and those who evaluate people already receiving benefits to see if they still qualify.

It's important that you understand the job of the claims examiner and the kinds of work pressure the claims examiners are under. Examiners are responsible for evaluating the nonmedical aspects of all claims—other than nonmedical eligibility issues that were already handled by the SSA Field Office. The number of nonmedical issues potentially involved in a claim is large. Some examples include:

- deciding the date you actually stopped work for disability purposes
- determining your vocational factors, including age, education, and work experience
- arranging for consultative examinations and coordinating your attendance
- contacting your treating sources for your medical records, and

- asking DDS medical consultants for advice on the nature and severity of your medical impairments, as well as on what kind of additional medical evidence is needed to decide your claim.

Examiners can have difficulty keeping up with the endless, changing rules. The Program Operations Manual System (POMS) includes the rules they must follow when processing claims. If the POMS doesn't have the answer to a question, the examiners ask their supervisors. If DDS staff don't know the answer, they send the question to the SSA Regional Office. You can access the POMS yourself online at www.ssa.gov, but you should be careful when interpreting it as some sections aren't up to date and it's loaded with very complex, bureaucratic terms.

C. DDS Organization

DDS offices have administrative personnel besides claims examiners. The other administrative personnel you might encounter include secretaries and vocational analysts. *Vocational analysts* are specially trained examiners who assess your ability to work based on the severity of your medical impairments, your work experience, and your education. Vocational analysts are often assistant supervisors of a group of examiners.

How Claims Examiners Work

Claims examiners are sometimes taught about basic medical principles by DDS medical consultants (who are doctors or psychologists). This helps them better understand the medical issues involved in claims, but it doesn't qualify them to make determinations about the medical severity of your impairments. Unfortunately, some examiners will still try. But under current regulations,examiners can't legally make medical determinations.

As might be expected, claims examiners vary greatly in how well they do their jobs. Some meticulously consider and document every detail. Others care only about processing claims as fast as they can with the least amount of work.

DDS offices have internal quality-assurance reviews that are supposed to catch poor work, and examiners have supervisors who should monitor their work. But supervisors also vary in how conscientious they are and in their willingness to make sure their examiners are doing a good job. In addition, a DDS office might not conduct the required number of internal quality-assurance reviews, which raises the likelihood of claims being done incorrectly and escaping the agency undetected.

If a DDS office is understaffed and under-funded, the number of cases an examiner has to handle increases. If your examiner has a caseload in the hundreds, the probability of errors increases greatly.

The more you know about the disability determination process, the more likely you'll be able to spot whether an examiner improperly handled your claim or an issue in your file was decided wrongly.

Here are some hints. Watch out if:

- You know a decision was made without sufficient medical information. For example, DDS denies your claim for a vision problem without requesting and reviewing your treating doctor's records or sending you for a consultative exam-ination of your eyes. It's illegal for a DDS office to ignore all of your medical claims.
- The examiner or a supervisor appears evasive or unable to answer your questions on the telephone.
- An examiner or a supervisor promises to call you back to answer a question and fails to do so.
- The examiner or a supervisor says there's no need to take your claim to a DDS medical consultant for an evaluation of your medical records, or won't tell you whether a doctor will be asked to look at your records. It's a violation of federal regulations for an examiner to make a medical determination of disability or to determine your residual functional capacity (see Chapter 8). But it happens.

Claims examiners are usually arranged into units, each with a supervisor and perhaps an assistant supervisor. The supervisors in turn answer to their supervisor—usually an operations manager, quality-assurance manager, or assistant director. The position titles may vary, but the general idea is that there is a bureaucracy with many levels of authority.

You ordinarily only meet your claims examiner, and in many cases, even that contact is limited to the telephone. A vocational analyst might also call you to discuss specific issues about the work you did or your education. You can also ask to speak to an examiner's immediate supervisor if necessary. You won't routinely come into contact with higher-level personnel, but it's possible. Claimants who are angry about their treatment and not satisfied by the supervisor could be referred to an assistant director. Other claimants don't wait for referral up through the chain of command—they call the DDS director on their own initiative.

The DDS director might be appointed by a state governor, which might mean frequent turnover, but the director sets the tone of the agency. How a particular DDS runs, therefore, depends on the director's integrity, intelligence, dedication, managerial ability, motivation, and desire to provide good public service. Agency directors don't have the legal authority to make the medical part of disability determinations—only an SSA medical consultant, disability hearing officer, or administrative law judge can do that.

D. Medical Consultants

Medical consultants are the people who ultimately review the medical aspect of your claim for disability benefits. A medical consultant must be a licensed medical doctor (with either an M.D. or D.O. degree) or a psychologist with a Ph.D. If you apply for disability based on physical impairments, a consultant with an M.D. or a D.O. will evaluate your file.

If you apply for disability based on a mental impairment, a consulting psychiatrist or a qualified psychologist will evaluate your file.

If you apply for disability based on both a physical and a mental impairment, a consulting psychologist can evaluate only the mental impairment. A consulting M.D. or D.O. must evaluate the nonmental impairment. The overall medical part of the determination of disability must be made by a consulting M.D. or D.O., unless the mental impairment alone would justify a finding of disability.

Federal law requires the SSA to have a qualified medical or psychological consultant review *all* initial claim applications (Public Law 114–74, 129 Stat. 584, 613, which is also known as the Bipartisan Budget Act of 2015). This law reversed the SSA's previous policy of letting disability examiners decide some claims without consulting a doctor.

It's important to understand that the 2015 law only applies to initial applications, not other types of evaluations. But the law used the word initial without clarifying, so it's not clear if the SSA is prohibited from letting claims examiners alone decide reconsideration appeals at DDS. If you feel it was possible that your reconsideration claim was denied because of a lack of professional medical evaluation, you could probably get it reviewed again without filing a formal appeal (which can take a long time) by contacting the DDS director or even your federal politicians. They can ask that DDS look at your claim again. (The author reviewed many such claims as a DDS chief medical consultant, no small number of which were reversed into allowances.)

If you have a question about your case, ask the local SSA Field Office or the state's disability determination agency.

1. The Medical Consultant's Job

A medical consultant's work is performed mostly at a desk, in an office. The consultant does strictly a paper review of your claim; the consulting physician or psychologist usually has no contact with you. The work of determining whether you qualify for disability or not includes the following:

- evaluating medical evidence to determine if your impairment meets the requirements of a listing in the Listing of Impairments (see Chapter 5, Section D1)

- assessing the severity of your impairments and describing your remaining physical or mental abilities (called your *residual functional capacity*, or RFC) and your limitations in abilities that are caused by the impairments (see Chapter 8)

- discussing with DDS other ways to get medical evidence, including suggesting ways to improve communication between DDS and the treating doctors and facilities. (For example, the medical records department of a hospital might tell a claims examiner that it doesn't have a biopsy report showing that a claimant has cancer. The medical consultant can suggest that the examiner call the pathology department of the hospital. Or a claims examiner might not be able to get a treating doctor on the telephone to ask questions about impairments that weren't covered in your doctor's medical records. A medical consultant, as a doctor, has a better chance of getting a treating doctor on the telephone. Because of time constraints, however, medical consultants don't usually talk to the treating doctors.)

- evaluating medical questions asked by a claims examiner. (For example, a claims examiner might need to know whether it's reasonable to award a particular SSI claimant presumptive disability. Or a claims examiner might need to know the probability that a medical condition will improve, in order to schedule a future review of the file. Or a claims examiner might need to know exactly what medical records are needed. The medical consultant would answer these questions.)

- reviewing requests for consultative examinations (CEs) to make sure they're necessary and will address the issue in question

- suggesting alternatives when a claimant can't (or won't) attend a CE, or doesn't cooperate with the disability determination in other ways. (For example, some claimants refuse to attend a CE, feeling that their treating doctor has the information. If the treating doctor hasn't provided DDS with the information, the medical consultant can suggest that the claimant visit the treating doctor and personally obtain the records. On the other hand, for example, if the claimant won't attend a CE because of agoraphobia—a fear of leaving the house—the medical consultant can intervene by having a consulting psychologist or psychiatrist sent to the claimant's home.)

- reviewing consultative exam reports that don't give enough medical information for a disability determination and recommending to the CE doctor ways to avoid deficient reports

- participating in the vocational rehabilitation screening and referral process, by advising whether you're medically capable of undergoing training for new job skills

- reviewing disability determinations to make sure that the decision is based on medical evidence, and

- signing disability determination forms.

If a Medical Consultant Has Been the Claimant's Doctor

Medical consultants who provide any of the medical evidence for a particular disability case (like when the consultant is also the claimant's regular physician) should disqualify themselves from working as a medical consultant on that specific case. This isn't as unusual a situation as it might sound. A doctor who works as a DDS medical consultant might also see patients privately, and one of their patients might apply for disability. In that case, the doctor can provide medical information as the treating doctor but can't act as the medical consultant for DDS in the disability determination for that claimant. This policy protects the doctor-patient relationship and attempts to ensure that the disability decision is made without any personal bias for or against the claimant.

2. Reviewing the Medical Consultant's Decision

Depending on the state, medical consultants may be employees of DDS or consultants who charge an hourly fee. Some medical consultants work only part time, which can be a problem. The complexities of Social Security medical evaluations can rarely be fully grasped by someone who does the work only part time.

If you're unhappy with the medical consultant's decision (that is, your claim is denied for a medical reason), what you can do about it depends on how strongly you feel about the matter. If you're concerned that your application received an inappropriate medical review, ask the director of DDS the following:

- the name and medical specialty of the doctor who reviewed your claim
- how long that doctor has worked for DDS, and
- the average amount of time the doctor spends at DDS per day or week.

The director should be able to answer these questions. In addition, the doctors' contracts are probably available as public records in your state's finance and administration department, because the doctors are paid through state coffers.

If you're really concerned about the doctor who reviewed your claim, ask the DDS director to have your records reviewed by a different medical consultant—specifically, one with more experience or knowledge of your medical condition. If the SSA has already denied your claim, ask the DDS director to recall your claim and reopen it. You can make this request for any reason up to a year after you've been denied benefits. (Reopenings and revisions are discussed in Chapter 12.)

E. If Your Claim Is Granted

The DDS medical consultant approves the medical part of the determination, and the examiner approves the nonmedical portions. Both the consultant and the examiner sign the appropriate final disability determination form. DDS then returns your file to the SSA Field Office. The SSA will complete any outstanding nonmedical paperwork, compute your benefit amount, and begin paying benefits.

The SSA is responsible for notifying you of the approval. A notice should be mailed to you between seven and ten days after the DDS decision. However, the time it actually takes for the necessary paperwork to be completed depends on workloads. Also, your claim could be slowed by months if, after the DDS decision, it's chosen for a quality review by an SSA Disability Quality Branch (DQB) located at an SSA Regional Office. You won't be told if your case has been selected for review, but you can find out by asking your DDS examiner. Still, there isn't anything you can do to speed up the process if your case has been chosen for review.

The SSA Field Office sometimes makes errors in calculating benefits. Chapter 13 contains information about benefit calculations, but this is a complex area. If you have any questions about receiving the right amount of money, don't hesitate to call your local Field Office and discuss it with them.

Remember that being found entitled to benefits doesn't necessarily mean you will get money at the same time. SSDI claimants can't get money until after a five-month waiting period, and SSI claimants can't get money until the month after they apply (see Chapter 10). An exception to the SSDI waiting period is for amyotrophic lateral sclerosis (ALS); claimants with ALS don't have a waiting period.

F. If Your Claim Is Denied

If DDS denies your claim, you might want to find out the details behind that decision. This information might be important to you if you plan to appeal. The SSA keeps disability information in an electronic folder, and much of that information is available to you. (Electronic folders are discussed in more detail in Chapter 12.)

If you get your folder, look for Form SSA831, *Disability Determination and Transmittal*—it's usually at the front of the folder. The DDS claims examiner and the medical consultant must complete this form in every initial and reconsideration application. If you've applied more than once, your folder (also called your disability file) will contain multiple forms.

Even if the form was signed by a medical consultant, it might not have been reviewed by a doctor. To see if the medical consultant who signed the form reviewed your disability file, look for medical notes or a residual functional capacity (RFC) rating form completed by the medical consultant. If you can't find notes or an RFC form, it's quite possible that your claim wasn't reviewed by the medical consultant. (Children don't receive RFCs, so no such form would be expected in their disability file, but you would still expect to find the medical consultant's notes.)

If it appears that your file wasn't reviewed by a medical consultant, write and call the DDS director. State that your file contains no evidence that your claim was reviewed by a doctor, except for a signature on the *Disability Determination and Transmittal Form*. Demand that your claim be recalled and reviewed by a medical consultant. If the director won't help you, contact your senator or congressional representative, as well as your governor and local state legislator. You have a right to have your medical records reviewed by a medical consultant.

Of course, your claim might be denied whether it's reviewed by a DDS medical consultant or not. (Chapter 11 contains a discussion of the different ways claims can be denied. Chapter 12 discusses the various types of appeal available to you.)

G. DDS Corruption and Incompetence

Corruption and incompetence involving DDS are probably the last thing on earth you want—or the SSA wants you—to think about. Still, it's possible that your claim is or will be denied for reasons unrelated to the criteria established under Social Security disability rules and regulations. This section helps you understand why corruption and incompetence might have an impact on your claim—and what you can do about it.

There are two basic reasons you should be interested in corruption and incompetence in DDS:

- As a claimant, you might be cheated out of a fair decision on your claim.
- As a taxpayer, your money might be spent in ways other than intended.

Unfortunately, anyone engaged in corrupt activity isn't going to make it easy for you to detect—but hopefully this section will help you know what to watch out for.

1. How Corruption and Incompetence Can Influence Your Claim

Honest errors and missing information can play a role in denials of deserving claimants. Unfortunately, denials might also result from corruption or incompetence. The SSA might not be aware of the corruption or incompetence in a particular DDS— or might overlook what it does know.

Here are some real-world examples of the kinds of activities that can go on.

a. Corrupt Directors

DDS directors are appointed by state governors, and some are appointed by governors with more interest in political goals than in delivering quality service. A corrupt director isn't necessarily as concerned with the overall allowance or denial of benefits as with which claims are allowed or denied. For example, a corrupt director might try to allow large numbers of claims that are politically sensitive—such as childrens' claims—while keeping a medical consultant in the agency who unfairly denies large numbers of adult claimants. A director or senior-level manager might pressure others into doing something wrong in order to hide the director's activities. A few specific instances of the practical application of corruption are given below.

Developing Illegal Policies. It's illegal for a director to manipulate DDS's allowance rate by pressuring medical consultants and other staff to allow a specific quota of favored types of claims. It's also against the law to speed up claim processing by giving examiners authority they don't have—such as:

- completing RFC forms
- making medical determinations on whether impairments aren't severe, or
- deciding whether medical conditions qualify under the Listing of Impairments.

Blocking Finished Claims. A corrupt DDS director can order DDS employees to hold finished claims and not forward the decisions to the SSA unless the decisions are what the director wants. For example, years ago a DDS director held back hundreds of finished claims that were denials. Only allowances were put into the DDS computer that was connected to the SSA. The result was an artificially high allowance rate, which allowed the agency to escape criticism by certain political action groups. Unfortunately, the denials sat for months and had many claimants wondering where their claims had gone. This prevented the denied claimants from going on to a timely appeal.

Controlling the Chief Medical Consultant. The chief medical consultant (CMC), as you might guess, is the head of the medical staff at a DDS. A corrupt director can anonymously control all medical determinations by influencing the CMC to approve medical policies that the director favors. If this happens, a medically unqualified person (the director) might be influencing your medical determination.

For example, a CMC might agree to pressure medical consultants to sign RFC forms that were actually completed by claims examiners, regardless of whether they agree with the claims examiners' opinions.

To make the process appear legitimate and give some cover to medical consultants, the medical consultants are told they will be required to sign such claims only if the claims examiner assures them that the examiner's medical assessment can't affect the decision (allowance or denial) outcome of the claim. So, if caught, a medical consultant could make the weak argument that "It didn't make any difference to the outcome," and people not familiar with how disability determinations are made might accept that excuse. However, federal regulations specifically require medical consultants to make the RFC determinations, and there's no legal excuse for not doing so. Indeed, state medical boards look unfavorably on doctors letting others use their signatures.

This kind of corruption is difficult to detect, even at higher review levels by the SSA or attorneys representing claimants, because there's no evidence in the file saying that a medical consultant signed an RFC they didn't agree with. If a paper RFC form was completed and the handwriting is that of the claims examiner, that is a strong hint. However, when such forms are completed on computer at a DDS, that clue is missing.

If your claim was denied based on medical ineligibility and no doctor was consulted, you should strongly insist that your claim be reviewed again, this time by a real doctor or psychologist. Also, if you appeal such a denial, lack of professional medical review of your file is a strong argument that you were denied a fair assessment.

b. Incompetent or Problematic Directors

Good administration of a DDS agency requires education, knowledge, skill, and experience. However, a governor might appoint an unqualified person to head DDS. For example, the director might have no experience with Social Security disability law or lack appropriate education. You should be able to find out about the director's qualifications by contacting the director or the governor's office.

Acting With Bias. Unfortunately, some medical consultants routinely deny claimants because of personal bias against people receiving disability. At one DDS years ago, a medical consultant commonly denied claimants with terminal cancer, terminal heart disease, severe arthritis, and terminal lung disease. He denied about 800 claimants a year who were legally entitled to benefits. Conscientious examiners stopped taking serious impairments to him, afraid that he would deny the claimants. Other examiners, however, were quick to give him cases in order to get fast decisions. No DDS director would terminate the medical consultant's contract because he—and those who were happy to work with him—moved along enormous numbers of cases. This DDS looked good in federal statistics—it had one of the fastest processing times in the country. This consultant's unfair tenure ended only when he died.

Stealing Time. Some DDS medical consultants work at other medical jobs while working at DDS. They might do consulting work or take calls from private patients while they're supposed to be reviewing disability files. Obviously, there are many problems with this. First, the doctor is "double-dipping" (getting paid by the government while not working for the government). Second, when the doctor has less time to review claims, the overall quality of each individual claim decreases.

Signers. Some medical consultants are known as "signers," meaning they'll sign medical assessments an administrator asks them to sign although they would otherwise have reached a different conclusion. For example, if a governor calls the DDS director and asks that DDS revisit a particular claim (not an illegal act), the director might feel pressured to please the governor, and make it clear to a medical consultant that the governor thinks the person is disabled. A signer will oblige, even if they don't agree.

Signers are an insidious form of corruption, and no DDS will admit they exist—but they do. The SSA doesn't have solid procedures for stopping them.

c. Problematic Claims Examiners

Some claims examiners focus more on quantity—keeping claims moving and their desk clear—than quality. DDS directors may have different performance standards, allowing poor claims examiners to keep their jobs when another office might need to let them go.

Because claims examiners see so many disability applications, some may become jaded and approve fewer claims over time. Other examiners might try to manipulate medical determinations by removing written medical opinions they don't like from files and then taking the claim to a different medical consultant, hoping for a different decision.

d. What Happens When DDS Disregards Federal Laws and Regulations

Federal regulations require the SSA to take the disability determination procedures away from a DDS that doesn't follow the law. It's rare, however, for the SSA to take such action. In the past, various DDS offices around the country have been found guilty of violations such as not reviewing medical information from treating doctors and not considering a claimant's age, education, and work experience. Unfortunately, many valid disability claims were caught in the crossfire, and the punishment was minimal—making DDS rereview the claims.

e. Political Pressure

Here's a historical example of how the SSA can mishandle the administration of its disability program.

In 1990, a U.S. Supreme Court decision (*Sullivan v. Zebley*) made the SSA change the way child disability claims were evaluated. Following the Court's order, the SSA created new child disability regulations that provided a way for children who didn't meet the listings to get benefits. Some DDS directors felt pressured to see the new regulations as an opportunity to allow most child claims. As a result, the number of approved child claims almost tripled. At many DDS offices, more than 90% of child claims were granted. Some medical consultants, however—particularly those with expertise in the diagnosis and treatment of child disorders—felt otherwise. A few resigned form their jobs. Others, especially those who tried to expose the problem, were terminated.

DDS offices with only a modest increase in the percentage of child claims allowed felt pressured into approving more claims. At the same time, reports of rising numbers of disability awards—along with stories of abuses of the program—made their way to the national news.

Congress established a commission in 1994 to investigate abuses and discrepancies in childhood disability determinations. Arguments were presented about legislation that would change the childhood disability standard, greatly reducing the number of children receiving benefits. In 1996, Public Law 104-193 (PRWORA) passed, resulting in about 15% of children on the disability rolls losing their eligibility for benefits under the new standard.

However, the SSA faced criticism for "kicking kids off of disability," just as it had for issuing too many "crazy checks" for children with mental health impairments. The burden of taking the negative press fell on local DDS offices, whose medical consultants and claims examiners had to undergo national retraining classes. After these sessions, thousands of cases were sent back to the DDS offices for ongoing review as often as was necessary until benefits were granted.

2. What You Can Do About Corruption and Incompetence

Your goal is to get a fair decision on your disability claim, not to get into a personal conflict with DDS personnel or to accuse them of malfeasance. But you have the right to have an intelligent, capable, and unbiased person review your claim. Here's how to minimize the effect of personnel problems on your claim.

You can try to prevent any problems by notifying DDS in writing that you expect only actions on your claim that are authorized by federal law, and only qualified, competent individuals to work on your claim. Send the letter (see the sample below) to DDS as soon as you file your application, with copies to your state and federal representatives. This alerts DDS personnel that you will pay careful attention to exactly what they do. This

alone will maximize your chance of a good quality review. DDS is required to make all correspondence from you a part of your file. If you have an attorney, having your attorney sign a letter like this will make DDS pay even more attention.

3. Remain Actively Involved in Your Claim

If you become aware of a specific problem involving the handling of your claim, you aren't helpless. Here are some suggestions on how to proceed:

- Call your claims examiner and that examiner's supervisor, if necessary, to discuss the problem. If, for example, the claims examiner didn't show your claim to a medical consultant, the examiner might do so when reminded of your right to such review—let the examiner know you will notify the agency director if you don't think your rights are being upheld. Be sure to follow up with a letter outlining your complaint. This ensures that your file contains your complaint and your understanding of what the claims examiner or supervisor said to you.

- Call the DDS director and state that if the problem isn't resolved to your satisfaction, you will write the governor's office and your state and federal representatives. Calling a director is effective because it puts the director on the spot—with you on the other end of the telephone, this

Sample Letter to DDS

Date: 12/12/24

Bob Smythe
Disability Determination Services
1234 Bobson Lane
Bobtown, VA

Dear Mr. Smythe:

I have applied for disability because of the following impairments:

1. Depression
2. Heart Disease
3. Lung Cancer

I hereby request assurance in writing that my claim will be reviewed by a licensed medical doctor (for physical impairments) or by a licensed psychiatrist or properly qualified psychologist (for mental impairments). I object to and want to be informed of nondoctors participating in the medical part of my disability determination. If my claim is not reviewed by a medical consultant, I hereby request that you tell me in writing the personal qualifications that allow the reviewing individual to make medical evaluations on my claim, including all licenses to practice medicine or psychology in this state.

If an examiner or consultant receives instructions from a supervisor who is not licensed to practice medicine or psychology regarding the medical severity of my impairments, I hereby object to the use of such instructions and request that I be notified of these instructions before a final determination on my claim is made.

Furthermore, I do not want my claim reviewed by any medical consultant DDS knows has problems that may interfere with his or her ability to review my file and make competent medical determinations. Specifically, I do not want my claim reviewed by a medical consultant with an uncontrolled physical or mental disorder that affects cognitive function; a medical consultant who is known to have an active drug or alcohol abuse problem; or a medical consultant who is unable to read my medical records or to see what documents to sign, unless that medical consultant has an aide who is qualified to interpret medical records.

I also do not want my claim reviewed by any medical consultant whom DDS knows or has reason to know is denial oriented—that is, who denies a significantly higher percentage of claims than do other medical consultants working in the same agency on the same types of claims. I demand a fair consideration.

I also request that my claim not be handled by a claims examiner who has any of the types of problems described above.

If this DDS office is involved in any type of special pilot project for the SSA that means my claim will be handled in ways different from the way claims are handled in other states, please inform me of the nature of such project so that I can protect my rights.

Finally, I request that this letter remain in my file for use in my appeal, if necessary. Under no circumstances do I authorize removal of this letter from my file.

Sincerely yours,

Bill Smith

Bill Smith
1234 William Drive
Williamsburg, VA

cc: Rep. Bobbie Williams (D-Va.)
Sen. Willa Williams
Rep. Woody "Will" Williamson

person is more likely to agree to take some action on your complaint than would be taken in response to a letter, which can be filed away and forgotten. But always follow up this call with a letter outlining your complaint and the director's response.

- Write your legislators and send a copy to the DDS director. Your complaint will become a part of your file, and the DDS director will know that you're serious—not just somebody who made a telephone call and gave up.

- Write the SSA's Office of the Inspector General (OIG), which is charged with investigating SSA (including DDS) wrongdoing—fraud, waste, abuse, and mismanagement. (Send copies to the DDS director and your state and federal representatives.) There is no guarantee that the OIG will think your complaint has merit, but you have nothing to lose by trying. Don't be afraid DDS will take some kind of revenge because you complained to the OIG; the opposite is more likely. If the DDS director knows you've gone so far as to complain to the OIG, the office will handle your claim with kid gloves.

The OIG can be reached in various ways:

SSA Fraud Hotline
P.O. Box 17768
Baltimore MD 21235
800-269-0271 (voice)
410-597-0118 (fax)
http://oig.ssa.gov

Also consider talking to your local newspaper. DDS offices and the SSA don't want bad publicity, and a mistreated claimant can often get a story in the newspaper. Too much bad publicity might embarrass the governor, and you can be sure the DDS director will be asked about it.

SEE AN EXPERT

You might find that attorneys are reluctant to spend too much time on the DDS process. A disability lawyer might tell you that it's not worthwhile to talk to DDS, since the agency denies most claims. But DDS officials typically allow about 30%–40% of initial claims and 10%–15% of reconsideration claims—almost half of all requests. So it makes sense to communicate with DDS. A good attorney will do everything possible to get DDS the information it needs about a claimant. Appeals beyond DDS can take a year or longer—even several years—so you want to avoid that if possible.

H. Quick Disability Determination Unit (QDD)

In DDS, a special unit known as the *Quick Disability Determination Unit* (QDD) might review your claim. If all of the important issues in your claim (such as your onset date—the date your disability began—and the degree of severity of your impairments) can be resolved within a month, then you could receive benefits quickly.

You can't refer your own claim to the QDD; DDS will make this decision internally. But because the disability claims examiner handling your file has input into whether your claim will go to the QDD, it can't hurt to ask the examiner whether your claim will go to the QDD and the reason for that decision.

You'll have the best chance of obtaining a favorable QDD review if you ensure all of the following:

- All of your important medical and nonmedical records have been provided to DDS.

- You aren't alleging a disability onset date that is far back in time (see Chapter 10 to learn more about onset dates).

- There are no complex vocational factors (age, education, or work experience) complicating a decision in your particular case (see Chapter 9 for more about these factors).

If the QDD doesn't approve your claim, or doesn't agree with your alleged onset date, the claim will be referred back to regular DDS functions so that any outstanding issues can be resolved.

How Claims Are Decided

Any time your claim for disability is evaluated—whether at Disability Determination Services (DDS), after a hearing with an administrative law judge, or in federal court—Social Security procedures require that specific issues be addressed in a specific order, in what's called the five-step *sequential evaluation process*. This process is used to make sure that everyone gets the same consideration. If at any point in the sequential evaluation process, the SSA determines that your impairments justify disability benefits, the evaluation ends. You can see how the process plays out in this chapter, which explains the sequence of events that occur at every level of the disability determination process. (See Chapter 12 for more on the different levels of disability appeals.)

Step 1. Are You Engaged in Substantial Gainful Activity?

If you're working and making a certain amount of money, you might be engaged in what Social Security calls *substantial gainful activity* (SGA). If so, you're not eligible for disability. (SGA is discussed in Chapter 1.) If you aren't performing SGA, the analysis proceeds to Step 2.

Step 2. Do You Have Severe Impairments?

The second step involves determining whether or not you have any medically determinable severe impairments. Severe impairments are any documented medical conditions that have more than a minimal impact on your activities of daily living. If your impairments don't (or shouldn't) significantly limit your ability to perform physical or mental tasks, your impairment will be considered not severe (or non-severe, mild, or slight). The SSA will deny your claim at Step 2 if you don't have at least one severe impairment.

Nonsevere impairments are typically easily managed with simple medical treatment. For example, somebody with headaches who takes over-the-counter drugs that successfully control their symptoms isn't likely to have a severe impairment. But the SSA will probably find that somebody who experiences frequent migraines that don't respond to prescription migraine medicine does have a severe impairment.

Similarly, a nearsighted person for whom everything is a blur without glasses (but clear with glasses) doesn't have a severe impairment. But if you have a retinal disease that greatly narrows your field of vision and can't be improved with surgery or corrected with glasses, your impairment wouldn't be nonsevere.

TIP

A claims examiner can't decide that your impairments aren't severe just because they're "normal for age." The SSA prohibits discrimination against older individuals by not allowing disability examiners and judges to consider some impairments normal for age. If you receive a denial notice with such wording, you have a strong basis for appeal.

At this stage, the SSA isn't necessarily looking at whether your medical conditions keep you from working. The agency just needs to see that your impairments have the potential to interfere with your ability to work, rather than being inconsequential or insignificant. As long as you have at least one severe impairment, the SSA will proceed to Step 3 of the sequential evaluation process.

Step 3. Do You Meet a Medical Listing?

If the SSA determines that you have one or more severe impairments, the agency will compare your conditions to a list—creatively called the "Listing of Impairments"—to see if your conditions are on it. Social Security can find you disabled at Step 3 if your medical record contains evidence that your impairments are severe enough to "meet or equal" the SSA requirements for certain medical conditions (called *listings*). The listings are federal regulations, found at 20 C.F.R. Part 404.

TIP

Remember: The Medical Listings are on Nolo's website (see Appendix D for the link). The listings contain the medical information the SSA uses to determine whether your particular impairment, such as coronary artery disease, meets the requirements to obtain disability benefits.

While the SSA at Step 2 is looking to see whether your impairments meet a minimum threshold of severity, at Step 3 the SSA is looking in the other direction—to determine whether your conditions are so severe that the agency considers them automatically disabling based on your medical record.

Each impairment in the listings contains a set of requirements or limitations—usually specific results from lab tests or medical imaging—that the agency presumes to be disabling. The listings differ for adults and for children, although there's significant overlap in the conditions listed.

Meeting a listing. The listings cover many common impairments. If any of your impairments exactly match the criteria of a listing, you'll be found disabled and granted benefits regardless of your age, education, or work experience. For example, say you have an aortic aneurysm. If an imaging test shows that the aneurysm is dissecting (meaning that the arterial lining is pulling away from the artery wall), and it isn't controlled by treatment, you'll be approved for disability benefits whether you have trouble working or not.

Reading the Listings

SSA staff, DDS examiners and medical consultants, hearing officers, administrative law judges, disability attorneys, and federal judges all refer to listing letters and numbers to identify specific listings. These numbers come directly from the federal regulations governing Social Security (20 C.F.R. Part 404). It is important that you understand this system so you can communicate clearly with the SSA and DDS. A typical listing is expressed using familiar letters and numbers:

#.##		
A.		
	1.	
		a.
		b.
		c.
	2.	
		a.
		b.
B.		
	1.	
	2.	
		a.
		b.

The #.## represents the listing number. Adult heart disease, for example, is listing 4.04. Each capital letter introduces a new condition that might qualify for a listing. The numbers further divide the condition into specific criteria. Usually, you'll qualify if you meet one of the numbers. For example, a judge might find that you meet listing 4.04(A)(1) because the results of your exercise test meet those criteria.

Some listing criteria are even more complex, and the SSA uses lowercase letters to identify them. In some cases, you must meet all of the lowercase conditions, while in other cases, you need to meet only one. For example, you might meet a listing if you match (A)(1)(a), (A)(1)(b), and (A)(1)(c). Or, you might meet a listing if you meet only (B)(2)(b). The exact qualifications vary from listing to listing.

Equaling a listing. If none of your impairments exactly meet the requirements of a listing, then the SSA must determine whether your impairments are equivalent in severity to the criteria for a similar impairment. (This is called *equaling a listing.*) Allowing benefits based on equaling a listing recognizes that it's impossible for the SSA to put every conceivable impairment in the listings. If the SSA finds that your symptoms are equally as severe as those of a listed impairment, you will be granted benefits.

In order for the SSA to find that your impairments are equal to a listing, the agency must find one of the following to be true:

- Your impairment isn't listed, but it's of the same medical severity as a listed impairment.
- Your impairment is listed, and although you don't meet the exact criteria of the listing, your medical findings have the same meaning as the listing criteria. For example, you might have a laboratory test not mentioned by the listing that shows the same thing as the type of test in the listing.
- You have a combination of impairments, none of which is severe enough on its own to meet a listing, but together, they're equivalent to a listing. For example, you have both heart and lung disease, which together cause you much greater limitations than either would alone.

- Children applying for SSI might have an impairment that's considered *functionally equal* to the listings. (Relatively few children have impairments that qualify as functionally equal.)

If your impairments or combination of impairments don't meet or equal any listing (or combination of listings), the SSA's analysis proceeds to Step 4.

Step 4. Can You Do Your Prior Job?

At Step 4, the SSA will consider whether your limitations are severe enough to prevent you from doing your past work (if you've worked before). The SSA looks back at 15 years when reviewing your work history.

To determine how severe your limitations are, the SSA will create a *residual functional capacity* (RFC) assessment for you. (RFCs are discussed in detail in Chapter 8.) Your RFC is a short paragraph that contains limitations on what you can do in a work setting.

The SSA compares your RFC with the demands of your past jobs do see if you could do them despite your current limitations. If you're still able to do your past work, the agency will deny your claim. But if you can't perform your prior work, the analysis proceeds to Step 5.

TIP
Keep in mind that the SSA isn't looking to see whether you could return to the exact same job. For example, if you used to work as a server for a restaurant that later closed, that doesn't mean that the agency won't find that you can't work as a server at another location. But if you used to work as a server and your new RFC limits you to sit-down jobs, the SSA will likely find that you can't return to your past work (since servers spend most of the day on their feet).

Step 5. Can You Do Any Other Job?

This is the final step in the sequential evaluation process. If your limitations prevent you from doing your prior work, then the SSA needs to determine whether other jobs in the national economy exist that you can do with your RFC. If so, the SSA will deny your claim because the agency thinks you can perform (or can learn to perform) less demanding jobs.

When deciding whether you can do other work, the SSA doesn't consider factors such as how much money you're used to earning or how close by the job site is. The agency will look only at whether you can physically and mentally perform the duties of any occupations that exist in significant numbers. Factors that the SSA *will* consider, however, include your age, education, and whether you have skills that you can transfer to other work.

(For more information about how the SSA determines whether you're expected to perform other work, see our discussion on *medical-vocational assessments* in Chapter 9.)

Whether You Can Do Some Work: Your RFC

f your medical impairments are more than slight or mild—but not severe enough to meet or equal a listing—then the SSA will need to determine your *residual functional capacity*, or RFC. (Listings are discussed in Chapter 7.)

An RFC analysis is an assessment of what the SSA thinks you're physically or mentally capable of doing despite the limitations from your impairments and the related symptoms. In other words, an RFC outlines both what you can still do as well as what activities you should avoid.

For example, an RFC might say that you can lift 50 pounds occasionally, but that you can't work in places where there is an excessive amount of dust and fumes.

The RFC analysis is a medical assessment, not a determination as to whether you are disabled. Your RFC doesn't state whether you can do specific types of jobs, but it can restrict you from doing work above a certain exertional level, such as sedentary work. SSA examiners and vocational analysts use your RFC rating to determine the types of work you might be able to do. Because your ability to perform work tasks is central to your RFC, assessments are only done on adult claims. Child claims have a different standard (discussed in Chapter 3).

Before we get into how the RFC analysis is done, let's look further at how it's used in the disability determination. If your residual physical and mental capabilities allow you to continue with your prior job, the SSA can deny your claim because you can return to that type of work. The SSA doesn't have to actually find you a job or call your previous employers and ask them if they will take you back.

If your RFC contains limitations that keep you from returning to your past jobs—say your RFC is for light work but your past jobs all required you to lift heavy objects—the SSA will consider *vocational factors* such as your age, education, and work experience to determine whether you can do any other work. If the SSA concludes that you can't, then the agency will award you disability payments. (Vocational factors are discussed in Chapter 9.)

Qualifying for benefits based on your RFC is sometimes referred to as getting a *medical-vocational allowance*. Conversely, if your claim is denied after this kind of analysis, you'll receive a *medical-vocational denial*.

The SSA won't pay the difference if your RFC restricts you to jobs with lower wages than you're used to earning. Unlike other disability programs, Social Security doesn't award partial disability payments—it's an all-or-nothing decision.

TIP

Learn who did your RFC. During your initial claim, reconsideration claim, or continuing disability review at DDS, a doctor or psychologist must determine your RFC. On appeal, an administrative law judge or federal judge can do the RFC assessment. If you were denied benefits after your initial application or the reconsideration, and the handwriting on the assessment doesn't match the doctor's or psychologist's signature, your claims examiner might have done your RFC. This would be a violation of current federal regulations. If you don't think a doctor or psychologist did your RFC, you should contact the SSA's Office of the Inspector General at 800-269-0271 or on the internet at https://oig.ssa.gov.

Your RFC is developed based upon all relevant evidence, including your description of how your symptoms affect your ability to function. In addition, the SSA might consider observations by your treating doctors or psychologists, relatives, neighbors, friends, coworkers, the SSA intake person, and others. The SSA uses your statement, the observations of others, and your medical records to decide the extent to which your impairments keep you from performing specific work activities. The SSA must have reasonably thorough medical evidence to make this decision.

The SSA assesses RFCs for physical impairments and for mental impairments. The medical consultant will not do a physical assessment if you have only a mental impairment. Nor will the consultant do a mental rating if you have only a physical impairment. Many claims, however, require both.

RFCs aren't assessed in numbers, percentages, or other scores. Instead, work abilities are put into categories. The lower your RFC category, the less the SSA believes you are capable of doing. For example, a physical RFC for light work is lower than a physical RFC for medium work. A mental RFC for unskilled work is lower than a mental RFC for semiskilled or skilled work.

Your RFC might be additionally reduced if you can't perform certain work-related activities very often, such as pushing and pulling.

The lower your RFC category, the less likely the SSA will say there is some work you can do. That's because the SSA can't say that you can do work that falls into a higher RFC category than the RFC you received. For example, if you receive a physical RFC for sedentary work, you can't be expected to do a job requiring light, medium, or heavy work. Similarly, if your mental RFC is for unskilled work, you can't be expected to do semiskilled or skilled work.

A. RFC Analysis for Physical Impairments and Abilities

This section focuses on how the SSA assesses a physical RFC in general. The downloadable files on Nolo's website (see Appendix D for the link) provide guidance on what an RFC might look like for various physical disorders. And how the SSA combines a physical RFC with the vocational factors of age, education, and work experience to do a medical-vocational analysis is discussed in Chapter 9.

When the SSA assesses your physical RFC abilities, claims examiners and medical consultants first make a judgment about the nature and extent of your physical limitations. If you have limited ability to perform certain physical activities associated with working—such as sitting, standing, walking, lifting, carrying, pushing, pulling, reaching, handling, stooping, or crouching—the SSA might conclude that you can't do your past work or any other work.

When determining your RFC, the medical consultant reviewing your application should consider any symptoms that you've reported—such as pain, nausea, and dizziness. (Symptoms that are important in making a disability determination are discussed in depth in Chapter 5.)

Your RFC should address the following:

- whether your symptoms are caused by a medically determinable impairment— that is, whether your symptoms have a source or cause that can be identified by medical testing
- whether the severity of your symptoms is reasonable based on the medical testing, and
- whether the severity of your symptoms is consistent with what you, your doctors, and other observers have to say about your ability to function (including in your application and your adult function questionnaire).

The SSA should recognize that your symptoms can limit your ability to work. For instance, joint and back pain are common symptoms associated with arthritis. But people vary considerably in the amount of pain they subjectively feel, and the SSA must evaluate each case on an individual basis. Even when an individual claimant reports a great deal of pain, the SSA isn't likely to add significant pain restrictions to their RFC due to pain if the claimant has very minor physical abnormalities.

While pain is one of the biggest limiting symptoms in an RFC, it's far from the only factor. Fatigue, weakness, numbness in the extremities, and medication side effects must all be taken into consideration when assessing your RFC. Failure of the SSA to consider all of your limitations in your RFC is the basis of many disability appeals.

The SSA must also address whether a treating doctor's statement about your physical capabilities is in your file. If so, the medical consultant, claims examiner, or disability judge has to explain whether they agree with your doctor's conclusions about what you can and can't do. If the SSA doesn't agree with your doctor, the agency must explain in detail the reason for discounting your treating doctor's opinion (see Chapters 6 and 12). Keep in mind that the SSA doesn't need to accept your treating doctor's opinion regarding your functional abilities, especially if that opinion isn't persuasive.

Do RFCs Take Age or Sex Into Account?

A physical RFC itself doesn't take your age into consideration, except in certain continuing disability review claims (see Chapter 14). In other words, your RFC won't be lower because you're 60 years old and not as energetic as you were at age 30. But the SSA doesn't ignore your age entirely. The agency considers how old you are when determining whether you can do other work during the medical-vocational analysis (discussed in Chapter 9). For example, if you're given a sedentary RFC, but your past jobs required heavy work and you're over 50, have no high school diploma, and only have unskilled work experience, the SSA will find that you're disabled.

Not only does your age not matter when assessing your RFC, but your sex and general fitness are also irrelevant. Here's how this plays out. Say you've never in your life been able to lift 50 pounds, much less 100 pounds. But if there is nothing significantly wrong with you, the SSA may give you an RFC saying you can lift 100 pounds. At first glance, this seems illogical and unfair. But restricting RFCs for nonmedical reasons would result in granting benefits to some people who have no significant impairments, and that would defeat the purpose of the disability system.

However, if your treating doctor's opinion about your limitations is supported by the evidence as a whole, the SSA will likely agree with your doctor and include those limitations in your RFC. And if those limitations rule out all jobs, it's likely that the SSA will approve your disability claim. (See Chapter 5 for more information about treating and examining source opinions.)

1. Exertion

The exertional level is the fundamental component of a physical RFC. To determine what exertional level your RFC should be, the SSA evaluates your ability to lift, carry, stand, walk, sit, push, and pull. Many claimants have exertional restrictions on their RFC because of medical impairments that affect their physical strength and stamina. Other claimaints—such as those who suffer from arthritis of the joints or spine—have reduced exertional ability on their RFC because of pain. Disorders of the nervous system, lung diseases, and heart and blood vessel diseases also account for large numbers of exertional restrictions due to fatigue and shortness of breath.

If your RFC restricts your exertion, the SSA must explain why limitations are justified because of your medical impairments.

Lifting or carrying exertional abilities are measured by the descriptive words frequently and occasionally. Frequently means you can lift or carry for at least one-third but less than two-thirds (cumulative, not continuous) of an eight-hour workday. Occasionally means you can lift or carry for less than one-third of an eight-hour workday.

Pushing and pulling exertional abilities are measured in terms of unlimited, frequently, and occasionally. Frequently means you can push or pull for at least one- third but less than two-thirds of an eight- hour workday. Occasionally means you can push or pull for less than one-third of an eight-hour workday.

A lot of jobs, especially those involving heavy equipment, require pushing or pulling. Any impairment that affects the use of your hands, arms, or legs could result in an RFC with pushing and pulling restrictions. Arthritis is probably the most frequent cause of pushing and pulling limitations. Strokes—because they tend to cause weakness in one arm and one leg on the same side of the body—are another common reason for limitations in the ability to push and pull.

Heavy work. Heavy work is defined as the ability to lift or carry 100 pounds occasionally and 50 pounds frequently and to stand or walk six to eight hours a day. The SSA rarely gives an RFC for heavy work. In general, the SSA believes that a person who can do heavy work has no exertional restrictions, and therefore doesn't have severe physical impairments.

Medium work. Medium work is the ability to lift or carry 50 pounds occasionally and 25 pounds frequently and to stand or walk six to eight hours daily. The SSA often gives an RFC for medium work to claimants whose exertional ability is moderately limited—a matter of medical judgment.

Light work. Light work is the ability to lift or carry 20 pounds occasionally and ten pounds frequently, and to stand or walk six to eight hours daily. The SSA gives an RFC for light work to claimants who can't do medium work but aren't restricted to sedentary work. Again, this is a matter of medical judgment.

If you can't stand or walk at least six hours daily, you won't be able to do light work. That means that your RFC can't be for more than sedentary work. Having a sedentary RFC is to your advantage as an applicant for disability benefits because it significantly limits the kind of jobs you can do.

Sedentary work. Sedentary work requires lifting no more than ten pounds at a time and occasionally lifting or carrying articles like small files or small tools. Although sedentary work is done primarily while seated, up to two hours per day of walking and standing might be necessary. A sedentary RFC is often given to claimants whose impairments aren't quite severe enough to qualify under a listing.

If the SSA says you can stand for four hours daily, then your RFC would be between sedentary and light work. Although this is possible, the SSA tries to avoid such blurry distinctions. Such an RFC would require a vocational analyst (see Chapter 9) to carefully evaluate how it affects your ability to return to your prior or other work.

Less than sedentary. *Less than sedentary* isn't an official RFC category, but the SSA (in particular, administrative law judges) sometimes gives it as an RFC rating. For example, while sedentary work doesn't involve much lifting or standing, sedentary jobs typically require good use of the hands and fingers for repetitive hand-finger actions (such as typing). If you're severely limited in the use of your hands, the SSA should give you a less than sedentary RFC instead of a sedentary RFC (we discuss fine manipulation in more detail below). Or, if you have a medical need to lay down, recline, or elevate your legs throughout the workday in order to relieve pain or discomfort, you'll likely get a less than sedentary RFC.

Having a less than sedentary RFC will almost always result in your disability claim being approved, because the SSA won't be able to identify any jobs that you can do (with some rare exceptions). Because sedentary work is the lowest exertional level, representing the least physically demanding types of jobs, in order to get a less than sedentary RFC, you'll need to show that you have additional, nonexertional limitations that rule out sit-down work.

Nonexertional limitations are restrictions in your RFC that aren't based on how much weight you can lift or how long you can be on your feet, but still restrict the types of jobs you can do. Most claimants with physical impairments will have a combination of exertional and nonexertional restrictions in their RFC. The following sections discuss the most common types of physical, nonexertional limitations.

2. Posture

In technical language, posture is the directional orientation of the body. Claimants with postural limitations will have difficulty bending, stooping, climbing, balancing, kneeling, crouching, and crawling.

Restrictions on postural abilities are described on an RFC as never, frequently, or occasionally. Frequently means you can do the activity at least one-third but less than two-thirds of an eight-hour workday. Occasionally means you can do the activity less than one-third of an eight-hour workday.

Bending. An ability to bend the back (or stoop) is often needed for jobs that require lifting and carrying.

How well you can bend your back is often the most important aspect of your physical evaluation, so make sure your range of motion is documented in your medical records. Some claimants can't bend their spine to any significant degree. This usually happens in people who have surgical fixation of the spine because of spinal fractures, advanced osteoarthritis of the spine, or an inflammatory disease known as ankylosing spondylitis. Many claimants with arthritis and degenerative disc disease will also have restrictions in bending due to back pain.

The worse your symptoms are, the stronger your restrictions will be. For example, claimants with serious back pain are almost always limited to only occasional bending. This restriction can be very important, because most medium or heavy work requires frequent bending. If you receive a medium level for lifting and carrying and an occasional restriction for bending, you'll likely receive an RFC for light work. Depending on your age, education, and experience, this limitation can make the difference between approval and denial of your claim.

Balancing and climbing. Difficulties with balancing are usually caused by inner ear disorders or impairments of the nervous system. When the medical records contain evidence of such conditions, the RFC should include restrictions on working at heights, around dangerous machinery, or for any job tasks that can't be performed safely without balancing. Climbing—except for steps with handrails—should also be prohibited when balancing is restricted.

Climbing should also be limited in cases of tingling or weakness in an arm or leg. Claimants with arthritis or joint instability in their hip or knee should also have an RFC that restricts climbing.

The RFC won't contain a blanket prohibition against all balancing or climbing. (That would mean that you wouldn't be able to remain upright at all, and if that were the case, you'd already qualify for disability under a listed impairment). Instead, the RFC will specify what kind of climbing is limited, such as ramps, stairs, ladders, ropes, or scaffolds.

Kneeling, crouching, and crawling. Limitations in kneeling, crouching, and crawling are most frequently caused by arthritis in the knees. The ability to crouch may also be decreased by back pain. Limitations in these areas can be useful in ruling out past work, but they don't usually prevent claimants from doing sit-down (sedentary) jobs.

3. Manipulation

Manipulation means the ability to use the hands, fingers, and arms for various tasks. *Reaching* means your ability to move your arms. *Gross manipulation* refers to your ability to use your hands to grasp and handle objects. *Fine manipulation* refers to your ability to use your fingers to feel and move small objects.

Manipulative abilities on an RFC assessment are generally limited to frequent (between one-third and two-thirds of the workday) or occasional (less than one-third of the workday). Because you need to be able to use your hands, fingers, and arms for pretty much every job, having a restriction to occasional manipulation in your RFC is very likely to rule out all the jobs you could do.

Reaching. Reaching is most often limited by arthritis or degeneration in the rotator cuff (shoulder) or elbow joints. Residual weakness in an arm following a stroke can also restrict your ability to reach.

Depending on your medical records, the SSA can limit your ability to reach overhead, in front of you, or to your sides. Restrictions on all these motions are called *omnidirectional* limitations.

Gross manipulation. Strokes, arthritis, bone fractures, and soft tissue damage are frequent causes of decreased gross manipulation due to weakness and numbness in the hands. Disorders that affect your ability to move your wrist or make a fist with your hand—such as cubital tunnel syndrome (ulnar nerve entrapment)—can also result in restrictions on handling.

Fine manipulation. Fine manipulation involves coordinated, precise movements of the fingers.

Impairments that don't cause much limitation in handling, such as diabetic neuropathy, can still affect fine manipulation. Tremors, burns, swelling, and numbness in your fingers can also impair your ability to pick up small objects, press keys, and write.

Wrist issues can affect fine manipulations as well. Fractures of wristbones can decrease the ability to perform fine manipulations, even after optimum healing. Carpal tunnel syndrome can cause pain in the wrist and numbness in the hands that affect manipulative ability.

While limitations on fine manipulation won't necessarily eliminate jobs at the medium or heavy exertional levels, restrictions on finger use become very important for jobs classified as light and (especially) sedentary. Because these jobs don't involve heavy lifting, the job duties are mostly activities such as typing or counting change—all tasks that require extensive use of the fingers. So if you have an exertional RFC for sedentary work but you can't perform fine manipulations, your claim will probably be approved.

4. Vision

RFCs don't describe visual impairments in terms of how long you can use your eyes. Instead, if you have medical documentation of decreased vision, your RFCs will describe your visual abilities as limited or unlimited. As with other impairments, if the SSA includes any restrictions related to vision in your RFC, the agency must explain why the impairments justify the limitations. (Visual tests and visual impairments are discussed in Part 2 of the Medical Listings on Nolo's website.)

RFCs for visual limitations take into account the following six metrics.

Near acuity means how well you can see close up. Near acuity is important for reading a book or typewritten papers.

While it may seem counterintuitive, good near acuity isn't required for many jobs (and in many cases is corrected with glasses or contacts), so being allowed disability on the basis of limited near acuity alone is unlikely. But a lack of near acuity can be important for some older claimants with cataracts and retinal diseases that can't be corrected with glasses or contacts.

Distance acuity means how well you see objects more than a few feet away. In most instances, decreased distance acuity can be corrected with glasses, contact lenses, or surgery.

But if your distance acuity is limited and can't be corrected with surgery or glasses, you might be unable to perform your prior work. For example, even a modest decrease in distance acuity can disqualify a person from having a commercial driver's license—which would rule out your past work if you were a truck driver. (Whether that alone would qualify you for disability depends on your other medical problems and your vocational factors, discussed in Chapter 9.)

Depth perception is the ability to perceive how far something is from you. RFC limitations on depth perception usually only come into play when a claimant is blind in one eye. A few jobs (such as being a pilot) require good depth perception, but many other jobs don't. Even if a claimant can't return to their prior work because of depth perception limitations, Social Security can usually name other jobs the claimant could do that don't require depth perception.

Accommodation means the ability of the eye's lens to change thickness in order to focus. The most common cause of an inability to accommodate is a stiff lens resulting from normal aging, easily correctable with reading glasses. Limited accommodation is rarely a basis for disability.

Color vision is the ability to distinguish different colors. Limitations in color vision (colorblindness) are usually genetic and are most often limited to green and red colors. Many people with color vision deficit can still see some color. Even if you suffer complete loss of color vision, the SSA can identify jobs that don't require color vision.

Field of vision (peripheral vision) refers to the ability to see objects out of the corner of your eye. Glaucoma, strokes, and diabetic retinal disease are the most common impairments that cause reductions in the visual field. Claimants who have significant restrictions in their peripheral vision—but not enough to meet or equal a listing— might still need to be restricted from work where lack of good peripheral vision can endanger their lives or the lives of others.

Specifically, their RFCs should contain limitations on driving, working at unprotected heights, or working around hazardous machinery.

5. Communication

The most important work-related communication abilities are hearing and speaking. On an RFC, communication abilities are described as limited or unlimited. Hearing and speaking impairments, as well as tests for those impairments, are discussed in Part 2 of the Medical Listings on Nolo's website.

Hearing. Awareness that someone is speaking and understanding the spoken word are both important in many jobs. Hearing problems, however, can often be improved with hearing aids. Most claimants who have hearing impairments don't qualify under a listing but have significant hearing loss that necessitates limitations in their RFC.

Common examples of hearing-related limitations in an RFC include restrictions in noise level at the job site. A claimant with hearing loss might not be able to work in a loud warehouse, for example, but could function in a quieter office environment.

Speaking. The ability to speak meaningfully enough to communicate with other people involves factors such as clarity, volume, and speed. Speech-related limitations in an RFC might include avoiding work where the following are required:

- speaking loudly (such as making public announcements)
- constant talking (such as telemarketing), or
- verbal clarity (such as for 911 dispatchers).

6. Environment

RFCs can contain environmental restrictions on the types of physical locations where a claimant can work. Factors that can result in environmental limitations include sensitivity to:

- extreme cold
- extreme heat
- wetness
- humidity
- noise
- vibration, and
- fumes (odors, dusts, gases, or poor ventilation).

Other environmental factors that might be in an RFC include the need to avoid certain dangers, such as working around hazardous machinery or at unprotected heights.

Restrictions on exposure to a particular environment can be expressed in an RFC as unlimited, avoid concentrated exposure, avoid even moderate exposure, and avoid all exposure.

As with all RFC restrictions, the SSA needs to explain why the limitation is supported by evidence in the claimant's record. But it can be difficult for a claims examiner to find evidence of environmental restrictions that should be included in an RFC. This is because a patient evaluated in an office or a hospital is in a special environment, one that may be very different from the environment found at many jobs. So when an examiner or vocational expert needs to determine whether you can return to your past work or do other work, they might need to ask you about the kinds of work settings you're used to.

Two physical impairments almost always result in environmental restrictions:

- **Epilepsy.** Claimants with epilepsy who have had a seizure in the past year are restricted from working around or driving hazardous machinery and from working at unprotected heights where they might injure themselves or others if they have a seizure.
- **Lung disease.** Claimants with significant lung disease symptoms are usually restricted from exposure to moderate dust and fumes. Restriction from all exposure isn't realistic because dust and fumes are unavoidable, even at home.

Two other common conditions might also give rise to environmental limitations in an RFC:

- **Heart or blood vessel disease.** Because temperature extremes can put dangerous stress on the heart and blood vessels, claimants with severe heart or vascular disease might be restricted from jobs involving concentrated exposure to extreme heat or cold. In some instances, a restriction to avoid even moderate exposure might be required.
- **Skin disorder.** Claimants with skin disorders that are affected by contact with water or sunlight (such as dermatitis) should be restricted from performing work that could worsen the condition. For example, an RFC for somebody with dermatitis that's aggravated by contact with water might include restrictions that eliminate working in a kitchen washing dishes. Or somebody with photosensitive skin who develops a rash from sun exposure might be prohibited from any outdoor work. Most RFCs for skin disorders will limit claimants from concentrated exposure to the environmental factor that could exacerbate the symptoms, but in very severe cases, the RFC might restrict the claimant from even moderate exposure to the irritant.

Vibration is an environmental factor that doesn't usually make a difference in the outcome of a claim, but it can in some cases. For example, a claimant with a restriction to avoid all vibration might be unable to perform their past work if it involved riding on a tractor. Depending on the rest of their RFC and their vocational profile, the inability to tolerate vibrations could make the difference between an approval and a denial.

Similarly, humidity isn't usually a deciding factor in disability claims, but a restriction on exposure to humidity could rule out past work performed in certain specialized environments (such as a greenhouse).

Noise level typically comes into play when a claimant has certain communication limitations (as discussed above). The SSA rates environmental noise levels on a scale of 1–5, with 1 being the quietest and 5 being the noisiest:

- Level 5 is **very loud**. Examples include a rock concert or a jackhammer at a construction site.
- Level 4 is **loud**. Examples include heavy traffic or bulldozers.
- Level 3 is **moderate**. Examples include many public retail environments, like a shopping mall or grocery stores.
- Level 2 is **quiet**. Examples include many private offices and libraries.
- Level 1 is **very quiet**. This is the level of an isolation booth used for a hearing test.

People with hearing impairments or speech impediments will likely have RFCs restricting them to a moderate or quiet environment. If their past work was done around loud or very loud equipment, a noise level limitation will rule out their past jobs.

B. Mental Impairments and Abilities

This section focuses on how the SSA assesses mental impairments in an RFC and how mental limitations affect the ability to work. (See Part 12 of the Medical Listings on Nolo's website for the SSA listings and RFCs for specific mental disorders.)

At the initial application, reconsideration, or continuing disability review (CDR) levels, a psychologist or psychiatrist reviews your records and creates a mental RFC for you. On appeal, an administrative law judge or a federal court judge reviews the mental RFC and decides whether your limitations are supported by the rest of the evidence in your records.

The objective of a mental RFC is to assess whether, despite your mental impairment, you can do skilled, semiskilled, or unskilled work—or whether you're incapable of doing even unskilled work. (See Chapter 9 for more on the definition of these types of work.) A claims examiner or vocational analyst uses the restrictions in your mental RFC to determine if you can return to your prior work or if you can perform some other kind of work.

Here's an example of how your mental RFC plays an important role in determining whether you can work (in particular, whether you can work a job that doesn't require any special skills).

EXAMPLE: Flora is a lawyer who suffered a traumatic brain injury after she was in an automobile accident, resulting in significant permanent mental impairment. Due to her brain damage, Flora can't perform skilled or even semiskilled work. Because Flora's past job as a lawyer was classified as skilled, the SSA found that Flora couldn't return to her past work. But Flora's doctor conducted some neuropsychological tests and found that Flora still was able to perform basic cognitive tasks, such as counting change and following simple instructions. The SSA determined that Flora had a mental RFC for unskilled work and no physical restrictions. Even though Flora was unable to return to her job as a lawyer, the SSA denied her claim because she could perform other, unskilled work.

On the other hand, a claimant who has severe depression despite ongoing treatment might not be able to do even unskilled work, because they'd be unproductive during the time they were on the clock or would miss too many days of work. In that case, the SSA would approve the claim, regardless of the claimant's age, education, or work experience.

Because of the large number of unskilled jobs in the economy, claimants with only mental impairments who have a mental RFC for unskilled work are rarely going to be awarded benefits. (For the few exceptions, see Chapter 9, Section C3.) This doesn't mean that mental RFCs that show a capacity for unskilled work—or even semiskilled work—are meaningless. These RFCs become important when the claimant also has physical limitations (discussed in Section C, below).

As with physical impairments, the SSA doesn't need to accept your treating doctor's opinion regarding your mental functional abilities, especially if the opinion is at odds with your medical records as a whole. If your psychologist or psychiatrist provided an opinion that the SSA disagrees with, the agency will explain why the mental limitations in your RFC don't reflect your doctor's or psychologist's conclusions. But if your doctor or psychologist's opinion makes sense within the context of the rest of your medical records, the SSA will likely use part or all of their assessment about your mental limitations in your RFC.

A mental RFC contains four categories of functioning to be assessed (covered in Sections 1 through 4 below). These categories are further divided into 20 functional items that cover the basic mental abilities needed for any job. The limitation assigned to each area is a matter of medical judgment, based on the evidence.

The Psychiatric Review Technique Form

For disability claims involving mental impairments, a DDS mental consultant must complete what's called a Psychiatric Review Technique Form (PRTF). This document is based on diagnostic categories of mental disorders and is intended to serve as a sort of checklist to help the person assessing your mental RFC—such as a consulting psychologist or an administrative law judge—to make sure all the relevant medical evidence has been considered.

You or your lawyer should pay special attention to your mental RFC or PRTF if you're reviewing your file and planning an appeal (see Chapters 6 and 12). Be on the lookout for opinions in the RFC or PRTF that aren't backed up by evidence in the file.

The SSA reviews mental impairment claims by determining how limited a claimant is in each assessed area. The more severe your mental symptoms are, the more limited you'll be.

If the SSA finds that you're not significantly limited in an area, your mental impairment interferes minimally with your daily routine. For example, if you're not significantly limited, you might feel anxious around large crowds, but can easily handle your symptoms by avoiding mass gatherings.

If the SSA finds that you're moderately limited in an area, your mental symptoms cause more than just a slight disruption to your life. Your anxiety may keep you from using public transportation or going shopping during busy times, for example, but you can still drive yourself and go to the grocery store when it's less crowded.

If the SSA finds that you're markedly limited in an area, your mental symptoms might prevent you from doing basic chores independently or certain activities altogether. Using the anxiety example once more, you might stop going to the grocery store by yourself entirely and instead have your food delivered. You might decline all invitations to social functions, even with close friends and family, because the thought of leaving your house brings on a panic attack. (Marked limitations are the most likely to result in an RFC that rules out unskilled jobs.)

If the SSA doesn't see anything in your medical records to indicate that you've experienced mental health symptoms, then the agency will find "no evidence of limitation in this category." If the SSA thinks that you might have a severe mental health impairment—say you mentioned to your physician on several occasions that you were feeling depressed but never got formal mental health treatment—the agency will find that your limitation is "not ratable on available evidence." The SSA is then obligated to obtain more information to determine what limitations, if any, you have in a particular area.

Most claimants don't have an across-the-board not significant, moderate, or marked limitation in all areas. Instead, mental RFCs typically have various combinations of severity, depending on the function affected. It's up to claims examiners and vocational experts at the SSA to decide whether an assortment of limitations prevents a claimant from returning to their past job or, if not, from doing other work. (The vocational application of RFCs is discussed in Chapter 9.)

Here are the four categories of functioning that will be assessed in a mental RFC.

1. Understanding and Memory

The SSA evaluates the following areas of understanding and memory abilities:

- remembering locations and worklike procedures
- understanding and remembering very short and simple instructions, and
- understanding and remembering detailed instructions.

A limitation—even if it's marked—in remembering detailed instructions doesn't usually prevent you from doing unskilled work, although generally the SSA will rule out skilled and semiskilled jobs with your RFC. Moderate limitations in remembering work procedures and remembering simple instructions will usually restrict you to unskilled jobs, while having marked limitations in those areas is a strong indicator that you can't do even unskilled jobs.

2. Sustained Concentration and Persistence

The SSA evaluates your ability to do the following tasks related to concentration and persistence:

- carry out very short and simple instructions
- carry out detailed instructions
- maintain attention and concentration
- perform activities within a schedule, maintain regular attendance, and be punctual within customary tolerances
- sustain an ordinary routine without special supervision
- work in coordination with or proximity to others without being unduly distracted by them
- make simple work-related decisions, and
- complete a normal workday and workweek without interruptions caused by mental symptoms and perform at a consistent pace without an unreasonable number and length of rest periods.

Having marked limitations in one or more areas in the concentration and persistence category is one of the most common ways that claimants with mental impairments qualify for disability. Because even unskilled work requires that you show up on time and complete your job duties, an inability to meet those basic expectations will rule out all full-time work. Vocational consultants keep track of employer tolerances for missing work, taking breaks, or a general lack of focus—what they call *off-task behavior*—on the job. A vocational consultant will help the SSA determine whether your limitations in these areas are beyond what employers generally tolerate in their employees. If your limitations exceed those tolerances, you'll likely be awarded benefits.

3. Social Interaction

The SSA evaluates your ability to engage in the following social behaviors:

- interact appropriately with the general public
- ask simple questions or request assistance
- accept instructions and respond appropriately to criticism from supervisors
- get along with coworkers or peers without distracting them or exhibiting behavioral extremes, and
- maintain socially appropriate behavior and adhere to basic standards of neatness and cleanliness—no general rule can be given for limiting this area because jobs vary so greatly.

Mild or moderate limitations in the above areas often result in restrictions against working in jobs that involve contact with the public, such as most retail and service industry jobs. However, the SSA will usually still find that you can do work that's relatively solitary—many janitorial jobs fit this bill. But if you're frequently showing up to work disheveled, fighting with your coworkers, or yelling at your supervisor in response to gentle suggestions, it's likely that the SSA will conclude that you have marked limitations in the above areas that rule out all jobs.

4. Ability to Adapt

Finally, the SSA evaluates your ability to manage yourself and adapt to changes— your general flexibility—in the following areas:

- respond appropriately to changes in the work setting
- be aware of normal hazards and take appropriate precautions
- travel in unfamiliar places or use public transportation, and
- set realistic goals or make plans independently of others.

This category is mostly a catchall of work-related mental items that haven't already been covered in the other categories. Somebody with marked limitations in these areas—who is unable to keep themselves out of danger or can't handle any deviation from a work routine—is also likely to have marked limitations in the other categories as well (or might meet a listed impairment).

C. Claims With Both Physical and Mental RFCs

Because of the large numbers of unskilled jobs in the economy, it's very rare for a claimant with a purely mental impairment who is capable of unskilled work to be granted benefits. In fact, all claimants must have additional physical limitations in order to be approved under the medical-vocational rules (see Appendix C). Of course, if you have a mental RFC for *less than unskilled work*, your claim will be approved notwithstanding any physical impairments you have or the medical-vocational rules.

Many claimants have both mental and physical limitations in their RFCs. Social Security is required to assess whether their mental and physical impairments combine to create more limitations together than each impairment would cause on its own. For example, many scientific studies show an overlap between the brain chemicals that control pain and those that control depression. Because the relationship between pain and depression can be a bit like a feedback loop—where depression increases pain and pain increases depression—these impairments combined can be greater than the sum of their parts.

Unfortunately, the SSA doesn't always pay enough attention to the intricate ways in which impairments interact with each other. Claimants who attend a physical consultative examination and a mental consultative examination will receive one physical assessment and one mental assessment, but they generally don't get a combined assessment unless they attend a hearing where a medical expert is present (which is uncommon). Even when a medical expert is available, many of them stick to their areas of expertise and are reluctant to give an opinion that they don't feel qualified to provide. While this is understandable, it can mean that the effect of your mental and physical impairments combined isn't fully evaluated, potentially resulting in a denial.

You can request copies of your consultative examination results from the SSA. Read them closely and make note of any physical symptoms that you think affect your mental health and any mental symptoms that could have an impact on your physical condition. That way, if your claim is denied because the SSA thinks you can still work despite your impairments, you'll have a persuasive argument to bring up in your appeal. And if you're restricted to sedentary work physically but unskilled work mentally, you should bring it to the attention of DDS so that a medical consultant qualified in both physical and mental impairments can consider the combined effects of your physical and mental conditions.

How Age, Education, and Work Experience Matter

As discussed in Chapter 8, if you have a severe impairment that doesn't meet or equal a listing, the SSA will determine what abilities you still have despite your limitations—known as your residual functional capacity, or RFC—to see if you can return to your past work. If you can't, the SSA will then consider your age, education, and work experience—what the agency refers to as *vocational factors*—to determine if you can do any other work. If you can't, then Social Security will consider you disabled and award you disability benefits. This chapter is about the *medical-vocational analysis* that the SSA performs to see if you can do (and learn how to do) any other work.

The SSA has published tables that take basic physical restrictions in an RFC (known as *exertional levels*) into consideration, along with age, education, and work experience. The tables direct the SSA to find someone disabled or not disabled, depending on their combination of medical factors (the limitations included in an RFC) and vocational factors. That's why the tables are formally called the *medical-vocational rules*, but you might hear claims examiners, judges, or attorneys refer to them informally as the grid. The grid rules appear in Appendix C of this book, along with instructions on how to use them. If the medical-vocational guidelines direct the SSA to find that you're disabled (using what the agency calls a *medical-vocational allowance*, you'll begin receiving disability benefits.

Table 1 considers sedentary work RFCs along with vocational factors. Table 2 deals with light work RFCs, and Table 3 with medium work RFCs. Heavy work RFCs aren't included in the medical-vocational rules because someone with a heavy RFC wouldn't be considered to have a severe physical impairment. (The SSA wouldn't find a claimant who is capable of doing heavy work to be disabled under the grid. The agency would need to find that the claimant had very significant mental limitations instead—a situation where the grid rules don't apply.)

Turn to Appendix C and look at Table 1. You can see that nine medical-vocational rules result in approvals when vocational factors are combined with sedentary RFCs. These are: 201.01, 201.02, 201.04, 201.06, 201.09, 201.10, 201.12, 201.14, and 201.17. Now turn to Table 2. Five medical-vocational rules result in approvals for claimants with light RFCs. These are: 202.01, 202.02, 202.04, 202.06, and 202.09.

Finally, look at Table 3. Now you see that only three medical-vocational rules result in allowance for claimants with medium RFCs. These are: 203.01, 203.02, and 203.10. This makes sense, given that being able to perform the physical demands of medium work means there's a greater chance that there's some job you could do.

Below, we'll discuss how age, education, and work experience are evaluated under the medical-vocational rules. This material will be clearer to you if you refer to the tables in Appendix C.

A. Age

Age is an important vocational factor that affects your ability to adapt to new work situations and to compete with other people.

Your disability application will be evaluated under one of the following age categories:

- younger than 50 years (younger individuals)
- age 50–54 years (closely approaching advanced age)
- age 55–59 years (advanced age), or
- age 60–64 (advanced age and also closely approaching retirement age).

Here's an overview of how the grid rules work. The lower your RFC at a particular age, the greater chance you'll be found disabled under a medical-vocational rule. For example, a 55-year-old claimant with a sedentary RFC has a better chance of being allowed than a 55-year-old with an RFC for light or medium work.

And the older you are, the greater the chance you'll be found disabled with a particular RFC. For example, a 55-year-old claimant with a sedentary RFC has a better chance of being allowed under the grid rules than a 50-year-old with the same RFC.

1. Sedentary Work and Age

Claimants 55 years of age and older are especially likely to be found disabled under a medical-vocational rule when they have RFCs for sedentary work. As Table 1 in Appendix C shows, the only not disabled claimants of this age group are those with past skilled or semiskilled work experience whose skills can be transferred to new jobs (or who have recent education training them to do skilled work.) Also, to be found not disabled in this age group, Table 1 requires that claimants be able to do a new job with little or no adjustment in their tools, work processes, work settings, or industry. In other words, Social Security can deny benefits to those 55 or older with a sedentary RFC, but only if they can fit into a new job with little difficulty and perform the work as if they had been doing it for years. The same rules apply for claimants 50–54 years old with a sedentary RFC.

What about claimants younger than 50 with a sedentary RFC? As Table 1 shows, these claimants will have a much harder time being granted a medical-vocational allowance.

If you're 45–49 years old, you can be found disabled with a sedentary RFC under Medical-Vocational Rule 201.17 only if both of the following are true:

- You are illiterate.
- Either you haven't worked in the past 15 years or your past work was unskilled and you can't do it any longer.

If you're between 18 and 44, under the SSA's grid rules, you won't be granted disability with an RFC that allows you to perform sedentary work. (But if you also have nonexertional limitations or a mental RFC, you might qualify for benefits if these additional limitations rule out all sedentary jobs.)

2. Less-Than-Sedentary Work and Age

RFCs for less-than-sedentary work aren't part of the medical-vocational rules, but such an RFC will almost always result in approval of benefits at any age, regardless of education and past work experience. Less-than-sedentary RFCs are discussed in Chapter 8, Section A1.

3. Other Work Levels and Age

If you're in the 60–64 age range, Social Security will find you disabled under the medical-vocational rules of Table 1 if you have an RFC for sedentary work and Table 2 if you have an RFC for light work, unless you have highly marketable, transferable skills or have had recent training for skilled work. Note also in Table 2 that many claimants ages 55–59 with RFCs for light work or sedentary work are allowed benefits.

In general, few claimants with an RFC for medium work are found disabled. But claimants 55 or older who have a medium RFC can be found disabled if they have a limited education—defined by the SSA

as completing the 11th grade or less—and a history of unskilled work (or don't have any past work). See Table 3, Medical-Vocational Rules 203.01, 203.02, and 203.10.

4. Age Examples

Age 55 is frequently the threshold that separates approval and denial of disability benefits. Two examples demonstrate this fact and show how approval or denial can turn on fine points.

EXAMPLE 1: Rita is 54 years old, has moderate arthritis in her spine so that she can't do more than light lifting, and receives an RFC for light work. Rita is a college graduate and has done desk work for most of her life. The SSA could find that Rita has skills that transfer to another desk job, and she'll be denied benefits under the appropriate grid rule for her closely approaching advanced age category, Medical-Vocational Rule 202.15. Unfortunately for Rita, even if she doesn't have any transferable skills, she'll still be denied benefits under a different Medical-Vocational Rule (202.14) because she can physically perform light jobs.

EXAMPLE 2: Lou is just a year older, 55, and has moderate arthritis in his spine so that he can't do more than light lifting. Lou is also a college graduate who has worked only desk jobs. As with Rita, if the SSA determines that Lou has transferable skills, he'll be denied benefits under the applicable grid rule for his advanced age category (in this case, 202.07). But unlike Rita, if Lou doesn't have transferable skills—and doesn't have recent training for a new skill set—he'll be awarded benefits under Medical-Vocational Rule 202.06.

B. Education

For Social Security purposes, education means formal schooling or other training that contributes to your ability to meet job requirements—such as reasoning ability, communication skills, and arithmetic skills. Lack of formal schooling doesn't necessarily mean that you are uneducated or don't have these abilities. You may have acquired meaningful work skills through job experience, on-the-job training, or other means that didn't involve formal school learning. Your past work experience and work responsibilities may show that you have considerable intellectual abilities, although you may have had little formal education. In addition, your daily activities, hobbies, or test results may show that you have significant intellectual ability that can be used for work.

1. How the SSA Evaluates Education

How much weight the SSA places on your education can depend on how much time has passed since you finished your education and when your health issues began, or how you used your education in your past work. The SSA is aware that a degree you earned many years ago may no longer be meaningful in terms of your ability to work. This is especially true regarding skills and knowledge that were a part of your formal education but that you haven't used in a very long time.

Therefore, the number (for example, 6th, 9th, or 12th) of the last grade you completed may not represent your actual educational level, which could be higher or lower. But if the SSA doesn't have evidence to show that your actual education differs from your grade level, the SSA will use the numerical level of the last grade you formally completed to determine your educational abilities.

When you file your application for disability benefits, you'll be asked about your education. The SSA will accept your word about your educational level, unless you've given them some reason to doubt it—like being a certified public accountant and saying you never completed the fifth grade. If you have any additional or written documentation about your education that you want in your file, give it to your SSA Field Office, and someone there will send it to DDS. Or, you can send it directly to the disability examiner at DDS handling your claim.

The SSA will classify your educational level into one of four categories based on how it has an impact on your ability to work.

Illiteracy means the inability to read or write. The SSA considers a disability applicant to be illiterate if they can't read or write a simple message such as instructions or inventory lists, even though they can sign their name.

Marginal education means having sufficient ability in reasoning, arithmetic, and language skills to do simple, unskilled types of jobs. The SSA generally considers formal schooling to the sixth grade or lower to be a marginal education.

Limited education means having some ability in reasoning, arithmetic, and language skills, but not enough to perform the complex job duties needed in semiskilled or skilled jobs. The SSA generally considers a formal education that ended somewhere between seventh and eleventh grade to be a limited education.

High school education and above. The SSA's definition involves having abilities in reasoning, arithmetic, and language skills acquired through formal schooling that included completing high school and may have included more education. The SSA generally considers someone with these educational abilities able to do semiskilled through skilled work.

2. Education and Medical-Vocational Rule Tables

Your education is an important vocational factor because it relates to the types of mental skills that you might be able to bring to a job. Turn again to Appendix C to see how various educational levels at sedentary, light, and medium work RFCs affect the allowance or denial of a claim. You can see that, for each table, applicants with lower educational levels are more likely to be found disabled. This is particularly true as age increases and work experience and skills decrease.

High school education. Whether you have a high school diploma, a GED, or postsecondary education (like a college degree), the SSA will apply the grid rules that correspond to a high school education. High school education is the highest level of education contemplated under the medical-vocational grid rules.

In order to qualify for disability under the grid rules with a high school education, you'll need to show that:

- you're at least 50 years old with a sedentary RFC, or at least 55 years old with a light RFC
- your education doesn't provide you with any skills you can easily use in a job (*direct entry into skilled work*), and
- you have a history of unskilled work or don't have a work history.

If all of the above apply, the SSA can use Medical-Vocational Rules 201.04 and 201.12 (Table 1) or Rules 202.04 and 202.06 (Table 2) to find that you're disabled with a high school education.

Keep in mind that if you have an RFC for medium work and a high school education, the SSA won't find you disabled under the grid rules even if you're 64. (Table 3, Rules 203.06–203.09).

Limited education. The SSA acknowledges that applicants without a high school level education can be at a disadvantage when it comes to employability. Using the grid rules, however, doesn't reveal much difference in outcomes between claimants who didn't graduate high school and those who did.

For example, every claimant over the age of 50 with a sedentary RFC and no transferable skills (or specialized training) from their past work will be found disabled, regardless of whether they have a high school diploma. (See Table 1.) The same goes for claimants over the age of 55 with a light RFC. (See Table 2.)

But one area where having a limited education is a decisive factor in a disability claim is for claimants 55 or older who are limited to medium work (see Table 3). For example, somebody who is 56 with an RFC for medium work, a high school education, and no work history would be found not disabled under Rule 203.14. But another 56-year-old claimant who—everything else being equal—has a limited education would be found disabled under Rule 203.10.

Marginal education and illiteracy. In a few cases, having a marginal education or being illiterate can be the deciding factor in determining disability using the grids. The only time a claimant younger than age 50 can be found disabled under the grids, for example, is when they are illiterate, limited to sedentary work, and don't have transferable skills. (See Rule 201.17.) And people over the age of 60 with an unskilled work history can be found disabled if they have a marginal education even if they can physically perform medium work. (See Rule 203.01.)

3. Education Examples

Two examples help illustrate the rules discussed above.

EXAMPLE 1: Dom has only a third-grade education, has done no work his entire life, is 55 years old, and has an RFC for medium work because of intermittent back pains and age-related degenerative changes in his spine. Medium work means Dom can lift up to 50 pounds and stand six to eight hours a day. That's more physical ability than many healthy people have. Yet Social Security will approve Dom for SSI benefits under Medical-Vocational Rule 203.10 because his chance of learning a new job that he can perform is small. (See Table 3 in Appendix C.)

EXAMPLE 2: Chuck is also age 55 but has a high school education and has worked in semiskilled jobs his entire life. He also has occasional back pains and age-related degenerative changes in his spine, and his RFC rating says the most he can do is medium work. Social Security is likely to deny his disability claim under Medical-Vocational Rule 203.15, 203.16, or 203.17 because his education will supposedly enable him to perform some type of work. Even if he had never worked, he could be denied under Medical-Vocational Rule 203.14 because of his education.

C. Work Experience

Work experience means the skills you've acquired through work you've done and indicates the type of work you could be expected to do. Your work experience should be relevant to your ability to perform some type of currently existing job.

The SSA has three considerations in deciding whether your past work experience is relevant:

- The SSA recognizes that the skills required for most jobs change after 15 years. Therefore, the general SSA rule is that any work you did 15 or more years before applying for disability isn't relevant to your current job skills.
- If you're applying for SSDI and your *date last insured* (DLI) is earlier than the application date, the SSA applies the 15-year rule to the DLI. (The DLI is the date at which your eligibility for SSDI benefits ran out, usually because

you stopped working some years earlier. If the date you filed your application is after your DLI, you can still receive benefits if you can show that your disability started before your DLI.)

- Your work experience must have lasted long enough for you to acquire actual experience.
- Your work must have been substantial gainful activity. (See Chapter 1, Section B1.)

1. Information About Your Work

Unless the SSA concludes that you meet or equal a listed impairment (in which case it doesn't matter whether you can do your past jobs), the agency will need to find out about the work you've done in the past. If you can't give the SSA all the information it needs, the SSA will try—with your permission—to get it from your employer or another person who knows about your work, such as a relative or a coworker. When the SSA needs to decide whether you can do work that is different from what you've done in the past, the SSA will ask you about all of the jobs you have had during the past 15 years.

You must tell the SSA the dates you worked, your duties, and the tools, machinery, and equipment you used. You also need to tell the SSA about the amount of walking, standing, sitting, lifting, and carrying you did during the workday, as well as any other physical or mental duties of your job.

2. Work in the National Economy

If the SSA denies your claim, saying you can perform a particular type of work, it means that the agency believes there are significant numbers of jobs open for doing similar work in the national economy. *Significant numbers* isn't an exact number. It's only meant to ensure that a reasonable chance exists that such work would be available. In other words, the SSA won't deny you benefits by referring to jobs that are isolated and exist in very limited numbers in relatively few locations (like raising sled dogs in Alaska). The SSA doesn't have to refer to a particular location in the country where you might find a job, however.

a. How the SSA Finds Job Information

The SSA must refer to reliable job information before saying there are jobs in the national economy that you can do. The agency looks at statistics from multiple sources—including state employment agencies, the Bureau of Labor Statistics, and the Census Bureau—but relies most heavily on the Department of Labor's *Dictionary of Occupational Titles* (DOT).

You can refer to the DOT yourself. It's a big book—nearly 1,500 pages—but it's available in most large public libraries, law libraries, university libraries, and online at https://occupationalinfo.org. The DOT was officially replaced by the O*NET, at www.dol.gov/agencies/eta/onet, but the SSA continues to use the DOT as its main reference for vocational analysis. Your claims examiner should have a copy to let you look at upon request.

The DOT lists various jobs along with the physical abilities required of the job tasks and the skills needed to perform them. An important consideration is the *specific vocational preparation* (SVP) for each job. The SVP is expressed as a number on a scale of 1 to 9. The lower the SVP number, the less skill is needed to do the job. For example, jobs listed in the DOT with an SVP of 1 or 2 are considered to be unskilled work.

The SVP represents the amount of time required to learn the techniques, acquire information, and get up to speed with the average performance quality expected in a specific job. The examiner or vocational analyst working on your claim will refer to the DOT to determine your SVP. Using the SVP, the examiner or vocational analyst can find out the skill level required in your past work experience, which is important when applying the medical-vocational rules.

b. Factors Not Considered in SSA's Work Decision

The SSA generally only considers whether you can do the physical and mental duties of a job when determining if jobs exist that you can perform. Factors that the SSA isn't concerned with include:

- lack of work in your local area
- hiring practices of employers

- technological changes in the industry in which you have worked
- changing economic conditions
- wages and salaries
- whether you would be hired for a job, even if you're capable of doing the work, and
- whether you want to do a particular type of work.

3. Skill Requirements for Work

Note: If you have a mental impairment, your mental RFC will contain limitations restricting the types of job skills you can do (see Chapter 8, Section B2).

Every job requires an ability to perform certain mental tasks and skills. The most basic, unskilled kinds of work don't require any advanced education or even work experience. You obtain more advanced skills through work experience and education.

The SSA classifies all jobs into three skill levels: *unskilled, semiskilled,* and *skilled.*

a. Unskilled Work

Unskilled work refers to jobs that involve little or no judgment. These jobs consist of simple tasks that can be learned in a short period of time. Unskilled jobs may or may not require considerable strength. The SSA considers a job to be unskilled if:

- the primary work duties are handling materials, machine tending, or placing or removing materials into or out of automatic machines or machines operated by others
- the job can be learned in 30 days or less, and
- little specific job skill preparation and judgment are needed.

You don't gain work skills by doing unskilled jobs. Jobs listed in the DOT with an SVP of 1 or 2 are considered unskilled work.

Some examples of unskilled jobs are fruit picker, warehouse stocker, and dishwasher. Determining whether work experience is unskilled isn't always simple, because some unskilled jobs might require abilities in common with semiskilled work. For example, a delivery driver might be required to provide summaries and reports of the daily delivery route.

The basic mental abilities needed to perform unskilled work are those required to perform even the simplest job. If you have no significant mental impairment, the SSA will assume that you don't have a significant limitation in your ability to perform unskilled work.

If you can't perform even the basic mental demands of unskilled work—in Social Security lingo, you've had a substantial loss of mental abilities—you'll be found disabled regardless of your age, education, or work experience. In this case, you might receive a mental RFC for less-than-unskilled work.

Special Rules for Many Years of Heavy, Unskilled Work

The SSA has a special rule for claimants who have performed only *arduous*, unskilled work for many years. These claimants can be granted benefits because they've "worn out" their bodies performing very strenuous work without acquiring any job skills.

To be classified as arduous unskilled work, a job must:

- be of a primarily physical nature, requiring a high level of strength or endurance (typically classified as heavy or very heavy work), or
- require a great deal of stamina or activity, such as bending and lifting at a very fast pace.

If all of your work in the past 35 years has been arduous and unskilled, you have a marginal (6th grade or less) education, and you can't return to your past work, the SSA will likely award you disability benefits. Disability attorneys often refer to this special medical-vocational profile as the *worn-out worker* rule.

EXAMPLE: Boris is a 60-year-old coal miner with a fourth-grade education. Boris has worked as a miner since he was 18. As a result, Boris has arthritis of the spine, hips, and knees. Medical evidence establishes that Boris can no longer work as a miner due to his impairments. Given his history of arduous, unskilled physical labor, the SSA will find Boris disabled on a medical-vocational basis.

b. Semiskilled Work

Semiskilled work requires some skills but doesn't involve complex work duties. For example, semiskilled jobs may require:

- alertness and close attention to watching machine processes
- inspecting, testing, or looking for irregularities, or
- tending to or guarding equipment, property, materials, or persons against loss, damage, or injury.

A job may also be classified as semiskilled when coordination and dexterity are necessary, such as when hands or feet must be moved quickly to do repetitive tasks.

Examples of semiskilled jobs include:

- quality control inspector
- typist
- receptionist
- security guard
- truck driver, and
- retail salesperson.

Some semiskilled jobs have elements of skilled work in them, so determining whether work experience is semiskilled or skilled can require the opinion of a vocational expert or consultant.

The SSA considers jobs listed in the DOT with an SVP of 3 or 4 to be semiskilled work.

c. Skilled Work

Skilled work requires that employees exercise judgment in completing complex tasks, such as determining what equipment to use and what operations should be performed in order to produce the correct form, quality, or quantity of material.

Skilled work may require some of the following:

- laying out work
- estimating quality
- determining the suitability and needed quantities of materials
- making precise measurements
- reading blueprints or other specifications, or
- making necessary computations or mechanical adjustments to control or regulate the work.

Other skilled jobs may require dealing with people, facts, figures, or abstract ideas at a high level of complexity.

Examples of skilled jobs include:

- engineer
- doctor
- pilot
- accountant
- attorney, and
- architect.

Skilled work isn't restricted to people who've been to college and have advanced degrees. Machinists perform skilled work, and some assembly-line work is considered skilled. Mechanics jobs and numerous other highly specialized technical jobs don't necessarily require a college degree.

Jobs listed in the DOT with an SVP of 5 or higher are considered skilled work.

d. Transferable Skills

The SSA won't award you disability benefits just because you can't do your former jobs. If you can't do any jobs you previously held because your RFC is for a lower exertional level than the type of work you used to do, then the SSA will next determine whether you have *transferable skills* from your past work that you could use for other work.

The SSA considers skills to be transferable when all of the following are true in another type of job:

- the same or a lesser degree of skill is required
- the same or similar tools and machines are used, and
- the same or similar raw materials, products, processes, or services are involved.

Transferability of skills is an important part of the medical-vocational analysis. If your skills can be usefully transferred to a new type of job, then Social Security will deny you benefits. If they can't be transferred, you might get benefits as a medical-vocational allowance, depending on your RFC and other vocational factors.

The degree of transferability ranges from very close similarities to remote and incidental similarities. A complete similarity of the three above factors isn't necessary for the SSA to consider you to have transferable skills, however. But if you have skills that are very specialized or have been acquired in an isolated work setting (like many jobs in mining, agriculture, and fishing), they wouldn't be readily usable in other jobs. In that case, the SSA is likely to find that they aren't transferable.

The SSA will only analyze whether skills are transferable for people who have done semiskilled and skilled work in the past. If your past work was all unskilled, the SSA doesn't consider transferability because unskilled work doesn't produce work skills in the first place.

D. Use of Vocational Analysts

The rules in Appendix C can help you figure out if you're likely to be considered disabled or not disabled on a medical-vocational basis. Remember from Chapter 8, however, that these rules will be applied exactly as written only if your RFC has only exertional restrictions. If you have additional nonexertional restrictions, the SSA must decide whether you're disabled based on your individual circumstances, within the framework of the rules. In order to see how nonexertional limitations in an RFC impact the grid rules, the agency seeks help from *vocational analysts.*

Vocational analysts have expert training in determining how vocational factors influence a claimant's ability to perform various kinds of jobs. For DDS, vocational analysts handle complex issues when RFCs or vocational factors don't exactly fit into the medical-vocational rules. At the appeal level, vocational analysts (called *vocational experts* at the hearing) help the administrative law judge reach a decision by answering the judge's questions about job duties. Unlike vocational analysts, who work for DDS, vocational experts are private consultants under contract with the SSA's Office of Hearings Operations.

EXAMPLE: Mary Ellen applied for disability based on lung disease and arthritis. Neither of Mary Ellen's impairments are severe enough to meet or equal a listing, so the SSA performed an RFC assessment. Because of her lung disease, Mary Ellen's RFC specifies that she can't do more than light work and must avoid exposure to excessive dust and fumes. Because of her arthritis, Mary Ellen can't use her hands to perform certain kinds of functions such as typing or pinching. At Mary Ellen's disability hearing, the judge asked the vocational expert how restrictions on fine manipulation would affect jobs at the light exertional level. The vocational expert stated that a restriction allowing only occasional manipulation would rule out all work. The judge must address the vocational expert's testimony when writing their decision about whether Mary Ellen is disabled.

You can request a copy of your file (see Chapter 2, Section E) and review your RFC to see if it contains all your medically documented restrictions.

Or, you can call your claims examiner and ask whether your RFC considers all of your medical limitations. Review every impairment you have with your examiner. Be specific in your questions—using the above example, Mary Ellen should ask if the RFC contains limitations on grasping small objects or turning knobs. Or, if you have lung disease, make sure your RFC restricts you from jobs involving excessive exposure to dust and fumes. Epilepsy symptoms should be addressed in an RFC by restrictions on working at unprotected heights or around hazardous machinery. Or if your back pain is so severe you can't bend over, your RFC should limit the amount of time you can bend.

If the claims examiner lets you know that an important work-related limitation isn't addressed on your RFC, ask the examiner to return the RFC to the medical consultant who prepared it to correct the oversight. If the examiner states that your treating doctor's medical records don't show a limitation or otherwise don't address your concern, insist that you do have a problem and you want it evaluated before your claim is decided. Ask to speak to the examiner's supervisor and, if necessary, call the DDS director. Federal laws and regulations require that every one of your complaints be fully addressed by the SSA.

Make Sure Your File Has Vocational Details

The devil is in the details. Not all SSA examiners are conscientious about getting vocational details from claimants about their prior work experience and skills, and vocational analysts can work only with the information they're provided. For example, your file might not include the fact that you needed special accommodations to perform your past work. Make sure everyone at the SSA handling your claim is aware of that fact.

Also, some medical consultants don't include important details on the RFC form for the vocational analyst. For example, you might have done a particular sewing job for many years and can do only jobs requiring similar skills. But now you have arthritis in your thumb joint because of the repetitive movement required by the job. The medical consultant may fail to note that you can't do work requiring frequent and repetitive thumb movement, although they restrict you to light work. When the vocational analyst gets your claim (with an incomplete RFC) and sees that your prior work was less than light, they might assume you can still perform your sewing job and send your file back to a claims examiner, who will issue a denial.

If you have medical restrictions from your treating doctor that aren't included in your RFC, ask the examiner to hold your file until you can contact your doctor and find out why your medical records are incomplete. You will probably get full cooperation from your doctor. If you don't, you must insist to the examiner that you have a problem and want it evaluated. This will almost certainly result in DDS ordering another doctor to evaluate you. If your claim is at the hearing level and your file doesn't contain information about all of your health problems, tell the administrative law judge that you have a problem that wasn't addressed by DDS when it denied your claim.

E. Vocational Rehabilitation

Vocational rehabilitation is the process of restoring a disabled person to the fullest economic usefulness of which that person is capable. The SSA can refer some disability claimants to vocational rehabilitation.

Vocational rehabilitation is a public program administered by an agency in each state that helps people with physical or mental disabilities become gainfully employed. A rehabilitation counselor evaluates your vocational factors (such as age, education, and past skills) and medical findings to determine if you're eligible for services. If you are, the counselor will work with you to plan a program of rehabilitation.

The SSA won't refer certain claimants to a vocational rehabilitation agency. This includes claimants who fall under any of the following categories:

- They have a terminal illness (one that can't be cured or treated).
- They have physical or mental impairments severe enough to prevent any work, even with additional training.
- They have chronic brain syndrome with marked loss of memory and understanding.
- They have a long-standing neurological or psychiatric impairment that doesn't respond to treatment, supported by evidence of poor employment or poor social history.
- They're of advanced age—usually older than 55—with little potential to adjust to or sustain work (for example, having a sparse work record or a record of performing arduous unskilled labor with a marginal education).
- They're younger than 16, unless the claimant's circumstances indicate a readiness to begin vocational rehabilitation services.

When Benefits Begin

The Social Security Administration (SSA) uses the term *onset date* to describe the date you became disabled. This date is important because the SSA may pay you SSDI benefits retroactively to the date you were disabled, even if you don't apply for disability until later. (The SSA doesn't pay SSI benefits until the first day of the month following the date of your application.)

Onset dates can get tricky. Choosing the right onset date isn't always clear, and involves both medical and nonmedical factors. To further complicate the issue, you might hear your disability claims examiner or attorney refer to three different kinds of onset dates, discussed below.

Alleged onset date (AOD) is the date on your disability application that you say ("allege") that you became unable to work due to your impairment. The SSA can agree with you that you've been disabled since that date, or the agency can pick another date that allows them to find you disabled (if they disagree your impairment was disabling at your AOD). You or your representative can change (*amend*) your alleged onset date at most points during the disability determination process.

Established onset date (EOD) is the date that the SSA determines that you became eligible to receive disability benefits. On this date, all of the following must be true:

- You must have satisfied the nonmedical eligibility factors for SSDI or SSI (see Chapter 1, Section A).

- You aren't engaged in substantial gainful activity (see Chapter 1, Section B).
- Your impairment must be expected to last at least 12 months or result in your death.
- Your impairment must be severe enough either to meet a listing or to rule out all work.

The EOD is the onset date used by the SSA to establish the amount of back pay you're owed. It might or might not be the same as your AOD, depending on your medical records, your work history, and whether you're applying for SSDI or SSI.

Medical onset date (MOD) is the date your medical condition became severe enough to meet Social Security's definition of disability. In many cases, this is the same date as your AOD. But the medical onset date can be earlier than your AOD if you aren't otherwise eligible for disability benefits due to nonmedical factors. For example, your income or resources might have been too high to qualify for SSI when you first became disabled.

A. Medical Evidence

Medical evidence is the main factor the SSA uses when determining your onset date. The agency reviews records from all of your medical sources (doctors, nurse practitioners, clinics, and so on) to determine when your impairment became disabling.

The EOD must be consistent with the medical evidence in your record. For example, if you claim that your disability began on May 1, 2022 but you didn't start seeing a doctor to treat your condition until August 1, 2024, the SSA will likely establish your onset date as August 1, 2024. If the SSA is unable to obtain sufficiently detailed medical reports from your treating doctors or hospitals, your EOD might not reflect your disability for as far back as you'd like. (See Chapter 5 for information on how to get good medical evidence into your file.)

B. Work Experience

The date you stopped working at the level of substantial gainful activity (SGA) is an important one for establishing your EOD. No matter how severe the medical evidence shows your condition to be, if you were still capable of working, the SSA is likely to set your EOD at the date your SGA ended. SGA is typically determined by the amount of money you make at your job. Under current Social Security regulations, any work that averages more than $1,550 a month is considered SGA (in 2024). If you're blind, the amount is $2,590. These amounts are adjusted annually.

The SSA sometimes uses other factors when determining whether your work was SGA. Social Security can consider the nature of your work duties, the number of hours you worked, how productive you were on the job, or any other factors related to the value of the services your work provided.

For example, if your employer had to provide special help for you to work, the value of the special assistance may be considered a subsidy and subtracted from your earnings in the SGA calculation. Additionally, any impairment-related work expenses (such as a prosthesis, service animal, or special transportation) you must pay for can be deducted from your earnings.

If you were working but not at what Social Security considers to be the SGA level, the agency might find your EOD to be a date while you were still employed.

EXAMPLE 1: After injuring his back, Caesar could no longer carry the heavy materials required for his construction job. With his employer's consent, Caesar's coworkers agreed to do the lifting and carrying for him. Six months after his injury, Caesar applied for SSDI benefits. When he was working, Caesar earned $1,600 per month—above the SGA limit—but the SSA deducted $450 per month because Caesar had needed special considerations in order to perform his job. With the deduction, the SSA found that the value of Caesar's earnings was really only $1,150 per month, well below the SGA level. The SSA then found that Caesar's EOD was the date he injured his back.

EXAMPLE 2: Suyan, a blind administrative assistant, was hit by a truck and paralyzed. A month later, she applied for SSDI disability benefits. Before her paralysis, Suyan could do her job only with special considerations. She used special software that read files to her, had a service dog that escorted her to business meetings, and had coworkers record documents for her to listen to. Suyan's employer estimated that the value of her special considerations was at least $5,000 per month, or $60,000 yearly. But Suyan's annual salary was $100,000, way over the SGA level, even with the $60,000 deduction. Therefore, Suyan's EOD could not be earlier than the date of her paralysis.

C. SSDI or SSI Claimant

Social Security sometimes distinguishes between the onset dates in SSDI claims and SSI claims. If you apply for both SSDI and SSI at the same time based on the same impairment, these concurrent claims may have different onset dates.

Failed Work Attempts

If you went back to work above SGA for a short time but couldn't work for longer because of your medical condition, the SSA won't count that period of earnings against you when determining your onset date. In other words, the date you originally quit work due to disability (or were fired) can be your onset date if the SSA considers your later attempt at work to be an *unsuccessful work attempt* (UWA). In order to qualify as an unsuccessful work attempt, you must have lasted less than six months at the job, and you must have left (or reduced your work below the SGA level) because of your medical impairment—either because you couldn't do the work or because any special conditions that you needed to do the work were removed. Special conditions include:

- assistance from other employees in doing your job
- special equipment to help do your job
- special arrangements, such as help getting you ready for work or getting to and from work
- permission to work irregular hours
- permission to take frequent rest breaks
- permission to work at a lower level of productivity than other employees
- work assignments tailored to your medical condition, or
- being allowed to work despite your impairment because of a family or past work relationship with your employer or other philanthropic reasons.

The SSA will decide if any of your earnings are considered to be part of an unsuccessful work attempt—you don't need to file a separate form.

1. Waiting Period for SSDI Claimants

If you're awarded SSDI benefits, you may be entitled to retroactive (past) pay if Social Security finds that your EOD is earlier than your application date. But the SSA doesn't pay you benefits from your EOD to the present. Social Security won't pay SSDI benefits until five full calendar months (known as the *waiting period*) have passed since your EOD.

Once the SSA establishes your EOD, it calculates your benefits from the first day of the month following your EOD (unless your EOD is on the first of the month). From that date, the agency then counts an additional five months to determine the date you can start receiving benefits. For example, if your EOD is March 2, 2023, the SSA doesn't count March as a part of your waiting period. Instead, your waiting period is made up of April, May, June, July, and August. The SSA will then pay disability benefits retroactively to September 1, 2023.

Because the SSA can't pay more than 12 months in retroactive SSDI benefits, if you have an EOD of 17 months (12 months plus the 5-month waiting period) before you apply for benefits, you'll be entitled to the maximum amount of past-due benefits.

Even if a doctor at the SSA states that your medical condition was disabling many years in the past, you won't be able to receive retroactive benefits greater the maximum 17 months.

EXAMPLE: Jerry, a 57-year-old bricklayer and long-time smoker with chronic obstructive pulmonary disease (COPD), stopped working on July 2, 2022—two years before applying for SSDI on July 1, 2024. Jerry stated that he had to stop work due to shortness of breath, and he had been financially supported by his children until recently. Jerry's medical records confirm lung disease and markedly decreased breathing capacity associated with emphysema.

Based on the evidence, Jerry's medical condition is severe enough to qualify for benefits when he stopped working in 2022. The DDS medical consultant reviewing Jerry's claim suggested an onset date consistent with the date Jerry stopped working on July 2, 2022.

However, because the examiner handling Jerry's claim knows that Jerry can only get 17 months of retroactive benefits, the examiner established an onset date of March 1, 2023. This date gives Jerry the full 12 months— after taking the five-month waiting period into consideration—of permissible benefits before his application date. (Unfortunately, Jerry can't get the benefits he could have had between July 2, 2022 and March 1, 2023 because he didn't apply soon enough.)

There are three exceptions to the waiting period rule for SSDI recipients. First, if you were approved for and started receiving SSDI, went back to work, stopped receiving benefits, and then become disabled again, you won't have to wait five months to receive benefits—as long as no more than five years have passed between your first onset date and your second onset date. (See Chapter 13.) Second, if you're awarded benefits as the child of a disabled worker, you aren't subject to any waiting period. (See Chapter 3.)

Third, people with amyotrophic lateral sclerosis (ALS or Lou Gehrig's disease) don't have a waiting period, so they can receive both cash and Medicare benefits right away.

2. No Waiting Period for SSI Claimants

The established onset date for SSI recipients can't be any earlier than the first day of the month following the date of application. This is true regardless of how long you've been disabled—unlike with SSDI, you aren't entitled to any retroactive payments before your application date. But you'll be paid benefits for the time it takes between when you filed your application and when Social Security decides that you're disabled. Because it can take many years of appeals before your claim is ultimately approved, these benefits can add up to a substantial amount.

> EXAMPLE: John has heart disease and arthritis. He applies for SSI benefits on July 5, 2023. On his application, John alleges an onset date of February 6, 2021. The SSA reviewed his medical records and determined that John's impairments began to be disabling in January 2020.
>
> But because John is only eligible for SSI, the SSA established his onset date as August 1, 2022—the first day of the month after the date he filed his application. John's claim was eventually approved on November 15, 2025. He will receive back payments from August 1, 2023.

Appeal of Onset Date

If you're awarded SSDI benefits, Social Security may establish an onset date later than you think is correct. In that situation, you can appeal by asking DDS to do a reconsideration of the onset date. But keep in mind that there's little point in arguing about onset date if the date the SSA established covers the full 17 months before your application. Also, you can't ask the SSA to review your onset date without running the risk that the agency decides it was wrong to award you disability benefits in the first place—the agency won't review only your onset date without reviewing the rest of your application. (For more information on appealing an onset date, see Chapter 12.)

Reasons You May Be Denied Benefits

When applying for Social Security disability, most people naturally think about the reasons why they should be granted benefits. You may find it useful, however, to turn the perspective around and understand the reasons why you might be denied benefits. In some cases, the reasons are beyond your control. But sometimes, you may be able to avoid doing something that results in a denial.

A. You Earn Too Much Income or Have Too Many Assets

The most basic reason for being denied benefits for SSDI or SSI is that you work above the substantial gainful activity (SGA) limit when you apply. This means you earn too much money. If you're an applicant who isn't blind, you're considered above the SGA limit if you make over $1,550 per month. If you're a blind SSDI applicant, you're considered above the SGA limit if you make over $2,590 per month. (These numbers are current for 2024. The limits adjust each year.) Income from investments doesn't count toward the SGA—only work income counts.

TIP

Once disability benefits begin, earning money doesn't always result in a termination of benefits. SSDI recipients can usually keep their benefits during a *trial work period.* Also, SSI recipients can sometimes receive cash in excess of the SGA amount provided they don't exceed SSI income and asset levels. (See Chapter 13.)

For SSDI, there's no such thing as partial disability based on how much money you earn. SSDI benefits are paid on an all-or-nothing basis. In other words, if you make $1,550 per month or less as a nonblind person, you'll receive the total amount of your SSDI disability check. If you make more than the $1,550 SGA limit, you won't receive any benefits. However, there are temporary exceptions for people receiving benefits and attempting to return to work (as described in Chapter 13). Keep in mind that Social Security doesn't count any impairment-related work expenses, such as the cost of a prosthesis or a service dog, towards the SGA limit.

For SSI recipients, SGA can be confusing because SSI eligibility is also dependent on an income limit. If you're approved for SSI, your SSI check will be reduced by part of your earnings. You could technically earn up to about $1,970 per month (in 2024) before your SSI will stop because you're over the income limit. If you make more than that, you would be financially ineligible for SSI.

But you are still subject to the $1,550 SGA limit when you apply for benefits. If you make over that amount, you will be *medically ineligible* for SSI.

(For additional information about SSI income and resource limits, see Chapter 1, Section D, and Chapter 13.)

B. Your Disability Won't Last Long Enough

Another reason you might be denied benefits is that the SSA thinks that your disability is only temporary. To qualify for SSI or SSDI benefits, the SSA must believe that your impairment is severe enough to last at least 12 months or result in your death. (The only exception to this duration requirement is for blind SSI applicants.)

Many claims—often based on bone fractures resulting from acute trauma, such as automobile accidents or workplace injuries—are denied because they aren't likely to still be disabling in 12 months. Almost all bone fractures heal in less than a year. But if you have severe bone fractures that haven't healed after six months, the SSA is more likely to think your impairment will last a year. There's no hard-and-fast rule, however—each case is evaluated on an individual basis.

EXAMPLE: Reg has an acute bone fracture from an automobile accident two months ago and he can't walk. After using up his sick days and unpaid leave from work, Reg applied for disability. Even though Reg can't work right now, the SSA denied his application because there's no evidence that Reg's fracture will take longer than 12 months to heal.

 TIP

You may be eligible for temporary disability benefits. A few states offer temporary disability benefits (TDI or SDI) for those who are unable to work for less than a year. If you live in California, Hawaii, New York, New Jersey, or Rhode Island, contact your state labor or employment department to apply.

C. The SSA Can't Find You

The SSA needs to be able to communicate with you about your application. The agency can deny your application if you're not responding to phone calls and written notices about critical matters, like scheduling a consultative examination or disability hearing. You can hire an attorney or disability advocate to handle your communications with Social Security, but be sure to stay in touch with your representative. Lawyers can remove themselves from representing lost clients if they can't reach you either.

If you move while your application is being considered, make sure the SSA knows how to contact you. Claimants get denied every day because the SSA can't find them.

D. You Refuse to Cooperate

Your medical records are key to your disability claim, so the SSA can deny your claim if you refuse to release those records to the agency.

Similarly, the SSA may need additional information about your medical impairments, either because your treating doctor's medical records are incomplete or because you don't have a regular doctor. In these instances, the SSA will request that you attend a *consultative examination* (CE) with an SSA doctor, on the agency's dime. The SSA might even schedule you for multiple CEs, and can deny your claim if you don't attend.

CEs are often scheduled without your input, so if you can't make it to a CE because of the time or location, talk to your claims examiner so DDS can schedule an exam at a time or place that's convenient for you. If you repeatedly fail to show up for a CE, however, your claim will most likely be denied. (See Chapter 5, Section C, for more on CEs.)

E. You Fail to Follow Prescribed Therapy

The SSA can deny you benefits when your doctor prescribes a treatment and you don't follow your doctor's recommendations— even though you have the ability to do so. In order for the SSA to deny your claim for failure to follow prescribed treatment,

the recommended treatment must be clearly expected to restore your ability to do economically meaningful work (substantial gainful activity). (For a child applying for SSI, the issue is whether the prescribed therapy will restore the child's ability to function in an age-appropriate manner.)

If your treating doctor doesn't think that the prescribed treatment is going to restore your ability to work, the SSA won't blame you for not following through, unless the agency disagrees with your doctor on that point because your doctor's opinion is clearly contrary to the general medical opinion.

But if, for example, you have debilitating migraines that keep you bedridden but you refuse to take medications generally known to reduce the frequency and intensity of the migraines, the SSA will likely deny your application—unless you can show that you have an acceptable excuse for refusing treatment.

The SSA does, however, recognize certain legitimate excuses for failing to follow prescribed therapy.

1. Acceptable Medical Excuses

Failure to follow prescribed therapy can be excused for reasons beyond your control. They include, but may not be limited to, the following:

- You have a mental illness so severe that you're unable to comply with prescribed therapy. Examples include mania, major depression, dementia, schizophrenia, and psychosis.

- You have cataracts from diabetes so severe that your vision is too poor to accurately measure your insulin dose.
- You have below-normal intelligence. For example, if your IQ is 70, you probably wouldn't be expected to self-administer home dialysis for kidney failure. But it's more likely that you could be expected to swallow a pill three times a day.
- You physically can't follow prescribed therapy without assistance—for example, because of arm paralysis.
- You have a fear of surgery so intense that surgery is *contraindicated* (medically not recommended). Your treating doctor must confirm the severity of your phobia to the DDS consulting doctor. If your treating doctor can't, the SSA may ask you to undergo a psychiatric examination. The SSA won't accept a refusal to have prescribed surgery as an excuse simply because its success isn't guaranteed or because you know someone for whom the surgery wasn't successful.
- The prescribed treatment is for major surgery and you've already undergone unsuccessful major surgery for this impairment.

- The prescribed treatment is cataract surgery for one eye, and your other eye has a severe visual impairment that can't be improved through treatment.
- The prescribed treatment is very risky because of its magnitude (such as open heart surgery or organ transplantation), unusual nature, or another reason.
- The prescribed treatment involves amputation of an extremity or a major part of an extremity.
- A doctor who has treated you advises against the treatment prescribed by another doctor.

> **CAUTION**
>
> **Parents or caregivers must follow the prescribed therapy for their children.** Young children can't be expected to reliably administer treatments to themselves or to take pills on a regular schedule. Parents or other caregivers are responsible for making sure their children follow prescribed therapy or they risk having the child's benefits denied.

The above list isn't exclusive. The SSA decides all potential instances of failure to comply on a case-by-case basis. Below are a few examples where the agency is unlikely to deny a claim based on failure to comply with treatment.

EXAMPLE 1: Sal, a young man in his twenties, applied for disability benefits due to a rare type of rapidly progressive rheumatoid arthritis that affected most of the joints in his body. After his diagnosis, Sal saw a new doctor seeking help for his unusual condition. The doctor prescribed Sal an antidepressant and recommended injections of vitamin B-12. Confused, Sal asked the doctor why he was being prescribed an antidepressant for what he understood to be an autoimmune disorder. The doctor said the combination of B-12 and antidepressants was a miracle cure for Sal's condition. Unimpressed with this answer, Sal didn't fill his prescription or return for the B-12 shots. The SSA will likely find that Sal has an acceptable excuse for not following the doctor's recommendation.

EXAMPLE 2: Susan has poorly controlled epilepsy. She takes her medications as directed, but the DDS medical consultant reviewing her file sees that her treating doctor gives her only older types of drugs used to treat epilepsy. Newer drugs will probably be very effective in reducing Susan's symptoms, but from the progress notes, it seems like the treating doctor doesn't even know they exist. Susan is granted benefits.

Keep in mind that the SSA will consider treatment prescriptions only from a licensed medical source (physician or nurse practitioner, for example) for a physical or mental disorder. If you have a mental impairment, your treating doctor could be a licensed psychologist with a Ph.D. degree. (This doesn't matter as far as not following prescribed medication, however, because psychologists can't prescribe medication.)

If an alternative practitioner is treating you, you won't be denied benefits for failing to follow a prescribed therapy if that treatment isn't a reasonable therapy generally recognized by the medical community.

EXAMPLE 3: Wilma has severe joint pains and suspects she has arthritis. She visits a naturopath, who suggests to Wilma that she visit her local health food store and buy certain herbs to cleanse the toxins from her body. A friend of Wilma's had been prescribed a similar treatment, which did nothing, so Wilma doesn't comply with the recommendation. In this case, Wilma won't be denied benefits for failing to follow prescribed therapy.

2. Acceptable Nonmedical Excuses

It's also possible that you can't follow a prescribed therapy for a reason that has nothing to do with your medical condition. Acceptable nonmedical excuses for failing to follow prescribed therapy are described below.

a. Lack of Money to Pay for Treatment

The SSA isn't allowed to deny you benefits based on failure to follow prescribed treatment if you don't have enough money to pay for that treatment.

It's very important to make sure the SSA knows that you don't have enough money to pay for medications, physical therapy, mental health counseling, or any other treatments for your impairments. Don't assume that a disability claims examiner will know about your financial plight. The SSA will want to see that you've tried all options, however, such as low- or no-cost clinics or sliding-scale options.

> **EXAMPLE:** Anna has frequent epileptic seizures because she can't afford the drugs necessary to control them. Anna's medical records show that her epilepsy is well controlled when she takes medication. However, Anna lives near a free clinic in a university medical center that is willing to give her free drugs and help her obtain transportation to the clinic for treatment. In this instance, Anna can't use lack of money as an excuse for failing to follow her doctor's prescribed treatment.

The SSA can also be wary of this excuse if the record suggests that you could afford to buy medications but you're spending your money elsewhere. Telling your doctor about the new luxury car you just bought one minute while claiming you can't afford pain relievers the next is probably going to raise a few eyebrows.

 CAUTION
Alcohol interferes with the action of antiepileptic drugs. If your medical records show that you drink alcohol despite advice to the contrary from your doctor, you're likely to be denied benefits. Not only would you be failing to follow prescribed treatment recommended by your doctor, but if you drink alcohol, the SSA will assume that your epilepsy would improve if you stopped drinking (see Section F, below, for more information).

b. Religious Reasons

Some people's religious convictions prohibit them from receiving medical therapy. The SSA won't deny you disability benefits for not following a prescribed therapy that is contrary to the established teaching and tenets of your religion. The SSA makes this determination by:

- identifying the church affiliation
- confirming your membership in the church, and
- documenting the church's position concerning the medical treatment by requesting relevant church literature or obtaining statements from church officials about the teachings and tenets of the church.

If you're a Christian Scientist, the SSA just needs to verify your membership in the church, because church teachings forbidding medical treatment are well established.

EXAMPLE: Dwight, a middle-aged truck driver, applied for disability benefits due to advanced kidney cancer. Dwight had seen a doctor in the earlier stages of the cancer who told him that the cancer could be easily removed with little chance of complications and a low rate of remission. Dwight, a Jehovah's Witness, refused the treatment because he would need to accept a whole blood transfusion, a procedure prohibited by the tenets of the religion. The DDS examiner evaluating Dwight's claim verified his church affiliation, confirmed his membership, and documented through church literature that a practicing Jehovah's Witness would decline the treatment. The examiner was satisfied that Dwight had a valid religious reason for not complying with recommended treatment and, because Dwight's medical records otherwise established disability, approved his application.

c. You Don't Have a Treating Doctor

The SSA shouldn't deny your claim for not following therapy for your condition if you don't have a treating doctor and, therefore, have no prescribed therapy, even if you have the money to see a doctor.

The SSA doesn't define what it means to have a treating doctor, but it usually means you have an established ongoing relationship with a doctor who is attempting to improve a particular health condition. (You can have more than one treating doctor if you have multiple impairments.) You don't have to see the doctor a specific number of times for them to be considered your treating doctor, but your visits should be frequent enough for the SSA to reasonably believe that the doctor has knowledge of your current condition. For example, if you saw a doctor several times, your medical condition stabilized with treatment, and you were given a return appointment for six months later, that doctor would likely be considered your treating doctor. But if you haven't seen a doctor for over six months, the SSA may conclude that you no longer have a meaningful treatment relationship with that doctor.

Doctors who perform SSA consultative examinations on you aren't considered treating doctors. You're not obligated to follow their treatment recommendations.

EXAMPLE: Hiro has cataracts and is blind. He applies for disability benefits. If he has the cataracts removed, Hiro will probably be able to see fairly well, but he doesn't have the money to pay for cataract surgery. Because Hiro can't afford to pay an eye specialist to submit a report to DDS, the SSA sends him to a consultative eye examination at the agency's expense. The examining doctor submits a report to DDS, stating that although Hiro is essentially blind, he would be able to see quite well with cataract surgery and placement of artificial lenses in his eyes. The doctor gave this recommendation to Hiro. The SSA shouldn't deny Hiro's claim on the basis of failing to comply with treatment because the prescribed treatment was recommended by the SSA doctor, not a treating doctor.

F. Drug Addiction or Alcoholism Contributes to Your Disability

The SSA will deny benefits to someone whose drug or alcohol abuse (DAA) is a material contributing factor to the disability. Basically, the agency needs to determine whether the claimant would be disabled if they stopped using drugs or alcohol.

In general, medical consultants who work for Social Security are responsible for making the determination about whether DAA materially contributes to a disability. Opinions from medical sources (including treating, nontreating, and nonexamining sources) can also be considered when making the determination. These opinions may be persuasive, but the medical consultants aren't obligated to give special significance to them.

1. Is the DAA Relevant to Your Impairment?

The SSA must decide if your drug addiction or alcoholism is relevant to your disability. This determination is separate from your disability determination, and is made only if all of the following are true:

- You're found to have medical impairments severe enough to be disabling.
- Medical evidence supplied by an acceptable medical source—such as a medical doctor or licensed psychologist—indicates that DAA is an issue.

- The medical evidence establishes the existence of DAA by satisfying the diagnostic requirements for substance abuse in the *Diagnostic and Statistical Manual of Mental Disorders*. This is a book published by the American Psychiatric Association and is found in most large libraries and bookstores. It is usually just referred to as the DSM-III, DSM-IV, or DSM-5, depending on the edition. The DSM describes the diagnostic criteria needed for various mental disorders and helps mental health professionals diagnose disorders. (The SSA's medical criteria for disabling mental impairments are based on the DSM.)

 CAUTION

Independent corroborative evidence of your drug or alcohol abuse is required. The most convincing and likely information that the SSA can use is from medical records of hospitalization for drug or alcohol abuse. A statement such as "I am an alcoholic," or "I take drugs"—even recorded in your medical records by a physician or a psychologist—isn't enough evidence of drug addiction or alcohol abuse. But addictive behaviors towards drugs or alcohol imply a pattern of compulsive use. (Note that DAA doesn't apply to children who have physical or mental impairments resulting from their mothers' use of alcohol or drugs during pregnancy.)

2. Making a DAA Determination

If you're found to have a drug or alcohol addiction that the SSA considers relevant, the agency will decide if that should prevent you from getting disability benefits. The key factor a medical consultant must consider when making a DAA determination is whether the SSA would still find you disabled if you stopped using drugs or alcohol. The medical consultant must consider two questions:

- Which of your current physical and mental limitations would remain if you stopped using drugs or alcohol?
- Would any of these remaining limitations be disabling?

EXAMPLE: Dot drinks alcohol heavily, resulting in inflammation of her liver (alcoholic hepatitis) that keeps her from working due to pain and nausea. Dot's doctor reviewed her medical evidence and told her that if she stopped drinking, her symptoms would likely improve significantly. If Dot's alcohol abuse is the only thing standing in the way of her ability to work, the SSA will deny her claim.

If you have a permanent impairment that would still be present if you stopped using alcohol or drugs, that impairment could still be the basis of a winning disability claim, even if substance abuse caused the condition in the first place.

EXAMPLE 1: Billy drank alcohol heavily for many years. As a result, his blood clots abnormally slowly, and he is physically weak. Billy's liver is so damaged from alcoholic scarring (cirrhosis) that it is shrunken and incapable of self-repair. Billy got treatment for his addiction and had been sober for three years at the time he applied for disability benefits, but the damage had already been done. Billy's condition was severe enough to meet the requirements of the listing for chronic liver disease. The SSA won't deny Billy's claim due to DAA, because his liver impairment remained disabling despite his abstinence from alcohol.

EXAMPLE 2: Gretchen is a frequent user of methamphetamine who struggles to stay clean. Gretchen seeks treatment at a rehabilitation center, a doctor discovers that Gretchen has a heart infection that resulted from using nonsterile needles to inject meth. The doctor notes that Gretchen's condition is irreversible and disabling. The SSA will likely find that DAA doesn't prevent Gretchen from receiving benefits because her heart damage would remain even if she stopped using drugs. (But the agency is likely to assign a representative payee to manage Gretchen's benefits on her behalf.)

G. You Have Been Convicted of a Crime

Certain conditions related to conviction of a crime or imprisonment will prevent you from receiving Social Security benefits. They are as follows:

- **Incarceration for a felony conviction.** You can't get disability benefits if you're in prison after being convicted of a felony. The one exception to this is if you're in a court-approved rehabilitation program that is likely to result in your getting a job when you get released from prison and your release is within a reasonable amount of time. For example, if you won't be leaving prison for another five years, the SSA won't grant you benefits.

- **Injured during a felony.** You can't get disability benefits for an injury you sustained while committing a felony (if you were convicted of the crime). You also can't get benefits because you had a preexisting injury that got worse while you were committing a felony.

- **Injured in prison.** You can't get disability benefits based on an injury you sustained—or an existing condition that worsened—while in prison for a felony. But you might be able to receive benefits after being released from prison.

H. You Commit Fraud

If you obtain disability benefits by dishonest means, the SSA can terminate your benefits and prosecute you for fraud. Anyone who helped you obtain benefits fraudulently can also be prosecuted.

Appealing If Your Claim Is Denied

I f the Social Security decides that you aren't eligible for benefits, that your current benefits will end, or that the amount of your payments should change, the agency will send you a letter explaining the decision. If you don't agree with the decision, you can ask a different DDS examiner to review the original decision and see if they reach a different result. This is the first level of the appeals process, known as *reconsideration*. When you request a reconsideration, a new DDS examiner will review the entire decision—even those parts that were in your favor—and come to their own conclusion.

If you disagree with the result of the re-consideration, you have additional options. You can appeal to an administrative law judge (see Section E3, below), then to the Appeals Council (see Section E4, below), and finally to a federal district court judge (see Section E5, below). Before filing an appeal, however, you should consider your chances of winning.

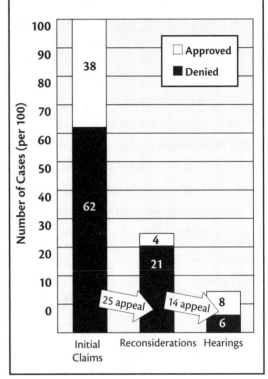

Progression of Cases Through the Disability Process

NOTE: Data based on total appeals in fiscal year 2022, not a longitudinal tracking of individual cases.

A. Deciding Whether to Appeal

A higher percentage of claimants are granted disability on appeal than at the initial application stage. See the chart below for a visualization of the SSA's statistics on how many cases are granted at each appeal level.

Here are some issues to consider when deciding whether to appeal.

TIP
There are no costs for filing an appeal with the SSA. This is true regardless of whether you're filing a request for reconsideration, asking for a hearing in front of an administrative law judge, or requesting review from the Appeals Council. And you can fill out the forms yourself and appear at your hearing to defend your case. If you choose to hire an attorney or an authorized representative, however, you'll have to pay for their services. And if you file an appeal in federal court, you'll need to pay court fees and other costs.

1. How Severe Are Your Impairments?

If you have a condition in Social Security's Blue Book of listed impairments and you think you could meet the listing, you have good reason to appeal. For example, if you have cancer and your medical evidence is close but not quite enough to meet the criteria of a listing, you have a good chance of being awarded benefits after an appeal. Part of the reasoning behind these improved odds is that your condition is unlikely to significantly improve in the months and years between appeals steps, and you're more likely to have medical imaging and lab tests that meet the requirements of a listing. (You can see the specific Medical Listings and the requirements for each on Nolo's website; see Appendix D.)

2. Is Your Impairment Going to Last at Least a Year?

Claimants often apply for disability benefits based on bone fractures or other injuries associated with accidents. Typically, these kinds of disabilities heal within several months. Because you'll need to show that you have an impairment that lasts for at least a year to qualify for disability benefits, your claim will be denied if the agency thinks you'll be better within a year. But if you were denied because the SSA didn't think you would meet the 12-month durational requirement, and you're still recovering from your injuries a year later, you'll have a better shot of winning on appeal.

3. How Old Are You?

The probability of getting benefits increases with age. If you're 50 or older, your chances of getting benefits are generally better than if you're younger than 50. Claimants under the age of 50 typically need to show that they can't do the least demanding work, while older claimants might be granted benefits even if they could physically perform easier jobs but they don't know how to do them (and can't learn). (See Chapters 7 and 8 for more on this issue.)

4. What Is Your Education?

If you don't have a high school education (and you're over the age of 50), you might have an easier time getting benefits under Social Security's *medical-vocational grid rules.* The less formal education or training you have, the higher the chances are that the SSA will find that you don't have skills that you can use in another job. So, if you have a high school education or more, your chances of obtaining benefits decrease, unless your medical condition is so severe that you meet an impairment listing or you get an RFC for less than sedentary work. (See Chapters 7 and 8 for more on this issue.)

5. What Is Your Work Experience?

The more skilled work experience you have, the greater the chances that the SSA will decide you can do some kind of work. The SSA will look back on work you've done in the past to see if you can use what you've learned on the job in a different area. If you've gained a lot of skills in your past jobs, the SSA is likely to find that you can use those skills elsewhere, in physically less demanding work. But if your past work was unskilled, that can reduce (and sometimes eliminate) the types of jobs that the SSA thinks you can do. Similarly, if symptoms from your medical impairment keep you from using your job skills, it's less likely that Social Security will identify work that you can do.

6. Can You File an Appeal on Your Own or Pay for Legal Help?

The Social Security disability appeals process can be lengthy and frustrating. You'll probably have to brace yourself for several denials and several years of appeals. Ask yourself if you're physically and mentally able to do the paperwork involved. Do you want to get involved in actively reviewing your file? Can you commit enough of your time to the appeal process? A disability lawyer or nonattorney representative can take a lot off your plate, but you need to be willing to pay them part of any past-due benefits you're owed from Social Security if you win your case.

7. Why Was Your Claim Denied?

Review your SSA file for incorrect statements or opinions that you can challenge. If your denial was based on obvious factual errors—for example, the SSA said that you don't have any objective evidence for your back pain, but they overlooked an MRI showing that you have severe spinal stenosis—you have a good chance of winning an appeal. Other factors that you should double-check for accuracy include which conditions you're getting treated for, your age, your education, and your work experience. If you can show that the SSA got something wrong that could change the outcome of your claim, your chances of winning an appeal are increased. (Keep in mind that if you spot only minor or clerical errors—like the SSA said you graduated from Cloverleaf High School when you actually graduated from Leaf Clover High—that isn't a strong argument on which to base an appeal.)

8. Is It in Your Best Interests to Appeal?

Appealing a denial isn't always the best option for everybody. Some claims simply don't yet have enough evidence to meet Social Security's definition of disability. (Disability attorneys may refer to these claims as being *unripe*, meaning they were filed too early but could be promising in the future.) Time spent appealing an unripe claim takes away from time that could be used to establish important medical evidence for a future application.

Financial considerations can also play a role in deciding whether to appeal. Some people can make more money working part time than they would by collecting disability benefits. And employers are required to provide reasonable accommodations for people with disabilities, which can make full-time work an accessible and appealing possibility.

Your decision to appeal shouldn't be based on just one of the above factors. Take them all under consideration. If you're younger than age 50, have more than a sixth-grade education, and don't meet the requirements of a listed impairment, then you'll likely get denied again on reconsideration. But if you don't mind a long wait for a hearing before an administrative law judge, then you'll reach the stage of the appeals process with the highest likelihood of approval. A few examples of cases and probable outcomes are given below.

EXAMPLE 1: Rick is 56 years old and has a fifth-grade education. He has done only arduous, unskilled, heavy work his whole life. He fell from a roof doing construction work and fractured his spine. After a lengthy hospitalization, it became clear to Rick that he couldn't return to his job, and he applied for Social Security disability. Rick's back pain intensifies if he sits or stands too long or lifts over 20 pounds, and he can't bend his back to tie his shoes. Rick was initially denied benefits because a DDS medical consultant erroneously ignored Rick's lifting and bending limitations and stated that

Rick could perform medium work, which involves lifting up to 50 pounds and has no restrictions on bending. Rick has a good chance of being approved for benefits.

Appeal Myths Versus Reality

Due to the large number of disability applicants, several myths have sprung up about the way the SSA and DDS agencies operate. One prevalent myth is that the SSA denies every initial application as a matter of policy. This isn't true. In reality, almost 40% of initial claims are granted, as are about 15% of reconsideration claims. That means hundred of thousands of claimants are approved by DDS each year.

Another example is the saying that "the SSA denies everybody twice." This statement refers to the fact that anyone who sees a judge has been denied initially and at reconsideration. But actually, only a small percentage of denied disability applicants make it to the hearing level, so this statement is a bit misleading. However, this common misconception is likely a reflection of the better chance claimants have of winning after a hearing in front of an administrative law judge. On average, judges allow about half of the claims they hear—higher than the approval percentage at either the initial or reconsideration stages. You'll have to wait a year or more to see a judge, however, so it's best to make sure your case is as strong as possible to get approved earlier.

EXAMPLE 2: Jay is 25 years old and suffered multiple bone fractures, wounds, and significant blood loss in a motorcycle accident. Because of his injuries, Jay can't return to his carpentry job for about six months. He applies for Social Security disability right away and is surprised to find that DDS denies his initial and reconsideration claims because his fractures are expected to heal in under a year. Unless Jay can successfully argue that his fractures aren't going to heal in 12 months, his chances of being allowed benefits even on appeal are small.

EXAMPLE 3: Jay's brother Jim, age 27, was also injured in the motorcycle accident, but he wasn't wearing a helmet and suffered a fractured skull. Jim was in the hospital for a month after brain surgery before he was finally allowed to go home to the care of his wife, Lorraine. Jim has significant difficulties with memory and thinking, characteristic of traumatic brain injury. With intensive rehabilitation, Jim has been slowly improving. Before he left the hospital, Lorraine filed for disability benefits on his behalf, but Jim's claim was denied. The denial notice indicated that, although Jim's brain injury was disabling at the present time, it was expected that he would recover in less than 12 months.

As Jim's guardian, Lorraine decided to review Jim's file and found that the DDS medical consultant had predicted that, based on Jim's slow improvement with rehabilitation, he would be capable of at least unskilled work within 12 months after his injury. Lorraine discovered two big problems with Jim's denial.

First, the DDS medical consultant was an orthopedist (a doctor who specializes in bone disorders), and shouldn't have been evaluating Jim's mental condition. Lorraine knew that the consultant was an orthopedist because of the specialty code entered on Form SSA-831-C3/U3: *Disability Determination and Transmittal* (see "DDS Medical Consultant Codes" in Section E1c, below, for the codes).

Second, because Lorraine had reviewed the requirements of listed impairment 11.18 for traumatic brain injury, she knew that SSA policy doesn't allow cases of severe traumatic brain injury to be denied on the presumption they will improve to not be disabling in 12 months. The SSA will delay making a decision on a traumatic brain injury until three to six months after the accident in order to get a better picture of the recovery time.

Lorraine helped Jim request reconsideration of his denial, pointing out both in writing and in telephone calls to the claims examiner and DDS agency director that Jim's application wasn't evaluated correctly. DDS assured Lorraine that on reconsideration, Jim's claim would be assigned to a medical consultant who would properly evaluate it. Within a month, Jim's claim for benefits was allowed, after being reviewed by a DDS psychiatrist who properly applied the criteria of listing 11.18.

EXAMPLE 4: Maude has been on disability for three years because of severe chest pain and weakness related to her blocked coronary arteries. Last year, Maude had coronary artery bypass surgery. Her chest pain has disappeared, and her heart tests show that Maude is now capable of considerably more physical activity than simply sitting. In her medical records, Maude's treating doctor made statements indicating that she has improved significantly. As Maude's physical condition currently appears compatible with work Maude used to do, the SSA ended her benefits. Maude has no real reason to appeal the SSA's decision because she is no longer disabled under the agency's definition.

B. Review the Rationale and Your File From the SSA

The SSA uses hundreds of specialized forms and notices to communicate with claimants and disability recipients. Here's an explanation of some of the paperwork you may receive from the SSA when your claim is denied.

1. Forms

Forms are the main method the SSA uses to obtain basic information, such as names, addresses, dates, and types of claims. The agency also uses forms to keep track of its internal processes (such as communications between claims examiners and medical consultants) or to transmit important information between the state DDS and the federal SSA. Many forms are designed to be completed by claimants, but some forms you won't see unless you review your file in preparation for an appeal.

2. Notices

Notices are SSA form letters used to communicate with claimants. The SSA must send a written notice to you whenever the agency makes a decision about your entitlement to benefits or when the agency is planning an action that will negatively affect your current or future entitlement to benefits.

For example, you may receive a notice telling you whether your claim is denied or allowed, or when you're going to be scheduled for a continuing disability review. Most notice forms have some type of identifier that begins with the letter L, such as SSA-L1675-U2, *Notice of Reconsideration.*

In addition to regular notices, the SSA sometimes sends out advance predetermination notices to SSDI claimants. These advance notices will:

- inform you of an action the SSA plans to take, like ending your benefits because you're working above the substantial gainful activity level
- summarize the evidence in your file that supports the reason the SSA is taking the action
- advise you how to present evidence that may change the planned action, and
- tell you how long you have to respond to the notice.

3. Rationales

Rationales are explanations of SSA determinations and are sent on Form SSA-4268. The form contains your name, Social Security number, type of claim (SSDI or SSI), and then a rationale—either a personalized explanation or a technical explanation.

The purposes of the rationales for disability determinations and hearing decisions are to:

- let you know which medical and nonmedical factors the SSA considered when arriving at a decision
- explain the process the SSA used to make the determination, and
- provide a record of evidence for the reasons underlying the conclusion.

Rationales are extremely important when your claim is denied. Any mistakes the SSA made in its rationales can help you understand what went wrong and provide the basis for an appeal.

a. Personalized Explanation Rationales

If you receive a notice of an unfavorable decision—such as one denying your application or ending your benefits—the notice will include a personalized explanation rationale. You may also receive an attachment with the notice, detailing additional reasons for your denial.

Personalized explanations are written to be understood by someone with a sixth-grade education. They're supposed to avoid abbreviations, jargon, technical terms, complex medical phrases, or personal statements about you that have nothing to do with your actual disability determination. Although the SSA uses some stock sentences in personalized explanations, your personal disability determination must be explained using the circumstances specific to you.

Your personalized explanation rationale must contain the following elements.

All medical and nonmedical sources used in evaluating your claim. All medical sources the SSA used to evaluate your claim, including doctors and hospitals, should be listed by name. Nonmedical sources—like school guidance counselors, welfare departments, vocational rehabilitation agencies, day treatment facilities, sheltered workshops, social workers, and family members—should be listed as evidence sources, but don't need to be identified by name.

An explanation for the denial. The explanation will depend on the specifics of your claim. For example, if you meet all the nonmedical criteria for the type of benefit (SSDI or SSI) you're applying for but the agency thinks you can still work, your explanation might say: "We have determined that your condition is not severe enough to keep you from working. We considered the medical record and other information, including your age, education, training, and work experience in determining how your condition affects your ability to work."

A list of the impairments evaluated. This will include the conditions (physical and mental) you listed on your disability application as well as any other impairments that the SSA found evidence of in your record.

For claimants with mental impairments who may be unaware of the exact nature of their condition, the rationale may be worded in such a way as to avoid causing upset or offense. For example, in denying your claim, the SSA might say something general such as, "The evidence does not show any other conditions that significantly limit your ability to work."

A brief description of your medical condition. The rationale will include a description of your impairments as the agency understands them. Read this carefully to see whether you agree with the description and to make sure nothing has been left out.

If you received a denial because the SSA doesn't think your condition will last for at least 12 months, the personal explanation rationale must address this issue.

If you were denied because the SSA believes you can do your prior work, the letter will include the job the agency thinks you can return to. The SSA doesn't have to include information about your residual functional capacity (see Chapter 8) if the SSA thinks you can return to your past work as it was generally performed. (See Example 1, below.)

The following three examples illustrate types of personalized explanation rationales that might be included with an initial claim denial notice. (These examples exclude doctor and hospital names that must be listed in actual notice rationales.) You should assume that, if the SSA doesn't list some of your important medical sources, they weren't used in your disability determination. This can be the basis for an appeal.

Form SSA-4268, Example 1

We have determined that your condition is not severe enough to keep you from working. We considered medical and other information, your age, education, training, and work experience in determining how your condition affects your ability to work. You said that you are unable to work because of a back condition. The medical evidence shows that you were operated on for a slipped disc. There are no signs of severe muscle weakness or nerve damage. While you cannot do heavy work, you are now able to do light work not requiring frequent bending. Based on your description of the job of rug inspector that you performed for the past 15 years, we have concluded that you can return to this job. If your condition gets worse and keeps you from working, write, call, or visit any Social Security office about filing another application.

If you were denied because the SSA agrees that you can't return to your past work, but believes you can do other jobs, the denial notice will include a statement that you have the ability to do work that is less demanding than your past work. The SSA will generally refer to your exertional level and skill level when stating that you can do a job that requires less physical or mental effort than your previous work. The SSA will say this in general terms, instead of listing specific jobs. For example, the agency might say, "You can do lighter work." (See Examples 2 and 3, below.)

Form SSA-4268, Example 2

We have determined that your condition is not severe enough to keep you from working. We considered medical and other information, your age, education, training, and work experience in determining how your condition affects your ability to work. You said that you were unable to work because of nerves. The medical evidence shows that you have anxieties that make it difficult to return to your prior work as a field representative. You also complained that you have arthritis in your hands and back.

We realize that your conditions prevent your return to any type of work requiring frequent interaction with the public or heavy lifting. However, your condition does not prevent you from performing other types of jobs requiring less mental stress or performing light lifting. Based on your age (45), education (high school graduate), and past work experience, you can do other work. If your condition gets worse and keeps you from working, write, call, or visit any Social Security office about filing another application.

Form SSA-4268, Example 3

We have determined that your condition is not severe enough to keep you from working. We considered medical and other information, your age, education, training, and work experience in determining how your condition affects your ability to work. You said that you are unable to work because of pain and stiffness in your knees and lower back.

The medical evidence shows that you have arthritis in your knees and back that causes you discomfort. We realize that your condition prevents you from doing any of your past jobs, but it does not prevent you from doing other jobs that require less physical effort. Based on your age (52), education (9th grade), and past work experience, you can do other work. If your condition gets worse and keeps you from working, write, call, or visit any Social Security office about filing another application.

Consider appealing if the SSA hasn't included the above elements in its personalized explanation rationale. An incomplete explanation can be a sign that the agency didn't consider all relevant information in your records when deciding your claim.

b. Technical Rationales

Technical rationales are medically complex, contain more detail than personalized explanations, and may refer to tools and regulations specific to Social Security, such as the *Dictionary of Occupational Titles* or the medical-vocational grid rules. The SSA doesn't send you a copy of the technical rationale, but it's a part of every claimant's file and can provide insightful information about why your claim was denied. They're very useful to review when considering whether to appeal a denial notice. We have included a number of actual technical rationales in Appendix B.

Personalized explanation rationales for denial notices you received in the mail won't be in your DDS file, but the technical rationales and official determination forms will be. Your DDS keeps your file for only about six months. After that, it's sent to a storage facility. You should ask your local SSA Field Office for help locating the file and getting you a copy.

You must appeal denials in writing within 60 days of the date that you receive the notice. The SSA assumes that you received the letter five days after the date printed on the letter, unless you can show you received it later. In other words, the appeal deadline is generally 65 days from the date the denial notice was sent.

If you don't appeal within 60 days, you risk losing your right to appeal the denial and will have to start from scratch. The SSA rarely makes exceptions for a late appeal, but if you have a good excuse, like an unexpected hospitalization, the SSA might overlook a late appeal request.

Continuing Disability Review Rationales

Personalized explanations for continuing disability review (CDR) denials will include the above information in addition to the dates and reasons you were granted disability in the prior decision and why the SSA no longer considers you disabled. Examples include determining that you have had medical improvement, finding that you resumed full-time work, or discovering an error in your prior determination. (CDR claims are covered in Chapter 14.)

TIP

If you miss the appeal deadline, you can always start over again with a new initial application, have it denied, and then appeal. Given the time involved, however, try to avoid starting over.

C. Appeal Basics

The SSA will enclose information on how to appeal the agency's decision with your denial or termination notice.

Beginning the appeal process isn't difficult. You simply call your local Social Security Field Office and tell them that you want to appeal a denial or termination of your benefits. The SSA will send you the proper forms and tell you where to mail them when they're completed. The different levels of appeal are discussed in detail in Section E, below.

You can also file an appeal online at www.ssa.gov/apply/appeal-decision-we-made. The online process is too lengthy to reproduce here, but the SSA guides you through the form step by step with instructions and examples. You can even complete part of the form at one time and come back later to finish it.

If you're nearing the 60-day deadline for filing the appeal forms, write a letter to the SSA stating that you will be appealing and asking for the forms.

If you live near an SSA Field Office, the easiest way to speed things along might be to go in person to complete the forms and ask any questions you might have of the Social Security representative. Even if you're filling out the forms at home, you can still call the Field Office for help completing them. Here are details on different types of appeals:

- To appeal from a denial of initial benefits, you must file Forms SSA-561-U2, SSA-3441-BK, and SSA-827. This starts your first level of appeal for reconsideration. (These forms are discussed in more detail in Section E1, below, and are filed at your local Social Security Field Office.)

- To appeal from an initial termination of benefits, you must file Forms SSA-789-U4 and SSA-3441-BK. This starts your first level of appeal for reconsideration. (These forms are discussed in more detail in Section E2, below, and are filed at your local Social Security Field Office.)

- To appeal from a denial by the SSA of a reconsideration claim, you must file Forms HA-501, SSA-3441-BK, and SSA-827. This starts your appeal to an administrative law judge (ALJ). (These forms are discussed in more detail in Section E3, below, and are filed at your local Social Security Field Office.)

- To appeal from denial of a claim before an ALJ, you must file Form HA-520. This starts your appeal to the Appeals Council. (This form is discussed in more detail in Section E4, below, and is mailed directly to the Appeals Council.)

- To appeal from denial by the Appeals Council, you can sue the SSA in federal district court, as discussed in more detail in Section E5, below.

It's possible to have your claim reopened and evaluated again without formally appealing. Reopenings are explained in Section F, below. Also, if you lose all of your appeals, you can file another initial claim and start all over again, as discussed in Section G, below.

1. How Long Appeal Decisions Take

The first level of appeal in most states— reconsideration of an initial denial by DDS—is the quickest, because your file is likely still at DDS.

In a reconsideration, your file is simply reviewed by a different medical consultant and examiner from the pair that made the original decision. If DDS doesn't have to wait for additional medical records and the agency's caseload is not too high, you might get a decision in as quickly as a month. However, a DDS agency with a heavy caseload could take five months or longer to complete the reconsideration review.

Similarly, if you're appealing a termination of benefits (where a disability hearing officer reviews the agency's decision to terminate), it might take less than a month to get a determination if the hearing officer doesn't have a large backlog of claims and all of the records you want reviewed are already in your file. But it's more likely that you'll have to wait several months.

Once you get to the next level of appeal after reconsideration (requesting a hearing with an administrative law judge), the process really slows down—you could easily wait for a year or longer before your hearing is scheduled. On further appeal to the Appeals Council, you'd probably be lucky to get any kind of answer within a year.

Appeals to a federal court typically take about a year to hear back, but several years is also quite possible. Federal court judges aren't like administrative law judges, who decide only disability claims. They have many kinds of cases on their schedule that have nothing to do with Social Security disability, so your claim will have to wait its turn.

2. Receiving Benefits While Appealing

If you're receiving benefits and the SSA decides to stop paying you after

a continuing disability review (see Chapter 14), you can continue receiving your benefits while you appeal to an administrative law judge (42 U.S.C. § 1383(a)(7)), if the SSA determined that one of the following situations applies:

- You are no longer eligible for SSDI because your condition has improved.
- You are no longer eligible for SSI.
- Your SSI will be reduced.

If you want your benefits to continue, you must tell the SSA within ten days of when you receive the denial notice, by signing and returning Form SSA-795. The local SSA Field Office should send you this form along with the termination notice. But beware: If you continue benefits through your appeals and lose, you may have to repay the SSA.

TIP

More information on appeals. If you have questions about your right to appeal, call the SSA at 800-772-1213 or call your local SSA Field Office. All calls to the SSA are confidential. You can also find a considerable amount of information about appeals, including many forms and pamphlets, on the official Social Security website at www.ssa.gov or at Nolo's sister website for disability resources, www.disabilitysecrets.com.

D. Your Right to Representation

Some people handle their own Social Security appeal. But you can appoint a lawyer, a friend, or someone else—called your *authorized representative*—to help you. The SSA will work with your lawyer or representative just as it would work with you. At the first level of appeal, many claimants don't have representation. But this changes the further along claimants move through the appeals process. By the time they're ready to see an administrative law judge, about 80% of claimants have decided to use a lawyer or another representative.

Your representative can act for you in most Social Security matters and will receive a copy of all SSA correspondence. Your representative cannot charge or collect a fee from your disability benefits without first getting the SSA's written approval. (For more information on using and paying a lawyer or representative, see Chapter 15.)

E. Four Levels of Appeal

There are four levels of appeal of an SSA decision. The appeal levels are:

1. reconsideration of your claim by DDS
2. hearing with an administrative law judge
3. review by the Appeals Council, and
4. filing a suit in federal court.

Each step is discussed below. The request for reconsideration is discussed twice—once for original claims, and once for terminations or reductions in benefits following a continuing disability review.

1. Request for Reconsideration of Original Claim

As mentioned above, Social Security must notify you when your claim is denied. The exact language of the notice depends on whether your claim is for SSDI, SSI, a combination of both, or additional sub-categories such as dependents benefits (see Chapter 1). The denial notice example below is for an initial SSDI claim, but you can expect similar language in any initial denial notice.

In addition to letting you know that you aren't entitled to benefits, the denial notice may explain other basic information about Social Security disability claims, as well as your right to appeal. A personalized explanation paragraph about your medical condition will be included either in the text of the denial notice or on a separate attachment.

Contact your local Social Security Field Office for help initiating your reconsideration appeal. Do not contact DDS directly, as they don't accept appeal applications. (The Field Office will send DDS your prior file for reconsideration and DDS will then contact you, as was done on your initial claim. Once a DDS reconsideration examiner has your file, you or your representative will communicate with the DDS officer.) You can still call the Field Office and ask any general questions about appeals that you want, but specific issues about your disability determination decision need to be taken up with the DDS examiner.

Notice From Social Security Administration Denying Initial DDS Claim (Page 1)

Social Security Notice

From: Social Security Administration

Date:

Claim Number:
- ☐ Disability Insurance Benefit
- ☐ Disabled Widow/Widower Benefits
- ☐ Childhood Disability Benefit

We have determined that you are not entitled to disability benefits based on the claim that you filed. The attached page explains why we decided that you are not disabled. However, you may appeal this determination if you still think you are disabled.

The determination on your claim was made by an agency of the state. It was not made by your own doctor or by other people or agencies writing reports about you. However, any evidence they gave us was used in making this determination. Doctors and other people in the state agency who are trained in disability evaluation reviewed the evidence and made the determination based on Social Security law and regulations. The law is explained on the back of this page.

In addition, you are not entitled to any other benefits based on this application. If you applied for other benefits, you will receive a separate notice when a decision is made on that claim(s).

YOUR RIGHT TO APPEAL

If you think we are wrong, you can ask that the determination be looked at by a different person. This is called a reconsideration. IF YOU WANT A RECONSIDERATION, YOU MUST ASK FOR IT WITHIN 60 DAYS FROM THE DATE YOU RECEIVE THIS NOTICE. IF YOU WAIT MORE THAN 60 DAYS, YOU MUST GIVE US A GOOD REASON FOR THE DELAY. Your request must be made in writing through any Social Security office. Be sure to tell us your name, Social Security number, and why you think we are wrong. If you cannot write to us, call a Social Security office or come in and someone will help you. You can give us more facts to add to your file. However, if you do

Notice From Social Security Administration Denying Initial DDS Claim (Page 2)

not have the evidence yet, you should not wait for it before asking for a reconsideration. You may send the evidence in later. We will then decide your case again. You will not meet with the person who will decide your case. Please read the enclosed leaflet for a full explanation of your right to appeal.

NEW APPLICATION

You have the right to file a new application at any time, but filing a new application is not the same as appealing this decision. You might lose benefits if you file a new application instead of filing an appeal. Therefore, if you think this decision is wrong, you should ask for an appeal within 60 days.

Enclosures:

SSA Publication No. 05-10058

Form SSA-L443-U2 (2-90)

The denial notice on the preceding pages is the kind you might expect to see if your initial DDS claim is denied.

a. Complete the Forms

The forms you need to request a reconsideration are:

- Form SSA-561-U2, *Request for Reconsideration*
- Form SSA-3441-BK, *Disability Report —Appeal,* and
- Form SSA-827, *Authorization to Disclose Information to the Social Security Administration (SSA).*

CAUTION

You must use forms provided by the SSA. You can get them at your local SSA Field Office or by calling the SSA hotline at 800-772-1213, Monday through Friday (except holidays), from 8:00 a.m. to 7:00 p.m. If you're deaf or hard of hearing, TTY service representatives are available at the same times at 800-325-0778. You can also download many necessary forms from the Social Security Administration website at www.ssa.gov. These forms aren't available from DDS. Each form comes with its own instructions. Also, if you ask, the SSA will help you fill them out.

TIP

You can request a reconsideration online. Instead of filling out the forms below, you can visit www.ssa.gov/apply/appeal-decision-we-made/request-reconsideration to handle the whole appeal online.

i. Form SSA-561-U2, *Request for Reconsideration*

If you're not sure whether this is the correct form to file, look at the letter you received from the SSA. Use this form if the letter says you have the right to file a request for reconsideration. If you have further questions, call 800-772-1213 or contact your local SSA office.

Here are instructions on how to fill out the form, with a completed sample at the end.

❶ **Name of Claimant:** Enter your name or the name of the person on whose behalf you're requesting reconsideration.

❷ **Claimant SSN:** Enter your Social Security number (or the number of the person you're filing for).

❸ **Claim Number:** Enter the claim number if it's different from the Social Security number.

❹ **Issue Being Appealed:** Simply put in the broad issue, such as "disability."

❺ **"I Do Not Agree. ... My Reasons Are:"** Briefly discuss the decision you disagree with and why you disagree with it. Use the back of the form or a continuation sheet if you need more room. For example, you could write, "I don't agree with Social Security's statement that I can lift 50 pounds and stand 6–8 hours daily. My doctor told me not to lift more than 20 pounds, and my back hurts if I stand longer than 30 minutes. I intend to submit more medical information, as well as my treating doctor's opinion about my limitations."

Form SSA-561-U2, *Request for Reconsideration* (Page 1)

Form **SSA-561-U2** (10-2022) UF
Discontinue Prior Editions
Social Security Administration

Page 1 of 4
OMB No. 0960-0622

REQUEST FOR RECONSIDERATION

NAME OF CLAIMANT:	CLAIMANT SSN:	CLAIM NUMBER: *(If different than SSN)*
❶ Myrtle Johnson	123-45-6789 ❷	❸

ISSUE BEING APPEALED: *(Specify if retirement, disability, hospital or medical, SSI, SVB, overpayment, etc.)*
❹ Disability

I do not agree with the Social Security Administration's (SSA) determination and request reconsideration.
My reasons are:

❺ Arthritis and my illness is chronic. Also, I reviewed my denial, and no real doctor in the SSA saw the evidence. I want a real doctor to look at my medical evidence and explain their reasoning, not just a bureaucrat.

SUPPLEMENTAL SECURITY INCOME (SSI) OR SPECIAL VETERANS BENEFITS (SVB) RECONSIDERATION ONLY
THREE WAYS TO APPEAL

I want to appeal your determination about my claim for **SSI** or **SVB**. I have read about the three ways to appeal.
I have checked the box below:

❻ ☒ **CASE REVIEW - You can pick this kind of appeal in all cases.** You can give us more facts to add to your file. Then we will decide your case again. You do not meet with the person who decides your case.

☐ **INFORMAL CONFERENCE - You can pick this kind of appeal in all SSI cases except for medical issues. In SVB cases, you can pick this kind of appeal only if we are stopping or lowering your SVB payment.** You will meet with a person who will decide your case. You can tell that person why you think you are right. You can give us more facts to help prove you are right. You can bring other people to help explain your case.

☐ **FORMAL CONFERENCE - You can pick this kind of appeal only if we are stopping or lowering your SSI or SVB payment.** This meeting is like an informal conference, but we can also get people to come in and help prove you are right. We can do this even if they do not want to help you. You can question these people at your meeting.

CONTACT INFORMATION

CLAIMANT SIGNATURE - *OPTIONAL:*	NAME OF CLAIMANT'S REPRESENTATIVE: *(If any)*
MAILING ADDRESS: ❼ 2300 Ilard Way	MAILING ADDRESS:

CITY:	STATE:	ZIP CODE:	CITY:	STATE:	ZIP CODE:
Baltimore	MD	43200			

TELEPHONE NUMBER: *(Include area code)*	DATE:	TELEPHONE NUMBER: *(Include area code)*	DATE:
❽ 1-(555)-555-5555	1/27/24		

TO BE COMPLETED BY SOCIAL SECURITY ADMINISTRATION

1. HAS INITIAL DETERMINATION BEEN MADE? ☐ Yes ☐ No	**FIELD OFFICE DEVELOPMENT (GN 03102.300)** ☐ NO FURTHER DEVELOPMENT REQUIRED
2. IS THIS REQUEST FILED TIMELY? ☐ Yes ☐ No	☐ REQUIRED DEVELOPMENT ATTACHED
(If "NO", attach claimant's explanation for delay. Refer to GN 03101.020)	☐ REQUIRED DEVELOPMENT PENDING, WILL FORWARD OR ADVISE STATUS WITHIN 30 DAYS
SOCIAL SECURITY OFFICE ADDRESS AND DATE APPEAL RECEIVED:	**SSI CASES ONLY - GOLDBERG KELLY (GK)** **(SI 02301.310)** RECIPIENT APPEALED AN ADVERSE ACTION: ☐ WITHIN 10 DAYS AFTER RECEIVING THE ADVANCE NOTICE; ☐ AFTER THE 10-DAY PERIOD AND GOOD CAUSE EXISTS FOR EXTENDING THE TIME LIMIT ☐ PAYMENT CONTINUATION APPLIES AND INPUT MADE TO SYSTEM

NOTE: Take or mail the **completed original** to your local Social Security office, the Veterans Affairs Regional Office in Manila, or any U.S. Foreign Service post and keep a copy for your records.

Claims Folder

❻ **Three Ways to Appeal:** This section explains the different ways to handle an SSI appeal. Read it and mark your preference here.

❼ **Mailing Address:** On the left side, sign the form (this is optional) and enter your address. If you have a legal representative handling your appeal (see Chapter 15), that person must sign on the right side and enter an address, and must complete and return Form SSA-1696, *Claimant's Appointment of Representative*. The SSA can't discuss your case with your legal representative until the agency receives Form SSA-1696.

❽ **Telephone Number:** Provide your daytime phone number.

ii. Form SSA-3441-BK, *Disability Report—Appeal*

Use this form to update your disability information when appealing. Here are instructions on how to fill it out. A completed sample, filled out by the claimant's spouse, follows (starting on page 3 of the form—pages 1 and 2 don't have any places for you to fill in information).

❶ **Section 1:** Complete this section to give the SSA your name, daytime telephone number, and other basic information.

❷ **Section 2:** Put the contact information here for someone like a spouse or friend. If there's no one you can put down, enter n/a.

❸ **Section 3:** Record any changes in your medical condition since you last completed a disability report form. Answer the questions as thoroughly as possible. Mention all changes in your impairments,

symptoms, limitations, daily needs, and daily activities. In the example given, the claimant's mental disorder has worsened and she was diagnosed with a new heart problem.

❹ **Section 4:** Provide any new information about your medical treatment and include information such as tests, hospitals, clinics, doctors, or other facilities involved in your treatment.

❺ **Section 5:** List other people who might have information about your condition. It could be almost anyone, such as attorneys, welfare agencies, vocational rehab services, insurance companies, and even correctional facilities. You aren't limited by the examples the form provides.

❻ **Section 6:** List the medications you're currently taking. Include the name, the date they were first prescribed, the reason why they were prescribed, the dosage, and any side effects you've experienced.

❼ **Section 7:** Describe any changes in your activities since the last disability decision. Specify here how your condition has worsened. For example, if you had to stop doing chores or gave up a hobby since your last decision, discuss why you can no longer do those activities here. If needed, you can include more detail in Section 10, Remarks.

❽ **Section 8:** Discuss any work or type of special job training or trade or vocational school you've had since you last completed a disability report form.

Form SSA-3441-BK, *Disability Report—Appeal* (Page 3)

Form **SSA-3441-BK** (01-2021) UF
Discontinue Prior Editions
Social Security Administration

Page 3 of 10
OMB No. 0960-0144

DISABILITY REPORT - APPEAL

For SSA Use Only - Do not write in this box.

Related SSN   Number Holder

If you are filling out this report for someone else, please provide information about him or her. When a question refers to "you", "your," it refers to the person who is applying for disability benefits.

❶ | SECTION 1 - INFORMATION ABOUT THE DISABLED PERSON

1.A. Name (First, Middle, Last, Suffix)
Anne Brown

1.B. Social Security Number
555-55-5555

1.C. Daytime Phone Number, including area code (include IDD and country codes if outside the U.S. or Canada) 303-555-5534

☐ Check this box if you do not have a phone number where we can leave a message

1.D. Alternate Phone Number, another number where we may reach you, if any

1.E. Email address (Optional) Brown11@yahoo.com

❷ | SECTION 2 - CONTACTS

Give the name of someone (**other than your doctors**) we can contact who knows about your medical conditions, and can help you with your claim (e.g., friend or relative)

2.A. Name (First, Middle, Last)
Sam Brown

2.B. Relationship to Disabled Person
Husband

2.C. Mailing Address (Street or PO Box), include apartment number or unit if applicable
472 11th Street

City	State/Province	ZIP/Postal Code	Country (if not U.S.)
Montrose	CO	80299	

2.D. Daytime Phone Number, including area code (include IDD and country codes if outside the U.S. or Canada) 303-555-5534

2.E. Can this person speak and understand English?   ☒ Yes   ☐ No

If no, what language does the contact person prefer?

2.F. Who is completing this form?

☐ The person who is applying for disability. (**Go to Section 3 - MEDICAL CONDITIONS**)

☒ The person listed in 2.A. (**Go to Section 3 - MEDICAL CONDITIONS**)

☐ Someone else (Please complete the information below)

2.G. Name (First, Middle, Last)

2.H. Relationship to Disabled Person

2.I. Mailing Address (Street or PO Box), include apartment number or unit if applicable

City	State/Province	ZIP/Postal Code	Country (if not U.S.)

2.J. Daytime Phone Number, including area code (include IDD and country codes if outside the U.S. or Canada)

Form SSA-3441-BK, *Disability Report—Appeal* (Page 4)

❸ **SECTION 3 - MEDICAL CONDITIONS**

3.A. Since you last told us about your medical conditions, has there been any **CHANGE** (for better or worse) in your previously described physical or mental conditions?

☒ Yes, approximate date change occurred: _____ A month ago _____   ☐ No

If yes, please describe in detail:
My wife has chronic schizophrenia. She is more withdrawn and seems to be more out of touch with reality. Her auditory hallucinations came back. Her psychiatrist had to increase her Clozaril.

3.B. Since you last told us about your medical conditions, do you have any **NEW** physical or mental conditions?

☒ Yes, approximate date of new conditions: _____ 10-11-21 _____   ☐ No

If yes, please describe in detail:
Anne developed a new heart condition--an abnormal heart rhythm that affects her ability to lift and carry. (See Section 10, Remarks)

If you need more space, use SECTION 10 - Remarks on the last page

❹ **SECTION 4 - MEDICAL TREATMENT**

4.A. Have you used any other names on your medical or educational records? Examples are maiden name, other married name, or nickname.

☐ Yes   ☒ No

If yes, please list the other names used:

4.B. Since you last told us about your medical treatment, have you seen a doctor or other health care provider, received treatment at a hospital or clinic, or **do you have a future appointment scheduled**?

☒ Yes   ☐ No (Go to SECTION 6 - MEDICINES)

4.C. What type(s) of condition(s) were you treated for, or will you be seen for?

☒ Physical   ☒ Mental (including emotional or learning problems)

If you answered "Yes" to 4.B., please tell us who may have **NEW** medical records about any of your physical or mental conditions (including emotional or learning problems).

Use the following pages to provide information for up to three (3) providers. **Complete one page for each provider.** If you have more than three providers, list them in SECTION 10 - REMARKS on the last page.

Please include
- doctors' offices
- hospitals (including emergency room visits)
- clinics
- mental health center
- other health care facilities

Only list the providers you have seen since you last told us about your medical treatment.

Form SSA-3441-BK, *Disability Report—Appeal* (Page 5)

SECTION 4 - MEDICAL TREATMENT (Continued)
Provider 1

4.D. Name of facility or office The Mental Health Group	Name of health care provider who treated you Dr. Claude Edwards

ALL OF THE QUESTIONS ON THIS PAGE REFER TO THE HEALTH CARE PROVIDER ABOVE

Phone Number 303-123-4567	Patient ID# (if known)

Address
10001 Forest View Drive

City Denver	State/Province CO	ZIP/Postal Code 80255	Country (if not U.S.)

Dates of Treatment (approximate date, if exact date is unknown)

Office, Clinic, or Outpatient visits at this facility	Emergency Room Visits at this facility	Overnight Hospital Stays at this facility	
First visit Jan. 3, 2020	Date	Date in	Date out
Last visit Dec. 1, 2021	Date	Date in	Date out
Next scheduled appointment (if any) March 2022	Date	Date in	Date out
	☒ None	☒ None	

What new or updated medical conditions were treated or evaluated?
Schizophrenia.

What new or updated treatment did you receive for the above conditions? (Do not list medicines or tests in this box.)
Medication and psychotherapy.

Has this provider performed or sent you to any tests? Please include tests you are scheduled to have in the future.   ☒ Yes (Please complete the information below.)   ☐ No (Go to the next page.)

KIND OF TEST	DATES OF TEST(S)	KIND OF TEST	DATES OF TEST(S)
☐ Biopsy (list body part)		☐ MRI/CT Scan (list body part)	
☒ Blood Test (not HIV)	10/21	☐ Speech/Language Test	
☐ Breathing test		☐ Treadmill (exercise test)	
☐ Cardiac Catheterization		☐ Vision Test	
☐ EEG (brain wave test)		☐ X-Ray (list body part)	
☐ EKG (heart test)			
☐ Hearing test		☐ Other (please describe)	
☐ HIV Test			
☐ IQ Testing			

If you need to list more tests, use SECTION 10 - REMARKS on the last page.

**If you do not have any more providers to describe, go to
SECTION 5 - OTHER MEDICAL INFORMATION on page 8.**

Form SSA-3441-BK, *Disability Report—Appeal* (Page 6)

Form **SSA-3441-BK** (01-2021) UF   Page 6 of 10

SECTION 4 - MEDICAL TREATMENT (Continued)
Provider 2

4.D. Name of facility or office Cardiology Associates	Name of health care provider who treated you Dr. Howard Stuckey

ALL OF THE QUESTIONS ON THIS PAGE REFER TO THE HEALTH CARE PROVIDER ABOVE

Phone Number 303-555-2222	Patient ID# (if known)

Address
Suite 200, 1201 Canyon Blvd.

City Denver	State/Province CO	ZIP/Postal Code 80302	Country (if not U.S.)

Dates of Treatment (approximate date, if exact date is unknown)

Office, Clinic, or Outpatient visits at this facility	**Emergency Room Visits at this facility**	**Overnight Hospital Stays at this facility**	
First visit August 2021	Date	Date in	Date out
Last visit October 2021	Date	Date in	Date out
Next scheduled appointment (if any) Jan. 2022	Date [X] None	Date in [X] None	Date out

What new or updated medical conditions were treated or evaluated?
Heart rhythm problem: atrial fibrillation.

What new or updated treatment did you receive for the above conditions? (Do not list medicines or tests in this box.)
Shock to restore normal rhythm.

Has this provider performed or sent you to any tests? Please include tests you are scheduled to have in the future.   ☐ Yes (Please complete the information below.)   ☐ No (Go to the next page.)

KIND OF TEST	**DATES OF TEST(S)**	**KIND OF TEST**	**DATES OF TEST(S)**
☐ Biopsy (list body part)		☐ MRI/CT Scan (list body part)	
☐ Blood Test (not HIV)		☐ Speech/Language Test	
☐ Breathing test		☐ Treadmill (exercise test)	
☐ Cardiac Catheterization		☐ Vision Test	
☐ EEG (brain wave test)		[X] X-Ray (list body part)	
[X] EKG (heart test)	Jan. 2022	Chest	
☐ Hearing test		[X] Other (please describe)	Jan. 2022
☐ HIV Test		Echocardiogram	
☐ IQ Testing			

If you need to list more tests, use SECTION 10 - REMARKS on the last page.

**If you do not have any more providers to describe, go to
SECTION 5 - OTHER MEDICAL INFORMATION on page 8.**

Form SSA-3441-BK, *Disability Report—Appeal* (Page 7)

SECTION 4 - MEDICAL TREATMENT (Continued)
Provider 3

4.D. Name of facility or office	Name of health care provider who treated you

ALL OF THE QUESTIONS ON THIS PAGE REFER TO THE HEALTH CARE PROVIDER ABOVE

Phone Number	Patient ID# (if known)

Address

City	State/Province	ZIP/Postal Code	Country (if not U.S.)

Dates of Treatment (approximate date, if exact date is unknown)

Office, Clinic, or Outpatient visits at this facility	Emergency Room Visits at this facility	Overnight Hospital Stays at this facility	
First visit	Date	Date in	Date out
Last visit	Date	Date in	Date out
Next scheduled appointment (if any)	Date	Date in	Date out
	☐ None	☐ None	

What new or updated medical conditions were treated or evaluated?

What new or updated treatment did you receive for the above conditions? (Do not list medicines or tests in this box.)

Has this provider performed or sent you to any tests? Please include tests you are scheduled to have in the future.　☐ Yes (Please complete the information below.)　☐ No (Go to the next page.)

KIND OF TEST	DATES OF TEST(S)	KIND OF TEST	DATES OF TEST(S)
☐ Biopsy (list body part)		☐ MRI/CT Scan (list body part)	
☐ Blood Test (not HIV)		☐ Speech/Language Test	
☐ Breathing test		☐ Treadmill (exercise test)	
☐ Cardiac Catheterization		☐ Vision Test	
☐ EEG (brain wave test)		☐ X-Ray (list body part)	
☐ EKG (heart test)			
☐ Hearing test		☐ Other (please describe)	
☐ HIV Test			
☐ IQ Testing			

If you need to list more tests, use SECTION 10 - REMARKS on the last page.

If you have been treated by more providers, use SECTION 10 - REMARKS on the last page.

Form SSA-3441-BK, *Disability Report—Appeal* (Page 8)

Form **SSA-3441-BK** (01-2021) UF   Page 8 of 10

⑤   **SECTION 5 - OTHER MEDICAL INFORMATION**

5. Since you last told us about your other medical information, does anyone else have medical information about any of your **physical or mental** conditions (including emotional and learning problems) or are you scheduled to see anyone else?

This may include:
- workers' compensation
- vocational rehabilitation services
- insurance companies who have paid you disability benefits
- prisons and correctional facilities
- attorneys
- social service agencies
- welfare agencies
- school/education records

   ☐ YES (Please complete the information below.)

   ☒ NO (Go to SECTION 6 - MEDICINES.)

Name of Organization	Claim or ID Number (if any)

Address

City	State/Province	ZIP/Postal Code	Country (if not U.S.)

Name of Contact Person	Phone Number

Date of First Contact	Date of Last Contact	Date of Next Contact (if any)

Reasons for Contacts

If you need to list more people or organizations, use SECTION 10 - REMARKS on the last page.

⑥   **SECTION 6 - MEDICINES**

6. Are you currently taking any medicines (prescription or non-prescription)?

   ☒ YES (Please complete the information below. You may need to look at your medicine containers.)

   ☐ NO (Go to SECTION 7 - ACTIVITIES.)

NAME OF MEDICINE	IF PRESCRIBED, NAME OF DOCTOR	REASON FOR MEDICINE	SIDE EFFECTS YOU HAVE
Clozaril	Dr.Claude Edwards	Treat schizophrenia	Sleepy, weak
Pradaxa	Dr. Stuckey	Anticoagulation	Bruise easily
MULTAQ	Dr. Stuckey	Control heart rhythm	Tired

If you need to list more medicines, use SECTION 10 - REMARKS on the last page.

Form SSA-3441-BK, *Disability Report—Appeal* (Page 9)

❼
SECTION 7 - ACTIVITIES

7. Since you last told us about your activities, has there been any **change** (for better or worse) in your previously described daily activities due to your physical or mental conditions? (Examples of daily activities are household tasks, personal care, getting around, hobbies and interests, social activities, etc.)

☒ Yes   ☐ No

If yes, please describe in detail:
```
Anne is now able to perform daily chores like cooking a simple meal and
cleaning. But she also has to be told to bathe and is less willing to
socialize with family members or guests.
```

If you need more space, use SECTION 10 - REMARKS on the last page.

❽
SECTION 8 - WORK AND EDUCATION

8.A. Since you last told us about your work, have you worked or has your work changed?

☐ Yes   ☒ No

If yes, you will be asked to provide additional information.

8.B. Since you last told us about your education, have you completed or are you enrolled in any type of GED classes, specialized job training, trade school, vocational school or college classes?

☐ Yes   ☒ No

If yes, what type?

Date(s) attended:

Degree(s) attained, if any:

Date of attainment (MM/YYYY):

If you need more space, use SECTION 10 - REMARKS on the last page.

❾
SECTION 9 - VOCATIONAL REHABILITATION, EMPLOYMENT, OR OTHER SUPPORT SERVICES

9. Since you last told us about your vocational rehabilitation, have you participated, or are you participating in:
- an individual work plan with an employment network under the Ticket to Work Program?
- an individualized plan for employment with a vocational rehabilitation agency or any other organization?
- a Plan to Achieve Self-Support (PASS)?
- an individualized education program (IEP) through an educational institution (if a student age 18-21)?
- any program providing vocational rehabilitation, employment services, or other support services to help you go to work?

☐ Yes (Please complete the information below.)

☒ No (Go to SECTION 10 - REMARKS.)

Name of Organization or School

Name of Counselor, Instructor, or Job Coach	Phone Number

Address

City	State/Province	ZIP/Postal Code	Country (if not U.S.)

Date when you started participating in the plan or program:

If you need more space, use SECTION 10 - REMARKS on the last page.

Form SSA-3441-BK, *Disability Report—Appeal* (Page 10)

Form **SSA-3441-BK** (01-2021) UF   Page 10 of 10

⑩   **SECTION 10 - REMARKS**

Use this space to provide any information you could not show in earlier sections of this form or additional information you feel we should know about. Please be sure to include the number of the question you are answering (For example, 3A, 4D, etc.).

3A. Anne needs almost constant supervision, will wander off if I don't watch her, and is increasingly suspicious of other people's motives. She wears her clothes in bizarre ways. Anne has a severe, chronic mental disorder. She can function minimally under the supervision and support of our family. Contrary to what the DDS stated when they denied her benefits, Anne's mental condition has not significantly improved and is even worse. Dr. Edwards emphasized we must provide a highly supportive home for Anne or she will decompensate even more. I think she is clearly worse and Dr. Edwards agrees. She's certainly not better, and her benefits should not have stopped. The DDS says she now can work. This is wrong as shown by medical records and Dr. Edwards' opinion. I wonder if a real medical specialist reviewed her records and why they didn't contact Dr. Edwards for a statement.

Anne's heart condition limits her physically now, in addition to her mental condition, and her medications make her lethargic. Dr. Stuckey says he can't completely control her rhythm and that she's at risk for stroke. Anne can sometimes do simple things like making a sandwich or doing a little dusting, but our daughters do most of the dusting and cleaning. Anne often refuses to help, saying "I'm just not interested."

I forgot to mention that Anne has a narrowed heart valve that causes her rhythm problem and also decreases her ability to do physical chores; she tires very easily. She certainly has not been able to work since her benefits were denied, in my opinion. Please contact her treating doctors.

Date Report Completed MM/DD/YYYY: 11/11/2021

❾ Section 9: Indicate whether you have had any vocational rehabilitation, employment, or other support services since you last completed a disability report form.

❿ Section 10: Use this space to continue your answer to any questions. Make sure you note the question number to which you are referring. You can also use this section to let the SSA know about any other information you think the agency should consider in the appeal process. For example, if DDS didn't evaluate a particular impairment or relied on incorrect information provided by your treating physician, state that.

If you run out of room, attach a blank sheet of paper as a continuation sheet. At the top of the sheet, write your name, Social Security number, and SSA-3441-BK, Continued.

iii. Form SSA-827, *Authorization to Disclose Information to the Social Security Administration (SSA)*

Use this form to allow your medical sources—doctors, hospitals, clinics, nurses, social workers, family members, friends, governmental agencies, employers, and anyone else who has medical information about you—to release protected information to the SSA. It's important to understand that Form SSA-827 releases all of your medical records, including information pertaining to drug abuse, alcoholism, mental disorders (excluding psychotherapy notes), and sexually transmitted diseases. You can't pick and choose what medical information is released under this form, but keep in mind that Social Security employees are trained to handle this information with sensitivity. The agency takes confidentiality very seriously, particularly with regard to medical records.

Here are instructions on how to fill out the form.

❶ Reading the Form. This section reminds you to read the form (Page 1) and associated legal comments on Page 2 (not included below).

❷ Information Being Disclosed. You should read the top part of the form carefully to make sure you understand what information will be available to the SSA when you sign the form.

❸ Signature. The claimant, legal guardian of a child claimant, or legal representative must sign the form in the block indicated. If the claimant isn't signing, specify the relationship of the person who is signing (such as parent or legal representative).

❹ Date, Address, and Daytime Phone Number. Enter the requested information.

❺ Signature of Witness. All forms must be witnessed. Many medical sources won't honor an authorization to release information unless it's witnessed. The witness can be any competent adult, including your spouse, neighbor, or a social worker. Include the address of the witness.

Form SSA-827, *Authorization to Disclose Information to the Social Security Administration (SSA)*

Form **SSA-827** (03-2020)
Discontinue Prior Editions

Page 1 of 2
OMB No. 0960-0623

Whose Records to be Disclosed	
NAME *(First, Middle, Last, Suffix)* Myrtle A. Johnson	
SSN 987-65-4321	Birthday *(MM/DD/YYYY)* 04/22/52

AUTHORIZATION TO DISCLOSE INFORMATION TO THE SOCIAL SECURITY ADMINISTRATION (SSA)

❶ ** PLEASE READ THE ENTIRE FORM, BOTH PAGES, BEFORE SIGNING BELOW **

❷ I voluntarily authorize and request **disclosure** (including paper, oral, and electronic interchange):

OF WHAT *All my medical records; also education records and other information related to my ability to perform tasks. This includes Specific permission to release:*

1. **All records and other information regarding my treatment, hospitalization, and outpatient care for my impairment(s)** including, and not limited to:
   - Psychological, psychiatric or other mental impairment(s) (excludes "psychotherapy notes" as defined in 45 CFR 164.501)
   - Drug abuse, alcoholism, or other substance abuse
   - Sickle cell anemia
   - Records which may indicate the presence of a communicable or noncommunicable disease; and tests for or records of HIV/AIDS
   - Gene-related impairments (including genetic test results)
2. **Information about how my impairment(s) affects my ability to complete tasks and activities of daily living, and affects my ability to work.**
3. **Copies of educational tests or evaluations,** including Individualized Educational Programs, triennial assessments, psychological and speech evaluations, and any other records that can help evaluate function; also teachers' observations and evaluations.
4. **Information created within 12 months after the date this authorization is signed,** as well as past information.

FROM WHOM

• **All medical sources** (hospitals, clinics, labs, physicians, psychologists, etc.) including mental health, correctional, addiction treatment, and VA health care facilities • All educational sources (schools, teachers, records administrators, counselors, etc.) • Social workers/rehabilitation counselors • Consulting examiners used by SSA • Employers, insurance companies, workers' compensation programs • Others who may know about my condition (family, neighbors, friends, public officials)	**THIS BOX TO BE COMPLETED BY SSA/DDS (as needed).** Additional information to identify the subject (e.g., other names used), the specific source, or the material to be disclosed:

TO WHOM The Social Security Administration and to the State agency authorized to process my case (usually called "disability determination services"), **including contract copy services, and doctors or other professionals consulted during the process.** [Also, for international claims, to the U.S. Department of State Foreign Service Post.]

PURPOSE Determining my **eligibility for benefits,** including looking at the combined effect of any impairments that by themselves would not meet SSA's definition of disability; and whether I can manage such benefits.

☐ Determining whether I am **capable of managing benefits ONLY** (check only if this applies)

EXPIRES WHEN This authorization is good for 12 months from the date signed (below my signature).

- I authorize the use of a copy (including electronic copy) of this form for the disclosure of the information described above.
- I understand that there are some circumstances in which this information may be redisclosed to other parties (see page 2 for details).
- I may write to SSA and my sources to revoke this authorization at any time (see page 2 for details).
- SSA will give me a copy of this form if I ask; I may ask the source to allow me to inspect or get a copy of material to be disclosed.
- **I have read both pages of this form and agree to the disclosures above from the types of sources listed.**

❸ PLEASE SIGN USING BLUE OR BLACK INK ONLY
INDIVIDUAL authorizing disclosure Signature

IF not signed by subject of disclosure, specify basis for authority to sign
☐ Parent of minor ☐ Guardian ☐ Other personal representative (explain)

(Parent/guardian/personal representative sign here if two signatures required by State law)

❹

Date Signed 10/22/21	Street Address 2300 Illiard Way		
Phone Number (with area code) (201) 472-0001	City Baltimore	State MD	ZIP 22212

WITNESS *I know the person signing this form or am satisfied of this person's identity:*

❺

Signature	IF needed, second witness sign here (e.g., if signed with "X" above)
Phone Number (or Address)	Phone Number (or Address)

This general and special authorization to disclose was developed to comply with the provisions regarding disclosure of medical, educational, and other information under P.L. 104-191 ("HIPAA"); 45 CFR parts 160 and 164; 42 U.S. Code section 290dd-2; 42 CFR part 2; 38 U.S. Code section 7332; 38 CFR 1.475; 20 U.S. Code section 1232g ("FERPA"); 34 CFR parts 99 and 300; and State law.

iv. Forward Forms to the SSA

Once you have completed all the forms, attach copies of any evidence showing that the original determination was incorrect, like medical records not included in the initial decision. Then fold all forms and documents in thirds, insert them in a standard business envelope, and mail to your local Social Security office. If you aren't sure where that office is, call 800-772-1213. Keep a copy of each form and the originals of your attached evidence for your records. You may use a nonstandard envelope if your papers won't fit into a standard one.

b. Reconsideration Appeal Process

The reconsideration is a complete review of your claim. It takes place at DDS, but it's done by a team made up of a medical consultant and a claims examiner who weren't part of the initial decision. This means that the examiner and medical consultant who were involved in the denial of your initial claim can't help decide your reconsideration claim.

The DDS reconsideration team will look at all the evidence submitted for the original decision, plus any new evidence you include with your reconsideration request.

c. Review Your File Before the Reconsideration

The SSA uses a computer system known as Electronic Records Express (ERE) that securely stores information about disability claims in a way that makes it easier to transfer between agencies. In the past, a paper file had to be physically shipped from one location to another—for example, from a claimant's local Social Security Field Office to DDS and many other potential destinations. This greatly slowed down the decision-making process. Now, every branch and component of the SSA has immediate access to data entered by any other component.

When you complete an application or appeal online, that information goes into a highly secure and confidential electronic folder assigned to your name and Social Security number. If you apply or appeal in person at an SSA Field Office, the official will scan the information into your electronic folder, even if you fill out a paper form. Perhaps most importantly, medical evidence—which can be extensive, and would be an unwieldy amount of paper to handle if printed out—is scanned into your electronic folder by either the Field Office or DDS.

The SSA still keeps any physical records that you submitted, but the agency no longer keeps its own decisional documents in a paper file. In the past, for example, you could find various medical consultant write-ups and administrative documents in the paper file. These are now in electronic form. So if you want to see how the SSA made its decision, you need access to your electronic disability records. Fortunately, the SSA recognizes your or your representative's right to information.

The access and disclosure policies are no different for paper and electronic records. SSA officials have the authority to copy appropriate disability information in your electronic file to a CD-ROM. You might have to go to your local Field Office to get a copy in person, or you may be able to get them to mail you a copy. If you don't have a computer, you might have to pay a fee to have the information printed.

If your appeal is at the hearing level and you have a representative, they'll likely be able to access your electronic file from a secure Social Security website that's frequently used to submit medical records. Your representative should review your electronic folder with you and make sure it contains all relevant documents.

As you review your file, note any inaccuracies and missing information. Ask the SSA to copy pages for you if necessary. You can't write directly on records in your file, but you can ask that information be added (such as new medical information and even your own statements about your condition).

Pay special attention to the following documents in your file.

Your medical records. Make sure all your important medical records are included. If your medical records contain comments from your treating doctor about your disability, note what they say. You or your representative might need to contact your treating doctor for clarification of a statement or to contest a comment you think is inaccurate.

EXAMPLE: Orris is a 53-year-old former electrician with heart disease who is being treated for heart failure. His regular doctor tells the SSA that Orris can do light work. But when Orris walks a half block, he gets short of breath, his heart races, he breaks out in a sweat, and he gets dizzy. Orris can't stand for more than ten minutes at a time without chest pain. He takes several medications, and the side effects make Orris feel even worse. Based on the statement from his doctor, the SSA decided that Orris could do light work, and denied his application for benefits. Orris's treating doctor might not know the SSA's definition of light work, which requires lifting up to 20 pounds and standing or walking six to eight hours a day. Orris must talk with his treating doctor, explain Social Security's definition of light work, discuss why he can't do it, and ask for a new letter accurately describing his limitations to be used in his reconsideration claim. This is especially important because, if the SSA hadn't found that Orris could do light work, he would have been awarded benefits due to his age, education, and work experience.

Sometimes, treating doctors don't provide information the SSA needs, even if they have it. Your doctor might have written down that you experience knee pain, but not that you have migraines. Or your doctor might give the SSA all the notes in their records, but the notes are too vague to provide helpful details. For example, say your doctor keeps records of every visit, but each progress note just mentions that you experience pain from arthritis. This isn't very helpful information for disability examiners, who need to determine how severe your arthritis is by looking at notes that contain examinations of swollen joints, range of motion, results of blood tests showing rheumatoid arthritis, and your doctor's considered professional opinion about what you can and can't do. If your doctor's notes are lacking, be sure the DDS reconsideration examiner at knows that your doctor didn't adequately evaluate your complaints. You can ask the examiner to send you to a consultative examination on the agency's dime to get a physical or mental evaluation.

Your work records. If DDS made inaccurate statements about your previous work history, you'll need to correct it. Compare your statements on any Form SSA-3369-F6, *Vocational Report*, or other forms, against those made by the SSA on your denial rationale. If necessary to correct your SSA file, ask your employer or coworkers to submit written information to DDS.

Form SSA-831: *Disability Determination and Transmittal.* This form is the official disability determination document used by DDS. One copy stays with your file and other copies go to other SSA offices, but you won't get a copy. Most of the information on the front of the form will be of little use to you anyway because of the number of internal codes used by the SSA. But it should contain the name and signature of both the disability examiner and the DDS medical consultant who worked on your claim.

Attached to Form SSA-831 (or on Form SSA-4268, *Explanation of Determination*) should be the technical rationale used in making your disability determination. Because the technical rationale contains a lot more detailed information than the personalized explanation rationale you were sent with your denial notice, it is in your interest to look it over, even though it might include bureaucratic language you don't understand. By reviewing the technical rationale, you can see the step-by-step reasoning that the SSA used to deny your claim. The DDS examiner handling your claim writes these rationales. (See Appendix B for examples of technical rationales.)

Note the name of the medical consultant who signed the SSA-831 and the number of the specialty code near their name. Specialty code information can be valuable if you suspect that the wrong kind of doctor reviewed your claim. For instance, claims for mental impairments should always be evaluated by a psychiatrist or psychologist, and children's claims for physical impairments should always be evaluated by a pediatrician.

Residual functional capacity (RFC) forms. You might not have an RFC form in your file if your claim was denied because your impairments were considered to be not severe (mild or slight). Otherwise, your file should contain a physical RFC (Form SSA-4734-BK, *Residual Functional Capacity Assessment*), a mental RFC (Form SSA-4734-F4-SUP, *Mental Residual Functional Capacity Assessment*), or both. Depending on how complex your claim is, you may have more than one of each type of RFC in your file.

Check the RFC forms to see if they accurately reflect all of your limitations. Do you agree with the medical consultant's assessment of what you can and can't do? Did the consulting doctor say that you can lift more weight or walk longer than your treating doctor thinks you can? Did they incorporate other restrictions in your RFC that were suggested by your treating doctor, like avoiding excessive fumes or restrictions on frequent bending of your back? Did the medical consultant underestimate your mental limitations by stating that you can complete tasks in a timely manner? If the consultant's RFC isn't in line with your treating doctor's opinion, the RFC form must include an explanation of why your doctor's recommendations weren't used. (See Chapter 8 for more on RFCs.)

Form SSA-2506-BK, *Psychiatric Review Technique Form* (PRTF). This form should be in your file if you have a mental health condition. The PRTF is meant to ensure that the DDS psychiatrist or psychologist considers all of the important information about your mental impairment. The PRTF should contain the following information:

- The dates covered by the assessment, the medical consultant's signature, and the date the form was signed.
- A medical summary of your claim (Section I).
- The medical consultant's record of pertinent signs, symptoms, findings, functional limitations, and effects of treatment that have a significant bearing on your case (Section II). This section should also include the medical consultant's reasoning about why you received a particular medical determination.
- The medical consultant's record of signs, symptoms, and findings that show the presence of the categories of mental disorders in the Listing of Impairments (Section III).
- The medical consultant's rating of functional limitations that are relevant to your ability to work (Section IV).

Look for any errors on the PRTF, such as the wrong treatment dates, an incorrect diagnosis of your mental condition, or statements made by the medical consultant that contradict statements made by your treating psychiatrist or psychologist. Check for any inaccuracies in the medical consultant's analysis of your medical history—for example, did the consultant say that you didn't have any episodes where your mental symptoms worsened, but you were hospitalized several times for auditory hallucinations?

Make sure you establish that a medical consultant—and not the claims examiner, who isn't a doctor—is the one who made the medical determination about what you can and can't do. You can do that by reviewing the medical consultant's notes to make sure they explain how the consultant reached their decision. If you don't see an explanation (or your file lacks these notes entirely), the determination may have been made by a claims examiner instead of a consulting doctor. When you file your appeal, insist that a medical consultant review your claim. (See Chapter 6 for suggestions on how to demand that a medical consultant review your file.)

You can also double-check the handwriting of the medical consultant to make sure that their signatures match the handwriting on the PRTF or RFC form. If they don't, the medical consultant may have simply signed a form completed by the examiner, and you should address this discrepancy in your appeal.

d. Reconsideration decision.

Not many disability claims are approved at the reconsideration level. If your claim is denied again, you'll receive a denial notice and explanation similar to the one you received when your initial claim was denied. The only difference is that the explanation should contain an evaluation of any new evidence or new claims brought up when you filed your request for reconsideration. The next step after a reconsideration denial is to request a hearing before an administrative law judge. (See Section E3, below.)

CAUTION
Medical consultant involvement in reconsiderations. Social Security rules require a medical consultant to be a part of every decision on the initial claim, but don't make it clear whether the requirement extends to reconsideration. If you don't think that a doctor was involved in making a medical determination that resulted in your claim being denied, raise this issue in your appeal.

DDS Medical Consultant Codes

Here is a list of the codes and the type of doctor each refers to.

1	Anesthesiology	29	Orthopedics
2	Ambulatory Medicine	30	Osteopathy
3	Audiology	31	Pathology
4	Cardiology	32	Pediatrics
5	Cardiopulmonary	33	Physiatry
6	Dermatology	34	Physical Medicine
7	E.E.N.T. (Eyes, Ears, Nose, and Throat)	35	Plastic Surgery
8	E.N.T. (Ear, Nose, and Throat)	36	Preventive Medicine
9	E.T. (Ear and Throat)	37	Psychiatry
10	Emergency Room Medicine	38	Psychology
11	Endocrinology	39	Public Health
12	Family or General Practice	40	Pulmonary
13	Gastroenterology	41	Radiology
14	Geriatrics	42	Rehabilitative Medicine
15	Gynecology	43	Rheumatology
16	Hematology	44	Special Senses
17	Industrial Medicine	45	Surgery
18	Infectious Diseases	46	Urology
19	Internal Medicine	47	Other
20	Neurology	48	Speech–Language Pathology
21	Neuro-ophthalmology	49	Child and Adolescent Psychiatry
22	Neuropsychiatry	50	Allergy and Immunology
23	Neonatology	51	Thoracic Surgery
24	Nephrology	52	Nuclear Medicine
25	Obstetrics	53	Neurosurgery
26	Occupational Medicine	54	Vascular Surgery
27	Oncology	55	Critical Care
28	Ophthalmology		

2. Request for Reconsideration of Continuing Disability Claim

Everybody who receives disability benefits has their case reexamined periodically to determine whether they're still disabled, a process known as a *continuing disability review* (CDR). (See Chapter 14 for more on CDRs.) The SSA can end your benefits after a CDR if the agency determines that your condition has improved and you can now work, or if you don't cooperate with the CDR.

The decision to end your benefits is made by a DDS medical consultant and examiner team. You'll receive a notice from the SSA explaining why the agency is stopping your disability payments. The notice will say something along the following lines:

We are writing to tell you that we have looked at your case to see if your health problems are still disabling. After looking at all of the information in your case carefully, we found that you are not disabled under our rules as of (*month/year*).

The notice will come with a brief explanation of how the DDS team reached its decision. If you want to appeal, you must use Form SSA-789-U4 to request a reconsideration of a CDR cessation (when the SSA stops your benefits following a review). The form lets the SSA know that you want to appeal your cessation at a hearing before a disability hearing officer (DHO). But before your claim goes to the hearing officer, a different DDS team will review the termination decision to see if it was incorrect. (See Subsection b, below). This team might reverse your cessation of benefits, in which case you won't need to have a hearing. But if the team agrees with the initial decision to end your benefits, you'll still get a chance to have a hearing officer review the cessation.

Although the DHOs aren't doctors or psychologists, they're allowed to form their own opinions about your medical impairments. In fact, some DHOs reverse half the CDR termination cases they hear, saving the claimants' benefits. They often aren't hesitant to disregard the judgments of two different DDS teams who thought your benefits should stop. So you have a fairly good chance that your benefits will be continued, and you have nothing to lose by appealing.

As you prepare for the hearing, keep in mind that the SSA must have good evidence that you've had significant work-related medical improvement (except for certain exceptions discussed in Chapter 14). Whether you've had medical improvement is the critical issue at your hearing—and it's a matter of medical judgment, so the SSA must consider your treating doctor's opinion. If your case is borderline, the SSA will likely resolve any inconsistencies in your favor, and your benefits should continue.

Beware of Copycat Reconsiderations

When you appeal a claim to DDS for reconsideration, the medical consultant and the examiner selected to review your file must be different from those who denied your initial claim. This doesn't mean the new DDS team will do a thorough examination—a few examiners and medical consultants are "copycats" who simply copy the initial denial determination instead of doing another review.

If your reconsideration is denied and you presented new evidence or had new issues you wanted considered, visit DDS and look at your file. Check the technical rationale and medical consultant review notes to make sure DDS didn't ignore the new information. If it looks like your claim was rubber-stamped without a thorough review, request that your claim be reopened and that the new medical and nonmedical evidence be considered. You have a right to request such a reopening (see Section F, below), which you can do with a telephone call or letter to the DDS director. If DDS refuses, you have an even stronger basis for appeal.

a. Complete the Forms

To request a reconsideration determination by a disability hearing officer, you must file Form SSA-789-U4, *Request for Reconsideration— Disability Cessation*, with your local Social Security Field Office. If it takes a while before your hearing is scheduled and you have new information you want the hearing officer to consider, you can update the information you originally provided on Form SSA-454-BK with Form SSA-3441-BK, which you must request from your local Social Security Field Office or get online. It's not available from DDS.

i. Form SSA-789-U4, *Request for Reconsideration—Disability Cessation*

Form SSA-789-U4 is easy to complete, and your local Field Office will be happy to help with any questions you have. The form is a multicopy form separated by carbon paper. A sample form with instructions on how to fill it out is included below.

The top of the form asks for the name and Social Security number of the claimant (you or the person receiving benefits for whom you're filling out the form). If the wage earner is different from the claimant—for example, in cases of dependents benefits—then the name of that person is required too, along with their Social Security number. If you're appealing cessation of SSI benefits, there's a blank space for your spouse's name and Social Security number. The blank space in the upper-right-hand corner is called "For Social Security Office Use Only" but has some important little boxes in it. If you let the SSA know that you want your notices sent in Spanish, the representative processing your claim should check the

Foreign Language Notice box. Or if you requested your benefits to continue during your appeal, the Benefit Continuation box should be checked. (See Section C2 for more information.)

Continuation of benefits applies only to appeals within Social Security (reconsideration, the ALJ hearing, and the Appeals Council). You can't continue to receive benefits while appealing to a federal court.

The Disability and SSI boxes refer to the type of benefit involved in your claim. Disability refers to Social Security Disability Insurance (SSDI) and SSI refers to Supplemental Security Income. Check the box under the Disability or SSI category (or both, if you have a concurrent claim) that reflects the specific kind of benefit you're receiving. For example, most adults on SSDI would check "worker" under the Disability category.

Next, the form asks you for the specific reasons you don't agree with the determination to stop your benefits. Remember, this is just a form to get your appeal started. You don't need to make long arguments here—just the basic facts. For example, you might say, "My arthritis has not improved, and the decision to stop my benefits ignored the opinion of my treating doctor that I haven't gotten better. I have additional information from my doctor showing that I haven't improved."

The next line lets you list any additional information you want to submit. For example, you can write "New medical

---

Getting Benefits During an Appeal

If you want your benefits to continue during your appeals, you have only ten days from the time you receive the CDR benefit cessation notice to file your appeal. The CDR benefit termination notice (see Chapter 14) will remind you of this fact. Since the SSA allows five days for mailing time, a more accurate way to count the days you actually have is to add 15 days to the date on the cessation notice.

If you continue receiving benefits through your appeals and ultimately lose, you may have to repay the SSA. In case you're asked to repay the benefits you were paid during appeals, you should also file Form SSA-632-BK, *Request for Waiver of Overpayment Recovery*, with your local Social Security Field Office. One of the exemptions for having to repay benefits is if you're unable to do so. Even if you eventually have to pay back some benefits, the amount can be as small as $10 per month.

Your benefits will usually stop if you lose your appeal before an ALJ. An exception to this rule is for claims that are also under Appeals Council or federal court review, and which are sent back (remanded) to the ALJ for a new decision. If you're already receiving benefits during this time, the Appeals Council or the court may require the SSA to continue your benefits until a final ALJ decision. (This situation doesn't apply to most claimants.) But if your claim is denied by an ALJ and later allowed by the Appeals Council or federal court, you might be able to collect back benefits, even if they were terminated.

Form SSA-789-U4, *Request for Reconsideration*

Form **SSA-789** (01-2019) UF
Discontinue Prior Editions
Social Security Administration

OMB No. 0960-0349

REQUEST FOR RECONSIDERATION - DISABILITY CESSATION RIGHT TO APPEAR
(SEE REVERSE SIDE FOR PAPERWORK/PRIVACY ACT NOTICE)

FOR SOCIAL SECURITY OFFICE USE ONLY
(DO NOT WRITE IN THIS SPACE)

NAME OF CLAIMANT Howard E. Walker	SOCIAL SECURITY NUMBER 888-88-8888

☐ FO Code _____

NAME OF WAGE EARNER OR SELF-EMPLOYED PERSON (if different from Claimant)

SOCIAL SECURITY NUMBER

☐ Benefit Continuation

SPOUSE'S NAME AND SOCIAL SECURITY NUMBER (COMPLETE ONLY IN SUPPLEMENTAL SECURITY INCOME CASE)
Helen Walker   SSN 777-77-7777

☐ Foreign Language Notice _____

TYPE OF BENEFIT	DISABILITY			SSI		
	☒ WORKER	☐ WIDOW	☐ CHILD	☒ DISABILITY	☐ BLIND	☐ CHILD

I DO NOT AGREE WITH THE DETERMINATION TO STOP DISABILITY BENEFITS AND I REQUEST RECONSIDERATION.
My reasons are (reasons should relate to the basis for stopping disability benefits and be as specific as possible):
NOTE: If the notice of the determination on your claim is dated more than 65 days ago, include your reason for not making this request earlier. Include the date on which you received the notice.

There has been no significant improvement in my impairments. Furthermore, the DDS ignored my treating doctor's opinion about my physical and mental abilities.

I AM SUBMITTING THE FOLLOWING ADDITIONAL INFORMATION (If "NONE" write "NONE")
(Attach additional page if needed):

Russell Crane, M.D.—see attached records

CHECK BLOCK 1 AND THE STATEMENTS THAT APPLY <u>OR</u> CHECK BLOCK 2

☒ 1. **I (and/or my representative) wish to appear** at a disability hearing. The disability hearing will be with a person called a disability hearing officer and it will let me explain why I do not agree with the decision to stop benefits.

☐ I need an interpreter at the disability hearing - Language _____
(If you need an interpreter, SSA will provide one at no cost to you.)

OR

☐ 2. **I do not wish to appear nor do I wish a representative to appear for me** at the disability hearing. I have been advised of my right to have a disability hearing. I understand that a disability hearing will give me a chance to present witnesses. It will also let me explain to the disability hearing officer why my disability benefits should not end. I understand that this chance to be seen and heard could help the disability hearing officer learn about the facts in my case. The disability hearing officer would give me a chance to have people who know about my condition give information and explain how my condition keeps me from working and restricts my activities. I have been told about my right to representation at the disability hearing, including representation by an attorney or other person of my choice. Although the above has been explained to me, I do not want to appear at a disability hearing, or have someone represent me at a disability hearing. I prefer to have the disability hearing officer decide my case on the evidence in my file, plus any evidence that I submit or that may be obtained by the Social Security Administration. I have been advised that if I change my mind, I can request a disability hearing prior to the writing of a decision in my case. In this case, I can make the request with any Social Security office.

Excerpt From Form SSA-773-U4, *Waiver of Right to Appear—Disability Hearing*

I have been advised of my right to have a disability hearing. I understand that a hearing will give me an opportunity to present witnesses and explain in detail to the disability hearing officer, who will decide my case, the reasons why my disability benefits should not end. I understand that this opportunity to be seen and heard could be effective in explaining the facts in my case, because the disability hearing officer would give me an opportunity to present and question witnesses and explain how my impairments prevent me from working and restrict my activities. I have been given an explanation of my right to representation, including representation at a hearing by an attorney or other person of my choice.

Although the above has been explained to me, I do not want to appear at a disability hearing, or have someone represent me at a disability hearing. I prefer to have the disability hearing officer decide my case on the evidence of record plus any evidence that I may submit or which may be obtained by the Social Security Administration. I have been advised that if I change my mind, I can request a hearing prior to the writing of a decision in my case. In this event, I can make the request with any Social Security office.

records from my treating doctor." Then give your doctor's name and address. If you don't have enough room to enter all the new information, the Social Security representative will put it on additional pages.

At the bottom of the page are checkboxes asking if you or your representative wish to appear at the disability hearing and whether you need an interpreter.

You don't want to waive your right to attend a hearing unless it's going to be impossible for you to attend. The hearing gives you the chance to personally explain to the hearing office why you believe you're still disabled. Also, the hearing officer may notice something about you (such as hand tremors or delayed speech) that isn't obvious from the medical file but supports your contention that you're still disabled.

Another SSA form, SSA-773, is also used to waive your right to personally appear at the hearing. If you do waive your right to appear on Form SSA-789-U4, the hearing officer may ask you to also sign Form SSA-773 to make sure that you understand what it means to waive your rights. Form SSA-773 contains language (see excerpt above) that explains the nature and importance of the rights you give up when you sign Form SSA-773 or the waiver section of Form SSA-789.

On page 2 of Form SSA-789 (not included above), sign your name and enter your address and phone number. Make sure you provide an address where the SSA can reach you. Also enter the name and address of your representative, if you have one. Your representative may sign the form for you. If you can only make an "X" for a signature, two witnesses who know you will also have to sign the form and provide their addresses.

ii. Form SSA-3441-BK, *Disability Report—Appeal*

Use this form to update your disability information. This is the same form you may have used when you filed for reconsideration of your initial claim. (Instructions for completing this form are discussed in Section E1, above.)

Even if you've already filed this form, you'll need to file it again. But all you have to do this time is include any changes in your medical condition that weren't included in your previous Form SSA-3441-BK. If you're not sure what has changed since the last time you completed an SSA-3441-BK, or if you've been receiving disability benefits for a long time and completed a different form in the past, go ahead and complete the form as thoroughly as you can. It's better to repeat some facts than to leave out something important.

If you haven't already filed a Form SSA-3441-BK, then complete the entire form.

b. DDS Review

As mentioned above, before a hearing officer can look at your case, a new DDS team—consisting of a medical consultant and a claims examiner—will review the initial decision to terminate your benefits. The purpose of the new review is to see if you can continue to receive benefits without having to go through the inconvenience of a hearing. The second team might reverse the first denial and grant you a continuation of your benefits, either because they think the first team made a mistake or because DDS received important additional information that changed the determination. In either case, the hearing is no longer necessary.

But if the second DDS team determines that the decision to end your benefits was correct, they will send an advisory decision to the hearing officer stating that you are to be considered medically improved and capable of performing some type of work.

c. Review Your File Before the Hearing

You'll want to review four categories of documents in your file.

Work activity records. Review Section E1c, above, for an explanation of what to look for.

Your medical records, including any letters sent to DDS by your treating doctor. (See Section E1c.)

RFC forms. Section E1c contains an explanation of what to look for.

Technical rationale. Technical rationales are internal SSA forms containing long explanations of DDS decisions. You can find an explanation of them in Section E1, above, and examples in Appendix B. The technical rationale will be on Form SSA4268, *Explanation of Determination,* or on one of the following forms:

- Form SSA-833-U3, *Cessation or Continuance of Disability or Blindness Determination and Transmittal (SSDI),* or
- Form SSA-834-U3, *Cessation or Continuance of Disability or Blindness Determination and Transmittal (SSI).*

Look also for SSA-831, *Disability Determination and Transmittal,* and an associated rationale from your initial disability determination. This form helps you understand DDS's reasoning in saying that you are no longer disabled.

d. Attend a Hearing With a Disability Hearing Officer

Disability hearing officers (DHOs) aren't medical doctors or psychologists, and don't need to have any formal medical training. Some are experienced disability examiners or examiner supervisors promoted into a hearing officer position and given administrative training on how to conduct hearings.

When the DHO receives your appeal, the DHO may allow your appeal for continued benefits without requiring a hearing. If so, you'll receive a written notice to that effect.

Otherwise, the hearing officer will send you a notice with the hearing date and location. If the DHO's office is far from your home, you can call that office to ask for a location closer to you. The notice will have the telephone number for the hearing office, which you can also obtain from your local Social Security Field Office.

Before the hearing, the DHO will send you a notice asking for a list of the people you expect to attend the hearing with you, including witnesses or a representative, such as a lawyer. Witnesses—including your spouse, other relatives, and friends who are knowledgeable about your limitations—can testify that your activities continue to be severely limited. This can be very helpful to your claim. You can't bring spectators to the hearing. If you bring people who don't have a legitimate reason to be present, the hearing officer has the authority to ask them to leave.

The hearing officer will make sure that your hearing takes place in privacy. Hearings are informal and don't take place in a court-room. Chances are you'll sit at a large table with the hearing officer and your representa-tive or attorney, if any. There won't be any-body present to argue against you or attempt to prove that you're not actually disabled.

DHOs may vary somewhat in how they handle hearings. However, they all must consider any new evidence you submit about your jobs and work experience, your medical impairments, your treating doctor's opinions, and your own statements about why you think the agency was wrong to end your benefits. The hearing officer must make sure that all of your allegations have been adequately developed in your file.

The DHO should introduce everybody, make sure all attendees understand why they're at the hearing, and briefly go over how the hearing will be conducted.

You will undoubtedly be asked why you think your benefits shouldn't be terminated. You have the right to ask questions during the hearing, and you'll want to ask DHO what significant medical improvement DDS claims that you've experienced that allows you to work and what level of work DDS thinks you can do. (Levels of work are explained in Chapters 8 and 9.)

You or your representative should review your file before the hearing so that you can show the hearing officer why the DDS decision was wrong.

For example, you can demonstrate that your medical records show you've had no significant medical improvement. Or you can show that your condition has improved somewhat, but not to the extent that you'd be able to do the jobs recommended in your cessation notice.

After the hearing has ended, you can expect a written decision from the hearing officer within a few weeks. If you're denied again, you'll receive a notice and explanation similar to those you received in your previous denials. You can appeal this denial to an administrative law judge, during which your benefits can continue. (See "Getting Benefits During an Appeal," above.)

3. Appeal to Administrative Law Judge

If your request for reconsideration—whether for an initial claim or a termination of benefits following a continuing disability review—is denied and you want to appeal further, you must request a hearing before an administrative law judge (ALJ) within 60 days after you've received the written notice of your denial. Because the SSA assumes you'll receive your notice in the mail within five days after it's sent, you actually have 65 days from the date on your denial notice to appeal. The ALJ can dismiss your case if you miss the appeal deadline without a good reason for doing so.

Your benefits can continue through the ALJ hearing process, as long as you choose that option when submitting your hearing request. But if you lose your appeal, you might have to repay the benefits you received during that time (see "Getting Benefits During an Appeal" in Section E2, above).

ALJs are attorneys who work for the SSA's Office of Hearings Operations (OHO) (formerly known as the Office of Disability Adjudication and Review, or ODAR). OHO is a division of the Social Security Administration, a federal agency, and is separate from state DDS agencies that evaluate initial disability applications, continuing disability reviews, and reconsideration claims. ALJs aren't like judges who work in the civil and criminal courts. Their powers are limited to Social Security matters. Most of their work involves upholding or overturning DDS decisions to deny or terminate disability benefits. There is no jury or opposing counsel in an ALJ hearing, and while the ALJ may consult medical or vocational experts to help make a disability determination, it's up to the ALJ alone to decide whether you're awarded benefits.

You might think that an ALJ's decision would be very similar to that of DDS or a hearing officer because they both use the same set of rules for determining disability. But ALJs usually pay little attention to DDS determinations. Because ALJs aren't doctors, however, it's sometimes difficult for them to decipher the technical terms doctors use and accurately evaluate medical information in a claimant's file. Although ALJs can ask consulting medical experts to help them better understand claimants' medical records, this is infrequently done. Some ALJs grant or continue benefits when a DDS doctor doesn't think a claimant has very many limitations. Overall, ALJs approve about half of the claims that reach them.

a. Complete the Forms

To request an ALJ hearing, you need three forms:

- Form HA-501-U5: *Request for Hearing by Administrative Law Judge*
- Form SSA-3441-BK: *Disability Report —Appeal,* and
- Form SSA-827: *Authorization to Disclose Information to the Social Security Administration (SSA)* (see Section E1a).

CAUTION
You must use forms provided by the SSA. You can obtain them at your local SSA Field Office or by calling the SSA hotline at 800-772-1213, Monday through Friday (except holidays), from 800 a.m. to 7:00 p.m. If you're deaf or hard of hearing, TTY service representatives are available during the same time at 800-325-0778. You can also download many necessary forms from the Social Security Administration website at www.ssa.gov. These forms aren't available from DDS.

TIP
You can request a hearing online. Instead of filling out the forms below, you can visit www.ssa.gov/apply/appeal-decision-we-made/request-hearing to handle the appeal online.

i. Form HA-501-U5, *Request for Hearing by Administrative Law Judge*

This is the form you use to request a hearing before an administrative law judge. Instructions and a completed sample follow.

❶ **Name of Claimant:** Enter your name or the name of another person on whose behalf this appeal is being filed.

❷ **Claimant SSN:** Enter your Social Security number or the number of the claimant requesting a hearing.

❸ **Claim Number:** Enter the claim number if it's different from the Social Security number.

Form HA-501-U5, *Request for Hearing by Administrative Law Judge*

Form **HA-501** (06-2022)
Discontinue Prior Editions
Office of Hearings Operations

OMB. No. 0960-0269
Page 1 of 2

REQUEST FOR HEARING BY ADMINISTRATIVE LAW JUDGE

*(Take or mail the **completed original** to your local Social Security office, the Veterans Affairs Regional Office in Manila or any U.S. Foreign Service post and keep a copy for your records)*

See Privacy
Act Notice

❶ 1. Claimant Name
Myrtle Johnson

2. Claimant SSN ❷
123-45-6789

3. Claim Number, if different ❸

❹ 4. I REQUEST A HEARING BEFORE AN ADMINISTRATIVE LAW JUDGE. I disagree with the determination because:
The reviewer did not consider my doctor's statement that I met the listing and my illness is even worse. Also, although a SSA doctor apparently signed my denial there is no evidence in my file showing a doctor did anything but sign what someone else wrote.

An Administrative Law Judge of the Social Security Administration's Office of Hearings Operations or the Department of Health and Human Services will be appointed to conduct the hearing or other proceedings in your case. You will receive notice of the time and place of a hearing at least 75 days before the date of hearing from the Social Security Administration, and 20 days before the date of hearing from the Department of Health and Human Services.

❺ 5. I have additional evidence to submit. ☒ Yes ☐ No

Name and source of additional evidence, if not included.
Paul Dogood,M.D.,455 Medical Way, Baltimore, MD 43407

Submit your evidence to the hearing office within 10 days. Your servicing Social Security office will provide the hearing office's address. Attach an additional sheet if you need more space.

6. Do not complete if the appeal is a Medicare issue. Otherwise, check one of the blocks **❻**

☒ I wish to appear at a hearing.

☐ I do not wish to appear at a hearing and I request that a decision be made based on the evidence in my case. (Complete Waiver Form HA-4608)

Representation: You have a right to be represented at the hearing. If you are not represented, your Social Security office will give you a list of legal referral and service organizations. If you are represented, complete and submit form SSA-1696 (Appointment of Representative) unless you are appealing a Medicare issue.

❼ 7. CLAIMANT SIGNATURE (OPTIONAL)
Myrtle Johnson

DATE
6/24/24

8. NAME OF REPRESENTATIVE (if any) ❽

DATE

RESIDENCE ADDRESS
2300 Illard Way

ADDRESS

CITY	STATE	ZIP CODE	CITY	STATE	ZIP CODE
Baltimore	MD	43202			

TELEPHONE NUMBER	FAX NUMBER	TELEPHONE NUMBER	FAX NUMBER
1-(555)-555-5555			

TO BE COMPLETED BY SOCIAL SECURITY ADMINISTRATION- ACKNOWLEDGMENT OF REQUEST FOR HEARING

9. Request received on _____ by: _____

(Date)   (Print Name)   (Title)

(Address)   (Servicing FO Code)   (PC Code)

10. Was the request for hearing received within 65 days of the reconsidered determination? ☐ Yes ☐ No
   If no, attach claimant's explanation for delay and supporting documents if any.

11. If claimant is not represented, was a list of legal referral service organizations provided? ☐ Yes ☐ No

12. Interpreter needed ☐ Yes ☐ No

Language (including sign language): _____

13. Check one: ☐ Initial Entitlement Case
☐ Disability Cessation Case or ☐ Other Postentitlement Case

14. HO COPY SENT TO: _____ HO on _____
☐ Claims Folder (CF) Attached: ☐ Title (T) II; ☐ T XVI;
☐ T VIII; ☐ T XVIII; ☐ T II CF held in FO ☐ Electronic Folder
☐ CF requested ☐ T II; ☐ T XVI; ☐ T VIII; ☐ T XVIII
(Copy of email or phone report attached)

16. CF COPY SENT TO: _____ HO on _____
☐ CF Attached: ☐ Title (T) II; ☐ T XVI; ☐ T XVIII
☐ Other Attached: _____

15. Check all claim types that apply:
☐ Retirement and Survivors Insurance Only   (RSI)
☐ Title II Disability - Worker or child only   (DIWC)
☐ Title II Disability - Widow(er) only   (DIWW)
☐ Title XVI (SSI) Aged only   (SSIA)
☐ Title XVI Blind only   (SSIB)
☐ Title XVI Disability only   (SSID)
☐ Title XVI/Title II Concurrent Aged Claim   (SSAC)
☐ Title XVI/Title II Concurrent Blind   (SSBC)
☐ Title XVI/Title II Concurrent Disability   (SSDC)
☐ Title XVIII Hospital/Supplementary Insurance   (HI/SMI)
☐ Title VIII Only Special Veterans Benefits   (SVB)
☐ Title VIII/Title XVI   (SVB/SSI)
☐ Other - Specify:

❹ **I Request a Hearing Before an Administrative Law Judge … :** State the specific reasons why you feel the decision to deny or end your benefits is incorrect. If you need additional space, use a blank sheet of paper and label it "Continuation Sheet."

❺ **Evidence:** If you have new evidence to submit, specify where you got the evidence from. You have ten days from filing this form to submit the new evidence, but it's best if you submit it when you file this form.

❻ **Check whether you do or do not want to appear at the hearing:** Check the appropriate box. If you don't want to attend the hearing, you also need to complete Form HA-4608, *Waiver of Your Right to a Personal Appearance Before a Judge*, which you can get from your local Social Security office.

Your representative, if you have one, can attend the hearing on your behalf (without you). When that happens, the ALJ will make a decision based on the information in your file and your representative's statements, unless the ALJ believes your presence is necessary. If you don't have a representative and don't want to attend the hearing yourself, the ALJ can make a decision based solely on the written information in your file. If you indicate on Form HA-501-U5 and Form HA-4608 that you don't want to appear at a hearing and you change your mind later, you can attend the hearing.

❼ **Claimant Signature:** Sign and date the form and enter your address, daytime phone number, and fax number (if you or your representative have one).

❽ **Representative:** If a legal representative is handling your appeal (see Chapter 15), enter their contact information here. The SSA can't discuss your case with your legal representative until it receives Form SSA-1696. Your representative should handle the paperwork associated with SSA-1696.

Leave the rest of the form blank. The SSA will complete it.

ii. Form SSA-3441-BK, *Disability Report—Appeal*

Use this form to update your disability information. This is the same form you likely used when you filed for reconsideration of your initial denial or cessation of benefits. (Instructions for completing this form are in Section E1, above.) Even if you've already filed this form, you'll need to file it again. But you only need to include changes in your medical condition that weren't included in your previous Form SSA-3441-BK. If you're not sure what has changed since the last time you completed an SSA-3441-BK, or if you've been receiving disability benefits for a while and completed a different form in the past, go ahead and complete the form as thoroughly as you can. It's better to repeat some facts than to leave out something important.

If you haven't already filed a Form SSA-3441-BK, then complete the entire form.

iii. Forward Forms to the SSA

Once you have completed all the forms, attach copies of any evidence you have that can help show that your denial or cessation of benefits was incorrect (such as new medical records). Fold all forms and documents in thirds, insert them in a standard business envelope, and mail to your local Social Security office. If you aren't sure where that office is, call 800-772-1213. Keep a copy of each form and the originals of your attached evidence for your records. If you can't follow these SSA instructions for mailing because your documents won't fit in a standard envelope, you can use a larger one.

b. Notice of Disability Review

The Office of Hearing Operations will send you a written notice after it receives your request for a hearing. The main points of the letter are to tell you that:

- Your request has been received and your case is in the queue for a hearing.
- You have the right to hire a lawyer or other representative.
- You should submit any new medical evidence you get (such as X-rays, blood test results, or treatment notes from recent doctors' appointments).

For more information about your rights to hire a representative, see the sample Notice of Disability Review, below.

c. Prehearing Conference

The ALJ might decide to hold a pre-hearing conference in order to aid the decision-making process. You can also ask for a prehearing conference, although the ALJ doesn't have to grant your request. Prehearing conferences are normally held over the phone, unless the ALJ decides that a different format, like an in-person meeting or videoconference, is desirable. You'll be given reasonable notice of the time, place, and manner of the conference.

At the conference, the ALJ may discuss relevant issues, such as obtaining and sub-mitting medical records, that can speed up the hearing. The ALJ will make a record of the conference. If neither you nor your representative appear at the prehearing con-ference without a good reason, the SSA can dismiss your request for a hearing. The SSA will consider the following to be *good cause* for missing the conference:

- Actions by the SSA somehow misled you about the conference (you should be able to explain how).
- You have physical, mental, educational, or language problems that prevented you from attending.
- Some other unusual, unexpected, or unavoidable circumstance beyond your control prevented you from attending.

Other circumstances might, if docu-mented, establish good cause. For example:

- You were seriously ill, and your illness prevented you from contacting the SSA in person, in writing, or through a friend, relative, or other person.
- There was a death or serious illness in your immediate family.

Sample Notice of Disability Review (Page 1)

Social Security Administration

Refer to:
(000-00-0000)

Addressee _____

Address _____

Dear _____ :

We have received your request for hearing. We will notify you in writing of the time and place of the hearing at least seventy-five (75) days before the date of the hearing. You have indicated that you are not represented.

YOU HAVE THE RIGHT TO BE REPRESENTED BY AN ATTORNEY OR OTHER REPRESENTATIVE OF YOUR CHOICE. A representative can help you obtain evidence and help you and your witnesses, if any, prepare for the hearing. Also, a representative can question witnesses and present statements in support of your claim. If you wish to be represented, you should obtain a representative AS SOON AS POSSIBLE so your representative can begin preparing your case. Please phone us at the number shown above if you decide to obtain a representative.

If there is an attorney or other person whom you wish to act as your representative, you should contact that person promptly to avoid any undue delay in scheduling your hearing. If you are unable to find a representative, we have enclosed a list of organizations that may be able to help you locate one. As indicated on the enclosed list, some private attorneys may be willing to represent you and not charge a fee unless your claim is allowed. Your representative must obtain approval from the Social Security Administration for any fee charged. Also, if you are not able to pay for representation, and you believe you might qualify for free representation, the list contains names of organizations that may be able to help you.

Sample Notice of Disability Review (Page 2)

If you have any evidence that you did not previously submit, please send it to this office immediately. If you are unable to send the evidence before the hearing, please bring it with you to the hearing.

You will be able to see all of the evidence in your file at the hearing. If you wish to see it sooner, or have any questions regarding your claim, please call this office at _____ .

Please have your Social Security number available whenever you call.

Sincerely,

Enclosures
(List of Representatives)
(Travel Expense Information)

- Important records were destroyed or damaged by fire or another accidental cause.
- You were trying very hard to find necessary information to support your claim but did not find the information within the stated time period.

d. Attorney Advisor Proceedings

A prehearing proceeding might be held by an *attorney advisor* instead of an ALJ. (20 C.F.R. § 404.942.) The SSA has expanded the use of attorney advisors nationwide after several years of testing them out in a few states. Attorney advisors can help relieve an ALJ's workload because they have the authority to exercise some of the functions of an ALJ. An attorney advisor may review your file when you appeal to an ALJ, contact you or your representative for more information, or schedule a conference regarding your case. They might also review your claim if:

- New and material evidence is submitted.
- There's an indication that additional evidence is available.
- There's a change in the law or regulations.
- There's an error in the file.
- There's an indication that a fully favorable decision could be issued.

The last item in the above list is important because Social Security regulations allow attorney advisors to overrule DDS on both medical and nonmedical issues and approve your claim. (*Fully favorable* means you get everything you ask for—ongoing monthly benefits and any back pay that you're entitled to based on your alleged onset date.)

If an attorney advisor approves your claim, the SSA will send you written notice of a favorable decision, and you won't have to go to an ALJ hearing. If, for some reason, you still want a hearing despite having your claim already approved, you have 30 days to request one. Otherwise, the hearing will be automatically dismissed. (It isn't clear why you'd want to have an ALJ hearing if an attorney advisor already approved your claim for benefits, but that option is available to you.)

An attorney advisor can't deny your claim, but if the advisor doesn't issue a fully favorable decision, then your ALJ hearing will proceed as scheduled. If an attorney advisor prehearing proceeding isn't completed before a scheduled ALJ hearing, then the hearing will still occur on the scheduled date—unless you ask for a delay.

So, if an attorney advisor gets your claim, it's just one more opportunity for a favorable decision, with zero downside. Importantly, it could mean that you get a favorable decision much sooner than you would with a scheduled ALJ hearing. Federal regulations don't prohibit you from asking for an attorney advisor case review, but they don't provide a method for you to do so.

e. Schedule the Hearing

If your case isn't resolved in your favor during the prehearing review, you'll receive written notice that your hearing has been scheduled. You should receive the notice with the time and place of the hearing at least 75 days before it's scheduled to take place. If you don't receive 75 days' notice, you can either waive the notice requirement (in which case your hearing will remain scheduled for that date) or ask that your hearing be rescheduled for a later date.

You must submit any new evidence you want the judge to consider at least five business days before the hearing, and the evidence (such as medical records) can't be edited or changed in any way.

The ALJ can change the hearing date if you or your representative can't make it on the scheduled date or time. You can avoid a conflict by calling the judge's office to discuss the hearing date before the ALJ mails the notice. The telephone number should be on all paperwork you receive. (You can also easily find the phone number for the judge's office by asking your local Social Security Field Office or looking online at the SSA's Office of Hearings Operations at www.ssa.gov/appeals/ ho_locator.html.)

ALJs typically have large backlogs of cases, so you may have to wait a year or more for a hearing. The SSA generally assumes that one ALJ can hear about 500 cases per year, and in the past, ALJs have been responsible for scheduling their own hearings. New regulations allow the SSA to take a more active role in scheduling hearings in an attempt to get cases decided faster, but because the backlog cases is largely due to the number of disability applications, the agency can only do so much to speed up the process. Although the SSA continues to expand options for ALJs to conduct hearings, you shouldn't expect a quick decision. That's why it's always better to be approved at the DDS stages of review (initial or reconsideration). Your medical, cash, and other benefits will start much sooner.

f. Where Hearings Are Held

Hearings are held in person, over the phone, or through videoconference. The SSA will consider your preference when setting the time and place of your hearing. Often, a telephone or video hearing can be scheduled sooner than an in-person appearance, making these attractive options. But you have the right to have your hearing held in person ("live"). If your notice of hearing says that your hearing is going to be held through videoconference or over the phone, you can request to have a hearing in person at a date and location determined by the ALJ. You must object to the hearing method in writing within 30 days of receiving the hearing notice.

You can also object to the time or location of the hearing up to five days (or 30 days after you received the hearing notice, if that's the earlier date) before it's scheduled to occur. The SSA will try to accommodate reasonable requests. You should state what location and time you want, along with the reason for your request. Good causes for missing the above deadlines are acceptable, like if you have a serious illness or your representative must be at a different hearing. Using this information, the ALJ will decide what's appropriate, taking into account all factors involved, including their own hearing schedules.

During the COVID-19 national health emergency, the SSA had to become more flexible with the manner of hearing. Because in-person hearings weren't an option, the agency relied heavily on phone and video hearings to make sure that hearings could continue. As a result, many ALJs shifted to video and phone hearings as their preferred manner of conducting hearings. In May 2023, the SSA issued a proposed rule change that allows for video and phone hearings to be as standard as in-person hearings. While the rule change hasn't yet been adopted as of the time of publication, disability applicants should expect video and phone hearings to become more common.

i. Video hearings

During a video hearing, you and the other participants can see and hear one another through large screens. The ALJ will be in their office, and a technician will be with you at the video hearing location to make sure the videoconferencing equipment works smoothly.

Except for the equipment, a video hearing isn't different from an in-person hearing. The judge can see and speak with you and anyone who comes to the hearing with you, like your representative. You can see the judge, anyone in the same office as the judge, and anyone at another videoconference site (such as a medical or vocational expert). The SSA ensures that the video hearing transmission is secure and that your privacy is protected. You shouldn't prepare for a video hearing any differently than you would if you were attending a hearing in person.

All states have video hearing locations. The SSA doesn't videotape hearings, but it does make audio recordings, as it does for all hearings.

At-Home Video Hearings

In some circumstances, the ALJ can hold a video hearing using videoconference software that you can access from your laptop or smartphone at home. In these cases, the SSA will send you a secure link that you click on at the specified time and date for your hearing. A hearing technician will let you into the virtual conference room, where you'll be able to see the judge, your representative, and any other witnesses. Some at-home videoconferences may be "mixed media," with some parties appearing by video and others calling in on their phone. The standard procedures for these hearings are the same as they are for in-person hearings.

ii. In-person hearings

Hearings are held throughout the United States, usually in a federal building in a major city that houses other federal offices— but separate from DDS and SSA Field Offices. If you're scheduled for an in-person hearing, it will usually be held as close to your home as possible.

iii. Telephone hearings

Phone hearings bring claimants, judges, and witnesses together on a conference call for the proceedings. If you have a phone hearing, you (and your representative) will receive a call from the SSA office at the date and time of your scheduled hearing. A hearing technician will make sure that all parties are present on the line and will set up the recording equipment. Once everybody has been connected, the hearing will begin.

Telephone hearings were used almost exclusively during the COVID-19 pandemic and they remain a popular way to conduct hearings. While ALJs used to allow telephone appearances only in extraordinary circumstances, judges will now grant most requests for a phone hearing or even suggest one themselves. Telephone conferencing doesn't remove your right to question, cross-examine, or object to witnesses.

iv. Expense reimbursement for hearings

The SSA can reimburse you if you have to travel more than 75 miles to get to the hearing location. This applies both to video hearings at a location other than your home and to hearings in person. Travel reimbursement for basic transportation expenses, such as bus fare or gasoline and tolls, is generally covered. Expenses for meals, lodging, or taxicabs may be covered, but you'll need to ask the ALJ to approve them either before the hearing (if you anticipate them) or during the hearing (if they're unexpected).

You must submit your reimbursement request in writing to the hearing office as soon as possible after the hearing. List what you spent and attach receipts. Keep in mind that if you requested a change in the scheduled location of the hearing to a location farther from your residence, the SSA won't pay for any additional travel expenses.

Let the ALJ know as far as possible before the hearing if you need money for travel costs in advance. The SSA can advance payment to you only if you show that without the money, you can't travel to the hearing and back. When you receive travel money in advance, you must give the ALJ an itemized list of your actual travel costs and receipts within 20 days after your hearing. If you didn't spend the entire advance payment, the SSA will send you a notice of how much you owe. You need to pay the amount due back to the SSA within 20 days of receiving the notice.

g. Prepare for the Hearing

It's a very good idea to have a disability lawyer with you at an ALJ hearing. While an administrative hearing is far less formal than a civil or criminal court hearing (see Subsection h, below), it's still a legal proceeding. You can hire a representative after you file your hearing request if you don't have one already (see Chapter 15).

As explained in Section E3, above, when you file your request for a hearing, you must submit new evidence you want the ALJ to consider. But between the time you filed the request and your hearing, you're likely to have gotten additional medical treatment. Obtain records of any updated treatment, such as doctors' notes or X-rays, and send them to the ALJ as soon as possible.

Prepare in advance to talk about your impairments and limitations with the ALJ by thinking about specific examples of your physical or mental limitations you want the judge to know about. This will help reduce your anxieties about the hearing and increase your chances of convincing the judge.

i. Review your file

Sections E1 and E2, above, explain how you can review your file. Before the hearing, you (or your representative) will want to review the technical rationales behind your denials and the residual functional capacity reports from medical consultants. Also, check to see if your condition is a listed impairment (the Medical Listings are available on Nolo's website; see Appendix D). If so, read up about the factors that qualify as meeting the listing. Then look at the reports to see if the medical consultants made any errors in determining that you didn't meet a listing. If you don't have a listed impairment, look at whether the medical consultant made mistakes such as overstating your ability to work or ignoring important mental symptoms and limitations.

ii. Request your record and the evidence

The SSA will generally give you a free copy of your record if you say that you need it for program purposes. But if your file is quite extensive, the agency may charge you a fee for printing it. You or your representative can ask to examine all the evidence that is going to be part of the hearing record before the hearing, in case you want to object to its admission or offer evidence to challenge it.

iii. Gather your medications

Gather together your medications so you can make a complete list of the medications you take, what the doses are, when the medications were first prescribed, and who prescribed them. You don't need to bring the physical bottles to the hearing with you.

iv. Figure out who all the witnesses will be

You'll receive a notice before the hearing if the ALJ plans to ask any expert witnesses to testify. The ALJ might have a medical expert or vocational expert testify about your medical condition or work abilities. ALJs don't often use medical experts, but they use vocational experts a lot. If you don't receive a witness notice at least a week before the hearing, call the ALJ's office and ask about experts. You shouldn't attempt to personally contact any expert witnesses.

You can bring witnesses, too. Inform the ALJ about who your witnesses are as soon as possible after you've chosen them. The Field Office can send the ALJ a list of witnesses you want, but neither the ALJ nor the Field Office is responsible for contacting your witnesses and making sure they show up at the hearing. Your witnesses are your responsibility. Don't overload the ALJ with witnesses. One is usually sufficient—two is pushing it in all but the most complex cases. Quality, not quantity, matters here. For example, your treating physician or a caregiver who sees you every day might know your condition better than anyone else. The majority of claimants have no witnesses and many of them still are awarded benefits, so don't worry if you can't bring a witness to your hearing.

h. Attend the Hearing

Hearing rooms and video hearing sites vary from location to location. Most likely, you'll be in a relatively small room with one or more tables. Remember, this is an informal hearing, not the kind of adversarial proceeding you might have in a trial. There won't be any government attorneys arguing against you.

If you have a representative, sit near them, and have your witnesses sit near you. In addition, follow these tips.

Arrive on time. The ALJ may cancel your hearing if you're late without a good reason. If you have good cause for being late or not showing up—such as a medical emergency or severe weather conditions—the ALJ can reschedule the hearing, but don't risk it. You can lose your claim by not showing up for a hearing. Even if it's rescheduled, it might be several months before you can have another one.

Avoid potentially missing your hearing and delaying your claim by checking the address of the Office of Hearings Operations at www.ssa.gov/appeals/ho_locator.html. This page has detailed maps and instructions on finding the ALJ's hearing office that you can print out. You can also call the ALJ's office or your local Field Office for directions.

Ask for an interpreter. You can request that an interpreter be present at your hearing if your English isn't strong enough to understand the hearing questions and procedures. If you requested an interpreter and they're not at the hearing, ask to reschedule.

Be aware that the hearing is recorded. ALJ hearings are tape-recorded. At no charge to you, the proceedings will be transcribed to hard copy if you lose at the hearing and appeal further. The only part of the hearing that might not be recorded is discussion *off the record*, but this should only relate to issues that aren't relevant to the hearing. Once the hearing goes back on the record, the judge must summarize what took place during the off-the-record discussion.

Don't bring spectators. Your hearing isn't open to the general public. Relatives or friends can come with you if you need assistance but they can't answer questions for you. Contact the ALJ's hearing office before the hearing if you have any questions about bringing someone.

Be comfortable and be yourself. There's no need to dress up. Also, if you're in pain from sitting too long and need to stand, go ahead.

Be courteous and respectful to the ALJ and everyone else present. Don't curse or use other foul or threatening language, no matter how angry you are.

Pay attention to what is happening. Don't read, eat, chew tobacco or gum, use your cell phone, or do anything else that might be distracting. If you want to be taken seriously, you must take the hearing seriously. Also, you can't answer questions properly if you don't know what's going on. Let the ALJ know if you have difficulty hearing the proceedings, and wear your hearing aid if you use one.

Be truthful. When asked questions, don't be vague or evasive. When asked questions, don't be vague or evasive. Vague and evasive answers are not helpful. They force the ALJ to make a decision on factors other than what you're saying, and can leave a bad impression. Avoid answering questions with "Not really," or "A little." The judge won't know if by "a little" weight you mean 5 pounds or 50 pounds.

Don't exaggerate your pain or other symptoms, but don't be too proud to express how your condition has made your life difficult. If you don't know the answer to a question, just say so.

Don't stage emotional outbursts. ALJs have seen it all before and won't be swayed by it if they think it's an act. Judges don't award disability based on how much claimants cry. But if you find yourself in tears as you explain your condition, don't be embarrassed—again, the ALJ has seen it all and knows that this can be the natural response of someone under stress.

i. Follow the Hearing Procedure

ALJs conduct hearings in various ways. Social Security doesn't require that the hearing be conducted in a specific sequence. This section gives you some idea of what to expect, although the order of your hearing may be different. If you have a representative who frequently appears before your ALJ, they should be familiar with the procedures of your ALJ and can fill you in on what to expect.

ALJs almost always start by introducing themselves and any staff or witnesses that are present. If you don't have a representative, the ALJ may then ask if you understand your right to have a representative. Unrepresented claimants can either choose to proceed with the hearing or ask to postpone in order to hire a lawyer.

The ALJ will also make a brief statement explaining how the hearing will be conducted, the procedural history of your case, and the issues involved. The ALJ will swear you in by asking you to raise your right hand and swear that your testimony shall be "the truth and nothing but the truth." The appropriate response is, "I do." Any witnesses will also be sworn to tell the truth before they testify.

As the hearing progresses, the ALJ will need to establish your name, age, address, education, work experience, and some details on your medical history, medications, symptoms, medical disorders, and limitations on your activities of daily living. The judge might ask you questions or have your representative ask you some questions. As emphasized earlier, give clear and concise answers and concrete examples of how your physical or mental impairments limit your ability to function. Saying "I can't do anything" is not informative. Everyone does something during the day, even if it's just sitting on the couch.

j. Your Witnesses

Once some basics are established, the ALJ will move on to your witnesses, if any. Anyone with some specific knowledge of the limitations imposed by your impairments can be a witness. One credible witness (or, rarely, two) should be enough to make the point to the judge—there's little value in having several people repeat the same thing over and over. As discussed in Section E3f, it's important that you review the chapters in this book concerning your impairments. Those chapters will help you understand how witnesses can help your case.

The ALJ will often be the first to question any witnesses you bring to the hearing. You or your representative may also question the witnesses. This means that you'll need to listen carefully during the judge's questioning and ask your witness only about whatever the judge left out. There's no need to bore the judge by going over the same territory. However, part of winning your case is making sure that the judge "gets" why you're disabled. For example, say your doctor is testifying about your back pain but the judge doesn't ask any questions about whether you experience any side effects from your medication. You (and your doctor) know that your medication causes severe drowsiness and mental fog, so be sure to ask your doctor questions about the side effects when your time comes.

Physical disorders. The best witnesses are those who have first-hand experience with your inability to perform certain activities because of your impairments.

EXAMPLE: Dwayne has chronic back pain related to degenerative arthritis and scarring around nerve roots from a prior surgery for a herniated disk. At his hearing, Dwayne's wife tells the ALJ that he tried to lift 30 pounds when moving boxes in their garage and was in excruciating pain for a week. She also discussed how Dwayne spends most of his day in a recliner because that's the most comfortable position for him, and that Dwayne no longer can help carry groceries in from the car, even when the loads are light and despite the short distance to the house.

Mental disorders. Your witnesses should discuss how any mental disorders you have limit your activities. What can you do and not do? Exercise independent judgment? Plan and cook a meal? Shop alone and return home without getting lost? Remember things, people, or obligations? Relate to other people? Bathe and dress alone? Finish tasks in a timely manner, if at all? Do your own grooming and hygiene? Pay bills? An employer or coworker in a mental disorder claim might testify that you can't remember work procedures or are too irritable to work with other people.

> EXAMPLE: Homer has progressive dementia of the Alzheimer's type, and his employer is a witness. The employer tells the ALJ that Homer slowly lost his ability to do his job as a supervisor in a furniture manufacturing facility—he couldn't remember procedures, didn't seem motivated to finish tasks, and he was irritable and short-tempered with the employees he supervised. As examples, the employer stated that Homer had left dangerous machinery running unattended, didn't return tools to their proper storage places, and blamed other employees for his shortcomings. Homer would have outbursts for no reason, which upset the other employees and disrupted the work schedule. On other occasions, Homer seemed to be unaware of dangers and walked right in front of a forklift carrying heavy boxes. The employer tried to give Homer simple jobs requiring minimal skill—such as counting boxes in the warehouse—but Homer still couldn't seem to do them without too many errors. The employer says he was sorry, but he had to lay Homer off work indefinitely.

Homer's son then testifies that he has the same kinds of problems around the house as he had at work. The son notes that Homer didn't seem interested in anything but watching TV, and stopped doing his favorite hobbies, fishing and playing his guitar. Homer did halfheartedly try to play his guitar once but angrily broke it against a wall when he couldn't remember the fingering for basic chords. Homer's son testified that Homer eats and sleeps poorly and gets confused doing simple jobs around the house. For instance, he was trying to repair an old chair and stopped for lunch. When he returned to the chair, he was confused about how to put it together and just left it unfinished. Homer can't drive any longer because he gets lost and almost had a wreck by running a red light. Of note, the son testified that Homer almost didn't recognize his daughter, who had come to visit from another city. Often, Homer doesn't remember to change his clothes or bathe unless his son reminds him.

Medical experts. Medical experts (MEs) are doctors in private practice hired by the SSA to help the ALJ understand the medical issues involved in a case. MEs are specialists in various medical disciplines and have medical licenses. A few MEs are also vocational experts (see below). The ME can't be a doctor who has seen you in the past.

An ALJ can ask an ME to review your file and provide a medical opinion before the hearing, or to testify at the hearing itself. The ALJ can't ask the ME for an opinion on vocational matters relating to your claim, even if the ME is also a vocational expert. The ALJ must include the ME in the witness list and send you copies of any correspondence between the ALJ and ME. If the ME gave the ALJ advice about your claim and isn't put on the witness list or brought to the hearing, this can be grounds for review by the Appeals Council.

At the hearing, you can cross-examine any medical expert involved in your case. But before you can cross-examine the ME, you need to have understood what they said. If the ME talks like a medical textbook, the ALJ is supposed to ask follow-up questions that require them to explain things in plain English. (You or your representative can remind the ALJ if they forget to do this.)

An ME may give a medical opinion as to whether you qualify for disability benefits, but the ALJ doesn't have to agree. MEs are paid only a small sum of money that's the same whether you win or lose, so they have little financial incentive for bias. Furthermore, MEs aren't paid by the SSA to argue against your claim for benefits. In some instances, an ME might argue that your claim should be allowed.

In fact, you can request that the ALJ call an ME to testify if you think it will help your case.

An experienced Social Security disability attorney can cross-examine an ME in a way that the ME agrees to certain facts that point toward your disability. If the ME won't agree to such facts, then it's important to get the ME to admit that the ME hasn't examined you.

Vocational experts. Vocational experts (VEs) are people with experience placing people in jobs. They evaluate your residual functional capacity (see Chapter 8) to determine if there are jobs in the national economy you can do. Like medical experts, some VEs are consultants for the SSA's Office of Hearings Operations.

The training and qualifications of a VE aren't standardized. A VE might have a background in a variety of fields, such as psychology, vocational education, vocational counseling, or vocational rehabilitation. Most VEs, but not all, have advanced college degrees in subjects such as vocational education. Various credential labels might appear after a VE's name, such as certified vocational evaluator or expert (CVE), certified rehabilitation counselor (CRC), certified case manager (CCM), certified disability management specialist (CDMS), or federally certified rehabilitation counselor for the U.S. Department of Labor. So you might see something like this: John Doe, Ph.D., CVE, CRC, CCM. Many VEs are members of the American Board of Vocational Experts (www.abve.net), a nonprofit organization with high standards for certification. (Note that vocational analysts used by DDS are usually trained by DDS and may have a much more limited vocational background than vocational experts in private practice.)

Medical Witnesses: Your Treating Doctor and SSA Medical Consultants

It's highly unusual for a claimant's treating doctor to attend an ALJ hearing. In the event your treating doctor will come, be sure to include the doctor on your witness list. If you don't, the ALJ can postpone the hearing. Even with the testimony of a medical expert, the ALJ must consider the opinion of your treating doctor. For example, suppose your treating doctor's opinion says you have greater functional limitations than what the medical consultant indicated during the initial determination of your claim. The medical consultant said you can lift 50 pounds and walk six to eight hours a day, but your doctor wrote that you can lift only 20 pounds and walk three to six hours a day. The ALJ must consider how persuasive your treating doctor's opinion is regarding your functional limitations, including whether the opinion is supported by medical documentation and is consistent with the other evidence in your file

If your treating doctor's opinion and the medical consultant's opinion are equally well supported, the ALJ must consider the length of your relationship with the doctor, how frequently you visited the doctor, the extent of examinations and testing performed by the doctor, whether the doctor is a specialist, and whether the doctor examined you in person. The ALJ must explain in writing how these factors were considered in determining the severity of your functional limitations and your RFC. It's important for you to point out that the medical consultant didn't examine you, doesn't know what you can and can't do physically and mentally, and doesn't have as much insight into your medical history as your treating doctor.

The opinions of a consultative examination doctor are harder to challenge, because that doctor did examine you. (See Chapter 5.) But if you have a strong relationship with your treating doctor and they provide an opinion that's consistent with and supported by the evidence in your medical records, the ALJ is likely to find the treating opinion more persuasive.

ALJs often use medical experts to help reconcile multiple conflicting medical opinions in a claimant's file. They're also frequently asked to provide an opinion on whether a claimant meets a listing or on other areas where SSA policies overlap with medical knowledge. You might not be able to challenge an ME on interpreting medical findings, but you can catch them if they make a mistake on SSA policies. For example, an ME might think that if your major epileptic seizures have been controlled for six months, then you don't have any environmental restrictions (such as not driving or working at unprotected heights). The ME is entitled to that opinion, but the SSA normally applies environmental restrictions for epilepsy for a period of 12 months. As this example shows, your representative needs to be alert to instances where the ME's opinion contradicts SSA policy.

It's very likely that the ALJ will have a VE at your hearing. You'll know by looking at the witness list that should have been mailed to you. You should also have been sent copies of any correspondence between the judge and the VE. Because a VE reviews your file and offers an opinion about your job capabilities, the VE is subject to cross-examination by you or your representative, same as a medical expert. And as with an ME, the judge is supposed to make sure that the VE speaks in plain English that you can understand.

In addition to answering questions at the hearing, the ALJ might send a VE *interrogatories* (written questions) about the vocational aspects of your claim, either before or after the hearing. If the ALJ gets the answers after a hearing and your claim is denied, you have a right to examine that evidence. The SSA should inform you about the existence of the interrogatories so that you can review them and use them in your appeal, if necessary.

The ALJ will ask the VE about the types of jobs you could do despite limitations from your medical impairments. You or your representative will have the chance to question the VE as well. VEs refer to the federal government's *Dictionary of Occupational Titles* (DOT), which describes the physical and mental requirements of various kinds of work. When there's a conflict between the VE's opinion and the DOT, the ALJ will ask the VE to explain why they disagree with the DOT.

Usually the VE will cite their professional experience and years working in job placement, if relevant. But the ALJ can't rely on the vocational expert's opinion over the DOT without finding the VE's explanation for the conflict to be reasonable.

Medical doctors and psychologists—your own, DDS medical consultants, and SSA medical experts—aren't typically VEs, and their opinion about whether you can do any job in the national economy carries little weight. Still, your treating doctor's opinion will be an important factor. Remember that the ALJ must consider your treating doctor's opinion about what you can do medically (lifting, walking, and so on), even when it conflicts with a medical consultant's or medical expert's opinion. If the VE didn't use your treating doctor's medical assessment, find out why. Ask what job recommendations the VE would make if using the doctor's assessment.

k. Consultative Examinations

If the ALJ needs additional medical information to evaluate limitations you discuss that aren't covered in your medical records, you might be asked to undergo a consultative examination by a physician or psychologist who does work for the SSA (see Chapter 5). The ALJ could request that you attend a consultative examination before the hearing, or they could decide on the need for more information during a hearing itself. In the latter instance, the ALJ would normally postpone the hearing until after the exam or schedule a supplemental hearing.

What the ALJ Might Ask the ME

Below is the Office of Hearings Operations' official list of suggested questions for ALJs to use when getting expert testimony from MEs. Studying these questions and the answers given by an ME can help you cross-examine the ME or respond to answers you think are not valid:

1. Please state your full name and address.
2. Is the attached curriculum vitae a correct summary of your professional qualifications?
3. Are you board certified in any medical field, and, if so, which field?
4. Are you aware that your responses to these interrogatories are sought from you in the role of an impartial medical expert?
5. Has there been any prior communication between the administrative law judge and you regarding the merits of this case?
6. Have you ever personally examined the claimant?
7. Have you read the medical data pertaining to the claimant that we furnished you?
8. Is there sufficient objective medical evidence of record to allow you to form an opinion of the claimant's medical status? If not, what additional evidence is required?
9. Please list the claimant's physical or mental impairments resulting from anatomical, physiological, or psychological abnormalities which are demonstrable by medically acceptable clinical and laboratory diagnostic techniques. In addition, please state your opinion as to the severity of each impairment, and the exhibits and objective findings which support your opinion.
10. Are there any conflicts in the medical evidence of record which affected your opinion? If so, please state how you resolved them.
11. Have we furnished you with copies of the pertinent section of the Listing of Impairments, Appendix 1, Subpart P, Social Security Regulations No. 4?
12. In your opinion, do any of the claimant's impairments, when taken individually, meet the requirements of any of the listed impairments? Please fully explain this answer and cite the appropriate sections in the listing. (Please specifically refer to listing sections.)
13. In your opinion, do any of the claimant's impairments present medical findings which are at least equal in severity and duration to a listed impairment in Appendix 1?
14. In your opinion, if the impairment(s) is a listed impairment or the medical equivalent thereof, on what date did the impairment(s) attain that level of severity?
15. Is there any evidence that the claimant has not properly complied with prescribed treatment?
16. Has any treatment been prescribed which may improve the claimant's condition?

What the ALJ Might Ask the ME (continued)

17. List the specific functional (exertional) limitations, such as sitting, walking, standing, lifting, carrying, pushing, pulling, reaching, and handling imposed by these impairments.
18. List the specific functional (nonexertional) limitations, such as environmental restrictions (sensitivity to fumes, etc.), or visual limitations, such as inability

to read small print or work with small objects, imposed by these impairments.
19. Please describe the claimant's visual acuity in terms of its effect on the claimant's ability to work safely.
20. Do you have any additional comments or information which may assist us in reaching a decision? If so, please state.

I. Await the ALJ's Decision

Don't expect the ALJ to give you a decision at the end of the hearing. The SSA will send you a copy of the ALJ's decision, which usually takes about two more months. If the ALJ denies your claim, you can appeal further to the Appeals Council.

CAUTION

Not all hearings end the day they begin. Various circumstances might cause you or the ALJ to suggest that the hearing be *continued* to another day. For example, the ALJ could decide that additional evidence is needed before making a decision on your case. You might have to gather and submit this evidence yourself, or the ALJ might order additional tests or opinions. If the ALJ gathers the additional evidence, you will be given an opportunity to look it over and request

a supplemental hearing if you think you need one. These posthearing conferences follow the same rules as prehearing conferences (discussed in Section 3b, above).

4. Appeals Council Review

If you're denied benefits by the ALJ, the final step in your administrative appeals process is with the SSA's Appeals Council (AC).

a. How to Appeal to the Appeals Council

To appeal to the AC, you must either file an appeal online at https://secure.ssa.gov/iApplNMD/oao or complete and return to the SSA Form HA-520-U5, *Request for Review of Decision/Order.* The SSA must receive the request within 60 days of when you receive your denial notice from the ALJ, or 65 days from the date on the ALJ's denial (five days are allowed for mailing).

What the ALJ Might Ask the VE

Below is the official list of suggested questions for ALJs to use when questioning a vocational expert. Use it to help prepare your own questions for the VE:

1. Please state your full name and address.

2. Is the attached curriculum vitae a correct summary of your professional qualifications?

3. Are you aware that your responses are sought from you in the role of an impartial vocational expert?

4. Has there been any prior communication between the administrative law judge and you regarding the merits of this case?

5. Has there been any prior professional contact between you and the claimant?

6. Have you read the evidence pertaining to the claimant that we furnished you?

7. Is there sufficient objective evidence of record to allow you to form an opinion of the claimant's vocational status? If not, what additional evidence is required?

8. Please state the following:

   a. Claimant's age, in terms of the applicable age category described in Sections 404.1563 and 416.963 of federal regulations. (See Chapters 8 and 9.)

   b. Claimant's education, in terms of the applicable education category described in Sections 404.1564 and 416.964 of federal regulations. (See Chapters 8 and 9.)

   c. Claimant's *past relevant work* (PRW); i.e., the claimant's work experience during the last 15 years, in terms of the physical exertion and skill requirements described in Sections 404.1567, 404.1568, 416.967, and 416.968 of federal regulations, and the *Dictionary of Occupational Titles*. (See Chapters 8 and 9.)

   d. The extent that any job during the last 15 years required lifting, carrying, pushing, pulling, sitting, standing, walking, climbing, balancing, stooping, kneeling, crouching, crawling, reaching, handling, fingering, feeling, talking, hearing, and seeing, as well as any environmental or similar aspects of the job (indoors, outdoors, extremes of heat or cold, wetness, noise, vibration, and exposure to fumes, odors, or toxic conditions). (See Chapters 8 and 9.)

   e. If the claimant's past relevant work was at either a skilled or semiskilled level, describe the skills acquired by the claimant during the performance of the job(s), and furnish a complete explanation for your opinion(s).

9. Hypothetical questions:

   a. Assume that I find the claimant's testimony credible, that because of his impairment he can only sit for up to three hours and stand or walk for no more than three hours before experiencing severe

What the ALJ Might Ask the VE (continued)

pain, and can lift no more than ten pounds, and then he must lie down for at least two hours in any eight-hour period to relieve the pain. If I accept this description of his limitations, could the claimant, considering his age, education, and work experience, engage in his past relevant work? Or, if not, could he transfer acquired skills to the performance of other skilled or semiskilled work?

b. Assume that I find that the claimant can sit for up to three hours at a time, stand or walk for no more than three hours, and lift up to ten pounds. Can he engage in his past work? If not, can he transfer any skills to perform other skilled or semiskilled work?

c. Assume that I find that the claimant can stand and walk for approximately six hours, and lift no more than 20 pounds at a time with frequent lifting or carrying of objects weighing up to ten pounds. Can he engage in his past work or, if not, can he transfer his skills to perform other skilled or semiskilled work?

d. If the claimant can transfer his skills to perform other skilled or semiskilled work, please provide some examples of these jobs and the frequency with which they are found in the national economy.

CAUTION

You must use forms provided by the SSA. You can obtain them at your local SSA field office or by calling the SSA hotline at 800-772-1213, Monday through Friday (except holidays), from 8:00 a.m. to 7:00 p.m. If you are deaf or hard of hearing, TTY service representatives are available at the same times at 800-325-0778. You can also download many necessary forms from the Social Security Administration website at www.ssa.gov. The form is not available from DDS.

Your other option is to simply write a letter, but it's best to use the official form so you include all necessary information.

If you decide to just write a letter, state: "I request that the Appeals Council review the administrative law judge's action on my claim because [state a reason, such as one of the following]":

- My ALJ hearing lasted only 20 minutes, and I didn't have a chance to present my evidence.
- I think the ALJ made a mistake in not considering my treating doctor's opinion.
- I have new evidence showing that the ALJ was wrong in denying my claim.
- The ALJ did not consider my mental problems.

If you send the form or letter by mail, attach to it copies of any evidence showing that the ALJ's decision was incorrect, like new evidence showing your condition is more severe than the ALJ thought. Then fold the documents in thirds, insert them in a standard business envelope, and mail them to your local Social Security Field Office. The Field Office will then mail your appeal papers to the Appeals Council, Office of Appellate Operations, 6401 Security Blvd., Baltimore, MD 21235-6401.

Keep a copy of your completed form and the originals of your attached evidence for your records. You may need a larger envelope if you have too many documents to follow the SSA's instructions about using a standard business envelope.

b. Will the Appeals Council Review Your Case?

The Appeals Council will examine your review request and notify you in writing of its intended action. It may grant, deny, or dismiss your request for review.

The AC can dismiss your case without reviewing it unless it finds any of the following:

- an abuse of discretion by the ALJ (like not allowing you to cross-examine the VE)
- an error of law (such as ignoring a treating doctor's opinion)
- the ALJ's decision not being supported by substantial evidence (for example, all medical imaging indicates that you

meet a listing but the judge decided you didn't), or

- a broad policy or procedural issue raised by the case (such as the ALJ not notifying a claimant that an expert witness would be present at the hearing).

If you file late, request a dismissal, or die, the AC might also dismiss your claim without reviewing it. The AC usually looks for a flaw in the ALJ decision before granting a review. In those situations, your chance of winning is only 2%–3%. The AC is not a place where you're likely to find success. For most people, the only reason to file a request with the AC is to exhaust all the SSA administrative appeal avenues, which you must do before you sue the SSA in federal court. (See Section E5, below.)

Appeals Council Can Initiate Review

Even if you don't appeal to the AC, the AC can select ALJ decisions for review at random or if referred from other divisions of the SSA. This means that on its own, the AC could review and grant a claim that had been denied by an ALJ, but it also means that the AC could reverse an ALJ allowance of benefits and deny your claim. When the AC decides to review a case on its own, you'll be notified of its proposed action (reversing or affirming) and given an opportunity to offer input. Although it's very unlikely that your case would fall into such a review sample, it does happen.

c. How the Appeals Council Conducts a Review

The Appeals Council judge will attempt to process your review request at the AC level. But if the AC feels the claim needs further factual development before it can issue a legally sufficient decision, it will return the case to the ALJ to gather the evidence, which provides the opportunity for you to have another hearing and for the ALJ to issue a new decision.

If the AC keeps your case for review at the AC level, it will look at the evidence of record (the evidence that was in your file when you asked for AC review), any additional evidence submitted by you, and the ALJ's findings and conclusions. The AC can also consult physicians (called medical support staff, or MSS) and vocational experts on its staff. When the MSS recommends granting your claim and the AC relies on that recommendation to reach its decision, the AC must add the MSS comments to your record.

If the MSS recommendation is unfavorable and the AC is going to use that recommendation to make its decision, the AC must offer the MSS report to you for comment before entering it into the record. If the AC doesn't use the MSS opinion to reach a decision, the AC doesn't make the MSS analysis a part of your record.

The AC uses its MSS in only about a fifth of its decisions, but has to use the MSS if it's going to award you benefits based on the fact that your impairments equal a listing. (See Chapter 7 for an explanation of listings.)

d. The Appeals Council's Decision

If the Appeals Council dismisses your case without reviewing it, it will send you a notice stating that it finds no basis to disturb the ALJ's decision. The ALJ's decision then becomes the final decision. This is the usual result of an AC review.

If the AC does review your case, it's important to manage your expectations. You probably won't hear back from the AC for a year, and the news isn't likely to be good. You might file a new application while you're waiting to hear back from the AC, but Social Security will just forward the application to the AC to be combined with your existing case. However, if you have a new critical or disabling condition, you can tell the AC that you want to file a new application, and it might allow you to file a new application before completing review of your existing appeal.

5. Sue the SSA in Federal Court

If you disagree with the Appeals Council's decision or the AC refuses to review your case, you can pursue your case further by filing a lawsuit—essentially suing the SSA—in U.S. district court. You need to file your complaint in a district court within 60 days after you receive notice of the AC's dismissal or 65 days from the date on the

AC's decision. You will almost certainly need an attorney if you haven't gotten one by now.

Federal judges hear disability cases without juries. The judge is supposed to review the case for legal errors by the SSA. District court judges reverse ALJs or the AC in at least a third of all cases, often with the reasoning that the SSA didn't give sufficient weight to a treating doctor's opinion, didn't consider pain and other symptoms, or should have asked for assessments of abilities from treating doctors.

The federal judge might allow your claim (approve benefits) or deny it (uphold the SSA's denial determination), but these aren't the court's only options. The court might also send your claim back to the ALJ—called a *remand*—to reevaluate your claim according to some special legal instruction. For example, the court might order the ALJ to reconsider the medical records or take additional vocational expert testimony at a new hearing. Since the AC declines to review most claims, most federal court reversals are of an ALJ's decision rather than the AC's decision.

Although you have a fair chance of winning an appeal in federal court, it's not an attractive option. Fewer than 1% of disability claimants actually take their cases to court. Suing the SSA is expensive and very time-consuming. Even if you win, it might take years to reach that level. Consequently, few attorneys are willing to file a disability case in federal court. You could represent yourself, but few nonattorneys have the skills, time, or money to do so, especially if they suffer from severe medical conditions.

Appealing to a Higher Court

If you lose a case in a federal district court, you can appeal to a circuit court of appeals. The U.S. federal court system is divided into circuits. Each circuit covers several states—for example, the 8th Circuit contains North Dakota, South Dakota, Nebraska, Minnesota, Iowa, Missouri, and Arkansas.

The decision of an individual circuit court is binding only on the district courts within its circuit. For instance, a decision by 8th Circuit Court of Appeals doesn't have to be followed in New York, and a decision by the 2nd Circuit Court of Appeals (which covers New York) isn't binding on federal district courts in Nebraska. This means that the outcome of your case could depend on where you live.

If you lose an appeal to a federal circuit court, you can theoretically take your case to the U.S. Supreme Court, but the Supreme Court only hears cases that it thinks warrant its special consideration. If your claim involves a broad legal or constitutional issue that potentially affects the entire country, the Supreme Court might consider hearing your case.

RESOURCE

Should you choose to appeal on your own, you can refer to *Represent Yourself in Court: How to Prepare & Try a Winning Case*, by Paul Bergman and Sara Berman (Nolo), for guidance.

If you do file in federal court, you can file a new initial claim at DDS while your case is pending, and the SSA will let the new claim proceed as long as the date you claim you became disabled on your new application is *after* the date of the AC denial or dismissal of the claim.

F. Reopening of Decisions

An alternative to appealing your case is to request a reopening of your claim—meaning you're asking whichever administrative level of the SSA has your claim to take a second look at it (and hopefully award you benefits this time). But you can only reopen your claim under certain circumstances. Here are the rules governing when you can reopen your case:

- If you make your request within 12 months of the date of the notice of the initial determination by DDS, ALJ, or AC, you can ask for a reopening for any reason.
- If you believe that the determination to deny you or terminate your benefits was based on fraud or a similar fault, you can request a reopening at any time.
- If you make your request within four years (for SSDI applicants) or two years (for SSI applicants) of the date of the notice of the initial determination, the SSA can reopen the case if it finds *good cause*. Examples of good cause include submission of new and material evidence, a clerical error in the computation of your benefits, or evidence of a clear error (like the claim is for somebody else).

Good cause doesn't include a change in the law that the decision was based on.

If the SSA agrees to reopen your case and issues a revised determination, that new determination is binding unless one of the following is true:

- You file a request for reconsideration or a hearing.
- You file a request for review by the Appeals Council.
- The Appeals Council reviews the revised decision.
- The revised determination is further revised.

G. Refiling an Initial Claim

You have the option to file another initial claim at any stage if you lose your appeal. Just go to your local Social Security Field Office (or online, for SSDI claims) and start the process over again. You'll have a better chance of winning your new claim if your conditions have worsened or you have a new condition.

Before you file a subsequent SSDI claim, be aware of a legal barrier known as *res judicata*, which means "the thing has been decided." DDS can use res judicata to avoid deciding a claim that's been previously determined if all the facts, issues, conditions, and evidence are the same.

If you file a new disability application with the same issues and no new facts or evidence, Social Security might be able to deny your application on the basis of res judicata. But res judicata can apply only if your *date last insured* (DLI) expired before the last denial you received (meaning you would no longer be eligible for SSDI benefits if you filed a new claim today). (See Chapter 9 for discussion of the DLI.)

So if your insured status is still active when you file a new claim, the SSA can't deny your claim due to res judicata. This is true even if you claim the same disability onset date, same impairment, and same condition.

Even if you're no longer insured for SSDI, res judicata won't apply if anything about your claim has changed, including the law or the evidence.

Here are some examples of when the SSA might be able to deny your claim for res judicata.

EXAMPLE 1—RES JUDICATA DOESN'T APPLY: You're denied on your first application on 1/30/22 and don't appeal. You file a second application on 1/30/24, before your date last insured expires (you've worked five of the last ten years leading up to January 2024). Even though you claim the same alleged onset date and submit no new evidence, the SSA wouldn't apply res judicata to your claim.

EXAMPLE 2—RES JUDICATA APPLIES: You're denied on your first application on 1/30/22 and don't appeal. You file a second application, claim the same alleged onset date, submit no new evidence, and show that you were last insured for benefits before 1/30/22. The SSA denies your claim on the basis of res judicata.

EXAMPLE 3—RES JUDICATA DOESN'T APPLY: The same example as above, except that you submit new evidence with your claim. The new evidence shows that your condition met a listing at the time of your last decision. The SSA would not apply res judicata to your claim.

However, in some cases where your date last insured had expired at the time of the last decision, rather than applying res judicata, the SSA might give you the benefit of the doubt and treat your new claim as a request for reopening (see Section F, above).

Once You Are Approved

A. Disability Benefit Payments

Once you're awarded disability benefits, you'll receive a Certificate of Award containing answers to many questions about Social Security payments. If any of your relatives are eligible for dependents benefits due to your disability (SSDI only), they'll receive a separate notice and a booklet about what they need to know.

1. When Benefits Start

For SSDI, you'll be paid monthly benefits starting five months after the time you're declared disabled (your established onset date). Your first payment might include some retroactive benefits going back to your established onset date, even if it was before you applied for SSDI. (However, you can't receive more than 12 months of retroactive benefits. How your retroactive benefits are calculated is covered in Chapter 10, Section C.)

SSI benefits begin the month following the month in which you qualify for disability benefits. You can't get retroactive SSI benefits going back to your date of disability. However, since it takes a while to get approved for SSI, you'll probably be owed some back payments going back to the month after which you applied for SSI. (See Chapter 10, Section C, for more details.)

2. How Much Benefits Will Be

How much your benefits will be depends first on whether you have an SSDI claim or an SSI claim, because each program uses different formulas to determine benefits. SSDI benefits are usually higher than SSI benefits.

a. SSDI Benefits

The SSA will tell you the amount of your benefits when it sends you notice that your claim has been approved. Your SSDI benefits are calculated using a complicated formula. The SSA first calculates your average earnings over a period of many years, known as your *average indexed monthly earnings* (AIME).

Your AIME is then used to calculate your *primary insurance amount* (PIA)—the basic figure the SSA uses in finding the actual benefit amount. The PIA is a total of fixed percentages of predetermined dollar amounts of your AIME. The dollar amounts increase yearly, but the percentages stay the same. For 2024, for example, the monthly PIA benefit for a disabled worker is the total of the following amounts:

Percentage of Amount in Right Column	Amount of AIME
90%	$0–$1,174
32%	$1,174–$7,078
15%	$7,078

EXAMPLE: Horace's AIME is $8,000. The SSA calculates his PIA as follows:

	$	1,174	×	90%	=	$	1,056.60
plus							
		7,078					
	−	1,174					
	$	5,904	×	32%	=	$	1,889.28
plus							
	$	8,000					
	−	7,078					
	$	922	×	15%	=	$	138.30
		TOTAL			=	$	3,084.10*

* round down to nearest $0.10 as required

Family members who were dependent on your income may also be eligible for benefits. For example, a child eligible to receive benefits on your record while you're alive is entitled to 50% of your PIA; if you die, the percentage increases to 75% of your PIA.

The *maximum family benefit* (MFB) is the total monthly benefit that can be paid to you (the wage earner) and any family members entitled to benefits on your record. The MFB doesn't affect the amount of your benefit. Instead, different amounts for each family member, based on a percentage of your PIA, are added to your PIA.

These dependent amounts will be reduced if the total of your benefits and your dependents benefits exceeds the MFB limit, which is 85% of your AIME, as long as the amount doesn't fall below your PIA. At the same time, the total MFB amount can't exceed 150% of your PIA.

Thee formula used to compute the family maximum consists of four separate portions of the worker's PIA. The dollar amounts increase yearly, but the percentages stay the same. For 2024, for example, the MFB for a disabled worker is as follows:

150% of the first $1,500 of PIA, plus
272% of PIA over $1,500 through $2,166, plus
134% of PIA over $2,166 through $2,825, plus
175% of PIA over $2,825.

This basic summary doesn't consider other factors that can influence the actual amount of your payment. It's not really practical for you to try to calculate your own monthly benefit, though. It makes more sense to let the SSA do the calculations. Of course, the SSA could make a mistake.

The following table can give you an idea of the approximate monthly amount of SSDI benefits paid to disabled recipients and qualified family members. The table also shows some other types of Social Security benefits for comparison.

Once you reach full retirement age, you'll receive retirement benefits rather than disability benefits. Be aware that these amounts can vary with individual eligibility circumstances.

The following table represents estimated average monthly Social Security benefits payable in 2024.

Type of Beneficiary	Award
Aged couple both receiving benefits	$3,033
Widowed mother and two children	$3,653
Aged widow(er) alone	$1,773
Disabled worker, spouse, and one or more children	$2,720
Disabled worker	$1,537
Retired worker	$1,907

The maximum a disabled worker can receive at full retirement age in 2024 is $3,822 per month (for high earners). (Also see Chapter 2 regarding how your benefit can be reduced by workers' compensation and other public disability or pension payments.)

b. SSI Benefits

Although your eligibility for SSI benefits depends on both your income and resources, only your income influences the amount of your monthly payment.

In 2024, the maximum SSI payment for a disabled adult is $943 per month and $1,415 for a couple. Some states supplement SSI payments with more money (called a state supplemental payment; see Chapter 1).

Your SSI check might not be the same every month. Each monthly amount depends on your other income and living arrangements. The SSA will tell you whenever it plans to change the amount of your check. See Chapter 1 for information on how your income and resources affect the amount of your SSI benefits.

3. When and How Payments Are Made

When and how benefits are paid depends on the type of benefit and whether the payment is by check or direct deposit to a bank account. If you don't have a bank account, your local SSA Field Office can help you find banks that offer low- or no-cost accounts to receive your SSDI or SSI benefits.

a. Check by Mail

SSI checks should arrive on the first day of the month. If you're receiving both SSI and SSDI, your SSI check should arrive on the first day of the month and your SSDI check on the third day of the month. If the first or third falls on a weekend or legal holiday, you should receive your check on the business day before. For example, if your payment date would fall on a Sunday, you should receive your check on the prior Friday instead.

SSDI recipients who started receiving benefits before 1997 get their payments on the third day of the month or the business day preceding it, if the third is a weekend or holiday. If you are awarded benefits after 1997, your SSDI payment will arrive on a day dictated by your birthday:

Birth Date Day of Month	Day SSDI Arrives
1st–10th	Second Wednesday
11th–20th	Third Wednesday
21st–31st	Fourth Wednesday

The SSA's site (www.ssa.gov) has a colorful calendar showing the exact dates you'll receive your payments if you live in the United States at www.ssa.gov/pubs/EN-05-10031-2024.pdf.

If you're living outside the United States, your checks may arrive later than the due date. Delivery time varies from country to country, and your check may not arrive the same day each month.

b. Direct Deposits

The SSA prefers that you have a bank (or savings and loan association or credit union) account so that your check can be deposited directly. If your deposit doesn't take place on the date scheduled, call the SSA at once, so they can put a trace on the payment. The deposit should always be in your account on the correct date.

If you don't have a bank account for direct deposit, the U.S. Department of the Treasury will send your benefits via the Direct Express® card program. Detailed information about the Direct Express program can be found at www.USDirectExpress.com.

c. Overpayments (Erroneous Payments)

If you receive a check or direct deposit payment to which you're not entitled—for example, for your spouse who died before the date the check was issued—you must return it to the SSA. If you return a check by mail, enclose a note saying why you're sending the payment back.

4. Paying Taxes on Disability Benefits

Social Security recipients must pay taxes on their benefits if they have substantial additional income. Specifically, if you file an individual tax return and your combined income—your adjusted gross income plus one half of your Social Security benefits—is between $25,000 and $34,000, you might owe taxes on 50% of your Social Security benefits. If your combined income is above $34,000, up to 85% of your Social Security benefits is subject to income tax.

If you file a joint return, you might owe taxes on 50% of your benefits if you and your spouse have a combined income between $32,000 and $44,000. If your combined income is more than $44,000, up to 85% of your Social Security benefits is subject to income tax.

If part of your benefits (between 50% and 85%) are taxed, they'll be taxed at your marginal income tax rate.

Most claimants don't make enough money to worry about paying taxes on their disability benefits. But situations vary; if you or your spouse has substantial additional income, consult a tax preparer.

SSI recipients are particularly unlikely to have a tax problem, because if they're liable for taxes, they probably make too much to get SSI.

5. How Long Payments Continue

Your disability benefits will generally continue as long as your impairment has not improved and you can't work.

But because of advances in medical science and rehabilitation techniques, increasing numbers of people with disabilities recover from serious accidents and illnesses. Some people recover enough to return to work. So your case will be reviewed periodically to make sure you're still disabled (see Chapter 14).

Your benefits may be reduced or terminated if you marry, receive certain other disability benefits, or move to certain countries where payments are prohibited (see Section B5, below). Also, if you're receiving SSDI when you turn full retirement age, your benefits will automatically be changed to retirement benefits, generally for the same amount. If you're receiving benefits as a disabled widow or widower when you turn 60, your benefits will be changed to regular widow or widower benefits.

For a broad discussion of Social Security issues, see *Social Security, Medicare & Government Pensions*, by Attorney Joseph Matthews (Nolo).

6. Eligibility for Medicare and Medicaid

Medicare is a health insurance program for eligible people who are age 65 or older or disabled. To be eligible for Medicare, you have to have worked and paid Social Security and Medicare (FICA) taxes for a certain number of years.

Medicare coverage doesn't start right away for SSDI recipients. Instead, you become eligible after you've been entitled to receive SSDI benefits for 24 months. If you have chronic kidney disease requiring regular dialysis, amyotrophic lateral sclerosis (ALS), or a transplant, however, you may qualify for Medicare almost immediately.

Medicare protection includes hospital insurance (Part A) and medical insurance (Part B). The hospital insurance part of Medicare pays hospital bills and certain follow-up care after you leave the hospital. Medical insurance helps pay doctor bills and other medical services.

There's no cost for the hospital insurance. If you want the medical insurance, you must enroll and pay a monthly premium, by having it withheld from your SSDI payment. If you choose not to enroll when first eligible and then sign up later, your premiums will be 10% more for each 12-month period you could have been enrolled but weren't (unless you received health care insurance through an employer or your spouse's employer).

If you receive Medicare and have low income and few resources, your state might pay your Medicare premiums and, in some cases, other out-of-pocket Medicare expenses such as deductibles and coinsurance. Contact a local welfare office or Medicaid agency to see if you qualify under a Medicare Savings Program.

Once you're covered by Medicare's medical insurance, if you want to cancel it, notify the SSA. Medical insurance and premiums will continue for one more month after the month you notify the SSA that you wish to cancel. For example, because Medicare generally doesn't cover health services you get outside the United States, you might want to either not sign up for coverage or cancel coverage if you plan to be abroad for a long period of time.

SSI recipients are eligible for Medicaid in most states. The SSA will automatically enroll SSI recipients in Medicaid in some states, but, in about 15 states, you have to apply separately for Medicaid. There's no Medicaid waiting period.

B. Reporting Changes—SSDI Recipients

Promptly report to the SSA any changes that might affect your or your family members' SSDI benefits. To let the SSA know the new information, you can call 800-772-1213 (voice) or 800-325-0778 (TTY), visit any SSA office (a clerk will help you), or complete and mail in the reporting form you received when you applied for benefits.

If you send a report by mail, be sure to include the following:

- your name or the name of the person on whose account your benefits are based
- your Social Security number or the Social Security number of the person on whose account your benefits are based
- the name of the person about whom the report is being made, if not you

- the nature of the change
- the date of the change, and
- your signature, address, and phone number, and the date.

If you don't report a change, you might miss out on money to which you're entitled or have to pay back money to which you were not entitled (called an *overpayment*). The SSA will withhold your monthly SSDI payment until the overpayment is paid off (unless you object because not getting your disability check would be a financial hardship).

Even if the SSA has no way to force you to repay an overpayment right now, the SSA will wait and deduct it from your tax refund or retirement benefits when you reach full retirement age.

In extreme situations—for instance, if you lie to the SSA to keep getting benefits—you could be prosecuted for Social Security fraud and fined, imprisoned, or both. The SSA has ways of finding out about true income and other factors affecting your eligibility for certain kinds of benefits—such as obtaining information from your employers and the Internal Revenue Service.

Here are the events that you must report.

1. You Move

As soon as you know your new address and phone number—even if it's before you move—let the SSA know. Include the names of any family members who also should receive their Social Security information at the new address.

Even if your benefits are deposited directly, the SSA must have your correct address to send you letters and other important information. Your benefits may end if the SSA is unable to contact you.

2. You Change or Establish Bank Accounts

If you receive your check by direct deposit and you change banks—that is, close one account and open another—you must report that to the SSA so your direct deposits continue. If you've been receiving your payments by Direct Express and you open a bank account, let the SSA know so it can set up direct deposit.

3. Your Condition Changes

If your medical condition improves or you believe you can work, you're responsible for promptly notifying the SSA. Failure to do so could mean that you would get payments you aren't entitled to receive—and might have to repay the SSA.

4. You Go to Work

Notify the SSA if you take a job or become self-employed, no matter how little you earn. You must tell the SSA if you start receiving wages that you haven't previously reported. The SSA has made this reporting easier by letting you report wage changes online by using the "My Profile Tab" after you set up a Social Security account on the SSA website. If you have a representative payee, they can also report your wages through their own Social Security account. (So far, this service is for SSDI only.)

If you're still disabled, you'll be eligible for a trial work period and can continue receiving benefits for up to nine months, even if you make over the SGA limit (see Section D, below).

If you return to work and incur any special expenses because of your disability, such as specialized equipment, a wheelchair, or some prescription drugs, let the SSA know. In some cases, the SSA will pay your expenses, or will at least deduct them from your income so that you remain eligible for benefits.

5. You Leave the United States

If you move abroad, the reporting requirements are the same as for other types of reportable changes as described in the introduction to this section.

If you leave the United States and have questions about your SSDI while you're out of the country, you have several places to turn to get assistance:

- SSA Federal Benefits Units at U.S. consulates and embassies or at the American Institute in Taiwan

- SSA representatives stationed at consulates and embassies in London, Athens, Rome, Mexico City, Guadalajara, Manila, and Frankfurt, or
- SSA Field Offices located in the British Virgin Islands, Canada, and Western Samoa.

a. Your Right to Payments When You're Outside the United States

Thousands of SSDI beneficiaries (and family members receiving benefits based on their work record) receive disability benefits while living outside of the United States. If you're not in one of the 50 states, the District of Columbia, Puerto Rico, the U.S. Virgin Islands, Guam, the Northern Mariana Islands, or American Samoa, you're considered to be outside the United States.

If you're a U.S. citizen and receive SSDI, you can continue to receive payments outside of the United States, as long as you're eligible for them, without having to return to the United States periodically (except if you go to a few countries where the SSA can't send payments, as discussed below). You don't have to notify the SSA of temporary trips outside of the United States, regardless of the length. But you must be able to receive mail from the SSA. If no one will keep track of your U.S. mail and you'll be outside of the United States for more than a month or two, give your local Social Security Field Office an overseas address. If you move permanently to another country,

definitely tell the SSA, as you're required to keep the SSA informed of your residence address.

Much more complicated rules apply to noncitizens receiving benefits. With some exceptions, an alien beneficiary who leaves the United States must return to the United States at least every 30 days, or for 30 consecutive days during each six-month period, in order to continue to draw benefits. If you're outside the United States for at least 30 days in a row, you're considered outside the country until you return and stay in the United States for at least 30 days in a row. In addition, if you're not a U.S. citizen, you might be required to establish lawful presence in the United States for that 30-day period after you return before you can receive disability benefits. Lawful presence means you're in the United States legally. (More specific requirements for lawful presence are given in Chapter 1, Section A1.)

There are some exceptions to this rule for noncitizens. For instance, if you're on active duty with the U.S. military or you move to a country that has a Social Security agreement with the United States, you may be able to continue to receive benefits when you're outside the United States.

Because of the large numbers of international treaties and agreements, there are different rules for receiving benefits in different countries. (See "Benefits When Living Abroad," below, for countries where noncitizens can continue to receive benefits.)

Benefits When Living Abroad

Category 1

If you're a citizen of one of the following countries, payments will continue no matter how long you're outside the United States, as long as you remain eligible.

Austria	Italy
Belgium	Japan
Brazil	Korea (South)
Canada	Luxembourg
Chile	Netherlands
Czech Republic	Norway
Estonia	Poland
Finland	Portugal
France	Slovak Republic
Germany	Slovenia
Greece	Spain
Hungary	Sweden
Iceland	Switzerland
Ireland	United Kingdom
Israel	Uruguay

Category 2

If you're a citizen of one of the following countries, payments will continue no matter how long you're outside the United States, as long as you remain eligible, unless you receive payments as a dependent or survivor.

Albania	Bulgaria
Antigua and Barbuda	Burkina Faso
Argentina	Colombia
Bahamas	Costa Rica
Barbados	Côte d'Ivoire
Belize	Croatia
Bolivia	Cyprus
Bosnia-Herzegovina	Denmark
Brazil	Dominica

Dominican Republic	Montenegro
Ecuador	Nicaragua
El Salvador	North Macedonia
Gabon	Palau
Grenada	Panama
Guatemala	Peru
Guyana	Philippines
Iceland	St. Kitts and Nevis
Jamaica	St. Lucia
Jordan	St. Vincent and the Grenadines
Latvia	
Liechtenstein	Samoa
Lithuania	San Marino
Malta	Serbia
Marshall Islands	Trinidad-Tobago
Mexico	Turkey
Micronesia	Venezuela
Monaco	

Category 3

If you're not a citizen of a country listed in one of the two charts above, your SSDI payments will stop after you've been outside the United States for six calendar months, unless one of the following is true:

- You were eligible for monthly Social Security benefits in December 1956.
- You're in the active military service of the United States.
- The worker on whose record your benefits are based had done railroad work qualifying as employment covered by the Social Security program (see Chapter 2, Section D, regarding the Railroad Retirement Act and the Social Security program).

Benefits When Living Abroad (continued)

- The worker on whose record your benefits are based died while in U.S. military service or as a result of a service-connected disability and was not dishonorably discharged.
- You're a resident of a country listed below with which the United States has a Social Security agreement. Note that the agreements with Austria, Belgium, Germany, Sweden, and Switzerland permit you to receive benefits as a dependent or survivor of a worker while you reside in the foreign country only if the worker is a U.S. citizen or a citizen of the foreign country.

Australia	Japan
Austria	Korea (South)
Belgium	Luxembourg
Canada	Netherlands
Chile	Norway
Czech Republic	Poland
Denmark	Portugal
Finland	Slovak Republic
France	Slovenia
Germany	Spain
Greece	Sweden
Hungary	Switzerland
Ireland	United Kingdom
Italy	Uruguay

- The worker on whose record your benefits are based lived in the United States for at least ten years or earned at least 40 earnings credits under the U.S. Social Security system, and you're a citizen of one of the following countries:

Afghanistan	Madagascar
Bangladesh	Malawi
Bhutan	Malaysia
Botswana	Mali
Burma	Mauritania
Burundi	Mauritius
Cameroon	Morocco
Cape (Cabo) Verde	Nepal
Central African Republic	Nigeria
	Pakistan
Chad	Senegal
China	Sierra Leone
Congo	Singapore
Eritrea	Solomon Islands
Ethiopia	Somalia
Fiji	South Africa
Gambia	South Sudan
Ghana	Sri Lanka
Haiti	Sudan
Honduras	Taiwan
India	Tanzania
Indonesia	Thailand
Kenya	Togo
Laos	Tonga
Lebanon	Tunisia
Lesotho	Uganda
Liberia	Yemen

Once your payments stop, they can't be started again until you come back and stay in the United States for an entire calendar month. This means you have to be in the United States on the first minute of the first day of a month and stay through the last minute of the last day of that month. For example, if you move back on July 2, you won't be eligible again for SSDI until September 1, after you've been in the United States for the full month of August. The SSA won't give you back payments for the months you missed.

The SSA has a useful screening tool for whether you can receive payments outside the U.S. at www.ssa.gov/international/payments_ outsideUS.html.

b. Additional Residency Requirements for Dependents and Survivors

If you receive benefits as a dependent or survivor of an SSDI recipient, special requirements might affect your right to receive SSDI payments while you're out- side the United States. If you're not a U.S. citizen, you must have lived in the United States for at least five years, during which time the family relationship on which benefits are based must have existed. For example, if you're receiving benefits as a spouse, you must have been married to the worker and living in the United States for at least five years.

Children who can't meet the residency requirement on their own might be considered to meet it if the SSDI recipient and their other parent (if any) meet the requirement. Children adopted outside the United States won't be paid outside the United States, however, even if the SSDI recipient meets the residency requirement.

The residency requirement for dependents or survivors benefits won't apply to you if one of the following applies:

- You were initially eligible for monthly benefits before January 1, 1985.
- You're a citizen of Israel or Japan.
- You're a resident of a country listed below with which the United States has a Social Security agreement:

Australia	Japan
Austria	Luxembourg
Belgium	Netherlands
Canada	Norway
Chile	Poland
Czech Republic	Portugal
Denmark	Slovak Republic
Finland	Slovenia
France	South Korea
Germany	Spain
Greece	Sweden
Hungary	Switzerland
Ireland	United Kingdom
Italy	Uruguay

- You're entitled to benefits based on the record of a worker who died while in the U.S. military service or as a result of a service-connected disease or injury.

c. How Payments Are Made When You Live Outside the United States

Social Security benefits can often be paid to qualifying U.S. citizens and noncitizens who move outside of the United States. Unless you're a U.S. citizen who never plans to reside in another country, it's important that you understand the basics of how international payments are made. Banking technology permits the SSA to establish direct deposit to pay beneficiaries who reside in certain countries through International Direct Deposit (IDD) or the Direct Express debit card.

International Direct Deposit payments. IDD involves the assistance of a sponsoring or processing bank—either the central bank of the foreign country or a large commercial bank in that country. Payments are deposited directly into your account at the financial institution in that country, in that country's currency. The benefits are calculated in U.S. dollars, and benefits aren't increased or decreased because of changes in international exchange rates. IDD is available in over 150 countries (see the full list at www.ssa.gov/international/countrylist6.htm).

If you move to an IDD country, the SSA will encourage you to open an account in the new country and receive payments in the new account. Contact the Federal Benefits Unit at the U.S. embassy in the country to which you move to get enrolled in IDD.

When you return from the IDD country, the IDD can't continue while you have a U.S. address. As soon as you return, open up a U.S. bank account and let the SSA know so it can arrange direct deposit into that account.

If You Move to a Prohibited Country

U.S. Treasury Department regulations prohibit sending payments to you if you're in Cuba, North Korea, Azerbaijan, Belarus, Kazakhstan, Kyrgyzstan, Moldova, Tajikistan, Turkmenistan, or Uzbekistan. The SSA can't send payments to these countries, and federal regulations also bar you from receiving payments by direct deposit or through a representative. Exceptions are possible for receiving payments to all of the above countries other than Cuba and North Korea. But exceptions aren't automatically granted, and specific conditions must apply. If you want the SSA to send you benefits in the above countries, you should contact an SSA Field Office for help.

If the SSA does learn that you are in Cuba or North Korea and the agency stops your payments, when you return, the SSA will send you the money it withheld while you were away, but only if you are a U.S. citizen. If you aren't a U.S. citizen, generally you can't receive payments for the months you lived in Cuba or North Korea.

Payment dates and amounts are a frequent source of confusion for overseas beneficiaries. Regular IDD SSDI payments generally are made on the third of the month. If that date is a nonbusiness day in the foreign country, payments generally are made the next business day.

Prior monthly accrual (PMA) payments are made on either the 12th or the 26th of the month. The PMA is a combined payment for all benefits due to you at the time your award is processed, and is paid immediately, subject to any delays by the U.S. processing partner, the Federal Reserve Bank of New York. The cutoff date for figuring out the PMA is about a week before the PMA payment date. PMA payments that arrive after the cutoff are scheduled for the next PMA payment date. Because the PMA payment includes the prior months' benefits, it could erroneously appear that these benefits are being paid incorrectly—especially because the check could arrive or be deposited after your first full monthly benefit check.

Direct Express. Another option is to receive your benefits on the Direct Express® debit card. Social Security can deposit your benefit payment directly onto the card account rather than a bank account. Call the toll-free Direct Express® international number (collect) at 765-778-6290 to set up Direct Express® services. Social Security also can help you sign up for the service.

d. Reporting Changes While Living Outside the United States

When you live outside the United States, you don't avoid the SSA's continuing disability reviews—a periodic process to determine whether you're still eligible for benefits. The SSA will send you a questionnaire (Form SSA-455, *Disability Update Report*) to fill out and return. You must return it to the office that sent it to you as soon as possible; if you don't, your payments will stop. (See Chapter 14.)

In addition to responding to the questionnaire, you're responsible for notifying the SSA promptly about changes that could affect your payments. If you fail to report something or deliberately make a false statement, you could be penalized by a fine or imprisonment. You might also lose some of your payments if you don't report changes promptly.

To report changes, contact the SSA in person, by mail, or by telephone. If you want to report by mail and you live in Canada, send your report to the nearest U.S. Social Security office. In Mexico, send your report to the nearest U.S. Social Security office, embassy, or consulate. In the Philippines, send your report to Veterans' Affairs Regional Office, SSA Division, 1131 Roxas Boulevard, Manila, Philippines.

In all other countries, you can contact the nearest U.S. embassy or consulate. If you'd rather send your report to the SSA in the United States, send it via airmail to Social Security Administration, Office of International Operations, P.O. Box 17769, Baltimore, MD 21235-7769, USA.

In reporting a change, include all of the following information:

- the name of person or persons about whom the report is being made
- what is being reported and the date it happened, and
- the claim number on the Social Security check (the nine-digit Social Security number followed by a letter, or a letter and a number).

6. You Receive Other Disability Benefits

If you're disabled and younger than 65, Social Security benefits for you and your family might be reduced if you receive workers' compensation or black lung payments or disability benefits from certain government programs. Let the SSA know if any of the following are true:

- You apply for another type of disability benefit.
- You begin receiving another disability benefit or a lump-sum settlement.
- You already receive another disability benefit and the amount changes or stops.

7. You Get a Pension From Work Not Covered by Social Security

Let the SSA know if you start receiving a pension from a job where you did not pay Social Security taxes. For example, state workers covered under a state or local retirement system might receive pension benefits related to work that didn't require the payment of Social Security taxes. Whether a particular state employee is covered under Social Security can vary from state to state and the type of agreements the particular state has entered into with the federal government. If you're not sure about your own situation, contact the official who manages your retirement plan.

Also, if you receive Social Security disability benefits and start to receive a monthly pension that is based in whole or in part on work that the U.S. Social Security system doesn't cover (such as a foreign social security pension), then your U.S. Social Security benefit may be reduced, because the SSA may use a secondary formula to figure your U.S. Social Security benefit. For more information, ask at any Social Security office (or U.S. embassy if you're out of the country).

8. You're a Spouse or Surviving Spouse Who Receives a Government Pension

If you're a disabled widow or widower or the spouse of someone getting disability benefits, your Social Security payments might be reduced if you worked for a government agency where you didn't pay Social Security taxes and you receive a pension from that agency. Notify the SSA if you begin to receive such a pension or if the amount of that pension changes.

9. You Get Married

Marriage might affect your disability benefits. Be sure to notify the SSA in the following situations:

- **You're an adult who was disabled before age 22 and you receive benefits on the Social Security record of a parent or grandparent.** Payments generally will end when you get married unless you marry a person who receives certain Social Security benefits. (Specifically, your benefits won't end if you're age 18 or older and disabled, and you marry a person entitled to child's benefits based on disability or a person entitled to old age, divorced wife's, divorced husband's, widow's, widower's, mother's, father's, parent's, or disability benefits.) Once your benefits end, they can't start again unless the marriage is declared void. (A void marriage is one that was illegal from the outset, such as if you marry someone who is already married.) If your marriage ends in a divorce or your spouse dies, you won't be eligible to have the benefits restart.
- **You receive benefits as the child of a disability recipient.** Your benefits will end when you marry.
- **You receive benefits on your own earnings record.** Your payments will continue, and you don't need to report the marriage. But report any name change so it will appear on your future mailings.
- **You receive benefits as a disabled widow or widower.** Payments will continue, but remember to report any name change. If your current spouse dies, you might be eligible for higher benefits on that partner's work record.

10. You Get a Divorce or an Annulment

Notify the SSA if your marriage is annulled or you get divorced. Divorce or annulment doesn't necessarily mean that your SSDI payments will stop. It depends on the circumstances.

If you're receiving payments based on your own work record, divorce or annulment of your marriage won't affect your payments.

If you're an ex-spouse age 62 or older and you were married to an SSDI recipient for ten years or more, your SSDI auxiliary payments will continue even if you divorce. But still contact the SSA if your name is changed as a result of the divorce, so that the SSA can put your new name on your payments.

11. You Can't Manage Your Funds

If you become unable to manage your funds, you must appoint a person or an organization, called a *representative payee*, to receive the benefits and spend them on your behalf. The payee is responsible for the following:

- properly using the benefits on your behalf

- reporting to the SSA any events that might affect your payments, and
- completing any reports the SSA requires.

If you appoint a representative payee because you have a drug or alcohol addiction, the SSA may refer you to a state substance abuse agency for treatment.

Note that if you've appointed someone to manage your finances or health care under a power of attorney, that person won't be qualified as representative payee simply because of the power of attorney. You must separately notify the SSA. Also, a representative payee isn't the same as an attorney or other representative who might help you pursue your claim.

The SSA prefers to appoint friends or family as payees, but if they're not available, the SSA can appoint a qualified organization, such as a social services agency, to be a representative payee. The SSA permits qualified organizations to subtract a fee from your benefits to cover the cost of services provided as your representative payee. This fee can't be more than 10% of the monthly benefit or $54 per month, whichever is less. However, if the SSA assigns a representative payee due to a claimant's drug or alcoholism condition, the fee can be up to $97 per month. These maximum fees are adjusted yearly based on the SSA's cost-of-living adjustment (COLA).

12. You're Convicted of a Crime

When you're convicted of a crime, the SSA should be notified if you're imprisoned or confined to an institution. Benefits generally aren't paid while you're imprisoned or institutionalized, although any family members eligible on your record may continue to receive benefits.

If Your Representative Payee Misuses Your Funds

What happens if your representative payee steals or otherwise misuses your benefit money? The SSA must repay you, provided that the representative payee handles the accounts of 15 or more beneficiaries. Otherwise, you'll need to prove that the SSA was fully negligent in following its own procedures for authorizing your representative payee. The SSA doesn't have any discretion in this rule—it's clearly specified by law. In other words, it isn't an issue that can be negotiated or argued.

However, representative payees are liable for both civil and criminal penalties if they misuse your benefits and can be required to pay back misused or lost benefits. (Details can be found on Social Security's website at www.ssa.gov/payee.)

Confinement to an institution without conviction doesn't result in a suspension of benefits if it results from a court or jury finding that you're one of the following:

- guilty by reason of insanity or similar factors (such as mental defect or incompetence), or
- incompetent to stand trial.

(Also see Section E4, below, regarding other laws applicable to prisoners.)

13. Recipient Dies

You must notify the SSA when an SSDI recipient dies. The deceased's survivors aren't entitled to keep the payment for the month in which the death occurred. For example, if Herman died in June, even on June 30, Herman's survivors must return the July payment, which is actually payment for the June benefit. If Herman and his wife Eloise receive a joint monthly payment, however, Eloise should contact the SSA before returning the payment, as she's entitled to a portion of it.

If the SSA was depositing the benefit directly into the recipient's bank account, be sure to notify the bank, so it can return any payments received after death.

If the deceased's family members received benefits on the deceased's record, those payments will change to survivors benefits. If an SSDI recipient also received benefits on

behalf of his or her children, the family will have to appoint a new representative payee for the children (usually the other parent, if there is one). The survivors will need to provide a death certificate or another proof of death to the SSA.

14. Child Reaches Age 18

Payments to a child will stop when the child reaches age 18 unless the child is unmarried and either disabled or a full-time student at an elementary or secondary school.

Twice a year, the SSA sends each student a form to be filled out and returned. If the form isn't sent back, the student's payments will stop.

If a child age 18 or older receives payments as a student, immediately notify the SSA if the student:

- drops out of school
- changes schools
- changes attendance from full time to part time
- is expelled or suspended
- is paid by an employer for attending school
- marries, or
- begins working.

If a child whose payments were stopped at age 18 either becomes disabled before age 22 or is unmarried and enters elementary or secondary school full time before age 19, the SSA can resume sending payments to the child. Also, disabled children who recover from a disability can have payments started again if they become disabled again within seven years.

15. Changes in Parental or Marital Status

If you adopt a child, let the SSA know the child's name and the date of the adoption. The child might be entitled to auxiliary benefits.

Also, payments to a child who isn't a U.S. citizen could stop or start if the child's natural or adoptive parent or stepparent dies, marries, or gets a divorce (or an annulment), even if the parent doesn't receive SSDI payments.

16. Child Leaves Your Care

If you receive benefits as a wife, husband, widow, or widower caring for a child who is younger than 16 or who was disabled before age 22, notify the SSA as soon as the child leaves your care. Failure to report this could result in a penalty, an overpayment, or an additional loss of benefits. A temporary separation doesn't affect your benefits as long as you retain parental control over the child. Also, let the SSA know if the child returns to your care.

17. Deportation or Removal From the United States

If you're not a U.S. citizen and are deported or removed from the United States for certain reasons, your Social Security benefits are stopped and can't be started again unless you're lawfully admitted to the United States for permanent residence. Even if you're deported or removed, your dependents can receive benefits if they're U.S. citizens.

If your dependents aren't U.S. citizens, they can still receive benefits if they stay in the United States for the entire month. But they can't receive benefits for any month if they spend any part of it outside the United States.

C. Reporting Changes— SSI Recipients

Your obligation to report any changes that might affect your SSI benefits is similar to the requirements described for SSDI recipients, above, with a few differences. For example, residents of California, Hawaii, Massachusetts, Michigan, New York, or Vermont have special reporting requirements described in Section C10, below.

You must report any required change to Social Security within ten days after the end of the month in which it happens. For example, if you move on November 5, you must let the SSA know by December 10. Make sure you notify the SSA of any address change as soon as you can.

SSI law has specific penalties for failing to make timely reports. These penalties can be deducted from your benefits—and you'll still have to return any overpayments. The penalty is $25 for the first failure to timely report, $50 for the second time, and $100 for each subsequent failure. Penalties won't be assessed if you were without fault or had good cause for the failure to report a change.

This section describes only the situations in which reporting changes are different for SSI recipients than for SSDI recipients. Be sure to read Section B, above, before you read the following additional requirements.

1. You Change the Number of People With Whom You Live

The SSA insists on knowing the number of people who live with you. This means that you must tell the SSA if someone moves into or out of your home, if someone you live with dies, or if you or someone you live with has or adopts a baby.

2. Your Income Changes

If you had a source of income other than your SSI when you applied for benefits, and the amount of that other income changes after you begin receiving SSI, tell Social Security. Similarly, if you start receiving income from another source while you're on SSI, you must tell the SSA. If you're married, you must notify the SSA if your spouse's income changes.

 TIP

Reporting wages from work. To report wages, you can use the automated toll-free SSI Telephone Wage Reporting system or the free SSI Mobile Wage Reporting smartphone app. Contact your local Social Security office to get set up.

If your child younger than 18 lives with you and receives SSI, notify the SSA of any of the following:

- changes in the child's income
- changes in your income
- changes in your spouse's income
- changes in the income of a child who lives with you but doesn't get SSI
- the marriage of a child who lives with you but doesn't get SSI, and
- changes in the student status (starts or stops attending school full time) of a child who is working or is age 18 to 20 and lives with you.

Changes in household income generally mean that your SSI benefit will be recalculated; the new amount will affect your SSI check two months later.

If you also receive Social Security (SSDI) benefits or retirement benefits, you don't have to notify the SSA of changes in the amounts of those benefits. (It already knows.) But if your spouse gets Social Security disability or retirement benefits, you do have to tell the SSA about benefit changes.

For SSI purposes, income includes cash, checks, and the equivalent if it can be used for food, clothing, or shelter. Income even includes items you wouldn't have to report for federal, state, or local income taxes. The following are examples of income:

- wages from a job
- net earnings from your own business
- value of any food, shelter, or clothing that someone provides for you (*in-kind support and maintenance*)
- money for food, shelter, or clothing (excluding food stamps and housing allowances)
- annuity or pension payments
- veterans benefits, railroad retirement, and railroad unemployment benefits
- workers' compensation, unemployment, black lung, or SSDI benefits
- prizes, settlements, and awards, including court awards
- life insurance proceeds
- gifts and contributions
- child support and alimony
- inheritances
- interest and dividends earned on deposit accounts and investments
- rental income, and
- strike pay and other benefits from unions.

The following items aren't considered income by the SSA:

- medical care
- social services
- cash from selling, exchanging, or replacing items you own
- income tax refunds
- earned income tax credit payments
- payments from life or disability insurance on charge accounts or other credit accounts

- bills paid by someone else for things other than food, clothing, or shelter
- proceeds of a loan
- replacement of lost or stolen items
- weatherization assistance (for example, insulation, storm doors, windows)
- income interest or dividends
- gifts used to pay tuition, fees, or other necessary educational expenses at any educational institution, including vocational and technical institutions
- income and interest on resources excluded under other federal statutes, and
- credit life and credit disability insurance policies issued to or on behalf of borrowers to cover payments on loans in the event of death or disability.

EXAMPLE: Frank Fritz, an SSI recipient, purchased credit disability insurance when he bought his home. Subsequently, Mr. Fritz was in a car accident and became totally disabled. Because of his disability, the insurance company paid off his home mortgage. Neither the payment nor the increased equity in the home is considered income to Mr. Fritz.

Some things the SSA normally counts as income aren't counted as income under certain conditions—such as food, clothing, shelter, or home energy assistance provided free or at a reduced rate by private nonprofit organizations. But you still must tell the SSA about income that you think falls in the "not counted" category; the SSA will make that judgment.

3. You Receive Assets

To qualify for SSI, a single person can own up to $2,000 of property, and a married couple can own as much as $3,000 worth. If you (or your spouse, if you're married, or your child if your child receives SSI) receive personal property or real estate, and the total value of what you own exceeds the limits, you must tell the SSA. You don't have to include property not counted toward these limits, such as your home or household goods. (See Chapter 1, Section A2.)

If you receive a check for back pay from the SSA to cover periods you were eligible for but didn't receive SSI or SSDI (past-due benefits going back to the month after your application date), Social Security won't count those payments as resources for nine months after the month you get the money. However, if you have any money left over after the nine-month period, it will count as resources. For example, Jillian starts receiving SSI on March 3; her first payment includes an extra $4,000 in back payments to cover the time she qualified for SSI before her payments began. If she has any of this money left over after December 3, she must tell the SSA. The SSA will consider it resources and count it toward her eligibility for future SSI benefits. If your past-due SSI benefits are paid in installments, you have nine months to spend each installment.

If your name gets added to a bank account with another person, the SSA will probably consider all the money yours even if it isn't (unless the co-owner also receives SSI). If someone wants to add your name to an account, check with the SSA first. If the money isn't yours or is for a special purpose such as paying your medical expenses, the SSA can tell you how to set up the account so it won't affect your SSI.

If you agreed to sell property to qualify for SSI, notify the SSA when you sell it. If you don't sell the property, it may count as an asset and you might not be eligible for SSI (and you might have to return checks already sent to you).

4. You Enter or Leave an Institution

You must tell the SSA if you enter or leave a residential institution, hospital, skilled nursing facility, nursing home, intermediate care facility, halfway house, jail, prison, public emergency shelter, or similar kind of institution. The SSA needs the name of the institution and the date you enter or leave. If you can't contact the SSA, ask someone in the institution's office to help you.

In most cases, you can't get SSI while you're in an institution, or your SSI payment will be greatly reduced. If you enter a medical institution, however, your SSI can probably continue if your stay is for 90 days or less. Your doctor must sign a statement about how long you'll stay, and you must sign a statement that you need to pay expenses for your home while you're in the institution. The SSA must receive both statements by the 90th day you're in the institution or the day you leave, if that's earlier.

5. You Marry, Separate, or Divorce

You must let the SSA know of any change in your marital status—that is, you marry, divorce, separate, or get back together after a separation. These changes can affect your income and, therefore, the amount of your SSI benefits.

6. You Leave the United States

If you leave the United States for 30 days or more, you usually can no longer get SSI. Before you leave, you're obligated to notify the SSA of the dates you'll be gone. Once you return, your checks can't start again until you've been back in the United States for at least 30 continuous days.

Dependent children of military personnel who leave the United States can continue to get SSI while overseas if they were receiving SSI in the month before the parent reported for overseas duty.

Note that, since Puerto Rico residents aren't eligible for SSI, if you go to Puerto Rico for more than 30 days, your SSI payments will stop even though Puerto Rico is part of the United States.

7. You're a Sponsored Immigrant

If you qualified for SSI as an immigrant sponsored by a U.S. resident, the SSA considered the income and assets of the following people when deciding whether you qualified for SSI:

- you (including items you own in your homeland)
- your spouse
- your parents if you're under 18
- your sponsor, and
- your sponsor's spouse.

For five years after you enter the United States, you must report any changes in the income and assets of the people on this list. After the five-year period, you have to report only changes in the income and assets of you, your spouse, and your parents if you're under 18.

This rule doesn't apply if you're a refugee or have been granted asylum. The rule also doesn't apply if you become blind or disabled after being lawfully admitted for permanent residence in the United States. Note that if you're not a citizen, the date you physically entered the United States isn't necessarily the same as the date in which you technically became lawfully admitted as a permanent resident.

8. You're Younger than 22 and Start or Stop Attending School

If you're younger than 22, notify the SSA of any date you start or stop attending school on a full-time basis.

9. You Become Addicted to Drugs or Alcohol

If you receive SSI based on disability and you become addicted to drugs or alcohol, the SSA may refer you to a state substance abuse agency for treatment. (Also, see Section E4, below, regarding the law affecting DAA cases.)

10. You Live in California, Hawaii, Michigan, or Vermont

Residents of California, Hawaii, Michigan, and Vermont have additional reporting requirements that can affect the state supplement portion of your SSI benefits. Here are the rules:

- **California.** You must let the SSA know if you were regularly eating your meals away from home and you now eat at home, or you were regularly eating at home and you now eat out. (Additional state payments may be available to people who can't cook or store food where they live or who are unable to cook for themselves.) Where you regularly eat means where you must eat, not how often you eat in one place or another. If you're able to prepare meals at home but eat out frequently, you're considered to regularly eat at home and you wouldn't qualify for extra benefits, because where you eat is a matter of choice for you, not a necessity. The actual rules are complex; report any change affecting your ability to prepare meals at home—including broken appliances.

- **Hawaii, Michigan, and Vermont.** You must notify the SSA if you live in a facility that provides different levels of care, and the level of care you receive changes. For example, Bernadette lives in a home that provides both assisted living and skilled nursing. Her health has deteriorated and she has been moved from the assisted living unit to the skilled nursing section. She must notify the SSA. Generally, if you're in a nursing home or another medical facility where Medicaid pays for more than half of the cost of your care, your federal SSI payment is limited to $30 a month. But some states' supplemental payment rules differ depending on the type of facility in which you live. If your level of health care changes, contact the SSA. You could be entitled to considerably more than $30 per month. (See also Chapter 3 regarding children in such facilities.)

D. Returning to Work

After you start receiving SSDI or SSI, you might want to try to return to work. Some people cite satisfaction from overcoming a disability through their job skills, connecting with people, and getting back into the mainstream.

TIP

Get help finding a job. The Employer Assistance and Resource Network on Disability Inclusion (EARN) has a website with many resources for job seekers with disabilities. Visit https://askearn.org/page/job-seekers-resources to find job boards for people with disabilities, college programs for students with disabilities, and organizations that can help you find a job.

But returning to work is a big step for a person with a disability. You might have questions and concerns like:

- How will my benefits be affected?
- Will I lose my Medicare or Medicaid?
- What if I need special equipment at work?

Special rules called work incentives can help you ease back into the workforce. These work incentives include:

- cash benefits while you work
- medical coverage while you work
- help with expenses your employer incurs because of your disability, and
- help with education, training, and rehabilitation.

1. SSDI Work Incentives

The SSDI work incentives are fairly extensive.

Trial work period. If you return to work, during the first nine months you'll continue to receive your SSDI benefits. At the end of nine months of work, the SSA will decide if you're doing substantial gainful activity (SGA)—earning at least $1,550 per month (in 2024). If you're self-employed, your income may not be the best measure of whether you're doing SGA. Often, more consideration is given to the amount of time you spend in your business than to the amount of your income. Either way, if the SSA determines that you're doing SGA after the end of your trial work period, you'll receive benefits for three more months and then they will stop.

Not all work counts toward the nine-month period. Generally, a month will count only if you earn more than $1,110 (2024) in gross wages (regardless of amount of time worked) or spend 80 hours working in your own business. In addition, for the SSA to consider stopping your benefits because you've worked for nine months, the nine months don't need to be in a row, but they must take place within a 60-month period. Note that these rules are different, and more lenient, from those the SSA used to determine whether you were doing SGA when you first applied for benefits. Issues involving the trial work period or SGA can be confusing and complex. If you have any questions, don't hesitate to call your local SSA Field Office.

Extended period of eligibility or reentitlement period. If you're still disabled but you continue to work after the nine-month trial work period, you'll receive special protection for the next 36 months. To avoid confusion, it's important to remember that this 36-month period, also known as the *extended period of eligibility* (EPE), begins only after the trial work period ends. (As explained in the preceding paragraph, the trial work period could end anywhere from nine to 60 months after you first return to work.)

During the extended period of eligibility (the 36-month period that follows the trial work period), the SSA will pay you your SSDI benefit in any month you earn below the SGA level, even if you stop working for a reason unrelated to your disability—for instance, you get laid off. You don't have to file a new application; you simply notify the SSA. If you stop working again because of your disability, your benefits will resume without your having to reapply. (See Section E1, below.)

EXAMPLE: Pamela, age 24, was receiving disability benefits of $943 a month based on a childhood condition that made it difficult for her to walk. She wanted to work but was afraid of losing her benefits and Medicare. After learning about the disability work incentives, Pamela started working in a local laundry earning $1,400 a month. Here's how her income changed.

First nine months of work—no change

Gross earnings		$ 1,700
Social Security check	+	943
Total monthly income		$ 2,643

Next three months of work
The SSA determined that Pamela's work after her trial work period ended was SGA—she made more than $1,550 per month. Her benefits continued for three more months and then stopped. (However, note that because Pamela is still considered disabled, her benefits could be reinstated anytime during the next 36 months if her earnings drop below $1,550.)

Following the first year of work
During the first year after her trial work period, Pamela's company relocated to a town not accessible by mass transit. She hired a neighbor to drive her to work and paid a coworker to bring her home. Her transportation expenses totaled $100 a month. In addition, Pamela purchased a special motorized wheelchair so she could get around the new suburban plant. This cost $75 a month.

Gross earnings		$ 1,700
Transportation expenses	–	100
Wheelchair cost	–	75
Countable earnings		$ 1,525

Because Pamela's countable earnings were less than $1,550 a month, the SSA reinstated her checks. Her total income changed as follows:

Countable earnings		$ 1,525
Social Security check	+	841
Total income		$ 2,468

Following the second year of work
After another year, Pamela paid off the motorized chair and received a raise to $2,500 a month.

Gross earnings		$ 2,500
Transportation expenses	–	100
Countable earnings		$ 2,400

Because her countable earnings exceed $1,550, her SSDI stopped. Her Medicare continued another 93 months past her trial work period.

The point of this example is to show that at each point in her working life, Pamela's total income was greater than it would have been had she not worked and simply received disability benefits.

Resumption of benefits if you become disabled again. If you return to work and become disabled again within five years after your benefits were stopped, they can begin again following the first full month you become disabled again. Although the SSA doesn't have to redetermine your eligibility, you do have to request expedited reinstatement. Social Security will pay you for provisional benefits for six months while your application is being processed. (See Section E1b, below, to learn more.)

Continuation of Medicare. If you're still disabled but you return to work for more than nine months and your benefits stop, your Medicare coverage can continue for another 93 months (7 years and 9 months). During this period, your hospital insurance coverage (Part A) is free. After the 93 months, you may be able to buy Medicare coverage by paying a monthly premium. (See Section E3, below.)

In addition, if you get Medicare and have a low income and few resources, your state might pay your Medicare premiums and, in some cases, other out-of-pocket Medicare expenses, such as deductibles and coinsurance, through a Medicare Savings Program. To find out if you qualify, contact your local welfare office or Medicaid agency. Having the government pay for these additional medical expenses makes it easier to become self-supporting when you're trying to leave the disability rolls.

Impairment-related work expenses. If you need certain equipment or services to help you work, the money you pay for them might be deducted from your monthly wages when Social Security calculates whether you're earning more than the SGA level. Costs for the following items can generally be deducted:

- equipment (such as a wheelchair or specialized work equipment)
- attendant care services (such as a personal attendant, job coach, or guide dog)
- prostheses
- prescription drugs, and
- transportation to and from work.

Only expenses you pay are deductible from your income as work expenses to determine whether you're making more than the SGA amount; expenses paid by your employer wouldn't be deducted from your monthly wages. If the deduction brings your monthly income to less than $1,550, you'll receive your SSDI benefit, and the month won't count toward your nine-month trial period, if you're still in your trial work period.

Recovery during vocational rehabilitation. If you participate in a vocational rehabilitation program that's meant to result in your becoming self-supporting, and your disability ends while you're in the program, your disability benefits generally will continue until the program ends.

Special rules for blind persons. If you're blind and you return to work and earn above the SGA level for blind people (above $2,590 per month for the year 2024), you're still eligible for a disability "freeze." This means that the years in which you have low or no earnings because of your disability won't be counted in figuring your future benefits, which are based on your average earnings over your work life.

If you're 55 or older and you're blind, the SSA figures your ability to perform SGA differently. After age 55, even if your earnings exceed the SGA level, your benefits will only be suspended, not terminated, when you work above the SGA level, if your work requires a lower level of skill and ability than work you did before age 55. The SSA assumes that your ability to do SGA is low and that you sometimes might be unable to work because of your disability. Thus, your eligibility for Social Security benefits might continue indefinitely, and the SSA will pay benefits for any month your earnings fall below the SGA level.

If you're blind and self-employed, the SGA level becomes the only measure of SGA. The SSA doesn't make a separate evaluation of the time you spend in your business, as it does for nonblind beneficiaries. This means you can be doing a lot of work for your business but still receive disability benefits, as long as your net profit doesn't exceed the SGA level.

If you're blind and self-employed, the SGA level becomes the only measure of SGA. The SSA does not make a separate evaluation of the time you spend in your business, as it does for nonblind beneficiaries. This means you can be doing a lot of work for your business but still receive disability benefits, as long as your net profit does not exceed the SGA level.

2. SSI Work Incentives

Like the SSDI work incentives, the SSI work incentives are quite extensive.

Continuation of SSI. If you return to work, you can continue to receive payments until your income exceeds the SSI income limits.

Continuation of Medicaid. If you return to work, your Medicaid coverage will likely continue until your income reaches a certain level. The level varies from state to state and reflects the cost of health care in your state. If your actual health care costs are higher than the average for your state, you might be able to keep your Medicaid. Be aware, however, that for Medicaid to continue after you go back to work, you must:

- need it in order to work
- be unable to afford similar health insurance coverage
- have a disabling condition, and
- meet the nonincome SSI disability requirements.

In addition, if you have low income and few resources, your state might pay your Medicaid premiums and other out-of-pocket Medicaid expenses, such as deductibles and coinsurance. (See Section E3, below, to learn about Medicaid expenses for disabled workers.)

Work expenses related to your disability. If you need certain equipment or services to help you work (impairment-related work expenses, or IRWE), the money you pay for them can be deducted from your monthly wages to determine your income level. Costs for the following items are generally deductible:

- equipment (such as a wheelchair or specialized work equipment)
- attendant care services (such as a personal attendant, job coach, or guide dog)
- prostheses
- prescription drugs, and
- transportation to and from work.

Only expenses you pay are deductible from your income as a work expense in determining whether you're earning more than the SGA level; expenses your employer pays aren't deducted from your monthly wages. If you're blind, the work expenses need not be directly related to the impairment (for instance, the cost of meals during work hours). Special rules for blind persons (see below) are even more favorable.

Plan for Achieving Self-Support. A special SSA rule called a *Plan for Achieving Self-Support*, or PASS, lets you put aside money and assets toward a plan designed to help you support yourself.

How Working Reduces Your SSI Amount

If you receive income from a job, the SSA doesn't count the first $85 in earnings you get each month. One half of what you earn over $85 is deducted from your SSI check.

If you have income in addition to job earnings and SSI, the SSA doesn't count the first $65 in job earnings you get each month. One half of what you make over $65 is deducted from your SSI payment. So is your other income, less $20.

If you have no income other than job earnings and SSI, you could earn over $1,971 a month (2024) before your SSI will stop (depending on your state—whether your state has a supplement matters in this calculation). If you have income in addition to job earnings and SSI, the amount you can earn before losing your SSI payment may be lower.

If you lose your job while you are still getting SSI, your SSI payments will increase. If you lose your job within 60 months of when your SSI payments stopped because of excess income, but you are still disabled, you can request your benefits to be started again without your having to reapply. (This is called expedited reinstatement.) If you lose your job after working more than 12 months from when your SSI has stopped for other reasons, you may have to reapply. (See Section E1, below.)

The money won't be counted toward your SSI eligibility and won't reduce your SSI payment. The goal of your plan might be to start a business or get a job.

If you're going to go back to work and your income might exceed the SSI eligibility level, a PASS could help you qualify. You can set aside income and assets you need to accomplish a work goal and reduce the money counted by the SSA toward your SSI eligibility or benefit amount.

Your vocational rehabilitation worker, your employer, an SSA staff person, or anyone else can help you write up a PASS. In general, the PASS must:

- **be in writing,** preferably on Form SSA-545-BK, *Plan to Achieve Self-Support*, and signed by you and, if applicable, your representative payee
- **state a specific work goal,** one that you have a reasonable chance of achieving given your strength and abilities (for example, "becoming a carpenter" or "becoming a programmer")
- **show a reasonable time frame,** including your projected beginning and ending dates, milestones along the way, and a last step that indicates how you'll get a job, and
- **specify the amount and sources of income or resources to be set aside,** including a description of expenses (reasonably priced) that are necessary to achieve your work goal.

EXAMPLE: Delano receives SSI payments of $943 each month. It's his only income. He's offered a job in a local fast food restaurant at $215 per month and contacts his local SSA office to see how this would affect his SSI payment. He's told that Social Security wouldn't count the first $85 of earnings and half of the earnings over $85.

Gross monthly earnings	$	215
First $85	–	85
Earnings over $85	$	130
SSI payment	$	943
Half of earnings over $85		
($130 ÷ 2)	–	65
New SSI award	$	878
Gross monthly earnings	+	215
Total monthly income		$ 1,093

After working 18 months, Delano gets a raise to $367 a month. He also purchases an electric wheelchair to help him get around at work, which he pays off at $52 a month.

Gross monthly earnings	$	367
First $85	–	85
Earnings over $85		282
Wheelchair cost	–	52
Balance	$	230
SSI payment	$	943
Half of balance ($230 ÷ 2)	–	115
New SSI award	$	828
Gross monthly earnings	+	367
Total monthly income		$ 1,195

Even though Delano's earnings went up by $152, his SSI payment was reduced by only $115 because of the work expense deduction for the wheelchair and the SSI work incentive. And his total income now is $1,195, substantially more than the $943 he had before he started working.

After a few more months, Delano decides that he wants to get a college degree. His sister helps him write a PASS describing his plans to work and save money for school. He wants to save $75 each month for school.

Gross monthly earnings:	$	367
First $85	–	85
Earnings over $85		282
Work expenses (wheelchair)	–	52
Balance	$	230
Half of balance ($230 ÷ 2)	$	115
PASS savings plan	–	75
Remainder after PASS deduction	$	40
SSI payment	$	943
Remainder after PASS deduction	–	40
New SSI award	$	903
Gross monthly earnings	+	367
Total monthly income		$ 1,270

Even though Delano's job earnings didn't change, his SSI checks increased because of the PASS.

Recovery during vocational rehabilitation. If you participate in a vocational rehabilitation program that's meant to result in your becoming self-supporting, and your disability ends while you're in the program, your SSI benefits generally will continue until the program ends.

Sheltered workshop payments. If you work in a *sheltered workshop*, a company that employs primarily disabled people, special rules allow the SSA to exclude some of your earnings when figuring your SSI payment.

Grants to disabled students. Most scholarships or grants used to pay for tuition, books, and other expenses directly related to getting an education won't be counted as income if you go to school or enroll in a training program. Students can also exclude up to $2,290 of earnings a month, up to $9,230 a year, in 2024. This amount is usually increased yearly.

Rules for blind persons. If your condition meets the legal definition of blindness, SGA isn't a factor for your SSI eligibility while you're receiving benefits. Your SSI eligibility continues until you medically recover or the SSA ends your eligibility because of a non-disability-related reason (for instance, you go over the SSI income or resource limits).

Also, most of your work expenses—not just those related to your disability—are deducted from your income when the SSA decides you're eligible for SSI and decides how much of your income should be deducted from your SSI payment. For example, the cost of special clothes needed on the job can be deducted.

Some other examples of *blind work expenses* (BWE) are costs for:

- guide dog
- transportation to and from work
- meals eaten at work
- federal, state, and local income taxes
- Social Security taxes
- attendant care services
- visual and sensory aids
- translation of materials into Braille
- professional association membership, and
- union dues.

EXAMPLE: Ahmed is 20 years old and receives SSI payments because he is blind. He receives $943 each month and has Medicaid coverage.

In January, Ahmed begins working part time during the evenings and on weekends for the veterinarian who cares for his guide dog. Ahmed is paid $425 a month to answer the phone, make appointments, and help with the care and feeding of animals boarded at the kennel.

Ahmed reports his work and earnings to his local Social Security office and reports the following blind work expenses:

Transportation to/from work	$	50.00
Care/feeding of his guide dog	+	35.00
Taxes	+	40.50
Total blind work expenses		$ 125.50

Here is how the SSA calculates Ahmed's SSI amount, based on his earnings and his blind work expenses:

Gross monthly earnings	$ 425.00
First $85	– 85.00
Earnings over $85	$ 340.00
Half of earnings over $85	$ 170.00
Blind work expenses	– 125.50
Countable income	$ 44.50
SSI payment	943.00
Countable income	– 44.50
	$ 898.50

This means that, even though Ahmed is earning $425 per month, he loses only $44.50 in SSI payments, and his Medicaid coverage continues. Ahmed's total monthly income becomes $1,323.50 ($898.50 SSI + $425 monthly earnings = $1,323.50).

In late March, Ahmed reports to the SSA that his employer has asked him to work longer hours and also is giving him a raise. Ahmed begins earning $700 per month in April. He tells SSA that he likes working with animals so much that he would like to go to school to learn to be a dog trainer and groomer. He plans to save $225 per month from his increased earnings so that he will have $1,125 saved to pay for books and tuition by September when the course begins at a local vocational school. The SSA helps Ahmed to write a PASS so that $225 per month is excluded from the income used to figure his SSI payment for the months from April through August.

Additionally, Ahmed reports that working longer hours and earning more will increase his transportation costs and his taxes. He reports the following blind work expenses beginning with April:

Transportation to/from work	$ 65.00
Care/feeding of his guide dog	+ 35.00
Taxes	+ 75.50
Total blind work expenses	$ 175.50

Here is how SSA computes Ahmed's SSI payment beginning with April:

Gross monthly earnings	$ 700.00
First $85	– 85.00
Earnings over $85	615.00
Half of earnings over $85	$ 307.50
Blind work expenses	– 175.50
Countable income	32.00
PASS adjustment	225.00
Countable income	$ 0.00

Because SSA was able to deduct so many of his work expenses, none of Ahmed's income is subtracted from his SSI payment. He receives $943, the maximum SSI payment in his state. Even though Ahmed is earning $275 more each month than he did in January, February, or March, his SSI check will increase from $898.50 to $943 because of his PASS. And his Medicaid coverage continues. Ahmed's total monthly income beginning in April is $1,643 ($700 monthly earnings + $943 SSI).

Ahmed begins a four-month course to learn to be a dog groomer and trainer in September. His PASS ended in August because he had saved the $1,125 to pay for books and tuition. But now he is an unmarried student under age 22 and he can use the student-earned income exclusion to reduce his countable income. He can exclude earnings of $2,290 per month up to a maximum of $9,230 annually. Because he'll be in school for only four months in the calendar year, he can use the exclusion for each of these months without exceeding the $9,230 annual maximum.

Ahmed continues to work for the veterinarian and receives another pay raise, which increases his earnings to $800 per month beginning in September. His blind work expenses for transportation and care and feeding of his guide dog are unchanged, but his increased wages cause his taxes to go up $12. His total blind work expenses, beginning in September, rise from $175.50 to $187.50 per month, including the $12 in additional taxes.

Here is how SSA figures Ahmed's countable income while he is a student from September through December:

Ahmed's earnings	$ 800
Student earned inc. exclusion	– 2,290
Countable income	$ 0

Ahmed continues to receive $943 per month from SSI in addition to his monthly earnings of $800, and his Medicaid coverage continues. Ahmed's total monthly income becomes $1,743 ($943 SSI + $800 earnings = $1,743).

E. The Ticket to Work and Work Incentives Improvement Act

A law called the Ticket to Work and Work Incentives Improvement Act (TWWIIA; Public Law 106-170) contains some provisions that affect how the SSA handles work incentives. The intention of the TWWIIA is to:

- increase the amount of choice that disability recipients have in obtaining rehabilitation and vocational services to help them go to work and attain their employment goals
- remove the barriers that required people with disabilities to choose between health care coverage and work, and
- ensure that more people with disabilities can participate in the workforce and lessen their dependence on public benefits.

Some of the more important highlights directly affecting disability recipients are described in this section. The SSA's regulations interpreting the law can be found at 20 C.F.R. Part 411.

1. Elimination of Work Disincentives

Although the SSA already offered work incentives, as discussed previously, Congress's intent in passing the TWWIIA was to further encourage those receiving Social Security disability benefits to return to the workforce by eliminating additional financial obstacles.

a. Work Activity as a Basis for Review

One of the worries for you, a disabled person returning to work, is the termination of your disability benefits if you start doing substantial gainful activity (SGA). The Ticket to Work law prohibits the SSA from using SGA as a means of triggering a continuing disability review (CDR) if you've been receiving benefits for at least two years. Regular, scheduled CDRs will still take place, however. This law:

- prohibits the use of SGA as a basis for review if you're entitled to disability insurance benefits under Section 223 of the Social Security Act (42 U.S.C.A. § 423) or monthly retirement or survivors insurance benefits under Section 202 of the Social Security Act (42 U.S.C.A. § 402) and you've received such benefits for at least 24 months, and
- allows for regular CDRs and for the termination of benefits if you're earning more than the SGA.

b. Expedited Reinstatement of Benefits

By speeding up reinstatement of benefits in the event that people need to get back on disability benefits quickly, the Ticket to Work law encourages claimants to try working. Provisions of this law and associated regulations include:

- **Applying for benefits.** If your SSDI or SSI is terminated because you're doing SGA or because of medical improvement, you can request a reinstatement of benefits without filing a new application if you're not able to work on account of your medical condition and you file the reinstatement request within 60 months of when your benefits ended. You must request expedited reinstatement of benefits in writing. You're permitted to apply for expedited reinstatement of benefits the same month you became unable to do SGA, so that you can obtain provisional benefits the very next month (see below). To obtain specific instructions, call your local SSA Field Office (you can get your Field Office number from the SSA at 800-772-1213). You'll need to complete Forms SSA-371 (SSDI), SSA-372 (SSI), or SSA-373 (SSI, Disabled Spouse). These are simple forms, mainly requiring addresses and Social Security numbers.

- **Medical standard of review.** Unlike a new disability application, when you request an expedited reinstatement of benefits, the SSA will consider only the impairments you had the last time you received benefits. The SSA will apply the *medical improvement review standard* (MIRS) as used in continuing disability reviews (see Chapter 14). Using this standard, it's likely that you'll be found disabled again—because the MIRS requires that in order to deny benefits, the SSA must find significant medical

improvement in your condition. The SSA's regulations acknowledge this fact, stating: "Under the medical improvement review standard, we will generally find that you're disabled." (20 C.F.R. §§ 404.1592b, 416.999.)

- **Unsuccessful work attempt.** The SSA considers that you've had an *unsuccessful work attempt* (UWA) if you tried to go back to work and your work attempt lasted no more than 6 months before you had to stop working or before your income fell below SGA levels. You don't apply for a UWA determination— it's something the SSA looks for internally—but it can affect your reinstatement, because earnings in a UWA period won't be applied to SGA determinations. That can affect when your benefits can begin again. For SSDI, UWA determinations by the SSA can apply either to claimants seeking expedited reinstatement of benefits previously received or to new claimants. For SSI, UWA determinations apply only to new claimants.

- **Provisional benefits.** While the SSA is deciding whether to reinstate your benefits, you can receive provisional benefits for up to six months. Provisional benefits begin the month you file your request, and the amount will be based on the amount of benefits you received in the month immediately before your benefits were terminated. If you were entitled to more than one type of benefit (SSDI and SSI), the SSA is supposed to pay you the higher one. Of course, you can fail to qualify for provisional benefits for a variety of reasons, such as working above the SGA level, being a prisoner, or not having previously received disability benefits.

• **Repayment of provisional benefits.** Generally, you don't have to repay any provisional benefits if your reinstatement request is denied. There are, however, some exceptions for fraud or mistake. For example, if you obtained provisional benefits that you knew you were unqualified to receive (such as by fraud), the SSA could demand the money back. If the SSA made a mistake (such as sending you a payment after deciding you couldn't have one, sending you a payment as a prisoner, or sending you a payment while you were doing substantial gainful activity), the SSA can demand repayment. Also, the SSA can deduct any Medicare premiums you owe from your provisional benefits.

• **Concurrent application for disability.** Applying for expedited reinstatement of benefits doesn't prevent you from filing a new application for disability. In the unlikely event your application for reinstated benefits is denied, the SSA will automatically consider the date you make the expedited reinstatement request as a protective filing date for a new initial application. Once you file the application, the SSA will begin reviewing all of your medical conditions to see if you're disabled.

• **What if your request Is denied?** You can appeal a denial for expedited reinstatement (but not provisional benefits) within 60 days of the date you receive the denial. You appeal by filing a *Request for Reconsideration* (Form SSA-561-U2). You may also need to submit additional documentation, such as a *Disability Report-Appeal* (Form SSA-3441-BK). You can call or visit your local Field Office and ask for help with the reconsideration.

• **24-month reinstatement period.** During the 24 months following the date your reinstatement request is granted, you won't receive benefits for any months in which you perform substantial gainful activity (for SSDI) or your income and resources are too high (for SSI). Following this 24-month period, your status will return to where it was when you originally received disability benefits. For example, you can again apply for work incentives, such as in the Ticket to Work program (see Section F, below), and can even reapply for expedited reinstatement of benefits at some point in the future.

2. Ticket to Work Website

The SSA has established a website to provide disabled beneficiaries with accurate information related to the Ticket to Work incentives. Visit https://choosework.ssa.gov to find information about the Ticket to Work program and current contact information for Ticket to Work service providers.

3. Expansion of Health Care Services

Loss of vital health care coverage is one of the biggest problems for disabled people trying to return to work. The following provisions give people additional assistance in decreasing health care cost barriers to working.

a. State Options Under Medicaid

The Ticket to Work law established a Medicaid buy-in option for states. For beneficiaries between 16 and 64, the law expanded funding for Medicaid for workers with disabilities by liberalizing the limits on resources and income and giving working people who have impairments the right to buy Medicaid, even though they're no longer eligible for SSDI or SSI. The states can require individuals to contribute to the cost on a sliding scale based on income. All but about five states are participating in the program.

b. Continuation of Medicare Coverage

Congress extended premium-free Medicare Part A coverage for SSDI beneficiaries who return to work for eight-and-a-half years (this includes the nine-month trial work period plus another 93 months).

c. Election to Suspend Medigap Insurance

The law allows workers with disabilities who have Medicare coverage and a Medigap policy to suspend the premiums and benefits of the Medigap policy if they have employer-sponsored health coverage.

F. Participation in the Ticket to Work Program

You might be eligible to participate in the Ticket to Work program, which can lead to new training and opportunities that allow you to return to work, if you're physically and mentally able.

1. Can You Participate in the Ticket to Work Program?

You're eligible to participate in the Ticket to Work program if you're either a Title 2 (SSDI) or Title 16 (SSI) beneficiary between 18 and 64 years of age. There are no other qualifications.

2. Should You Participate?

The Ticket to Work program offers extensive benefits to those who might be able to perform some type of work. It's another way that you can receive vocational rehabilitation services that could allow you to ultimately earn more money than you're able to receive in disability benefits.

Many people receiving disability benefits could perform less physically demanding jobs if they had the training. Some beneficiaries worry, however, that if they try to return to work before they're ready, they risk losing their disability benefits or their medical coverage under Medicare or Medicaid. The Ticket to Work program offers numerous safety net features to prevent the loss of disability benefits.

It's important to understand that the program is entirely voluntary. Its purpose is to offer you greater choice when it comes to finding work or earning more money—not to force you into working. If you decide that you're not interested in the program or aren't able to work, you don't have to take part. Your decision will have no effect on your disability benefits.

There are numerous benefits to enrolling in the program, including the following:

- Social Security will pause continuing disability reviews on your claim
- you'll have access to free legal assistance

- you'll get free planning and assistance in evaluating your work alternatives, and
- you'll receive free training.

The SSA sends out letters about the Ticket to Work program to all recipients, along with what they call tickets, which you can use to access services.

You should receive only one ticket. However, it's possible that you could receive a new ticket, or even multiple tickets over your lifetime, if your benefits are stopped and then restarted.

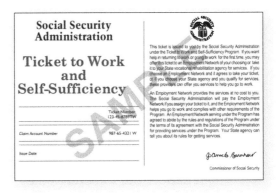

TIP

Don't toss your ticket. Even if you don't think you want to take part in this program now, keep any ticket the SSA sends to you in a safe place. Having this ticket will make things easier if you decide later to take part in the program.

3. Working Shouldn't Affect Your Disability Status

Ordinarily, the SSA reviews your case from time to time to see if you're still disabled—and stops your benefits if it thinks you can work. But if you choose to participate in the Ticket to Work program, the SSA won't conduct its usual medical reviews, which should protect you from Social Security finding that you're no longer disabled.

To avoid these medical reviews, however, you must be actively using your ticket—that is, engaging in the activities outlined in your employment plan on a regular basis and in the approximate time frames set forth in the plan (see Section 8, below).

4. Getting a Ticket

If you're interested in taking part in the Ticket to Work program but haven't yet received a ticket, visit the Ticket to Work website at https://choosework.ssa.gov. You can also call the Ticket to Work Help Line at 866-968-7842 or 866-833-2967 (TTY) if you have questions.

You don't actually need a paper ticket to participate. The employment network (EN) you select (see below) will be able to verify your eligibility to participate in the program.

An employment network might also contact you directly, asking whether you want to participate. Of course, you can always say "no."

TIP

Shop around before you assign your ticket to a provider. You don't need to sign up with the first EN you speak to. If you have multiple ENs in your area, talk with their staff members about the services they provide and about your goals. Make sure you've found an EN you're comfortable with before you assign them your ticket.

5. Where You'll Go for Services

Unlike previous SSA programs, you'll no longer be referred directly to state vocational rehabilitation agencies for rehabilitation services. Instead, you'll be able to use your ticket to go to an approved service provider of your choice, called an *employment network* (EN). The EN can be a private organization or a public agency (such as a state vocational rehabilitation agency) that has agreed to work with the SSA to provide vocational rehabilitation, employment, and other support services to assist beneficiaries in going to work and remaining on the job.

You can search for employment networks in your area by visiting https://choosework.ssa.gov/findhelp.

6. What to Expect From the Employment Network

At your first formal appointment with the EN you've chosen, expect to be asked a number of questions about your disability, your work history, and other subjects. Although the EN may already have received information about you from the SSA, these questions are necessary so the EN can consider how it can help you. Feel free to ask any questions of the EN about its role in assisting you to reach your employment goal.

After you've met with an EN staff person, the two of you will develop and sign an individual work plan (IWP). The SSA regulations require that your completed IWP include statements of:

- your vocational goal, including goals for earnings and job advancement
- the services and support you need to achieve your vocational goal
- any terms and conditions related to the provision of these services and supports
- the EN's acknowledgment that it can't receive any compensation directly from you for the cost of services and support
- the conditions under which the EN can modify your IWP or terminate its relationship with you
- your rights under the Ticket to Work program, including your right to take back your ticket if at any time you're dissatisfied with the EN
- the remedies available to you, including the availability of the protection and advocacy system (discussed in Section F8, below) for the resolution of disputes
- your right to amend your IWP, if the EN is also in agreement
- your right to privacy and confidentiality, and

- your right to have a copy of your IWP, in an accessible format chosen by you.

You'll notice that you have a number of important rights under the IWP, including the right to change your plan and the right to move to a different EN. (See Section 8, below, for how to switch to a new EN.)

7. How the EN Gets Paid— and How This Affects You

An EN can choose between two primary methods of payment for providing services under the Ticket to Work program:

- the *outcome payment system,* or
- the *outcome milestone system.*

Under the outcome payment system, the EN can choose to be paid for each month (up to a maximum of 36 months for SSDI and 60 months for SSI beneficiaries) during which you don't collect federal disability benefits because of your work and earnings. By contrast, if the EN selects the outcome milestone system, the EN can receive some payments before your benefits stop, but after you start working. Payments are made when you achieve one or more milestones toward permanent employment, with a limit of 60 months of outcome payments. Overall, the EN stands to make more if it chooses the outcome payment rather than the outcome milestone system.

Why should you care about this? Because it may help explain the EN's behavior and what sort of plan or activities it's steering you toward.

> ### You Can Still Receive Vocational Rehab Services Without a Ticket
>
> State *vocational rehabilitation* (VR) agencies will continue to exist, and you don't need a ticket to use their services. Don't be confused by the fact that they also participate in the Ticket to Work program. Your state's VR agency might call your plan for returning to work an *individualized plan for employment* (IPE) instead of an individual work plan (IWP), but the two plans are very similar.

8. Your Progress Toward Self-Supporting Employment

The purpose of the Ticket to Work program is to provide you with the services and support you need to work—with the ultimate goal of reducing or eliminating your dependence on SSDI or SSI benefits. That means that the SSA will keep an eye on you to determine whether you are, in fact, making timely progress on your work plan. At a certain point, the SSA will expect you to start working. To better understand what will be required, you need to first understand what the SSA means by timely progress and what it will count as work.

a. Definition of Timely Progress

What is timely progress? In general, the SSA asks you to show an increasing ability, year by year, to work at levels that will reduce or eliminate your dependence on disability benefits. The SSA has a very specific calendar of what it considers timely progress.

The SSA's regulations (20 C.F.R. § 411.180) define *timely progress* as follows:

1. 12-month review requires three months' work at the trial work level ($1,110/month in 2024) or 60% of a full-time course load at a college or vocational training program or earning a GED.

2. 24-month review requires six months' work at the trial work level or 75% of a full-time course load at a college or vocational program.

3. 36-month review requires nine months' work earning more than SGA-level income, or completion of a vocational training program, a two-year college program, or a full-time academic year at a four-year college.

4. 48-month review requires nine months' work earning more than SGAlevel income, or another full-time year at a four-year college.

5. 60-month review requires six months of receiving no disability benefits from the SSA or another full-time year at a four-year college.

6. 72-month review requires six months of receiving no benefits from the SSA or completion of a four-year college program.

7. Future reviews every 12 months require six months of receiving no benefits from the SSA.

b. Definition of Work

Whether you're said to be working under the Ticket to Work program depends on the type of benefits you're receiving and various other individual factors.

SSDI nonblind beneficiaries. If you're receiving SSDI for a disability other than blindness, then during your first and second 12-month progress reviews, the SSA will consider you to be working during any month in which your earnings from employment or self-employment are at or above the SGA level for nonblind beneficiaries.

During your third 12-month progress review period, and during later 12-month progress review periods, the SSA will consider you to be working during any month for which Social Security disability benefits aren't payable to you because of your work or earnings.

SSDI blind beneficiaries or beneficiaries in trial work period. If you're receiving SSDI and are blind, or are in a trial work period, then during your first and second 12-month progress reviews, the SSA will consider you to be working during any month in which your earnings are at the SGA level for nonblind beneficiaries, if either of the following is true:

- Your gross earnings from employment are at the SGA level for nonblind beneficiaries, before deductions for impairment-related work expenses.
- Your net earnings from self-employment are at the SGA level for nonblind

beneficiaries, before deductions for impairment-related work expenses.

During your third 12-month progress review period, and during later 12-month progress review periods, the SSA will consider you to be working during any month for which SSDI isn't payable to you because of your work or earnings.

SSI beneficiaries. If you receive SSI, then during your first and second 12-month progress reviews, the SSA will consider you to be working during any month in which your:

- gross earnings from employment are at the SGA level for nonblind beneficiaries, before any SSI income exclusions, or
- net earnings from self-employment are at the SGA level for nonblind beneficiaries, before any SSI income exclusions.

During your third 12-month progress review period, and during later 12-month progress review periods, the SSA will consider you to be working during any month in which your earnings from employment or self-employment are sufficient to preclude the payment of SSI cash benefits for one month.

Concurrent SSDI and SSI nonblind beneficiaries. If you're receiving SSDI and SSI at the same time for something other than blindness, then during your first and second 12-month progress reviews, you'll be considered working during any month in which your earnings from employment or self-employment are at the SGA level for nonblind beneficiaries.

Concurrent SSDI and SSI blind beneficiaries or beneficiaries in trial work period. If you're receiving SSDI and SSI concurrently and are blind or are in a trial work period, then during your first and second 12-month progress reviews, you'll be considered working during any month in which your:

- gross earnings from employment, before any SSI income exclusions or deductions for impairment-related work expenses, are at the SGA level for nonblind beneficiaries, or
- net earnings from self-employment, before any SSI income exclusions or deductions for impairment-related work expenses, are at the SGA level for nonblind beneficiaries.

During your third 12-month progress review period, and during later 12-month progress review periods, the SSA will consider you to be working during any month in which your earnings from employment or self-employment are enough that you don't need SSDI or SSI cash benefits for the month.

c. If You Fail to Make Timely Progress

If you're not making timely progress toward self-supporting employment, the Ticket to Work program manager will conclude that you're no longer using your ticket. Your ticket will be deactivated, and you'll once again be subject to continuing disability reviews (CDRs).

But you can reenter the Ticket to Work program under certain conditions, depending on how far you had gotten in your work plan when the failure to make timely progress occurred. The various re-entry rules are complicated, but they basically require you to start actively participating in your plan again and doing some type of work. For help in understanding how the rules apply in your case, contact your EN or the program manager.

To re-enter "in-use" status, you'll need to submit a written request to the program manager. If you're approved, you'll receive a written decision reinstating you to in-use status for your Ticket to Work. If the program manager denies your request, you can appeal to the SSA within 30 days. (You'll receive instructions with the denial letter.) If the SSA agrees with you and reverses the denial, then the SSA will send you a notice and inform the program manager. In that event, you'll be reinstated as of the date of the SSA's decision.

9. Dissatisfaction With Your Employment Network

The transition from receiving disability benefits to supporting yourself through employment is bound to involve difficulties and frustrations—it's no easy task. With any luck, you'll receive the assistance you need from your employment network, but the EN itself may also frustrate you through errors, decisions you don't agree with, or bureaucratic hassles.

a. Changing Employment Networks

You can decide to decide to switch employment networks at any time. You'll need to unassign your ticket by filling out a ticket unassignment form (available at the choosework.ssa.gov website).

But if you want to keep medical continuing disability reviews from starting up again, it's important that you reassign your ticket to a new EN within 90 days.

b. Internal Grievance Procedures

Before you switch employment networks, there are several internal steps you can take if you're having a problem with your EN. Your EN is required to have a grievance process through which unhappy clients can voice their dissatisfaction and receive a reply. If you don't get a satisfactory reply, you can call the program manager and ask them to resolve your grievance informally. If the program manager can't help, they will pass the matter on to the SSA.

You also can request an agency in the protection and advocacy system in your state (see below) to help you if you're unhappy with an EN. You can ask your state agency to help you at any stage of the grievance process.

If your EN happens to be a state vocational rehabilitation agency, the agency must give you a description of the services available through the client assistance program. It also must give you the opportunity to resolve your grievance through mediation or an impartial hearing.

c. Outside Help: Your State Protection and Advocacy System

In every state, various organizations have been designated to help you navigate the Ticket to Work system. Collectively, they're referred to as the system for Protection and Advocacy for Beneficiaries of Social Security (PABSS), but the particular organization you contact will no doubt go by a different name. Search for PABSS organizations in your state at https://choosework.ssa.gov/findhelp.

Your state protection and advocacy agency can give you help and personal representation on matters like:

- information and advice about vocational rehabilitation and employment services
- specific advice about selecting an EN
- information about special rules called work incentives, which are designed to support your efforts to work
- assistance in resolving any complaints against your EN or other associated provider, and

- assistance with any problems that arise with the work plan you develop with your EN.

The protection and advocacy agencies are mainly concerned with advocacy and advice about work incentives, rehabilitation opportunities, and dispute resolution from a legal perspective. For example, you might wish to dispute the legality of an EN's terminating your Ticket to Work for reasons you think are unfair. Or you might just have a question about the difference in the way the SSA evaluates income earned under the Ticket to Work program compared to income earned by a person not in the program.

d. Help From Work Incentives Planning and Assistance Program

Social Security's Work Incentives Planning and Assistance (WIPA) program can help you answer questions about the SSA's work incentives and decide whether you're ready to start working. It's run through local community organizations, which are paid by the SSA. Each WIPA agency has benefits specialists on its staff who can deal with complex issues, such as how working will affect your benefits payments and what additional federal, state, and local supports are available to help you in your effort to work.

In contrast to the legal guidance and advocacy a protection and advocacy agency offers, the major purpose of the WIPA program is to provide planning information and assistance regarding work incentives that may be appropriate for you personally. For example, you might want expert advice on the kind of rehabilitation and work goals that would be most appropriate in view of your impairments and limitations. Go to the SSA's list of service providers, at https://choosework.ssa.gov/findhelp, for a list of WIPA organizations and their contact information.

10. Advising the SSA When You Go Back to Work

If you go back to work, or you begin to earn more money, you must notify your local Social Security office. The Ticket to Work program doesn't replace the special rules, called *work incentives*, that help serve as a bridge between Social Security and SSI disability benefits and financial independence. These work incentives include:

- cash benefits while you work
- Medicare or Medicaid while you work, and
- help with any extra work expenses you may have as a result of your disability.

(See Section D, above, for more information about work incentives.)

11. When Your Ticket Can Be Terminated

You've already read about one of the reasons that your participation in the Ticket to Work program can be canceled—your inability to make timely progress on your work plan (see Subsection 7, above). However, the SSA can stop your participation (or, in their language, "terminate your ticket") for other reasons. These are summarized below; to read the list in full, see 20 C.F.R. § 411.155.

a. Ticket Termination for Reasons Other Than Work or Earnings

Your ticket can be terminated for any of the following reasons, as early as the first month involving one of them:

- Your entitlement to SSDI or widow's benefits based on disability has ended for reasons other than your work activity or earnings (such as reaching retirement age or having significant medical improvement).

Summary of Ticket to Work Program

Here's a summary of the important features of the Ticket to Work program:

- The program is designed to help both SSDI and SSI Social Security disability beneficiaries make a transition to work.
- The program is entirely voluntary, and you can stop at will. There's no expense to you.
- An employment network of your choosing will help you develop an individual employment plan, and your progress will be evaluated on a regular basis.
- While participating in the program, you won't be subject to continuing disability reviews for the purpose of determining whether your medical condition has improved. Nor will your earnings trigger a CDR—even if they're over the SGA maximum.

- Free legal assistance will be available to you through a protection and advocacy agency for disputes or other legal questions you may have with your employment network.
- Free planning and knowledge assistance regarding rehabilitation and vocational alternatives will be available to you through the Work Incentives Planning and Assistance (WIPA) agencies available in each state.
- Participation in or successful completion of the Ticket to Work program and return to full-time work doesn't eliminate your entitlement to work-incentive provisions, as discussed in Sections D1 and D2, above. For example, you'll still have prolonged access to Medicare or Medicaid health care coverage and other privileges, even when you return to full-time work.

- Your eligibility for benefits under SSI based on disability or blindness has ended for reasons other than your work activity or earnings (such as reaching retirement age or having significant medical improvement or excess resources). Note that although the SSA won't review your condition for medical improvement while in the Ticket to Work program, you might declare your own improvement to SSA and return to regular work. That's why medical improvement is mentioned here as a possible reason for ticket termination.

b. Ticket Termination Because of Work or Earnings

Your ticket can also be terminated for reasons having to do with your work and earnings. Remember that the purpose of the program is to help you return to work full time. When you've successfully completed the Ticket to Work program, subject to the work incentives discussed in Section D, above, you'll be performing SGA, and your disability benefits will cease. This is the type of ticket termination you're hoping to achieve if you're in the program.

The relationship of your work and income to your receipt of benefits can be difficult to puzzle out, so if you have any questions, the protection and advocacy agencies and WIPA agencies are there to help. The SSA Field Offices can also help you clear up any questions. There is plenty of expert advice available—all you have to do is ask.

Continuing Disability Review

Your case will be reviewed from time to time to see if you still qualify for benefits. If you have experienced significant medical improvement and are capable of working, you may lose your benefits. This review process is called *continuing disability review* (CDR). If you receive benefits for many years, expect to go through many CDRs. (See Section A, below, for more on how often reviews are performed.)

When it's time for your CDR, either you'll receive a notice in the mail or someone from your local Social Security office will contact you to explain the process and your appeal rights (see Section B, below).

The CDR process is complex, and improperly trained reviewers are prone to making errors. So be sure to study this chapter closely before you undergo a CDR.

CDRs are initially done by a team from Disability Determination Services (DDS)—the state agency that reviews files for the SSA—including a disability examiner and a doctor known as a medical consultant. The team reviews your file and asks you to provide information about any medical treatment you've received and any work you've done. Based on what you tell them about your updated condition, the DDS team will ask your doctors, hospitals, and clinics for reports about your health. They'll want to see the results of any new medical tests, how effective your treatments have been, and how your health problems limit your activities.

DDS is concerned not only with improvements since your last review or initial disability award, but also with any new health problems you might have. If the DDS medical consultant needs more medical information, you might be asked to undergo a special examination or test known as a *consultative examination*. The consultative examination is paid for by the SSA.

If your health has improved, DDS will want to know if you can work. The CDR evaluation measures whether your overall health affects the kind of work you can do—both the work you did in the past and any other kind of work. (See Chapters 8 and 9 for the elements considered in evaluating your ability to work.)

If you're appealing a CDR decision, whoever is hearing the appeal—whether an administrative law judge or federal court judge—should obey the CDR principles set forth in this chapter. (See Chapter 12 for a comprehensive discussion of the appeals process.)

Child CDRs are evaluated in essentially the same way as CDRs for adults. (The minor differences are covered in Section D, below.)

A. Frequency of Reviews

How often the SSA reviews your case depends on the severity of your condition and the likelihood of improvement. The frequency can range from six months to seven years. The award letter you received when the SSA approved your claim for benefits shows when you can generally expect your first review. The exact date (and that of subsequent reviews) depends on how the SSA classifies your disability.

1. Medical Improvement Expected (MIE)

If, when your benefits first start, the SSA expects your medical condition to improve, your first review is likely to be six to 18 months later.

> EXAMPLE: Betty was in a car accident and suffered severe fractures in her leg and arm, along with other injuries. Sixteen months after her injury, Betty's fractures hadn't healed properly, and she developed a bone infection that left her unable to walk without help. At the time Betty was approved for disability benefits, her orthopedic surgeon had planned several more operations to restore Betty's ability to walk and predicted that she would need at least six more months to heal. Because of the high probability that Betty's condition would improve, the SSA scheduled a CDR six months after she was granted benefits.

Your age can affect whether you will be put into the MIE category. Younger people are more likely to have their health improve to the point that they're able to return to work. If you'll be 54½ years of age or older at the scheduled review date, the SSA generally won't use the MIE category, unless either of the following is true:

- You have an impairment that is almost certain to result in great improvement or full recovery, such as sprains and fractures or cancers with a high cure rate (like certain lymphomas and types of leukemia). In these cases, you could

get an MIE review up to age 59½. After age 59½, it's unlikely you'll get another review.
- You receive SSI and are legally blind but are expected to improve. You could get an MIE review up to age 64½.

2. Medical Improvement Possible (MIP)

If, when your benefits first start, the SSA believes it is possible for your medical condition to improve, but the SSA cannot predict when that improvement might happen, your case will be reviewed about every three years. Examples of disorders in which improvement is possible include conditions such as increased thyroid gland activity (hyperthyroidism) and inflammatory intestinal diseases like regional enteritis or ulcerative colitis.

> EXAMPLE 1: After several weeks of having dull, aching pains in the center of his chest, especially when he exerted himself or got excited, Livan woke up one morning feeling like an elephant was on his chest. Livan was rushed to the nearest hospital in the middle of a life-threatening heart attack. Treatment stabilized his condition, but he has severe blockages in multiple major arteries supplying his heart muscle. Despite optimum medical treatment, his heart disease is crippling, and his symptoms of chest pain, shortness of breath, weakness, and fatigue are so severe that the SSA considers him disabled. Livan has refused heart surgery because he is scared—his uncle died on the operating table during a similar procedure. Livan is relatively

young at age 50, and medical improvement with surgery could make a big difference in his ability to work. The SSA knows that medical improvement is possible if Livan has surgery and that there's a good chance Livan will change his mind about the operation. The SSA will review Livan's case a few years after he began receiving benefits.

EXAMPLE 2: Sharon has had high blood pressure and diabetes for years. She tried to treat herself with various herbal remedies. Her kidney function got progressively worse, and Sharon eventually qualified for disability benefits due to complete kidney failure. The SSA put Sharon's case in the MIP category because a kidney transplant could result in marked medical improvement. But if Sharon's doctor reported that she was going to have a kidney transplant within a few months, the SSA might put her case in the MIE category.

3. Medical Improvement Not Expected (MINE)

If the SSA doesn't expect your medical condition to improve, your case will be reviewed about every five to seven years. You're most likely to fall into this category if any of the following apply:

- You will be older than 54½ years when the CDR is scheduled.
- You have already had several CDRs.
- You have multiple severe impairments or an irreversible condition with no known treatment.

Examples of disorders that the SSA puts into a MINE category include the following:

- amputation
- ankylosing spondylitis of the spine
- autism
- blindness or glaucoma
- cerebral palsy
- chronic myelogenous leukemia
- deafness
- degenerative nervous system diseases
- diabetic eye disease
- diabetic nerve damage
- Down syndrome
- mood disorders, such as major depression
- mental disorders caused by organic brain disease
- intellectual disability
- multiple sclerosis
- Parkinson's disease
- peripheral vascular disease (arteries or veins)
- polio with permanent residuals
- psychotic mental disorders, such as schizophrenia
- rheumatoid arthritis
- stroke, or
- traumatic spinal cord or brain injuries.

EXAMPLE 1: Doug is 55 years old, has degenerative arthritis throughout his lower spine, and suffers pain and stiffness. Surgery would not relieve his symptoms, and other forms of treatment have been only moderately effective. Doug has a limited education and has worked only in jobs lifting and carrying 50 pounds or more. In his condition, he can't lift more than 20 pounds, but he isn't qualified for jobs with that kind of restriction. He's already had two CDRs, and his disability benefits were continued each time. The SSA will put him in the MINE category.

EXAMPLE 2: Sally is 52 years old and was diagnosed with severe depression at age 40. Following an initial recovery, Sally's medical records show years of only partially successful treatment with a variety of medications and six hospitalizations. She continues to live with her elderly parents but can't help much with chores. She spends much of her day watching television but has trouble following plots and remembering characters. Her parents manage her disability benefits, and she can't function outside of her parents' home without her condition worsening. Sally continues to show serious signs of depression, such as lack of pleasure, weight loss, feelings of hopelessness, poor sleep, lack of general interests, and some continuing suicidal thoughts. Sally has had two CDRs and is seen weekly at a community mental health center, with only marginal improvement.

Don't be surprised if you aren't notified about a CDR when you're expecting it, based on the MIE, MIP, or MINE time limits. When the SSA runs short of operating money, it typically stops performing CDRs rather than cut back on vital operations. The result is that your CDR might come later than would otherwise be the case—sometimes years later.

B. How the SSA Contacts You

A CDR begins when you receive a notice stating that the SSA is reviewing your disability claim. The important thing is to remain calm, understand that this is a regular part of the process, and know that you haven't been singled out. Don't assume that you will be automatically terminated from the program.

1. Form SSA-455, *Disability Update Report*

Accompanying the CDR notice will be Form SSA-455, *Disability Update Report*. A sample copy of the form follows. Be sure to read the SSA's instructions before filling out the form. You must return the completed form within 30 days.

 CAUTION
You must use forms provided by the SSA. You can obtain them at your local SSA Field Office or by calling the SSA hotline at 800-772-1213, Monday through Friday (except holidays), from 8:00 a.m. to 7:00 p.m. If you are deaf or hard of hearing, TTY service representatives are available at the same times at 800-325-0778. You can also download many necessary forms from the Social Security Administration website at www.ssa.gov.

Once the SSA Field Office receives your Form SSA-455, the agency will decide whether your benefits should simply

Sample Notice of Continuing Disability Review (Page 1)

Office of Disability Operations
1500 Woodlawn Drive
Baltimore, Maryland 21241

Date: June 14, 2024

Claim Number: 000-00-0000

We must regularly review the cases of people getting disability benefits to make sure they are still disabled under our rules. It is time for us to review your case. This letter explains how we plan to start our review of your case.

What You Should Do

Please complete the form enclosed with this letter. Answer all the questions on the form because they are very important. They ask about your health problems and any work you did within the last two years.

We have enclosed an envelope for you to use. If there is no envelope with this letter, please send the signed form to us at the address shown above.

If We Do Not Hear From You

You should return the form within 10 days after you receive it. If we do not hear from you in that time, we will contact you again.

If you don't give us the information we need or tell us why you cannot give us the information, we may stop your benefits. Before we stop your benefits, we will send you another letter to tell you what we plan to do.

When We Receive the Completed Form

- If we need more information, we will call you. If you do not have a telephone, please give a number where we can leave a message for you.
- The information you give us now will help us decide when we should do a full medical review of your case. We will let you know within 90 days after we receive the completed form whether or not we need to do a full medical review now.

Sample Notice of Continuing Disability Review (Page 2)

Important Information

If we decide to do a full medical review of your case:

- You can give us any information which you believe shows that you are still disabled, such as medical reports and letters from your doctors about your health.
- We will look at all the information in your case, including the new information you give us.
- We may find that you are no longer disabled under our rules, and your payments will stop. If this happens, you can appeal our decision. You can also ask us to continue to pay benefits while you appeal.

Things to Remember

Do you want to work but worry about losing your payments or Medicare before you can support yourself? We want to help you go to work when you are ready. But work and earnings can affect your benefits. Your local Social Security office can tell you more about how work and earnings can affect your benefits.

If You Have Any Questions

If you have any questions, you may call us at 800-772-1213 or call your Social Security Office at 000-000-0000. We can answer most questions over the phone. You can also write or visit any Social Security office. The office that serves your area is located at:

12345 Main Street
New York, NY 10000

If you do call or visit an office, please have this letter with you. It will help us answer your questions. Also, if you plan to visit an office, you should call ahead to make an appointment. This will help us serve you more quickly.

Michelle A. King
Michelle A. King

Deputy Commissioner for Operations
Enclosures:
Form SSA-455, *Disability Update Report*
Return envelope

Form SSA-455, *Disability Update Report* (Page 1)

*

Disability Update Report

DATE: June 30, 2024

Social Security Administration, P.O. Box   , Wilkes-Barre. PA 18767-

FORM APPROVED
OMB NO. 0960-0511

PAYEE'S NAME AND ADDRESS

John Smith
123 4th Street
Baltimore, MD 21241   PSC:

REPORT PERIOD
From: 12-31-23   To The Present

BENEFICIARY   John Smith

TELEPHONE NUMBER   CLAIM NUMBER
201-123-6789

Please be sure to **use black ink or a #2 pencil to print your answers.** Also, **read the enclosed instructions** before completing the form. Finally, remember that when answering the questions, **the "REPORT PERIOD" for which we need information about you is from** 12-31-23 **to the present.** If you have any questions, call 1-800-772-1213 or TTY for the hearing impaired at 1-800-325-0778.

1. a. Since 12-31-23   have you worked for someone   YES   NO
    or been self-employed? ⟶   ☐   ☒

    b. If you answered "YES" to 1.a., please complete the information below.

	WORK BEGAN		WORK ENDED		MONTHLY EARNINGS
	Month	Year	Month	Year	Dollars Only, No Cents
Most Recent Work 1.	☐	☐	☐	☐	$ ☐,☐
2.	☐	☐	☐	☐	$ ☐,☐
3.	☐	☐	☐	☐	$ ☐,☐

2. Have you attended any school or work training program(s)   YES   NO
    since 12-31-23 ?   ☐   ☒

3. Since 12-31-23   to the present...*(Please place an 'X' in one box only):*

    ☐ my doctor and I have not discussed whether I can work.

    ☒ my doctor told me I cannot work.

    ☐ my doctor told me I can work.

4. Place an "X" in only one box which best describes your health now as compared to 12-31-23 .

    ☐ BETTER   ☐ SAME   ☒ WORSE

Form SSA-455-OCR-SM (10-2013)   Continued on the Reverse ⟶

Form SSA-455, *Disability Update Report* (Page 2)

FOR SSA USE ONLY
AC?

5. a. Have you gone to a doctor or clinic for treatment (including evaluations, checkups, counseling, prescriptions, or medicine) since 12-31-23 ? ⟶   YES [X]   NO [ ]

b. If you answered "YES" to 5.a., please list:

		Reason For Visit:	Month	Year
Most Recent Visit	1.	C H E S T P A I N	0 1	2 4
	2.	S H O R T B R E A T H	0 1	2 4
	3.	A R T H R I T I S	0 2	2 4

6. a. Have you been hospitalized or had surgery since 12-31-23 ? ⟶   YES [X]   NO [ ]

b. If you answered "YES" to 6.a., please list:

		Reason For Hospitalization or Surgery:	Month	Year
Most Recent	1.	H N P	0 3	2 4
	2.			
	3.			

REMARKS: If you use this space to further answer questions 1. through 6., place an "X" in the box to the right and print on the lines below.   [X]

Back pain from HNP surgery persists. I can't lift over 10 lbs.
and carry it very far without both chest and back pain. My heart
doctor says I may need more testing to see if I have heart artery
blockages. Please contact my doctors for more information.

I declare under penalty of perjury that I have examined all the information on this form, and on any accompanying statements or forms, and it is true and correct to the best of my knowledge. I understand that anyone who knowingly gives a false or misleading statement about a material fact in this information, or causes someone else to do so, commits a crime and may be sent to prison, or may face other penalties, or both.

SIGN HERE ➤ *John Smith*	TODAY'S DATE 6-30-24
	TELEPHONE NUMBER *(include Area Code)* 201-123-6789

Form SSA-455-OCR-SM (10-2013)

continue—in which case the CDR process ends—or whether a full medical review of your claim is necessary. You have no other participation in this screening procedure. In either event, you'll receive another written notice. If a full medical review of your claim occurs, when it's complete, you'll receive notice of whether your benefits will continue or end.

2. Form SSA-454-BK, *Continuing Disability Review Report*

If the SSA chooses a full CDR, you'll be sent SSA-454-BK: *Continuing Disability Review Report* to complete.

Along with the form will be a notice inviting you to contact a Social Security representative at your local Field Office. Such contact is meant to protect your rights and assure that you fully understand the questions on the form. It will also give you the opportunity to ask questions that you might have about your CDR.

You can complete the form and mail it back to your local Field Office. If you need help filling out the form, the SSA prefers face-to-face contact, but you can do it by telephone if you wish. The Field Office will allow you to skip the personal contact if:

- You (or your representative payee) agree or request that the CDR be conducted by mail.
- You have an official representative payee (for example, the payee is an institution or a government agency).

- You reside in a foreign country, unless you're in a country that has a U.S. district office for Social Security.

Form SSA-454-BK is 10 pages long, but filling it out is more time-consuming than difficult. In addition to the help available at the SSA Field Office, an attorney or other representative can fill out much of the form for you. A copy of the form (starting on page 3) and instructions on how to complete it are below. For all questions, the SSA wants to know what has happened since the time you filed your original disability application or had your last CDR.

Don't worry about the little code boxes asking for the types of entitlement. The SSA Field Office representative can complete that information.

❶ **Section 1.** Provide your name, address, contact information, and so on.

❷ **Section 2.** Provide contact information for a person (other than your doctors) who knows about your medical conditions and is available for the SSA to contact about your claim. A spouse is a good example, but it could be a friend or relative. If there's no one you can put down, enter n/a.

❸ **Sections 3A, 3B, 3C.** List the physical or mental disorders that you feel limit your ability to work, along with your height and weight. Do not provide additional details or the medications you take. For example, you could just name "heart disease, emphysema, hearing problem, and arthritis."

❹ **Sections 3D, 3E.** This section asks for information about visits to doctor's offices and hospitals in the last year. List contact information, diagnoses, hospitalizations, clinic visits, tests given, treatment, and so on, for only the prior year. The SSA doesn't want earlier information, which they probably already have. In the examples given, the claimant has a cardiologist, pulmonary specialist, and orthopedist. The SSA only wants general information, not a lot of detail. If you had tests that aren't listed on the form, describe them under the Remarks section of the form (Section 9).

❺ **Section 3F.** List your medications, what they were prescribed for, and who prescribed them. Again, the SSA wants only information for the previous year. Do not provide any additional details. The SSA only wants to get an updated overview of your condition. If there isn't enough room for all your medications, or you want to say more about them, use the Remarks section on page 11 of the form.

❻ **Section 3G.** Check the boxes for any of the listed assistive devices that you use. Importantly, state the health care provider who prescribed the device. It's important that your assistive device be documented as medically necessary, but if you got an assistive device on your own, then still list it. You can put "Self" in the column for prescriber and explain in the page 11 Remarks why you need the device. It may also be helpful to explain why you had to get the device

for yourself, rather than having your doctor prescribe it. For example, perhaps you felt you needed the device right away and couldn't wait for a doctor's appointment to open up. You should keep in mind that the SSA regards the need for an assistive device more favorably when it's prescribed by a medical professional. But the SSA's medical consultants will also make a decision themselves about whether you need an assistive device, so it's not absolutely necessary to have a prescription from your doctor.

❼ **Section 4.** This section has straight-forward questions about whether you've done any work since your last decision. If so, you might want to provide details in the Remarks section on page 11. You don't have to explain your answers on this form, but SSA will be asking for details at some point.

❽ **Section 5.** List any services you've had since your last disability decision that involve vocational rehabilitation, job placement, or anything else that might relate to helping you return to work, such as the Ticket to Work program or a *Plan to Achieve Self Support* (PASS). As with the other questions, you'll need to provide names, dates, addresses, and phone numbers of the programs or employers. If you've had physical exams, vision or hearing tests, work evaluations, psychological tests, or other medically related employment tests, the SSA wants to know about them. Don't worry about describing the results—the SSA will obtain the tests and come to its own conclusion about what they mean for your case.

❾ **Section 6.** This section asks for other medical information, but only for adult disability recipients older than 18). Here the SSA wants to know if there are any organizations—like vocational rehab facilities, attorneys, workers' compensation, or social welfare services—that have any information about your medical condition. Simply provide the contact information if your answer to the question is "yes." Otherwise, check "no" and go to the next section. This section wants only information about the prior year—don't provide earlier information, as it is likely to only duplicate what the SSA already knows. If the SSA needs earlier information, the agency will ask for it.

❿ **Section 7.** The SSA wants to know about any additional education or training you've had since your last disability decision. This information could be from before the past year.

⓫ **Section 8.** The SSA has a long list of daily activities. First check "yes," and then check the box for any activity you have difficulty doing, and then use the white space to explain what you have difficulty with. You can always explain in more detail using the Remarks section. Some examples are given on the sample form below on how to do this, and here are some additional issues you might want to consider when completing this section.

Section 8 gives you an opportunity to describe in detail how your medical disorders affect your ability to function during a typical day. This section is one of the most important on the CDR form. It gives you the chance to describe to the SSA in your own words any difficulties you have in performing *activities of daily living* (ADLs). Take your time and write something in every section. Tell the SSA what activities you're limited in performing, to what degree those activities are limited, and how the limitations are caused by your medical condition. If you need more room, use the Remarks section and add more pages if you want. Examples are given on the sample form in Section 11, but here are some specific suggestions.

Personal mobility. Write down the specific things you have difficulty doing, like walking, getting out of a chair, or moving about in some other way. Next, describe the symptom or problem that causes your limitation—such as weak-ness or paralysis, numbness, pain, poor balance, dizziness, or lack of coordination. Finally, describe the degree of severity of your symptoms— such as inability to stand for more than 30 minutes because of back pain, inability to walk more than two blocks due to leg pain, or shortness of breath.

Personal needs and grooming. Describe any difficulties you have. Don't underestimate the importance of these everyday activities that many people take for granted. For example, if you've had a stroke, you may be unable to button your shirt with one hand. Inability to button a shirt or pick up coins tells the SSA that you have difficulty with fine movements of your fingers, movements that are critical in many kinds of work.

Form SSA-454-BK, *Continuing Disability Review Report* (Page 3)

Form **SSA-454-BK** (06-2023) UF
Discontinue Prior Editions
Social Security Administration

Page 3 of 12
OMB No. 0960-0072

CONTINUING DISABILITY REVIEW REPORT

For SSA Use Only - Do not write in this box.
Date of your last medical disability decision:

❶ **SECTION 1 - INFORMATION ABOUT YOU**

When a question refers to "you" or "your" it refers to the person receiving disability benefits. If you are completing this report for someone else, please provide information about them.

1.A. NAME (First, Middle, Last, Suffix) Jesse Chang	**1.B.** SOCIAL SECURITY NUMBER 111-11-1111

1.C. In the last 12 months, have you used any other names on your medical or educational records? Examples include maiden name, other married names, other names, or nickname.

☐ YES

☒ NO

If YES, please list names used

1.D. MAILING ADDRESS (Street or PO Box) Include apartment number if applicable.
1234 Pasadena Way

CITY Dallas	STATE/Province TX	ZIP/Postal Code 82221	COUNTRY (if not USA)

1.E. Is your residence address the same as your mailing address? ☒ YES ☐ NO - Complete RESIDENT ADDRESS below

RESIDENT ADDRESS (Include apartment number if applicable.)

CITY	STATE/Province	ZIP/Postal Code	COUNTRY (if not USA)

1.F. DAYTIME PHONE NUMBER(S) where we can call to speak with you, or leave a message, if needed. (Include area code, or IDD and country code if outside the USA or Canada.)

Primary: (901)-555-5555   Secondary: (901)-555-5556
(If available)

1.G. EMAIL ADDRESS
None

1.H. Can you speak and understand English?	☒ YES	☐ NO

If NO, what language do you prefer? _____

If you cannot speak and understand English, we will provide an interpreter free of charge.

1.I. Can you read and understand English?	☒ YES	☐ NO
1.J. Can you write more than your name in English?	☒ YES	☐ NO

❷ **SECTION 2 – SOMEONE WE CAN CONTACT**

Please provide the name of someone (other than your doctors) we can contact who knows about your medical condition(s), and can help with your case and can help us reach you if you become unavailable. Examples include a family member, friend, or neighbor.

2.A. NAME (First, Middle, Last, Suffix) Sue Chang	**2.B.** Relationship to Person in **1.A.** wife

Form SSA-454-BK, *Continuing Disability Review Report* (Page 4)

Form **SSA-454-BK** (06-2023) UF   Page 4 of 12

2.C. MAILING ADDRESS (Street or PO Box) Include apartment number if applicable.
1234 Pasadena Way

CITY	STATE/Province	ZIP/Postal Code	COUNTRY (if not USA)
Dallas	TX	82221	

2.D. DAYTIME PHONE NUMBER (as described in **1.F.** above)   (901)-555-5555

2.E. Can this person speak and understand English?   ☒ YES   ☐ NO

    (If NO, what language is preferred?)

❸   **SECTION 3 - MEDICAL INFORMATION**

Please provide us with general medical information to assist us with any records requests. We will use this information to see what additional questions or forms we may need to send you.

3.A. Separately list each physical and/or mental health condition that limits your ability to work. **If under age 18**, list the physical and/or mental health condition(s) that limit the child's ability to do the same things as other children the same age.

1. Heart disease: coronary arteries blocked. Bypass surgery in 2018
2. Emphysema
3. Hearing problem
4. Arthritis in hands
5. High blood pressure

If you need more space to list additional conditions go to Section 9 – Remarks

3.B. What is your height?	5	8	OR	
	feet	inches		centimeters
3.C. What is your weight?	180		OR	
	pounds			kilograms

❹ **3.D. Within the last 12 months,** have you seen or received treatment from a health care provider (doctor, hospital, clinic, psychiatrists, nurse practitioners, therapists, physical therapists, or other medical professionals)?

    ☐ NO (**Go to 3.F.**)

    ☒ YES (**Complete the following section below.**)

You may find this information on medical bills or the internet. If you don't have the full street address, give as much as you can remember. **Example: "On Main St. next to the Courthouse."**

1. NAME OF FACILITY OR OFFICE	NAME OF HEALTH CARE PROVIDER THAT TREATED YOU
The Cardiology Group	Emily Crowe (cardiologist)

What medical conditions were treated or evaluated?

Heart disease. Follow-up after bypass surgery and treatment of my high blood pessure.

PHONE NUMBER		DATE LAST SEEN	07 / 2024
(111) 444-4444		(IF KNOWN)	MM / YYYY

STREET ADDRESS			
412 11th Street			

CITY	STATE/Province	ZIP/Postal Code	COUNTRY (if not USA)
Pasadena	TX	93870	

Form SSA-454-BK, *Continuing Disability Review Report* (Page 5)

Form **SSA-454-BK** (06-2023) UF

2. NAME OF FACILITY OR OFFICE The Pulmonary Clinic	NAME OF HEALTH CARE PROVIDER THAT TREATED YOU Dr. Glen Rose

What medical conditions were treated or evaluated?

Emphysema and bronchitis

PHONE NUMBER (111)122-1234	DATE LAST SEEN (IF KNOWN)	09 / 2024 MM / YYYY

STREET ADDRESS 82 Oak Cove			
CITY Pasadena	STATE/Province TX	ZIP/Postal Code 82221	COUNTRY (if not USA)

3. NAME OF FACILITY OR OFFICE The Orthopedic Specialists	NAME OF HEALTH CARE PROVIDER THAT TREATED YOU Dr. Jane Barr

What medical conditions were treated or evaluated?

Back pain and hand arthritis

PHONE NUMBER (333) 333-3333	DATE LAST SEEN (IF KNOWN)	08 / 2024 MM / YYYY

STREET ADDRESS 920 Freeway Drive			
CITY Pasadena	STATE/Province TX	ZIP/Postal Code 82221	COUNTRY (if not USA)

4. NAME OF FACILITY OR OFFICE	NAME OF HEALTH CARE PROVIDER THAT TREATED YOU

What medical conditions were treated or evaluated?

PHONE NUMBER	DATE LAST SEEN (IF KNOWN)	MM / YYYY

STREET ADDRESS			
CITY	STATE/Province	ZIP/Postal Code	COUNTRY (if not USA)

5. NAME OF FACILITY OR OFFICE	NAME OF HEALTH CARE PROVIDER THAT TREATED YOU

What medical conditions were treated or evaluated?

PHONE NUMBER	DATE LAST SEEN (IF KNOWN)	MM / YYYY

STREET ADDRESS			
CITY	STATE/Province	ZIP/Postal Code	COUNTRY (if not USA)

Form SSA-454-BK, *Continuing Disability Review Report* (Page 6)

If you need to list more facilities or doctors, use **Section 9 – Remarks**.

3.E. Within the last 12 months, did any of the providers listed in **3.D.** order any medical tests for you? (Include tests already performed and those scheduled in the future, and the healthcare provider, or facility, that scheduled them.)

☐ NO (**Go to 3.F.**)

☒ YES (**Complete the following section below.**) – If you need more space, use **Section 9 – Remarks**.

TEST	NAME OF HEALTHCARE PROVIDER OR FACILITY
Blood test (not HIV)	The Cardiology Group, Dr. Emily Crowe
Breathing test	The Pulmonary Clinic, Dr. Glen Rose
Cardiac catheterization	
EEG (brain wave test)	
EKG (heart test)	The Cardiology Group, Dr. Emily Crowe
Hearing test	
HIV test	
Speech/language test	
Treadmill (exercise test)	The Cardiology Group, Dr. Emily Crowe
Vision test	
Psychological/IQ test	
Biopsy (list body part, if known):	
MRI/CT scan (list body part, if known):	
X-ray (list body part, if known):	
Other – please specify:	

❺ 3.F. Within the last 12 months, have you taken or are you now taking any prescription or non-prescription medicines? Please put any side-effects you may have in **Section 9 - Remarks**.

☐ NO (**Go to 3.G.**)

☒ YES (**Complete the following section below.**) – Look at your medicine containers, if necessary. If you need more space, use **Section 9 – Remarks**.

NAME OF MEDICINE	IF PRESCRIBED, GIVE DOCTOR NAME (IF KNOWN)	REASON FOR MEDICINE (IF KNOWN)
1. Theophylline	Dr. Rose	Bronchitis
2. Ibuprofen	Dr. Barr	Back and hand arthritis
3. Losartan	Dr. Crowe	High blood pessure
4.		
5.		
6.		

Form SSA-454-BK, *Continuing Disability Review Report* (Page 7)

❻ 3.G. Do you use an assistive device?

Note: Even if you do not always use an assistive device at home, if you always use it when outside your home, please select "always."

☒ NO (**Go to Section 3.H.**)

☐ YES (**Complete the following section below.**) If you need more space, use **Section 9 – Remarks**.

DEVICE	FREQUENCY OF USE		NAME OF HEALTH CARE PROVIDER, IF PRESCRIBED (IF KNOWN)
☐ Braces	☐ Always	☐ Sometimes	
☐ Canes	☐ Always	☐ Sometimes	
☐ Crutches	☐ Always	☐ Sometimes	
☐ Eyeglasses	☐ Always	☐ Sometimes	
☐ Hearing aid	☐ Always	☐ Sometimes	
☐ Screen reader	☐ Always	☐ Sometimes	
☐ Walker	☐ Always	☐ Sometimes	
☐ Wheelchair	☐ Always	☐ Sometimes	
☐ Other:	☐ Always	☐ Sometimes	

3.H. Is the person receiving disability benefits listed in **1.A.** under age 14?

☒ NO (**Go to Section 4**)

☐ YES (**Go to Section 10**)

❼
SECTION 4 – WORK INFORMATION
Complete only if you are age 14 years old or older

Please tell us if you have worked since the date of your last medical disability decision. If we have any additional questions about your work, we may contact you.

4.A. Since the date of your last medical disability decision have you worked? (See date on top of **Page 3**.)

☒ NO (**Go to 4.B.**)

☐ YES (**Complete following section below.**)

Are you currently working?

☒ No

☐ Yes

Select all types of work you had since your last medical disability decision:

☐ Wages from employer

☐ Self-employment

4.B. Is the person receiving disability benefits listed in **1.A.** under age 18?

☒ NO (**Go to Section 5**)

☐ YES (**Go to Section 10**)

Form SSA-454-BK, *Continuing Disability Review Report* **(Page 8)**

❽

SECTION 5 – SUPPORT SERVICES
Complete only if you are age 18 years or older

Please provide the information about your participation in support services. Examples of support services can include:
- **An Individualized Education Program (IEP) through a school (if a student age 18-21)**
- **An individualized work plan with an employment network under the Ticket to Work Program**
- **A Plan to Achieve Self-Support (PASS)**
- **An individualized plan for employment with a vocational rehabilitation agency or any other organization.**

5.A. Since the date of your last medical disability decision, have you participated or are you participating in any support services mentioned above or any other vocational rehabilitation, employment services, or other support services to help you return to work? (See date on top of **Page 3**.)

    ☒ NO (**Go to Section 6**)

    ☐ YES (**Complete the following section below.**)

FACILITY OR ORGANIZATION NAME	PHONE NUMBER

COUNSELOR, INSTRUCTOR, OR JOB COACH NAME

MAILING ADDRESS (Street or PO Box) (Include Suite, Building, etc.)

CITY	STATE/Province	ZIP/Postal Code	COUNTRY (if not USA)

5.B. Are you still participating in the plan or program? (Select answer below. If date not known, use best estimate.)

☐ YES - Date began: ___ / ___ MM / YYYY	Expected completion date: ___ / ___ MM / YYYY
☐ NO - Date began: ___ / ___ MM / YYYY	Date stopped: ___ / ___ MM / YYYY

Reason stopped:

5.C. What types of services, tests, or evaluation were provided?

Select all that apply:

☐ Vision test   ☐ Psychological/IQ test   ☐ Work classes   ☐ Hearing test   ☐ Work evaluation
☐ Other - Please explain:

❾

SECTION 6 - OTHER MEDICAL INFORMATION
Complete only if you are age 18 years or older

Please provide the contact information for anyone else or any other organization that may have medical information about your physical or mental health condition(s) that you did not list in Questions 3.D. or 5.A.

6. Within the last 12 months, does anyone else (other than your medical providers) have your medical information or are you scheduled to see anyone else? Examples include places like social services agencies, case workers, welfare agencies, attorneys, prisons, workers' compensation, insurance companies who have paid you disability benefits.

    ☒ NO (**Go to Section 7**)

    ☐ YES (**Complete the following section below.**)

Form SSA-454-BK, *Continuing Disability Review Report* (Page 9)

Form **SSA-454-BK** (06-2023) UF   Page 9 of 12

NAME OR ORGANIZATION	PHONE NUMBER

MAILING ADDRESS

CITY	STATE/Province	ZIP/Postal Code	COUNTRY (if not USA)

NAME OF CONTACT PERSON	CLAIM NUMBER (if any)

Date of Last Contact (in last 12 months, if known)	Date of Next Contact (if any)

Reason(s) for Contacts

If you need to list other people or organizations use Section 9 - Remarks and give the same detailed information as above for each one you list.

⑩   **SECTION 7 – EDUCATION, TRAINING, AND LITERACY**
                          Complete only if you are age 18 years or older

Please provide any information about your education, training, and literacy since your last disability decision. Information about Individualized Education Plans (IEPs) or other support services should be recorded in "SECTION 5 - SUPPORT SERVICES".

7.A. Have you received any **education** since your last disability decision? (See date at the top of **Page 3**.)
    ☒ NO (**Go to 7.B.**)
    ☐ YES (**Complete the following section below.**)

NAME OF SCHOOL

DATE(S) OF ATTENDANCE If date not known, use best estimate. ___ / ___ to ___ / ___
                                                   MM YYYY   MM YYYY

MAILING ADDRESS

CITY	STATE/Province	ZIP/Postal Code	COUNTRY (if not USA)

TYPE OF PROGRAM/DEGREE

Date Completed (or scheduled to be completed) If date not known, use best estimate. ___ / ___
                                                        MM YYYY

7.B. Have you received any type of **training** (specialized job, trade, or vocational training) since your last disability decision? (See date at top of **Page 3**.)
    ☒ NO (**Go to 7.C.**)
    ☐ YES (**Complete the following section below.**)

NAME OF TRAINING FACILITY	PHONE NUMBER

MAILING ADDRESS

CITY	STATE/Province	ZIP/Postal Code	COUNTRY (if not USA)

TYPE OF PROGRAM	Date Completed (or scheduled to be completed) If date not known, use best estimate. ___ / ___ MM YYYY

Form SSA-454-BK, *Continuing Disability Review Report* (Page 10)

7.C. What written language do you use every day in most situations (at home, work, school, in community, etc.)?

7.D. READING - In the language you identified in **7.C.**, can you <u>read</u> a simple message, such as a shopping list or short simple notes?   ☐ YES   ☐ NO

7.E. WRITING - In the language you identified in **7.C.**, can you <u>write</u> a simple message, such as a shopping list or short simple notes?   ☐ YES   ☐ NO

If you need to list other education information or training facilities use Section 9 - Remarks and provide the same detailed information as above.

⑪
SECTION 8 - DAILY ACTIVITIES
Complete only if you are age 18 years or older.

Please tell us how your conditions affect your everyday life. This will help us further understand your medical condition(s).

8. Do your medical conditions cause you to have difficulties doing any of the following? You should think about the difficulty you experience in performing these tasks alone and without assistance from other people or assistive devices. If other people or assistive devices help you perform a task or perform a task for you because it would be difficult for you to perform the task without the assistance, choose "Yes".

☒ YES   ☐ NO

If YES, please select any tasks that you need help with or have difficulty doing.

☒ Dressing	☐ Taking medicine	☒ Doing chores (inside/outside of house)
☒ Bathing	☐ Preparing meals	☐ Driving or using public transportation
☐ Caring for hair	☐ Feeding self	☐ Understanding or following directions
☒ Walking	☐ Shopping	☐ Managing money
☒ Standing	☐ Lifting objects	☐ Getting along with people
☒ Sitting	☐ Using arms	☒ Using hands or fingers
☐ Concentrating	☐ Remembering	☒ Seeing, hearing, or speaking

Please explain anything you marked you need help with or have difficulty doing:
In dressing, my wife has to help me with button, because I can't handle small things due to my arthritis.
I take showers only, because have trouble getting out of tub due to my back pain.

I can't stand or walk more than a half hour because of back pain. Also, if I stand more than two hours at a time, my back hurts.

I can only do a few light chores because of my hand and back arthritis. I can't carry heavy things or finish things that take more than an hour, because my back and hands hurt and I get short of breath and start wheezing.

If you need more space, use **Section 9 – Remarks**.

Form SSA-454-BK, *Continuing Disability Review Report* (Page 11)

⑫

SECTION 9 - REMARKS

Please provide any additional information you did not give in earlier parts of this report, that you think would help us understand your disability and how it affects you. If you did not have enough space in prior sections of this report to provide the requested information, please use this space here to provide the additional information requested in those sections. For example, if you experience any side effects from the medication listed in 3.F., please provide that information in this section. Be sure to note the name of the section (and question number) you are referring to.

Continued from Sec. 9 about my daily activities

I talk to neighbors if they walk by and watch the neighbor's kid cut my lawn as I can't do it anymore. In the afternoon, I take a nap or go with my wife to the store. I don't lift anything heavy. If it's cold, I stay inside. At night, I read or watch TV, but have to change sitting or standing because of my back pain; can't stay in one position more than an hour.

My doctors say I'm getting slowly worse and will provide the lung tests and x-rays to show it, if the SSA asks them. Dr. Rose said I should avoid dust and fumes like I was exposed to during 25 years of farm work. He also said to avoid very hot or cold environments because of the stress to my heart and lungs. If it's very hot or cold outside, or if there's much ozone pollution I get more short of breath and sometimes chest pain.

Dr. Barr has always said I have severe arthritis in my spine as well as degenerative discs. She said I should never lift over 20 lbs. and should avoid excessive bending of my back. She said I should avoid activities that jar my back, like riding heavy equipment such as tractors.

A claimant with a profound mental disorder, such as severe dementia from Alzheimer's disease, might require help in even basic personal needs. Be sure to note if you have a caregiver providing help. And if you're completing the form for a disability recipient with a mental disorder, ask the caregiver for insight into what the recipient can and can't do.

Household maintenance. The SSA is not so much interested in whether you actually do things around the house—the SSA wants to know if you *can* do these things. For example, the fact that you don't cook is not an argument that you can't cook. It's more significant that you could previously cook but aren't able to any longer because you can't stand for very long and your kitchen isn't wheelchair accessible; you can't use your fingers to open jars, cans, or packages; you're forgetful and burn food; or your anxieties keep you from going out to shop.

With a physical disorder, you might have difficulty standing or using your hands to perform routine household activities—for instance, the pain in your hands is so severe you can't turn a wrench or hold a paintbrush, or your loss of coordination means you can't hit a nail to do repairs around the house. Maybe you can't vacuum because you get short of breath or pushing the vacuum cleaner causes pain in your shoulder.

Whatever the limitation, be specific and give the reason for the limitation. For example, you might write, "I can rake leaves slowly for 30 minutes before I get so exhausted I have to rest for the same length of time."

Social contacts. The SSA is looking at your ability to interact with other people. Social skills are important in determining the type of work you can do, especially when evaluating the severity of a mental disorder.

The SSA will want to know if you lost interest in social activities that you'd previously enjoyed—for example, if you were active in your weekly book club but no longer go because of depression, paranoia, or fear of leaving home. The agency isn't as concerned about activities you don't do that you never really liked in the first place.

Mental disorders aren't the only reason you might limit your social contacts. Fatigue, muscle weakness, or pain are examples of physical symptoms that can limit your desire and ability to interact socially.

❷ **Form Section 9.** In this Remarks section, you can add any additional information you think the SSA should know about how your physical or mental disorder affects your ability to function. Be as specific as possible. If you state that you have some limitation in your ability to function, it's to your advantage to have medical documentation from your treating doctors that support your statement. Make sure you discuss your problems with your doctors in your appointments so there will be documentation of your limitations when the SSA brings up your claim for a continuing disability review.

Remarks. Describe any other problems you haven't previously discussed for example, if you have epilepsy and can't drive, difficulties with balance that prevent you from riding a bicycle, confusion that makes it difficult for you to travel on public transportation, or memory problems that keep you from going out alone without getting lost.

Some example text is written on the sample form, but it's just for general guidance. Write what you think is best for a realistic picture of your problems.

Remember to date the form at the end.

C. Medical Improvement Review Standard

The SSA evaluates your case using what it calls the *medical improvement review standard* (MIRS). The MIRS governs how the SSA evaluates CDRs.

You need to understand the MIRS because some medical consultants, examiners, and others who conduct CDRs aren't adequately trained in the MIRS. Someone could incorrectly terminate your benefits.

The MIRS isn't applied under certain circumstances (see Section C2, below).

! CAUTION

Insist on a medical review. If DDS terminates your benefits, ask to review your file. If necessary, insist that a DDS medical consultant review your claim. Otherwise, a disability examiner who is not a doctor might be responsible for stopping your benefits. (See Chapter 6, Section G. Also see Chapter 12 on how to review your file and file an appeal.)

Under the MIRS, your CDR will be evaluated quite differently from your original application for disability benefits. During your initial application, you had the burden of proof to show that you were disabled. But in a CDR, the burden shifts to the SSA. This means that your benefits will continue unless the SSA can clearly show that you have medically improved to the extent you can work. The MIRS requires the SSA to meet two separate requirements before the agency can terminate your benefits. The agency must show that:

- You have significant medical improvement related to your ability to work, as determined by a DDS medical consultant (see Subsection a, below).
- You can actually perform substantial gainful activity, as determined by a DDS claims examiner or vocational specialist (see Subsection b, below).

1. Medical Improvement Related to Your Ability to Work

Medical improvement means that your symptoms have gotten less severe since your last CDR. Sometimes an improvement is only minor, in which case it would be unfair for the SSA to say your condition has gotten better in any meaningful sense. (See the example regarding trivial impairments, below.) Therefore, federal regulations require that there be *significant* medical improvement.

Disorders Showing Temporary Improvement

If the severity of your symptoms fluctuates, the SSA is supposed to take this into consideration when considering whether you've had any medical improvement in your condition. For example, let's say your rheumatoid arthritis flares up every three or four months and then is better for several months. Your "good period" should be stable for six months to a year before the SSA decides you have improved enough to have your benefits terminated. Multiple sclerosis and systemic lupus erythematosus (SLE) are examples of other physical conditions that can act in this way.

Mental impairments such as bipolar disorder can also show a lot of variation in severity. The SSA must look at all of your medical history *longitudinally* (meaning the agency will evaluate how your impairments affect you over a period of at least 12 months) before making a decision to stop your benefits.

In most instances, any significant improvements will be naturally related to your ability to work. However, this isn't always true, and "related to the ability to do work" is important legal language used by the SSA. For example, if you have a marked improvement in the medical severity of one of your various disorders that has nothing to do with your ability to work (such as a hair transplant for alopecia), the

SSA shouldn't say you have had significant medical improvement related to your ability to work. No matter how much some things improve, they might have little to do with the ability to work. The reason federal regulations use the phrase "related to your ability to work" is to make sure that the MIRS standard isn't applied to medical improvements that are irrelevant or trivial.

a. Comparison Point

The date that your claim was last reviewed and your benefits allowed or continued is called the *comparison point decision* (CPD). Depending on the history of your claim, the CPD could be the date of your initial allowance, the date you were allowed at some appeal level, or the date of a previous CDR.

The DDS medical consultant shouldn't be concerned with how or why you were placed on disability or reapproved after your previous CDR, or who made the decision (with some exceptions discussed in Subsection 2b, below). The MIRS applies only to the medical severity of your impairments at the CPD date as compared to those same impairments at your current CDR.

If you don't have significant medical improvement in your impairments, then your benefits will continue.

b. New Impairments

If you do have significant medical improvement, this doesn't necessarily mean that your overall medical condition has significantly improved. If you suffer from new impairments that began after the last CPD date, the medical consultant will consider the impact of the new impairments on your ability to work. (New impairments are further discussed in Subsection 4d, below.) Of course, if you don't have significant medical improvement in the impairments that got you disability, then your benefits will continue, and there will be no point in reviewing your new impairments.

c. Evaluating Evidence

The SSA evaluates *symptoms, signs, and laboratory abnormalities* to determine the medical severity of your impairments and whether they have improved:

- **Symptoms** are your own description of your physical or mental impairment. Common examples include, "My back hurts," "My abdomen hurts," "I have chest pain," "I'm cold," "I'm tired," "I'm dizzy," "I'm short of breath," "I'm scared," and "I feel worthless." For children who can't describe their symptoms, the SSA accepts the statements of parents or guardians who know the child best.
- **Signs** are physical or psychological abnormalities that can be observed apart from your statements (symptoms). Examples of signs include missing limbs, skin rashes, abnormal reflexes, fast pulse rate, sweating, struggling to breathe, bleeding, tremors, seizures, decreased

emotional expression, agitation, paranoid delusions, or many other things.
- **Laboratory findings** are physical or psychological facts that can be shown by use of diagnostic techniques such as chemical tests, X-rays or other imaging studies, EKGs, or psychological tests. The SSA evaluates signs and laboratory findings using methods generally acceptable to the scientific medical community. For example, the SSA wouldn't accept reports claiming to diagnose liver disease by examining the colored part of the eye (iridology) or as a result of "therapeutic touch," because these types of reports are not acceptable to the scientific medical community.

d. When Improvement Might Be Found

Below are some examples of how the SSA applies the MIRS to cases involving physical disorders, mental disorders, and a combination of the two.

Physical disorders. Chapters 7 and 8 explain the Listing of Impairments and residual functional capacity (RFC), and how they affect whether you qualify for disability benefits. If you move up at least one exertional level of severity (such as from sedentary work to light work, or from light work to medium work, or from medium work to heavy work), or if you no longer meet or equal a listing, then you clearly have experienced a significant medical improvement.

EXAMPLE: Two years ago, after Kota's diseased heart valve resulted in heart failure, she was granted disability benefits. In her RFC rating, Kota was restricted to sedentary work. Subsequently, she had heart surgery with placement of a new valve. During the CDR, the DDS medical consultant found that Kota was now able to lift and carry up to 20 pounds, meaning she was capable of performing light work. The medical consultant found that Kota had significant medical improvement.

Medical improvement that doesn't change the exertional level of your RFC might or might not be significant. In the following example, the claimant's improvement is significant even though the exertional level remains at light work.

EXAMPLE: At Rick's previous CDR, he was given an RFC for light work because of asthma and arthritis in his spine. Since then, Rick has had treatment for the asthma and breathes much better, according to both his symptoms and objective pulmonary function tests. While Rick's had significant medical improvement because of his improved breathing, his arthritis still restricts him to light work.

Mental disorders. If you move up at least one mental skill level of severity (such as from unskilled work to semiskilled work, or from semiskilled to skilled work), or you no longer meet or equal a mental health listing, then you've experienced a significant medical improvement.

EXAMPLE: Julie is a 35-year-old college-educated accountant with a ten-year history of successful skilled work who was diagnosed with major depression. Julie was initially granted benefits a year before her current CDR because she met the listing for major depression. Julie has received intensive ongoing treatment, and while she still has some signs of depression, Julie's mental health has significantly improved to the extent that she now has a mental RFC for unskilled work. Although Julie hasn't fully recovered from depression, her ability to do unskilled work represents significant medical improvement.

Medical improvement that doesn't change the skill level of your mental RFC might or might not be significant. As discussed in Chapter 9, disability claimants with solely mental impairments who can still perform semiskilled or skilled work are rarely granted benefits. Even claimants who are limited to unskilled work don't usually get benefits unless there are other vocational factors at play (such as age, education, and work experience) in addition to physical restrictions. Because vocational factors don't improve over time—you won't get younger before your next CDR, for example—these same factors would probably result in a your benefits being continued on review.

Combined physical and mental disorders. If you were awarded disability benefits based on a combination of physical and mental impairments, a decrease in the severity of either condition can, by itself, be enough to establish significant medical improvement.

> **EXAMPLE 1:** Paul is a 34-year-old worker who fell off a roof and suffered a severe fracture of his spine. Even after maximum healing of the injury, he was physically capable of only sit-down work, and Paul's doctors didn't expect any further improvement in his range of motion or pain level. Paul also suffered significant anxiety that was worsened by his accident. Paul was awarded disability two years ago based on this combination of anxiety and back surgery that kept him from performing even unskilled, sedentary jobs. Following treatment of his anxieties with psychotherapy and medication, Paul's mental impairment has improved to the point where it's no longer severe. Even though Paul's back injury hasn't gotten better, he has experienced significant improvement in his mental condition.

> **EXAMPLE 2:** Cindy is 50 years old with 25 years' experience as a laundry worker, a job that the SSA has classified as unskilled. Cindy had suffered a fractured tibia that was somewhat slow in healing, and the SSA awarded her benefits based on her unskilled work history, age, and the limitations caused by her fracture. Cindy's fracture is now completely healed without any significant residual problems, so the SSA determined that there has been significant medical improvement.

Trivial impairments. If you have a *trivial impairment* that gets much better, the DDS team shouldn't consider that to be a significant medical improvement.

> **EXAMPLE:** Maria was originally granted disability because of a heart disease. At the same time, she also had a case of athlete's foot. At her CDR, the medical consultant determined that Maria's athlete's foot was cured but that her heart disease was the same. Maria has not had significant medical improvement. If the heart disease had improved significantly, then the SSA would find that she has had significant medical improvement.

2. Your Ability to Work

Even if the medical consultant finds that you have experienced significant medical improvement, your benefits won't be automatically terminated. A DDS examiner or vocational analyst must also show that you're capable of performing some work available in the national economy. The DDS examiner must take into account your original impairments and any new impairments you might have. (See Subsection 4d, below, regarding new impairments.)

> **EXAMPLE:** Max is 55 years old, has a tenth-grade education, and has always done heavy work. He was originally allowed benefits because of multiple unhealed fractures and arthritis in his spine. By the time of his CDR, Max's fractures had healed, and DDS found significant medical improvement. But Max's spinal arthritis still restricts him to an RFC

for light work. Max will continue to receive benefits because the SSA won't be able to show that Max can perform any jobs, given his RFC, age, education, and work experience.

Your mental impairments and vocational factors help determine the skill level of jobs that you can do. Common symptoms of mental impairments, such as forgetfulness and fatigue, can rule out jobs requiring detailed or complex problem-solving tasks (generally found at the semiskilled and skilled levels). Or if you're over 50 and you've only done simple unskilled jobs in the past, the SSA might not expect you to learn how to do a skilled job.

3. Age and Time Receiving Disability

The SSA knows that older recipients may be affected by aging and long periods of inactivity from not working. Aging and inactivity are often associated with decreased heart and lung function, muscle weakness, joint degeneration, and decreased general exercise capacity.

The SSA considers age and inactivity if you're over age 50 and have been receiving disability benefits for at least seven years. DDS can consider these factors in determining your RFC and whether you've had significant work-related medical improvement. Your age and how long you've been receiving disability benefits can tip the scales in your favor when the decision is a close call.

4. When the MIRS Doesn't Apply

Under certain conditions, the SSA doesn't have to apply the MIRS to your CDR evaluation. In these following cases, it's possible—but not certain—that you might be able to keep your benefits without a DDS review for medical improvement.

a. Your Impairment Meets or Equals a Listing

If you're an adult and your impairment continues to meet or equal the same listing in the Listing of Impairments (see Chapter 7, Step 3) as it did at the time you obtained disability benefits or at your last CPD, then the SSA can simply continue your benefits without having to consider the MIRS.

You'll continue to receive your benefits, even if the requirements of the listing have been changed and you don't meet these new listing requirements. This is extremely important to keep in mind, because many disability recipients, especially those with heart disease or other cardiovascular disorders, were granted benefits under listings that are now out of date. Make sure that your DDS medical consultant doesn't overlook this grandfather clause and terminate your benefits.

Similarly, if you qualify as an adult under any newer listings in effect at the time of your CDR—even if you originally qualified under older, different listings—your benefits will continue without a medical improvement evaluation. Moreover, meeting or equaling the listings in effect at the time of the CDR can also include any

The Lesser the Disability, the Less Room There Is for Improvement

One of the amazing things about the MIRS is that if you were granted benefits in a situation in which you really weren't entitled to them, they can't be taken away except in limited situations (discussed in Section 4, below). Through errors in judgment by someone working in the SSA, it is possible for people who actually have moderate impairments to be initially approved for benefits by being judged as much worse than they actually were. Because the law doesn't allow the judgment of past decision makers to be questioned, you can be in benefit status the rest of your life (as long as you're not working above the SGA level).

How can this happen? Once you get to the ALJ level of appeal, your claim, the judge might disagree with the DDS claims examiner. For example, an ALJ might approve your claim under a less-than-sedentary rating after a DDS medical consultant gave you a higher RFC rating (say for medium work).

Now look at what happens when your claim later comes up for CDR evaluation. The ALJ has given you a rating for less-than-sedentary work, which would allow benefits

for any claimant with any age, education, or work experience. The DDS medical consultant who looks at your claim on CDR might think, "There's nothing really seriously wrong with this person medically." But remember, the medical consultant must determine if there is any medical improvement in your moderate condition. If there isn't, you could be entitled to benefits indefinitely, because no matter how many CDRs you have in the future, there may never be significant improvement.

In reality, there is no question that medical doctors know more about medicine than ALJs or other nondoctors deciding appeal cases.

But knowing this to be true, a DDS medical consultant might try to say there has been medical improvement when there really is none, and the ALJ may believe it. However, it is not legal to ignore the medical improvement requirement in such instances.

Watch out for this kind of intentional ignoring of the MIRS if you feel you're disabled. You still get the protection of the law, if at one point an ALJ gave you a less-than-sedentary RFC.

new impairments you have acquired since your CPD and wouldn't require a medical improvement evaluation.

In children, the rules are a little different. Whether a child qualifies for benefits under a listing is decided only after a determination that there has been significant medical improvement. (See Section D, below.)

b. You Are No Longer Disabled or Never Were

If DDS finds that you're no longer disabled, or that you never were disabled, the SSA can terminate your benefits without applying the MIRS if you're performing substantial gainful activity (SGA) (see Chapter 1, Section B) or you're capable of doing so. Group I exceptions to the MIRS rule include the following.

You have undergone vocational therapy related to your ability to work. If you're no longer disabled and can engage in SGA, your benefits can be terminated without going through the MIRS. (This exception doesn't apply to SSI recipients.)

> EXAMPLE 1: Tanya was found to be disabled when her impairment allowed her to do only work with a sedentary level of exertion. Her prior work experience was in work that required a medium level of exertion, and her age and education at the time she was awarded benefits would not have qualified her for work below the medium level. Since then, Tanya has completed a specialized training course that qualifies her for a job

as a computer programmer. During her CDR, DDS concluded that Tanya has had no medical improvement and can still do only sedentary work. But because a computer programmer's work is sedentary in nature, Tanya is now able to engage in SGA and is no longer eligible for Social Security disability.

> EXAMPLE 2: Jacques qualified for disability because the medical evidence and RFC showed he could do only light work. Jacques' prior work was heavy, and his age, education, and prior work qualified him for jobs at the medium or light exertional level. The current evidence and RFC show no medical improvement and that he can still do only light work. Since Jacques was originally awarded benefits, his vocational rehabilitation agency successfully enrolled him in a trade school course, and he can now do small appliance repair. This is considered light work. With these new skills, Jacques is now able to engage in SGA even though his RFC has not changed.

Based on new or improved diagnostic or evaluative techniques, your impairment isn't considered to be as disabling as it was at the CPD. If your condition is no longer considered disabling, your benefits can be terminated without going through the MIRS. For this exception to apply, the new or improved techniques must have become generally available for medical use after the last CPD.

EXAMPLE: Ginger has heart disease. At the time of her last CPD, her heart function was measured with the Master's Two-Step Test. Since then, the EKG Exercise Test has replaced the Master's Two-Step Test as a measurement of heart function. Using the EKG Exercise Test, Ginger's condition is not considered as disabling as was previously thought. If Ginger can engage in SGA, she would no longer be considered disabled even though she's had no medical improvement.

A prior disability decision is incorrect.
If a prior decision is found to be wrong, your benefits can be terminated without going through the MIRS, under certain conditions. DDS must find clear evidence that a prior decision granting you disability was in error—a difference in judgment between the past and current reviewers isn't enough. DDS can make this determination in one of three ways:

- Clear evidence (not open to judgment) already documented in your file shows that the decision in question should not have been made.

EXAMPLE: Rory was granted benefits when the SSA determined that his epilepsy met Listing 11.02 in the Listing of Impairments. Listing 11.02 requires a finding of tonic-clonic seizures about once every month. On a review of Rory's original SSA file, the DDS team finds that Rory's seizures occurred once or twice a year, which isn't frequent enough to meet the listing requirements.

The previous decision that Rory met the listing was clearly incorrect, and whether Rory now will be considered disabled depends on whether he can engage in SGA.

- New evidence is available that shows how severe your impairment is that wasn't available at the time of the CPD, and if the evidence had been present at the time of the CPD, you wouldn't have been found disabled.

EXAMPLE: Lance was originally found disabled due to chronic obstructive lung disease. The severity of his breathing impairment was documented primarily by a pulmonary function test. Spirometry results showing a specific measurement of reduced breathing capacity called an FEV1, although required by SSA regulations, weren't obtained at the time of the CPD. A review of the FEV1 value later obtained during the CDR shows that the test was invalid. Lance's current pulmonary function test, supported by an FEV1 value showing normal lung function, reveals that his condition doesn't limit his ability to perform basic work activities in any way. Lance is no longer entitled to disability.

- New evidence relating to your allowed claim shows that your condition isn't as disabling as originally thought, and if the new evidence been present at the time of the CPD, you wouldn't have been found disabled.

EXAMPLE: K'ia was originally awarded benefits due to a lung tumor doctors thought was cancer. Because she had other health problems at the time, the doctors didn't do a biopsy of the tumor. After K'ia began receiving benefits, she had a biopsy, and the tumor proved to be benign. K'ia is no longer entitled to disability.

Remember that just having the past and current reviewers disagree about your disability isn't enough to determine that a mistake was made, as illustrated by the following example.

EXAMPLE: Tim was previously granted disability benefits for his diabetes mellitus, which the prior DDS medical consultant believed was equal to a listed impairment. At the time of the CPD, Tim was taking insulin for hard-to-control (*brittle*) diabetes. Tim was spilling extra sugar into his urine and his blood sugar would occasionally drop drastically when he exerted himself doing household chores.

During Tim's CDR, the current medical consultant didn't find any change in Tim's symptoms, signs, and laboratory results, but didn't agree that Tim's diabetes equaled a listing. Regardless, Tim will continue to receive disability benefits, because the CDR medical consultant can't substitute their opinion for another.

You currently engage in SGA. If you're currently working above the SGA level, your benefits can be terminated without going through the MIRS. This exception doesn't apply to SSI recipients, and it doesn't apply if you receive SSI or SSDI during a trial work period or reentitlement. (See Chapter 13 for a discussion of these terms.)

You are the beneficiary of advances in medical or vocational therapy or technology related to your ability to work. Because such advances usually result in significant medical improvement, this exception rarely has a practical application. It doesn't apply to SSI recipients eligible to receive special SSI cash benefits.

c. Something Other Than Disability Disqualifies You

In a few rare situations, you may automatically lose your entitlement to SSI or SSDI for reasons unrelated to your disability. These are called the *group II exceptions*. The SSA can apply these exceptions without considering your medical improvement or ability to work. Group II exceptions are as follows.

The SSA is unable to find you. If the SSA can't find you, the SSA will find that your disability has ended (see Chapter 11, Section C).

You don't cooperate with the SSA. If the SSA asks for medical evidence, for other evidence, or for you to undergo an examination by a certain date and you refuse without good reason, the SSA will find that your disability has ended (see Chapter 11, Section D).

You fail to follow a prescribed treatment that is expected to restore your ability to engage in SGA. If you can't show a good reason for not following treatment, the SSA will find that your disability has ended (see Chapter 11, Section E).

You committed fraud. Committing fraud means you gave the SSA false or misleading information during any prior decision about your benefits (see Chapter 11, Section H).

d. New Impairments

The SSA does not consider any new impairments you develop after the CPD date as part of the medical improvement decision. In adults, new impairments are evaluated either after the issue of significant medical improvement is decided (see Section 1, above) or after they meet or equal a listing (see Subsection 4a, above).

In children, new impairments are evaluated only after the SSA makes a determination of whether there is significant improvement (see Section D, below).

But what if you develop a significant new impairment during or near the time you're having your CDR? In this case, your medical condition could be unstable, making the disability determination more difficult. The following example illustrates the procedure that should be followed.

> EXAMPLE: Rima was originally awarded disability benefits for lung cancer. Three years ago, she underwent successful surgery to remove a lung, and her cancer showed no sign of recurrence. Because the SSA will need to determine how severe Rima's respiratory symptoms currently are, the agency sent her notice of a CDR. Two weeks after Rima received noticed of the CDR, she was hospitalized for a heart attack and her doctors recommended heart surgery within the next month. On the SSA's end, the DDS medical consultant can choose to postpone or carry out the CDR. If the medical consultant believes that Rima is still so limited from her lung disease that her benefits are likely to continue, the CDR could be held. But if it's unclear how Rima's recovery from her heart attack will affect her respiratory disorder, the CDR should be postponed.

D. Children and CDRs

SKIP AHEAD

Children younger than 18 who receive benefits as dependents of an SSDI recipient don't undergo CDRs because these benefits don't depend on the child's health. This section applies only to CDR evaluations for child SSI recipients.

CDR evaluations for children receiving SSI differ in some ways from the CDR evaluations of adult SSDI or SSI claims. For example, the medical improvement determination in SSI children doesn't involve changes in RFCs because children aren't given RFCs. (The SSA doesn't evaluate how the health of minor children affects their ability to work.) Additionally, the order of CDR steps is a little different—whether a child has shown medical improvement is considered before determining whether the child meets or equals a listing.

Still, the main question is whether the child has experienced significant improvement in impairments. The SSA uses the following analysis:

Step 1. Has the child experienced significant medical improvement in the impairments present at the CPD? If "no" and none of the exceptions apply, benefits will continue. If "yes," proceed to Step 2.

Step 2. Do the impairments still meet or equal the severity of the listing that was met or equaled at the time of CPD? If "yes" and none of the exceptions apply (as described in Section C4, above), then benefits will continue. If "no," proceed to Step 3.

Step 3. Considering all of the child's current impairments—both those present at the CPD and new ones—do the impairments meet or equal a current listing? If "yes," then benefits will continue. If "no," benefits will end.

E. Appealing a CDR Decision

Once the SSA makes its CDR decision, you'll receive a written notice. If the SSA decides you're still disabled, your benefits will continue.

If the SSA determines that you're not still disabled, the SSA will send you a personalized explanation explaining how it reached its determination. If you don't appeal, you'll receive benefits for the remainder of the month in which your disability ended, plus two more months. In no case, however, can your benefits be taken away earlier than the date it was decided to terminate your benefits.

This prevents the SSA from demanding back benefit repayment from you by saying that your disability ended before the agency even conducted your CDR. For example, suppose you were significantly improved and able to work a year before the SSA did a CDR evaluation of your claim. That is the SSA's fault, not yours, and you won't have to repay the money you received during this year. The only exception would be if you had committed fraud to obtain benefits. In that case, the SSA could demand that you repay all benefits you received.

What if the SSA decided that your disability ended on the same day the SSA gives you notice that your benefits ceased? In that case, your benefits would continue for three more months and then be stopped. (See Chapter 12 for information on appealing denied claims.)

Your Right to Representation

You don't need to represent yourself in a disability claim. You can appoint someone in writing to be your authorized representative to deal with the SSA on your behalf. (42 U.S.C. § 406; 20 C.F.R. §§ 404.1700, 416.1500.) SSA personnel will work with your representative, just as they would work with you. Your authorized representative's primary role is to pursue your claim for benefits under SSDI or SSI. Authorized representatives can be disability lawyers, professionals who work for a disability firm, or other types of nonlawyer representatives.

TIP
An authorized representative is different from a *designated representative*, who is a person you can appoint to look at your medical records. An authorized representative is also different from a *representative payee*, who is a person you can appoint to handle your benefit checks. You can name the same person to be your authorized representative, designated representative, and representative payee, however. (Designated representatives are discussed in Chapter 2, and representative payees are discussed in Chapters 3 and 13.)

A. When Do You Need an Authorized Representative?

Many people are perfectly capable of applying for disability benefits themselves, and some claimants do just that. They have the time and ability to complete the paperwork, meet with the claims examiner, contact their treating doctors and hospitals for their medical records, and follow up on any requests from the claims examiner, medical examiner, or medical consultant.

Other people appoint authorized representatives to handle their applications for benefits. Typical reasons for appointing such a person include the following:

- You just don't want to handle your own claim.
- Your medical condition prevents you from effectively representing yourself.
- You don't have the time to represent yourself.
- You have limited education or English skills and want someone to help with the paperwork.

Many people decide to appoint authorized representatives only after their initial claims for benefits (and perhaps reconsideration) have been denied and they want to appeal. Most claimants hire disability lawyers to represent them at the appeal hearings, but a few claimants do handle their hearings on their own. (Chapter 12 has complete information on appealing.)

Going through the entire appeals process means you'll need to argue your case before an administrative law judge (ALJ), an attorney who works for the SSA and reviews Disability Determination Services (DDS) decisions. If you lose your case before the ALJ, you can request review by the Appeals Council. If you're denied an Appeals Council review, you can file a lawsuit in a federal district court. At that point, it's almost always in your best interest to hire an attorney as your authorized representative. (See Section D, below.)

Ultimately, the decision of whether to hire a representative requires judgment on your part—a judgment that often relates to money. Authorized representatives work on *contingency*, meaning they only get paid if you win your case. The SSA will set aside a portion of any back pay you're owed to pay your representative. You won't have to pay your representative out of pocket, and fees are capped by the SSA. So if, after reading this book, you conclude that you have a really good chance of being awarded benefits, then you might not want to hire a representative in order to maximize the amount of past-due benefits you could receive. But if you're uncertain, or you've been denied benefits and want to appeal, then hiring an authorized representative may make sense. You need to balance the fee you'll have to pay the representative against the amount of money you potentially could recover if you're awarded benefits. (Fees are discussed in Section G, below.)

B. What Can an Authorized Representative Do?

An authorized representative can act for you in most Social Security matters, including the following:

- helping you fill out the paperwork

- accompanying you—or attending on your behalf—any interview, conference, or hearing with the SSA or DDS
- helping get medical records or information from your treating sources to support your claim
- obtaining information from your Social Security file
- requesting reconsideration of your claim, a hearing, or an Appeals Council review
- helping you and your witnesses prepare for a hearing
- presenting your case at a hearing and questioning any witnesses, and
- if your representative is an attorney, filing an appeal in federal court.

If you hire a representative, all correspondence will be sent to both you and your representative. However, it's a good idea for you to inform your representative of any communications from the SSA in case, by some error, the representative doesn't get a copy. Even though you have appointed a representative, you (through your representative) remain legally obligated to provide Social Security with accurate information.

A representative typically doesn't sign an application for disability benefits on your behalf, but the representative can help you fill out the forms.

Many unrepresented claimants submit incomplete forms to Social Security. If you hire a representative before you get a denial, the representative can help you fill out the paperwork, track down important medical records and test results, and obtain detailed statements from your doctor.

Note that if there is a good reason why you can't sign the application, the SSA may accept an application signed by your representative.

> **EXAMPLE:** Joe is a 55-year-old who had a heart attack a few days before the end of the month and was unable to file an application for SSI disability benefits. However, Joe had hired an authorized representative, Sinclair, to help him with his claim. The Social Security office accepted an application for Joe signed by Sinclair, because it wouldn't be possible to have Joe sign and file the application until the next calendar month— which would mean that Joe would lose one month's benefits.

C. Who Can Be an Authorized Representative?

Authorized representatives generally fall into two categories—attorneys and nonattorneys. Your Social Security office has a list of organizations that can help you find an authorized representative.

1. Attorney Representatives

Any attorney in good standing, licensed to practice in the United States, can serve as your representative in dealing with the SSA. The only exceptions are if the attorney has been disqualified or suspended from acting as a representative in dealing with the SSA

(see Section 3, below) or is otherwise prohibited by law from acting as a representative.

If the attorney you hire is a member of a law firm or organization, you can appoint a second or third person within the firm (corporation, LLC, or partnership) or organization as an additional representative to handle your case if your first representative is unavailable. Note that Social Security rules don't allow you to appoint a firm, corporation, LLC, partnership, or organization as a whole to act as your authorized representative—you must name a specific person.

2. Nonattorney Representatives

You can appoint anyone you want to be your representative in dealing with the SSA as long as that person has a good character and reputation, can give you valuable help with your claim, has not been disqualified or suspended from acting as a representative in dealing with the SSA (see Section 3, below), and isn't otherwise prohibited by law from acting as a representative. The law doesn't define what "good character" is, but it most likely means the person has not been convicted of any serious crimes.

You may be able to find a disability advocate, one type of nonattorney representative, to help you with your claim. Some disability advocates are registered to receive payment from Social Security for claims that they work on (they have to take a Social Security test to be able to receive payments from the SSA).

Some disability firms have a staff of both nonlawyers and lawyers to assist you. The nonlawyers help you file your application and gather medical records and your employment history, while the lawyers help you at your appeal hearing if you get denied.

3. Suspended or Disqualified Representatives

On occasion, the SSA suspends or disqualifies people from serving as authorized representatives. This can happen when a representative knowingly and willingly provides false information to the SSA or charges an unauthorized fee for their services. If you attempt to name someone as your authorized representative who has been suspended or disqualified, the person's name will pop up in the SSA's computers as suspended or disqualified. If you want to check beforehand, call the SSA hotline (800-772-1213). Tell the person who answers that you want to find out if the person you're considering appointing to be your authorized representative has been suspended or disqualified by the SSA.

D. Should Your Authorized Representative Be an Attorney?

If you want to appoint an authorized representative, you must decide between an attorney and a nonattorney. The same general analysis suggested at the end of Section A, above, applies here—if

you're at the initial application stage and don't foresee too many problems, then a nonlawyer representative might serve you fine. There are very capable and highly experienced nonattorney representatives who can help you with your application.

If your case isn't cut-and-dried from the start or you've been denied benefits already and are filing an appeal, then it might be to your advantage to have a disability attorney as your representative. An attorney doesn't charge any more than a nonattorney (see the discussion on fees below), but often knows more about Social Security law.

Attorneys with extensive disability experience should be well equipped to handle the legal issues that arise in your claim. They know a lot about the SSA and its regulations. They can make sure that you don't miss deadlines, can help you obtain medical records that hospitals or treating doctors won't give the SSA, and can call the examiner handling your file and ask questions on your behalf. And if you're planning on appealing your claim to federal court, you have to hire an attorney.

Attorneys vary in their competence, skill, and experience. Some attorneys are new to the field of Social Security disability. Disability law is an extremely specialized area, and attorneys can't quickly review a few law books and capably represent your claim.

You should be cautious in retaining attorneys who only take disability cases occasionally, while most of their time is spent in another kind of law practice. Some attorneys have not only extensive disability case experience representing claimants but a history of working in some other capacity that gives them additional valuable insights—such as being a former SSA attorney, administrative law judge, or DDS supervisor or examiner. You can call an attorney's office and find out the answers to these questions before making an appointment.

E. How to Find a Disability Representative

You can find a competent local disability representative in a variety of ways: through a personal recommendation, in a directory, or through a lawyer referral service. If you use a referral service, make sure it guarantees its lawyers are active members of its state's bar in good standing.

Two sites that are part of the Nolo family, Lawyers.com and Avvo.com, provide excellent and free lawyer directories. These directories allow you to search by location and area of law, and list detailed information about and reviews of lawyers. You can visit www.lawyers.com/find-a-lawyer or www.avvo.com/find-a-lawyer to find out more.

When considering whether to hire an attorney, you should ask yourself whether the attorney:

- is easy to relate to
- listens to what you have to say
- seems genuinely concerned with your disability problem
- is friendly, and
- is willing to answer your questions in a way you can understand.

Many attorneys use paralegal assistants or staff members to help them with disability claims. This should be acceptable to you as long as the attorney adequately supervises the paralegal, keeps up with what is happening in your claim, and personally handles any significant legal events, such as hearings. After all, you're supposed to be paying for attorney representation.

Make sure that your potential representative has a good working relationship with each level of the Social Security Administration that you'll be dealing with. You don't want your attorney or nonlawyer representative to be needlessly adversarial with the claims examiners at DDS or the staff at the administrative law judge's office.

Your representative should be honest with you about your chances of success. For example, if an attorney or nonlawyer representative says that DDS denies everyone and that your only chance is at the hearing level, be skeptical. While disability claims do indeed have a good chance of getting approved after a hearing, it gives the wrong impression about your chances at DDS. In sheer numbers, more claims get approved at the initial application level than any other level, even though the odds of getting approved are better with a hearing—for the relatively small numbers of claimants who make it to the hearing stage.

Your representative should be maximizing your odds of success at every level instead of waiting for a judge's decision (which can take years).

Attorneys and disability firms don't accept all cases that come to them. And because they get paid only if you win benefits (see Section G, below), they need to decide whether you have a reasonable chance of being awarded benefits before they'll take your case. For example, if you're 25 years old and in good health except for an artificial leg that you walk well on, an attorney isn't likely to take your case, because anyone experienced in the Social Security system knows that your chance of being awarded benefits is slim. On the other hand, if you have multiple physical and mental impairments, are over the age of 55, and have worked in manual labor your whole life, you probably have a strong case.

If an attorney says you don't have a chance, you can visit another attorney or disability firm for a second opinion.

F. Notifying the SSA of Your Choice for Representative

Once you choose a representative, you must tell the SSA in writing by completing Form SSA-1696, *Claimant's Appointment of Representative*. Your representative will help you fill out the form.

CAUTION
You must use forms provided by the SSA. You can obtain them at your local SSA Field Office or by calling the SSA hotline at 800-772-1213, Monday through Friday (except holidays), from 8:00 a.m. to 7:00 p.m. If you're deaf or hard of hearing, TTY service representatives are available at the same times at 800-325-0778. You can also download many necessary forms from the Social Security Administration website at www.ssa.gov.

On the form, give the name and address of the person whom you're appointing as your representative. If your representative isn't an attorney, the form must show the representative's name and state that the representative accepts the appointment. Both you and the representative must sign the form. Provide your address, Social Security number, and telephone number. For SSDI claims, if the claimant isn't the same person as the wage earner (such as a parent signing for a child), fill in the Social Security numbers for both.

Depending on what stage of the disability determination process (DDS, hearing, or Appeals Council) your claim is currently at, you'll need to send your appointment of representative form to a specific office. If your claim is at the DDS level, you should send the form to a Social Security Field Office. If you've requested a hearing, the form should be filed with the Office of Hearings Operations (OHO). If you're appealing an administrative law judge's decision to the Appeals Council, the form should be sent to the Appeals Council. Your representative should take care of these details for you.

G. When and How Your Representative Is Paid

Your representative is paid out of any past-due benefits you're entitled to if your claim is approved. If you lose your claim, in most cases, you don't have to pay your authorized representative. This fee structure is called a *contingency* arrangement because whether your representative ultimately gets paid depends (*is contingent*) on the outcome of your case. Representatives generally aren't allowed to collect more than 25% of your past-due benefits in fees, up to a maximum of $7,200.

Be clear on the nature of the fee agreement before you hire someone as your representative. Fee agreements often include a paragraph stating that you will pay any out-of-pocket office costs associated with handling your claim, even if you lose. These costs may include long-distance telephone calls, copying birth and death certificates, travel expenses, or postage.

1. SSA Approval of Fee Agreements

The SSA must approve in writing all fee agreements between claimants and their authorized representatives. Your authorized representative must file a copy of the agreement with your Social Security Field Office before a decision has been reached on your claim. After your claim has been decided favorably (resulting in payment to your representative), the SSA will typically approve your fee agreement as long as the agreement isn't in excess of the fee cap and you both signed it.

Your representative must provide you with a copy of the fee agreement sent to the SSA. The SSA will consider the fee agreement and let you and your representative know of its decision.

> **EXAMPLE:** If it took 17 months from your onset date to get your claim approved, the SSA would owe you a year's worth of benefits. If that amount was more than $28,800, your representative could get only $7,200 (25% of $28,800 is $7,200, so anything over that amount would exceed the fee cap.)

Both attorney and nonattorney representatives use fee agreements. A single agreement covers both SSDI and SSI claims—your representative can't collect $7,200 from your SSDI back pay and another $7,200 from your SSI back pay.

How the representative actually gets paid for their work depends on several factors (see Section 3, below). Keep in mind that once you appeal to federal court, the SSA-specific fee agreement—and the fee cap—might not apply. (See Section 4, below.)

And at any level, you may have to pay for your representative's out-of-pocket expenses.

If the SSA doesn't approve the fee agreement, it will notify you and your representative that your representative must file a fee petition. (See Section 2, below.) Any representatives who forget to request approval of a fee agreement must also use the fee petition process. Because fee petitions are time-consuming and delay payment, most representatives prefer fee agreements.

RESOURCE
To read more about fee agreements and see sample language that the SSA suggests for these agreements, visit the SSA's website at www.ssa.gov/representation.

2. SSA Approval of Fee Petitions

While fee agreements are fairly simple—most are only a few paragraphs long—fee petitions can be lengthy documents. In a fee petition, your representative must state, in detail, the amount of time spent on each service provided to you.

The representative must give you a copy of the fee petition. If you disagree with the information shown, you must contact the SSA within 20 days. (The SSA won't accept a fee petition until a final decision has been made on your claim.) You should contact your SSA Field Office in writing and follow up with a telephone call a few days later to make sure it has your letter.

When evaluating a fee petition, the SSA looks at the reasonable value of the services provided. The SSA may approve your representative's request to charge you, but not at the amount in the petition. In that case, the SSA will tell you and your representative the approved amount. Your representative can't charge you more than the approved amount (except for out-of-pocket expenses). If you or your representative disagrees with the approved amount, the person who objects can ask the SSA to look at the petition again.

A representative who charges or collects a fee without the SSA's approval, or who charges or collects more than the approved amount, may be suspended or disqualified from representing anyone before the SSA and can face criminal prosecution.

3. How Your Representative Is Paid

For attorney representatives, the SSA usually withholds 25% of your past-due benefits to put toward your attorneys' fee and sends you anything left over after the lawyer is paid. If the SSA doesn't withhold the attorneys' fee, you must pay the attorney out of your benefit amount. If you don't pay, the SSA can withhold the amount you owe your attorney from future benefits.

You must pay your representative directly when:

- Your representative isn't an attorney or appointed representative (registered with Social Security).

- Your attorney didn't request fee approval or didn't request it on time.
- The fee is for more than the amount the SSA withheld, in which case you must pay the balance.

In certain cases, including where you agree to pay your representative directly, your representative can accept money from you to be placed in an escrow (holding) account. Some representatives might do this to make sure that you pay their fees or costs. In the past, the SSA didn't withhold a representative's share of benefits in SSI claims, so representatives ran the risk of not getting paid. However, this is no longer much of an issue. Because most disability representatives work on contingency, you don't have to offer any money for an escrow account. The SSA will pay the attorney if you win your claim—and there is no cost to you if you lose your claim. But a different payment structure is likely to apply if you and your representative take your claim to federal court.

4. Attorney Representation in Federal Court

You can appeal your case to federal court if your claim is denied at the highest level of administrative appeal for the Social Security Administration (the Appeals Council). A federal court can order the SSA to approve your claim, or it can instruct the SSA to obtain more information or rehear the case. To get your claim into federal court, you must file a formal lawsuit using an attorney.

If you appeal to federal court, the court can allow reasonable attorneys' fees for the part of your representation that involves the court proceedings. These attorneys' fees are in addition to any fees allowed by the fee agreement you and your attorney might have with the SSA. Remember that the courts and the SSA are two different organizations—when you enter the federal court system, you leave the SSA behind. Whether you have to pay your attorney extra for representing you in federal court depends on the payment arrangement you have. The SSA doesn't have the authority to approve or disapprove attorney charges for federal court representation.

Many attorneys, however, use *two-tier fee agreements* that allow the attorney to petition for fees if the case is appealed to federal district court. A two-tier agreement allows the lawyer to be paid the usual maximum fee of 25% of your back pay, capped at $7,200, if you are approved at the initial application, reconsideration, or ALJ hearing stage. If the case goes further, the attorney is free to petition for fees beyond the $7,200 cap.

It costs money to go to federal court, and claimants often can't pay an attorney's hourly rate if they're not working on contingency. Therefore, an attorney is unlikely to take your case to federal court unless they think you have a reasonable chance of winning—because if you lose, the attorney might have to pay court costs in addition to not getting paid for representing you.

If the payment arrangement you have with your attorney says that you'll have to pay for federal court representation, then the attorney's fee could be your burden—the arrangement might be that you pay only if you win, or you might have to pay whether you win or lose.

If the federal court approves your claim, the court will order the SSA to consider you disabled and start paying you benefits. Based on when the federal judge decides the onset date of your disability was, you'll also be entitled to some past-due benefits from the SSA. For SSDI claims, your past-due benefits could extend back to a time before you even applied for disability. For SSI claims, the earliest onset would be the month after you applied for benefits (see Chapter 10). If you have both SSDI and SSI claims (concurrent claims), you can receive past-due benefits for both. Note that the judge can order the SSA to take the attorneys' fees out of your past-due benefits, provided there is enough money to cover the fees.

Otherwise, you and your attorney will have to work something out regarding payment for court representation.

Remember that when a federal court approves a claim, there are two payment issues that come up at the same time: the fee for your attorney for previously representing you before the SSA, and the fee your attorney will charge you for federal court representation. It's not likely that an attorney is going to represent you in federal court unless you have enough past-due

benefits to make it worthwhile or can make other arrangements for payment. Most attorneys, however, will file a claim under the Equal Access to Justice Act, which will pay part of the attorneys' fees if you win your claim (see below).

You should be aware that attorney payment issues can be complex and potentially controversial. The comments in this section are meant to guide you in the most important general principles. They aren't a substitute for expert legal advice. You should discuss payment issues in detail with your attorney until you feel comfortable with what you should expect to pay.

a. Attorney Payment for SSDI Claims Allowed or Denied in Federal Court

i. Payment for SSA representation

To receive payment by the SSA from your past-due benefits in an SSDI claim, your attorney must file a request for direct payment and submit this request to a Social Security office within 60 days of when you get the notice awarding you benefits. Remember, this is only for the SSA part of your representation. If your attorney doesn't meet the 60-day deadline, the SSA will send you and your attorney written notice that the SSA will send all past-due benefits to you unless the lawyer asks for the fee within another 20 days. If your attorney still doesn't file the request on time, the SSA will send you all of your past-due benefits and the attorney must seek payment from you independently.

ii. Payment for federal court representation

The amount of fees you might owe your attorney if you win in federal court is addressed in 42 U.S.C. § 406(b). Under this provision, the court part of your charges cannot exceed 25% of your total past-due SSDI benefits.

Payment for federal court representation differs from payment for representing you solely within the SSA. Within the SSA, your representative is generally limited to 25% of your past-due benefits, up to $7,200. At the federal court level, however, attorneys representing SSDI claimants who win aren't limited by the same fee cap that applies to agency representation. *Culbertson v. Berryhill*, 586 U.S.___ (2019.) In other words, payments for representation before the SSA and the federal courts are calculated separately—unless you have a fee agreement covering the cost of federal court representation, your attorney can charge you up to 25% of your back benefits for the SSA representation and another 25% for the federal court representation. The attorney can even charge you if you lose your case in federal court, depending on your agreement.

The judge who hears your disability case must approve the amount of the attorney's fee for the court representation. Your attorney can then ask the SSA to take this money out of your back benefits.

If you lose your case in federal court, the SSA won't pay your attorney out of your past-due benefits, because you won't have any money coming.

b. Attorney Payment for SSI Claims Allowed or Denied in Federal Court

i. Payment for SSA representation

If you win SSI benefits in federal court, Social Security must approve the fee agreement concerning the part of your representation before the SSA. As mentioned previously, the SSA has no authority over attorneys' fees for court representation.

ii. Payment for federal court representation

Again, payments for representation before the SSA and the federal courts are separate. Your attorney can charge you up to 25% of your back benefits for the federal court representation in addition to the 25% of your back benefits for representation at the SSA.

The judge who hears your disability case must approve the amount of the attorneys' fee. Your attorney can then ask the SSA to take this money out of your back benefits.

5. If Someone Else Pays Your Fee

If someone will pay your attorneys' fee for you—for example, a long-term disability insurance company—the SSA still must approve the fee, except in the following cases:

- A nonprofit organization or government agency will pay the fee.

- Your representative provides the SSA with a written statement that you won't have to pay any fees or expenses.

6. The Equal Access to Justice Act

The Equal Access to Justice Act (EAJA, found at 5 U.S.C. § 504, 28 U.S.C. § 2412), is an additional way attorneys can collect fees—at the rate of $125 per hour—for representing you before a federal court, thereby lowering your own costs. Whatever amount your lawyer can collect under EAJA isn't taken out of your back pay benefits. EAJA fees are paid directly to you, not to your attorney, and then you pay your attorney with that money.

If you're planning on appealing to a federal court, you can ask your attorney to file an application for EAJA fees in order to help pay legal bills. Applications for EAJA assistance can be filed within 30 days of the court's judgment, but in practice, applications may be filed between 61 and 90 days after the court's judgment.

You will get paid EAJA expenses only if you win your case—that is, if the court reverses your prior SSA disability denial into an approval. If you lose your appeal as a federal court denial, then you could owe your attorney money, depending on the type of payment agreement you have.

If the court remands your claim to an administrative law judge instead of reaching a decision, you can still collect EAJA fees. Generally, unless the court finds that the SSA was *substantially justified* (had a good reason) to deny you benefits, you'll be awarded EAJA fees.

Note that court filing and administrative fees can be hundreds of dollars. EAJA typically doesn't cover these expenses, unless you ask and the court believes you are financially unable to pay them yourself.

Note that attorneys can't collect fees from your back pay and from EAJA for the same federal court representation, although some district courts may allow *netting*, where the EAJA fees are subtracted from the attorneys' fees that are taken out of your back pay.

TIP
More information. If you have any questions about your right to representation, call the SSA at 800-772-1213.

H. Keeping Up on the Law Yourself

With or without a lawyer, you should realize that the material in this book can change between printings. The U.S. Congress and the Social Security Administration are constantly updating and revising the rules that affect you. You can stay on top of legal developments in Social Security disability law by visiting www.nolo.com.

Glossary of Bureaucratic Terms

Adjudication. The process of determining a disability claim.

Adjudicator. A person officially involved in making the disability determination.

Administrative law judge (ALJ). An SSA employee and attorney who holds hearings at the first level of appeals above the state agency (DDS).

Allegations. The medical problems that a claimant puts forth as the basis for wanting disability benefits.

Alleged onset date (AOD). The date a claimant states that he or she became unable to work due to impairments.

Claimant. The person who applies for disability benefits.

Closed period. If an impairment does not qualify as severe enough for benefits at the time of adjudication, benefits can still be given for prior periods of at least 12 months during which there was sufficient severity.

Concurrent claims. Two claims filed at the same time, under different aspects of the law. Usually, concurrent claims are SSDI/Title 2 and SSI/Title 16 claims filed at the same time.

Consultative examination (CE). Physical or mental examination of a claimant at the expense of the SSA.

Consultative examination (CE) doctor. A doctor or another health professional paid by the SSA to perform a consultative examination. See "consultative examination."

Continuing disability review (CDR). The process by which the SSA reevaluates the severity of a claimant's impairments to determine whether there has been significant medical improvement.

Diary. A term that has two meanings:
- the interval of time until a claim is reevaluated after benefits are allowed, and
- the interval of time a state agency holds a claim to determine the outcome of some medical problem or treatment, before a final determination is made. When a claim is held to determine an outcome, the state agency will send the claimant a letter saying that a final decision has been delayed for a specified amount of time, usually not more than three months.

Disability determination. The determination that an adult is unable to work and qualifies for benefits or that a child qualifies for benefits.

Disability Determination Services (DDS). A state agency. See "state agency."

Disability hearing officer (DHO). An experienced disability examiner who interviews claimants receiving disability payments to determine if benefits should continue. Claimants appear before a DHO to appeal the termination of disability benefits when they are about to lose them.

Duration. How long a claimant has had an impairment severe enough to qualify for Social Security disability benefits.

Equal. Allowance term meaning that a claimant has an impairment as severe as required by the listings, although no specific listing exactly applies to his or her claim. The equal concept can be applied to single or multiple listings, as well as single or multiple impairments, as appropriate to a particular claim.

Examiner. A DDS examiner is specially trained to make initial, reconsideration, and continuing disability review determinations regarding nonmedical evidence from a claimant's file. Examiners physically control individual claimant files that are assigned to them, as well as communicate with claimants or their representatives. (See Chapter 5.)

Impairments. The medical problems that a claimant has, either mental or physical.

Initial claim. The first application for disability benefits.

Listings. Lists of rules giving the medical criteria that must be fulfilled for benefits to be granted without consideration of age, education, or work experience. Separate listings exist for adults and children. Listings are found in the Listing of Impairments in federal regulations (Code of Federal Regulations, Title 20, Part 404, Subpart P, Appendix 1, and reinterpreted in this book's online Medical Listings in Parts 1 through 14).

Medical consultant (MC). A medical doctor, osteopath, or psychologist who works under contract or as an employee of a state agency (DDS), or who works in some similar role at some other level of the SSA. The SSA may refer to those who evaluate mental disorders as "psychological consultants." The MC is specially trained by the SSA and other MCs to make the "overall determination of impairment severity" in initial, reconsideration, and continuing disability review determinations. This determination must be done according to federal rules, regulations, and other written guidelines based on the medical and nonmedical evidence. All medical evidence used in these determinations is obtained from medical and other sources outside of the state agency. MC determinations should not be biased; therefore, the MCs do not meet, talk to, or treat claimants concerning their individual claims. Medical consultants are not the same as doctors who do consultative examinations. Consultative examination doctors examine claimants for a fee paid by the SSA. Unlike MCs, they do not make disability determinations.

Medical-vocational allowance. Allowance of disability benefits based on a combination of RFC, age, education, and work experience.

Meet. Allowance term meaning that a claimant's impairment exactly fulfills the requirements of a listing.

Not severe (nonsevere). Term that means all impairments considered together are still not sufficient to produce any significant restriction in the functional capacity of a claimant. Describes a mild or slight impairment.

Onset. The date at which a claimant's impairments are sufficiently severe to qualify for disability. This is not necessarily the same as the date when the impairment first arose.

Presumptive disability. A privilege of SSI/Title 16 claimants in which they can receive benefits (and sometimes Medicaid) for up to six months before a final decision is made on their claim by a state agency. SSDI/Title 2 claimants cannot have presumptive disability.

Projected rating. The opinion of the SSA about the level of residual impairment severity that is expected to exist 12 months after the onset of allowance-level severity. Allowance-level severity must persist 12 months before benefits are granted. Such a projected rating could result in either allowance or denial, depending on medical or vocational factors. If a projected rating is a denial, it is a way of saying that while an impairment may be severe enough to be disabling at the present time, it is expected to improve to nonallowance severity in less than 12 months.

Quick Disability Determination (QDD). A procedure to speed up case decisions for people who have such extreme impairments that their claims are almost certainly going to be approved.

Reconsideration claim. A denial of benefits or an unfavorable decision made by DDS that is being reconsidered at the request of the claimant. Reconsideration is not automatic; a claimant must request it.

Residual functional capacity (RFC). A claimant's maximum mental or physical capabilities as determined by a DDS medical consultant in instances in which the impairment does not meet or equal a listing but is more than "not severe" (slight). See "medical consultant."

State agency. One of the agencies in each state funded by the Social Security Administration to make decisions on disability claims. The examiners and other administrative personnel are state employees, even though they're funded with federal dollars. Also known as Disability Determination Services (DDS).

Substantial gainful activity (SGA). The standard for determining a claimant is making too much money through work to be eligible for disability benefits. Blind claimants can make more than nonblind claimants. The amount that you can earn without losing benefits is increased yearly.

Treating doctor. Any medical doctor or psychologist who treats a claimant at the claimant's own request and is not paid by the SSA. A treating doctor can also be the claimant's CE doctor, if the treating doctor has agreed with the SSA to do such exams. See "consultative examination." According to federal regulations, your treating doctor is not involved in making disability determinations.

Trial work period (TWP). An interval of time for claimants already on the disability rolls in which they can work and continue to draw benefits until it is clear they can actually perform jobs well enough to take care of THEMSELVES.

Vocational analyst. At DDS, an experienced disability examiner with special training in evaluating the combination of RFC, age, education, and work experience regarding a claimant's ability to perform various jobs.

Examples of Technical Rationales for Denials

We have included this appendix of technical rationales for denials to give you added insight into how and why the Social Security Administration issues denials in specific cases. In the following examples, the doctor and hospital names and dates have been removed or changed. Names and dates must, however, be listed in actual notice rationales. If DDS fails to list some of your important medical sources, you can assume that they were not used in your disability determination. This can be the basis for an appeal. Explanations of abbreviations and medical terms have been added in brackets so the rationales are a little easier to follow.

Form SSA-4268, Denials From Initial Application

Example 1: Impairment(s) Not Severe

The only source of medical evidence provided by the claimant was the Mercy Hospital outpatient treatment report. Since this report was incidental to the claimant's alleged impairments and no other medical evidence existed, two consultative examinations (CEs) were arranged: one to evaluate the claimant's general health, the other to assess the possibility of organic brain damage due to apparent alcohol abuse. The claimant alleges disability since January 2, 20xx, due to "bad lungs, high blood pressure,

and forgetfulness." There is no indication that the claimant has worked since that date.

A review of the Mercy Hospital report indicates the claimant was treated for a bruised arm. An X-ray was taken due to complaints of pain in her arm. The X-ray was negative. She was treated for abrasions and released within hours of admittance.

The general CE was done by Dr. Meyer. Dr. Meyer's report notes the claimant alleged constant fatigue and an inability to remember recent events. She admitted to drinking about two six-packs of beer every day and to smoking one to two packs of cigarettes daily for at least three years. Medical examination shows the claimant's height as 66 inches and her weight as 140 pounds. Her blood pressure is 124/85 repeated; pulse 76 and regular. Some increased A/P [anterior-posterior or front to back] diameter of the chest, distant breath sounds, and scattered rhonchi [a type of abnormal breathing sound, heard through a stethoscope] are noted. The chest X-ray is consistent with chronic obstructive pulmonary disease (COPD) with somewhat flattened diaphragms. No infiltrates are noted. PFTs [pulmonary function tests] were obtained and show FEV1 [forced expiratory volume in 1 second] of 1.6 liters and MVV [maximum voluntary ventilation] of 75 L/min, both recorded after inhaled bronchodilators. The EKG [electrocardiogram] is normal, as is the neurologic examination. Extremities show no muscle wasting or weakness. Slight hepatomegaly [enlarged liver] is noted; however, LFTs [liver function tests] are normal with the exception of an elevated SGOT [a liver enzyme] of 75 units. The CBC [complete blood count] is normal with the exception of an MCV [mean corpuscular volume] of 110.

Analysis of findings based on the above medical summation shows the claimant's breathing capacity, as evidenced by PFT values, is not significantly diminished. In addition, despite some liver enlargement and elevated SGOT, other liver studies were normal. The neurological system was essentially intact, and blood pressure was within normal limits. Consequently, no impairment related to these findings exists, because they are essentially normal.

To assess the possibility of organic brain syndrome, the claimant was referred to Dr. Johnson. His assessment includes use of a WAIS [Wechsler Adult Intelligence Scale], the Wechsler Memory Scale, and the Bender-Gestalt. No indication of memory loss or psychosis is shown to exist. The claimant tested to be above average intellectually with a full-scale IQ of 110.

Dr. Johnson's report indicates the claimant admitted to drinking to steady her nerves, but she did not report any disorder of thought or constriction of interest. She appeared to have good personal habits. According to Dr. Johnson's report and the report by the DO [district office, same as

Field Office], her daily activities are not restricted. She does not appear withdrawn or isolated. She helps her mother take care of the house and does the shopping.

The above medical summary indicates the claimant's mental functional restrictions are present only during acute intoxication. The claimant has above-normal intellect and normal memory and thought processes. She does not behave bizarrely. There is no indication she cannot understand and follow directions. Appropriate daily activities show there is no significant restriction of work-related functions. There is no evidence that the individual cannot perform basic work-related functions on a sustained, longitudinal basis.

For an impairment to be considered severe, it must significantly limit the individual's physical or mental abilities to do basic work activities. Medical evidence does not demonstrate an impairment that is severe, nor does the combined impact of respiratory, liver, and psychiatric impairments produce a severe impairment. Accordingly, the claimant is found not disabled because she has no severe impairment or any combination of impairments that is severe.

Example 2: Can Perform Past Work

The claimant has said that he became unable to work as of 6/15/2015 due to "a heart condition." He was in the hospital when he applied and was to have bypass surgery. There is no work issue.

The medical evidence documents the presence of coronary artery disease. The claimant was hospitalized 6/15/2015 due to chest pain, with EKG changes suggestive of ischemia. Cardiac catheterization showed 75% obstruction of the left main coronary artery. He was discharged to await bypass surgery. Triple bypass surgery was performed 6/30/2015. Three months after surgery, the treating physician reported that there was no chest pain. No treadmill test had been done and none was planned. The doctor said the claimant should limit lifting to 10–20 pounds.

The evidence documents the presence of a severe cardiovascular impairment. However, the findings do not meet or equal the severity of any of the listed impairments. While Listing 4.04C1.b was met at the time of the angiogram, the bypass surgery improved the condition, and there is no longer any chest pain. The claimant would be restricted from lifting more than ten pounds frequently or more than 20 pounds occasionally due to his heart condition. There are no other medically imposed limitations or restrictions. The individual is capable of performing light work.

After a military career that ended in 2005, the claimant did no work until 1/2008 when he was employed as a cashier in a discount liquor house. This was full-time work at SGA [substantial gainful activity] levels until 1/2010. From 1/2010 until AOD [alleged onset date], 6/15/2015, he worked on weekends only, and that work was not SGA. The period 1/2008–1/2010 lies within the relevant 15-year period and was of sufficient duration for him to gain the job experience necessary for average job performance. Therefore, his job as cashier has current relevance.

Demands of the job included sitting most of the day while operating a cash register, observing the merchandise being purchased, taking the customers' money, and making change. These duties entailed the abilities to sit, see, talk, reach, handle, finger, and feel. He also demonstrated an elementary knowledge of mathematics and cash register function. It was occasionally necessary for him to stand and walk a few feet to secure a register tape and then insert the tape into the machine.

With the exertional capacity to do light work, and in the absence of any nonexertional limitations, this individual is able to do his past relevant work as he described it. Therefore, he is not disabled.

Example 3: Can Perform Other Work

The claimant has alleged disability since 5/1/2020 due to "diabetic, hearing, heart." When he has diabetic attacks, he has cold sweats, shakes, and acts drunk. He has no chest pain. The DO claims representative noted that he had a hearing aid and occasionally needed questions repeated. The claimant is not engaging in any work activity.

Medical evidence reveals the presence of insulin-dependent diabetes. There are allegations of frequent diabetic attacks, but there are no medical records to support this. A general consultative examination was obtained, as there was insufficient evidence from the treating source to evaluate severity. This revealed the following abnormal findings: Corrected vision was 20/25 with grade one over four diabetic changes of the fundi [retinas]. He wore a hearing aid and had difficulty hearing a tuning fork. Pulses were two plus over four. The lower extremities showed some mild chronic venous insufficiency but no varicose veins. There was no evidence of diabetic neuropathy. No heart problem was documented. There is X-ray evidence of an abdominal aortic aneurysm. This is asymptomatic, and surgery is not anticipated. There is no complaint of chest pain. A consultative hearing evaluation was done because further documentation of severity was needed. The audiogram showed bilateral hearing loss between 65 and 85 decibels. Speech discrimination is 88 percent, and a hearing aid is recommended and used by the claimant. He can hear loud conversational speech and can hear over the phone.

None of the above impairments is of the severity described in the Listing of Impairments. The combination of impairments also does not meet or equal the listed impairments.

The evidence reveals the presence of diabetes, aortic aneurysm, and a hearing deficit. Per SSA-4734-F4, dated September 10, 2014, heavy lifting would be precluded due to the aneurysm. The claimant can lift and carry 25 pounds frequently and up to 50 pounds

occasionally. The hearing deficit and alleged insulin reactions would preclude work around dangerous machinery or at heights.

The claimant is 60 years old and has completed nine years of school, which is considered to be limited education. He has worked for 34 years as a wire drawer for a wire company.

This heavy, semiskilled work performed in a noisy and hazardous work setting required him to be on his feet all day, frequently lift 50-pound coils of wire, and occasionally lift coils that weigh 100 pounds. It also required frequent pushing, pulling, stooping, crouching, reaching, handling, and fingering for purposes of situating the coils on the wire-drawing machine and drawing the desired finished product. The claimant set up the machine, demonstrated knowledge of the characteristics of various metals, and assessed conformance to specifications. Demands of his past relevant work correlate to those of Wire Drawer (wire), DOT 614.382-010 [job description in the *Dictionary of Occupational Titles*].

The claimant's exertional limitations in themselves as translated into a maximum sustained RFC for medium work would prevent him from doing his past relevant work. The special medical-vocational characteristics pertaining to those cases that feature arduous, unskilled work, or no work are not present. The exertional capability to do medium work presents a potential occupational base of approximately 2,500 unskilled sedentary, light, and medium occupations, which represent a significant vocational opportunity. This individual's hearing impairment and the medical restriction to avoid working around dangerous machinery and at heights would only minimally narrow that potential occupational base; age, education, and past work experience under the framework provided by [Medical-Vocational] Rule 203.04, he is expected to effectuate a vocational accommodation to other work.

Some examples of unskilled occupations that are within his RFC include: Bagger (ret. tr.), DOT 920.687-014, Turner (can. & preserv.), DOT 522.687-038, and Crate Liner (furn.), DOT 920.687-078. According to data shown in County Business Patterns for 1982, Harris County, Texas, had over 230,000 employees working in the retail trade industry, over 30,000 of which were employed in grocery stores. Both the furniture manufacturing and wholesale furniture industries combined employed over 5,000 individuals. Another 200–500 worked at canning and preserving fruits and vegetables. Based on these figures, which pertain only to one county, it can be inferred reasonably that the cited occupations exist as individual jobs in significant numbers not only in the region in which the individual resides, but also throughout the national economy. Therefore, since he has the capacity to do other work, disability is not established.

 TIP

More technical rationales from real Forms SSA-4268 are below. These are from decisions to end benefits following a continuing disability review (CDR) and illustrate the many reasons benefits may be terminated. Again, explanations of abbreviations and medical terms have been added in brackets so the rationales are a little easier to follow.

Form SSA-4268, *Denials From Continuing Disability Review (CDR)*

Example 1: Not Severe; Medical Improvement (MI) Occurred

The beneficiary was found to be disabled beginning 8/10/2014, because of a fractured left femur with slow healing. The impairment met the requirements of Listing 1.06. Current evaluation is necessary because medical improvement was expected. He indicates that he is still unable to perform work activity due to a left leg problem. He has not engaged in any substantial gainful activity since onset.

Current medical evidence reveals that the disabled individual had full weight-bearing status at an examination in February 2016. X-rays interpreted at that time revealed that the fracture was well healed. A consultative orthopedic evaluation was secured because range-of-motion data were needed. The consulting orthopedic surgeon reported that the individual had good range of motion of both lower extremities. He walked with a normal gait and experienced no difficulty in getting on and off the examining table. His impairment does not meet or equal listing severity.

At the CPD [comparison point decision] the individual was unable to walk without crutches, and X-rays did not show the expected amount of healing. His impairment has decreased in severity because he is fully weight bearing, and an X-ray shows solid union; therefore, medical improvement has occurred. Since the beneficiary met a listing at the CPD but currently no longer meets that listing, the medical improvement is related to the ability to work. Although he alleges a left leg problem, his current impairment is not severe, as he now has no significant restrictions on standing, walking, lifting, or other work activities.

As medical improvement has occurred and the individual is able to engage in SGA, disability ceases April 2016, and benefits will terminate in June 2016.

Example 2: MI Occurred; Can Perform Past Work

This individual was found to be disabled beginning 8/17/2013 because of coronary artery disease. The impairment equaled Listing 4.04A1. The beneficiary has completed a nine-month trial work period. She continues to work as a telephone solicitor, with earnings indicative of SGA. Benefits have been stopped as indicated on SSA-833-U5 on 11/13/2015. She feels she still has a severe heart condition that limits activity. A current medical decision is needed to determine "impairment severity" and, thus, entitlement for an extended period of eligibility.

Medical evidence indicates that the beneficiary underwent bypass surgery in June 2014. Although she initially progressed well, she subsequently began to complain of chest pain and shortness of breath. She underwent a second bypass surgery in April 2015. Current examination revealed normal heart sounds with only occasional premature ventricular contractions. The beneficiary experiences chest pain infrequently with heavy exertion. The pain is relieved with nitroglycerin or rest. The doctor stated that the patient would not be able to return to work activity. The treating cardiologist reported in March 2016 that the beneficiary performed a stress test to 7 METS [metabolic equivalents]. A chest X-ray revealed only mild cardiomegaly. The treating doctor assessed that because of the beneficiary's history of heart disorder, she should avoid lifting in excess of 25 pounds.

The record reveals that the patient underwent two bypass surgeries for her heart disorder. Chest pain of cardiac origin is experienced infrequently, but a treadmill exercise test was negative at 5 METS. It showed abnormalities at 7 METS. Therefore, the evidence does not show current findings that meet or equal the listed impairments. The second bypass surgery improved circulation to the heart, and symptoms have decreased. Therefore, medical improvement has occurred.

At the time of the CPD, a listing was equaled. Since the impairment no longer meets or equals that listing, the medical improvement is related to the ability to work.

The record reveals that the beneficiary continues to have a severe cardiovascular impairment that limits her ability to perform basic work activities. There is a current capacity to lift a maximum of 20 pounds occasionally and 10 pounds frequently.

The beneficiary is limited to light work activity. Her past work from 3/2005 to 8/2010 was that of a laundry marker, which involved such activities as sorting laundry, putting names on articles, etc. This is a light, nonstressful job. Accordingly, she can return to her past relevant work, as she has the functional capacity to do light work.

Although the beneficiary's treating physician stated she would not be able to return to work, the weight to be given such statements depends upon the extent to which they are supported by specific and complete clinical findings and are consistent with other evidence in the beneficiary's case. The clinical findings and other evidence do not support the conclusion that the beneficiary is disabled for any gainful work.

Because medical improvement has been demonstrated by a decrease in medical severity related to the ability to work, and because the beneficiary is able to engage in SGA, impairment severity ceases in 3/2016.

Example 3: MI Occurred; Can Do Other Work

The beneficiary has been disabled since 2/6/2012 because of musculoskeletal injuries sustained in a motorcycle accident. He was found to be limited to sedentary work and [Medical-]Vocational Rule 201.09 directed a finding of disabled. He has not worked since his established onset date. The beneficiary alleges he remains unable to return to any work activity because he still has knee pain. Current evaluation is needed because medical improvement was expected.

The treating physician reported that he continued treating the beneficiary for complaints of pain to the lower extremities. He states that he treated the beneficiary with medication and advised him to exercise. X-rays taken at the examination on 1/8/2015 revealed only spurring in the right knee, in addition to old healed fractures. A consultative examination was arranged to obtain range of motion. Evidence from the consulting orthopedist dated 3/1/2015 reveals that the beneficiary continues to walk with an abnormal gait. Flexion of the right knee is limited to 120 degrees. The left can be fully flexed. Range of motion of the hips and ankles is normal. The impairment does not meet or equal the requirements of the listings.

At the comparison point, the beneficiary was unable to ambulate for short distances as a result of his right knee impairment. X-rays revealed that all other injuries were healed except the right knee, which did not have complete healing. Current medical evidence demonstrates a decrease in severity since an X-ray revealed that the right knee fracture is well healed with minimal spurring and there is only mild limitation of motion. Therefore, medical improvement has occurred, as there is a decrease in medical severity. He now has the ability to stand and walk six out of eight hours and to lift 20 pounds occasionally and ten pounds frequently, which is a wide range of light work. The medical improvement that has occurred is related to his ability to work, because he could only do sedentary work activity at the CPD. The beneficiary's impairment imposes significant restrictions on his ability to perform basic work activities and is severe.

Although the beneficiary alleges pain in the right knee, the fracture is well healed, with minimal spurring and mild limitation of motion. He is restricted to light work, but the clinical findings do not establish an impairment that produces pain of such severity as to prevent the beneficiary from performing any gainful activity.

The disabled individual is 53 years of age, has a limited education, and has a 20-year work history as a general laborer in a foundry, which is unskilled work involving heavy lifting and carrying. Since the beneficiary is limited to light work, he would be unable to perform his past work due to the exertional demands involved. The special medical-vocational characteristics pertaining to those cases

that feature arduous, unskilled work or no work are not present. The facts in this case correspond exactly with the criteria of [Medical-]Vocational Rule 202.10, which directs a finding of not disabled. Since there is medical improvement and the individual has the ability to do SGA, disability is ceased in 2/2015, and benefits will be terminated as of 4/2015.

Example 4: MI Occurred; Multiple Not Severe Impairments; Combined Effect Is Severe, but One Impairment Is a Subsequent Impairment; Can Perform Other Work

The beneficiary has been under a disability since 10/19/2013 due to rheumatic heart disease with mitral stenosis [narrowing of the mitral heart valve] and peptic ulcer [of intestine], which led to an allowance in the framework of [Medical-] Vocational Rule 202.10. The case is being evaluated now because medical improvement is possible. The beneficiary believes he is still disabled because of his heart condition, plus recent pulmonary disease. He attempted working a few years ago but had to stop after three weeks. There is no SGA issue.

Medical evidence reveals a history of rheumatic heart disease that required hospitalization for congestive heart failure. This has responded to treatment, and currently there is no chest pain and no evidence of pulmonary or peripheral edema, according to his physician. There are no symptoms related to peptic ulcer disease, since diet has been adjusted. Recently, shortness of breath has been increasing. He had been smoking two packs of cigarettes a day for 20 years but has stopped because of respiratory problems. A consultative examination was scheduled for evaluation of his respiratory impairment with pulmonary function testing.

On physical examination, height was 69 inches and weight was 180 pounds. Breath sounds were diminished, with prolonged expiration and an expiratory wheeze. The chest was otherwise clear. On examination of the heart, a diastolic rumble [abnormal heart sound] at the apex. An EKG showed a prominent wide P-wave suggestive of left atrial enlargement, which was confirmed on the chest X-ray. The heart size otherwise was within normal limits. The lung fields were hyperaerated [over-expanded] and diaphragms were somewhat flattened [signs of emphysema]. Ventilatory function [breathing test] studies done by the consultant revealed that post-bronchodilator [drugs], FEV1 was 1.9 liters and MVV 76 liters per minute [abnormally low results indicate emphysema, but not at listing-level severity].

Current medical findings do not meet or equal the findings described in any listed impairment. There is no current evidence of congestive heart failure and no active ulcer. This shows medical improvement, as there is a decrease in the medical severity of impairments present at the CPD. At that time, the functional capacity was for light work activity. The current RFC, considering only the rheumatic heart disease and peptic ulcer, shows full capacity to do all work activities, and these impairments are now not severe. Therefore, medical improvement related to ability to do work is demonstrated.

Although the heart and digestive impairments are not severe when considered alone, considering their effect on ability to perform work activities in combination with a respiratory impairment, the beneficiary would be restricted to lifting up to 50 pounds occasionally and 25 pounds frequently. The beneficiary now has the capacity to perform a full range of medium work. He cannot perform his prior work as baker helper (heavy, unskilled work). It involved much lifting of things, such as bags of flour (up to 100 pounds), racks of baked items, and piles of unfolded boxes. Although his most recent work was arduous and unskilled, it lasted only 17 years, and he previously did semiskilled work. Therefore, the special medical-vocational characteristics pertaining to those cases, which feature arduous, unskilled work, or no work, are not present. He is of advanced age (56) with limited education (grade 6) and meets [Medical-]Vocational Rule 203.11, which indicates the ability to do SGA. Because there is medical improvement, demonstrated by decreased medical severity and related to the ability to work, and the individual has the ability to do SGA, disability is ceased on 4/2015. Benefits will be terminated 6/2015.

Example 5: MI Occurred; It Is Obvious That the Vocational Exception Also Applies; Can Perform Other Work

The beneficiary was initially allowed disability benefits from 12/7/2013, because of injuries received in a motorcycle accident. At the time of the CPD, he had a traumatic left above-the-knee amputation with persistent stump complications, inability to use a prosthesis, and a right recurrent shoulder dislocation. The impairment was found to meet Listing 1.05B. The current evaluation is necessary because medical improvement was expected. The beneficiary states that he is still disabled because of the left leg amputation and difficulty walking with his prosthesis. He has not worked since the onset date.

The medical evidence reveals that following his left above-the-knee amputation in 12/2013, the beneficiary experienced persistent pain and tenderness about the stump and underwent three stump revisions. The most recent revision was 2/1/2015 for excision of a bony spur and painful scar. Office notes from the beneficiary's treating physician show that following the latest stump revision, the beneficiary was able to wear his prosthesis over an extended period of time without much discomfort. Recent examination of the stump revealed that there were no neuromas [painful nerve tangles] or other abnormalities. An X-ray did not demonstrate any bony spurs or complications. Furthermore, the beneficiary has had no recent problems with right shoulder dislocation. He had full range of motion of his shoulder without pain or instability. The beneficiary no longer has an impairment that meets or equals the level of severity described in the listings.

The beneficiary was unable to use his prosthesis at the time of the comparison point decision because of repeated stump complications. Current medical findings show that these complications have resolved, and the beneficiary is able to ambulate with his prosthesis over an extended period of time without discomfort. Therefore, medical improvement has occurred. Although he alleges difficulty walking with his prosthesis, the beneficiary has the residual functional capacity to stand and walk for two hours and to sit for six hours with no further restrictions. Since his current condition no longer meets or equals Listing 1.05B, his medical improvement is related to the ability to work.

The beneficiary received evaluation and counseling through the Department of Vocational Rehabilitation. He obtained funds to attend a two-year program at Central University. In December 2015, he received an associate degree in computer science. The combination of education and counseling constitute vocational therapy.

The beneficiary has a severe impairment that limits him to the performance of sedentary work. The beneficiary is 30 years old, with 16 years of education. He has four years of relevant work experience as a painter. This job involved standing and walking at least six out of eight hours. The beneficiary is unable to perform his past work because of limitations on standing and walking. The special medical-vocational characteristics pertaining to those cases that feature arduous, unskilled work or no work are not present. Additionally, his ability to perform sedentary work has been enhanced by vocational therapy; therefore, the vocational therapy exception applies. The beneficiary meets [Medical-]Vocational Rule 201.28, which directs a decision of not disabled. Medical improvement is established, the vocational therapy exception applies, and the beneficiary is able to engage in SGA. Therefore, the beneficiary can no longer be considered disabled under the provisions of the Social Security Act as of May 2016, and benefits are terminated as of July 2016.

Example 6: MI Is Not Related to Ability to Do Work, but Vocational Therapy Exception Applies; Can Perform Other Work

The beneficiary was found to be disabled beginning 8/3/2013 as a result of a crush injury with fracture of his left ankle. He was restricted to the performance of light work and thereby met the requirements of [Medical-]Vocational Rule 202.06, which directed a decision of disabled. Current medical evidence was obtained because medical improvement was expected. The beneficiary states that he continues to be disabled because of left ankle pain and

difficulty standing and walking. He has not worked since onset of his disability.

Recent medical information from the beneficiary's physician shows that the beneficiary continues to have pain and numbness in his left foot. An ankle fusion was done 9/2014 to provide a stable joint and to permit weight bearing. He is fully weight bearing now but walks with a prominent limp. In order to further document severity and obtain a current X-ray, the beneficiary was examined by a consulting orthopedic physician. Clinical examination of the left ankle revealed some thickening of the heel, but the fusion appeared to be stable. Ankle movements are limited to 10 degrees dorsiflexion [upward movement] and 20 degrees plantar-flexion [downward movement]. An X-ray was consistent with a healed subtalar arthrodesis [surgical ankle fusion] and moderate traumatic degenerative changes. Neurological evaluation revealed an absent left ankle jerk and inability to walk on heels and toes. There was decreased sensation over the lateral and dorsal [upper] aspects of the left foot and decreased strength of the left extensor hallucis longus [muscle that moves the great toe upward].

The beneficiary's impairments do not meet or equal the level of severity described in the listings. An X-ray shows that arthritis has developed at the fracture site. The beneficiary continues to experience left ankle pain. Further, he has an abnormal gait and limitation of motion of his ankle. However, since the ankle fusion, the beneficiary is fully weight bearing, which is medical improvement since the CPD. His left ankle impairment continues to restrict his ability to stand and walk to six hours during an eight-hour day. The beneficiary remains limited to the performance of a wide range of light work, lifting 20 lbs. occasionally and ten pounds frequently. This is the same RFC as that at the CPD. Therefore, the medical improvement is not related to his ability to work.

Since the comparison point decision, the beneficiary underwent vocational counseling through the Department of Rehabilitation Services and enrolled in an 18-month training program on small appliance repair. He completed the course on 11/30/2015, after working on appliances such as radios, electrical tools, and a variety of small household appliances.

The recent completion of this specialized training course, in conjunction with counseling, constitutes vocational therapy. This therapy has enhanced the beneficiary's ability to perform work because he has acquired a skill that provides for direct entry into light work.

Although the beneficiary continues to experience left ankle pain, he is fully weight bearing and is able to perform light work. The clinical findings do not establish an impairment that results in pain of such severity as to preclude him from engaging in any substantial gainful activity.

The beneficiary has a severe impairment that restricts him to light work. He is 57 years old with 12 years of education. He has six years of relevant work experience as a truck driver, which is a medium semi-skilled job. The beneficiary is unable to perform work as a truck driver because of the exertional demands of the job, and there are no transferable skills. The special medical-vocational characteristics pertaining to those cases which feature arduous, unskilled work or no work are not present. However, as a result of vocational therapy since the comparison point decision, the beneficiary has obtained job skills that are useful in the performance of light work and, therefore, meets [Medical-]Vocational Rule 202.08, which directs a decision of not disabled. He can do such occupations as an Electrical-Appliance Repairer (DOT 723.381-010), a Radio Repairer (DOT 720.281-010), or an Electrical Tool Repairer (DOT 729.281-022), all skilled light work in the electrical equipment industry. According to the Labor Market Trends Bulletin and the Virginia Department of Labor and Industry, over 30,000 individuals are employed in the electrical equipment industry in Virginia, and the cited occupations are well represented throughout that industry. It can be inferred that the occupations exist as individual jobs in significant numbers in the region where the individual lives and throughout the national economy.

Although there has been no medical improvement in the beneficiary's impairment related to the ability to work, the vocational therapy exception to medical improvement applies, and the beneficiary is able to engage in SGA. The beneficiary is no longer disabled as of 3/2016, and benefits are terminated as of 5/2016.

Example 7: No MI; Not Severe Impairment(s), but Error Exception Applies

The beneficiary was initially allowed disability benefits from 6/21/2016 because of chronic obstructive pulmonary disease and asthma. She was restricted to light work and [Medical-]Vocational Rule 202.09 was applied. Current findings were obtained because medical improvement is possible. The beneficiary alleges that she is still unable to work because of emphysema and has not worked since her onset.

A report from the beneficiary's treating physician states that the beneficiary has chronic obstructive pulmonary disease and complains of shortness of breath. She also has been diagnosed as having asthma, allergic sinusitis, and hay fever. These conditions are controlled with medications. A consultative exam was necessary to obtain ventilatory studies. A chest X-ray revealed mild chronic obstructive pulmonary disease. Pulmonary function studies [4/2/2016] showed FEV1 of 1.7 and MVV of 75. A physical exam showed a height of 5 feet 2 inches and weight of 120 pounds. There were decreased breath sounds; otherwise, the chest was clear [normal] to percussion [thumping] and auscultation [listening].

The impairment does not meet or equal the level of severity described in the listings.

The beneficiary was receiving treatment for asthma and COPD at the comparison point. She was hospitalized in October 2016 for an asthma attack. Ventilatory studies done during the admission showed a functional restriction to light work, and the claim was allowed using a [Medical-]Vocational rule. Review of the records demonstrates that the studies were done while the beneficiary was in an acute phase of asthma. Wheezes and rales [abnormal breath sounds] were noted, and no bronchodilator [drug] was administered prior to testing. Documentation guidelines in effect at the CPD prohibit the use of ventilatory studies performed in the presence of bronchospasm [narrowed airways]. Outpatient records sent later reveal that ventilatory testing was repeated in December 2016. These studies show an FEV1 of 1.9 and MVV of 84. Medical improvement has not occurred [because there is no significant difference between the 4/2016 and 12/2016 breathing test results]. However, the error exception applies because the beneficiary was allowed ventilatory studies performed in the presence of bronchospasm without the administration of bronchodilators, and additional evidence that relates to the CPD shows that if that evidence had been considered in making the CPD, disability would not have been established.

The beneficiary does not have any restrictions on standing, walking, or lifting as a result of her breathing impairment, and her impairment is not severe. Therefore, the beneficiary retains the capacity to do SGA.

The error exception of the Medical Improvement Review Standard (MIRS) applies, and the beneficiary has the ability to perform SGA. Disability ceases April 2016, and benefits will terminate as of June 2016.

Example 8: Failure to Cooperate

The beneficiary has been under a disability since 4/13/2010 due to histiocytic lymphoma of the ileum [lymph node cancer affecting the third part of the small intestine] that equaled the listing. Current evaluation is necessary because medical improvement is possible. There has been no work since onset. The beneficiary says he is still disabled because of stomach problems. He had chemotherapy and radiation therapy after his operation. Because he has ulcers, he must avoid certain foods.

The only treatment source given by the beneficiary was Wadsworth Memorial Hospital. The Oncology [cancer] Clinic notes indicate he had completed chemotherapy. He was last seen 12/8/2015, at which time he was progressing satisfactorily. He weighed 170 pounds with height of 6 feet. Lymph nodes were shotty [small and hard, like shot], and the liver was enlarged. Since no current medical evidence was available, a consultative examination was scheduled for February 10, 2016.

The beneficiary failed to keep the consultative examination. He was contacted, and another appointment was scheduled, which he again failed to keep. On 3/1/2016 personal contact was made by the District Office at the beneficiary's home. The need for current medical evidence and for his cooperation in going for a CE was explained. There was no indication of any mental impairment or other condition that would make him unable to cooperate. Since he agreed to keep a CE, another appointment was scheduled for 3/9/2016. The beneficiary did not keep the CE, and DDS was unable to contact him by telephone. On 3/15/2016, written notice that failure to cooperate could result in termination was sent to the beneficiary. He did not respond.

At the CPD, the beneficiary had malignant lymphoma of the ileum with metastasis. The most recent available evidence from 12/8/2015 indicates satisfactory progress. There is no current medical evidence available to determine if medical improvement has occurred, and the beneficiary has repeatedly failed to cooperate in efforts to obtain current medical evidence. Therefore, since there is failure to cooperate, a group II exception to medical improvement, disability is ceased 3/2016, the month the beneficiary was notified that failure to cooperate could result in termination of benefits. Disability will terminate 5/2016.

Medical-Vocational Rules

I f you aren't eligible for disability based solely on your illness or injury, the Social Security Administration looks at other issues to determine whether you meet eligibility requirements in another way.

The SSA uses the following tables of medical-vocational rules to decide whether physical impairment claims should be approved or denied based on a combination of how much work you can do (called your *residual functional capacity*, or RFC), age, education, and work experience. These rules are applied only in claims where the RFC is for sedentary, light, or medium work without other restrictions. If the RFC has additional special restrictions, then a vocational analyst will need to look at the claim. Other restrictions can include almost anything, such as the claimant's inability to work around excessive dust and fumes, inability to do fine movements with the fingers, inability to bend the back frequently, or inability to use leg controls.

At Disability Determination Services (DDS), a vocational analyst is an experienced disability examiner who has special training to evaluate the combination of RFC, age, education, and work experience

in relation to a claimant's ability to perform various jobs.

Claimants capable of heavy work can do such high levels of physical exertion that the SSA considers them to have "not severe" (mild or slight) impairments, and so they don't actually receive RFCs for heavy work.

If your physical impairments are significant but not severe enough to meet any listing, the medical-vocational rules will give you a good idea whether you could still be eligible for benefits. You can find out what your RFC is from the SSA after a determination has been made on your claim.

The medical-vocational rules in these tables are applied only when your RFC is so physically restrictive that you can't return to your prior work, if you had any. The medical-vocational rules help determine whether you could do any other kind of work. (If you can return to your prior work based on your RFC, the SSA will simply deny your claim, stating that you can return to your prior work.)

The rules are a consistent way for the SSA to determine disability. There are no similar medical-vocational rule tables for mental impairments.

If you're less than six months away from your next birthday, your age will be counted as if you have reached that day. For example, if you're 49½ years old, the SSA will consider you 50 years old.

Review Chapter 8, "Whether You Can Do Some Work: Your RFC," and Chapter 9, "How Age, Education, and Work Experience Matter," for information that will help you use these tables.

Abbreviations	
AA	Advanced age (55 and older)
CAAA	Closely approaching advanced age (50–54 years old)
CARA	Closely approaching retirement age (60 and older)
YI	Younger individual (less than 50 years old)
M	Marginal education (6th grade or less)
LL	Limited or less education (grades 7–11)
HSG	High school graduate or more (high school graduate, college graduate, or equivalent special training)
US	Unskilled
SS	Semiskilled
S	Skilled
N	None
I	Illiterate

Table No. 1: Sedentary RFC				
Rule	Age	Education	Previous Work Experience	Decision
201.01	AA (55 and older)	LL	US or N	Disabled
201.02	AA (55 and older)	LL	S or SS—skills not transferable	Disabled
201.03	AA (55 and older)	LL	S or SS—skills transferable	Not disabled
201.04	AA (55 and older)	HSG—education does not provide for direct entry into skilled work.	US or N	Disabled
201.05	AA (55 and older)	HSG—education provides for direct entry into skilled work.	US or N	Not disabled
201.06	AA (55 and older)	HSG—education does not provide for direct entry into skilled work.	S or SS—skills not transferable	Disabled
201.07	AA (55 and older)	HSG—education does not provide for direct entry into skilled work.	S or SS—skills transferable	Not disabled
201.08	AA (55 and older)	HSG—education provides for direct entry into skilled work.	S or SS—skills not transferable	Not disabled
201.09	CAAA (50–54)	LL	US or N	Disabled
201.10	CAAA (50–54)	LL	S or SS—skills not transferable	Disabled
201.11	CAAA (50–54)	LL	S or SS—skills transferable	Not disabled
201.12	CAAA (50–54)	HSG—education does not provide for direct entry into skilled work.	US or N	Disabled
201.13	CAAA (50–54)	HSG—education provides for direct entry into skilled work.	US or N	Not disabled
201.14	CAAA (50–54)	HSG—education does not provide for direct entry into skilled work.	S or SS—skills not transferable	Disabled
201.15	CAAA (50–54)	HSG—education does not provide for direct entry into skilled work.	S or SS—skills transferable	Not disabled
201.16	CAAA (50–54)	HSG—education provides for direct entry into skilled work	S or SS—skills not transferable	Not disabled

Rule	Age	Education	Previous Work Experience	Decision
	Table No. 1: Sedentary RFC (continued)			
201.17	YI (45–49)	I	US or N	Disabled
201.18	YI (45–49)	LL	US or N	Not disabled
201.19	YI (45–49)	LL	S or SS—skills not transferable	Not disabled
201.20	YI (45–49)	LL	S or SS—skills transferable	Not disabled
201.21	YI (45–49)	HSG	S or SS—skills not transferable	Not disabled
201.22	YI (45–49)	HSG	S or SS—skills transferable	Not disabled
201.23	YI (18–44)	I	US or N	Not disabled
201.24	YI (18–44)	LL	US or N	Not disabled
201.25	YI (18–44)	LL	S or SS—skills not transferable	Not disabled
201.26	YI (18–44)	LL	S or SS—skills transferable	Not disabled
201.27	YI (18–44)	HSG	US or N	Not disabled
201.28	YI (18–44)	HSG	S or SS—skills not transferable	Not disabled
201.29	YI (18–44)	HSG	S or SS—skills transferable	Not disabled

Rule	Age	Education	Previous Work Experience	Decision
		Table No. 2: Light RFC		
202.01	AA (55 and older)	LL	US or N	Disabled
202.02	AA (55 and older)	LL	S or SS—skills not transferable	Disabled
202.03	AA (55 and older)	LL	S or SS—skills transferable	Not disabled
202.04	AA (55 and older)	HSG—education does not provide for direct entry into skilled work.	US or N	Disabled
202.05	AA (55 and older)	HSG—education provides for direct entry into skilled work.	US or N	Not disabled
202.06	AA (55 and older)	HSG—education does not provide for direct entry into skilled work.	S or SS—skills not transferable	Disabled
202.07	AA (55 and older)	HSG—education does not provide for direct entry into skilled work.	S or SS—skills transferable	Not disabled
202.08	AA (55 and older)	HSG—education provides for direct entry into skilled work.	S or SS—skills not transferable	Not disabled
202.09	CAAA (50–54)	I	US or N	Disabled
202.10	CAAA (50–54)	LL	US or N	Not disabled
202.11	CAAA (50–54)	LL	S or SS—skills not transferable	Not disabled
202.12	CAAA (50–54)	LL	S or SS—skills transferable	Not disabled
202.13	CAAA (50–54)	HSG	US or N	Not disabled
202.14	CAAA (50–54)	HSG	S or SS—skills not transferable	Not disabled
202.15	CAAA (50–54)	HSG	S or SS—skills transferable	Not disabled
202.16	YI (18–49)	I	US or N	Not disabled
202.17	YI (18–49)	LL	US or N	Not disabled
202.18	YI (18–49)	LL	S or SS—skills not transferable	Not disabled
202.19	YI (18–49)	LL	S or SS—skills transferable	Not disabled
202.20	YI (18–49)	HSG	US or N	Not disabled
202.21	YI (18–49)	HSG	S or SS—skills not transferable	Not disabled
202.22	YI (18–49)	HSG	S or SS—skills transferable	Not disabled

	Table No. 3: Medium RFC			
Rule	**Age**	**Education**	**Previous Work Experience**	**Decision**
203.01	CARA (60–64)	M or N	US or N	Disabled
203.02	CARA (60–64)	LL	N	Disabled
203.03	CARA (60–64)	LL	US	Not disabled
203.04	CARA (60–64)	LL	S or SS—skills not transferable	Not disabled
203.05	CARA (60–64)	LL	S or SS—skills transferable	Not disabled
203.06	CARA (60–64)	HSG	US or N	Not disabled
203.07	CARA (60–64)	HSG—education does not provide for direct entry into skilled work.	S or SS—skills not transferable	Not disabled
203.08	CARA (60–64)	HSG—education does not provide for direct entry into skilled work.	S or SS—skills transferable	Not disabled
203.09	CARA (60–64)	HSG—education provides for direct entry into skilled work.	S or SS—skills not transferable	Not disabled
203.10	AA (55–59)	LL	N	Disabled
203.11	AA (55–59)	LL	US	Not disabled
203.12	AA (55–59)	LL	S or SS—skills not transferable	Not disabled
203.13	AA (55–59)	LL	S or SS—skills transferable	Not disabled
203.14	AA (55–59)	HSG	US or N	Not disabled
203.15	AA (55–59)	HSG—education does not provide for direct entry into skilled work.	S or SS—skills not transferable	Not disabled
203.16	AA (55–59)	HSG—education does not provide for direct entry into skilled work.	S or SS—skills transferable	Not disabled
203.17	AA (55–59)	HSG—education provides for direct entry into skilled work.	S or SS–skills not transferable	Not disabled
203.18	CAAA (50–54)	LL	US or N	Not disabled
203.19	CAAA (50–54)	LL	S or SS—skills not transferable	Not disabled

Table No. 3: Medium RFC (continued)

Rule	Age	Education	Previous Work Experience	Decision
203.20	CAAA (50–54)	LL	S or SS—skills transferable	Not disabled
203.21	CAAA (50–54)	HSG	US or N	Not disabled
203.22	CAAA (50–54)	HSG—education does not provide for direct entry into skilled work.	S or SS—skills not transferable	Not disabled
203.23	CAAA (50–54)	HSG—education does not provide for direct entry into skilled work.	S or SS—skills transferable	Not disabled
203.24	CAAA (50–54)	HSG—education provides for direct entry into skilled work.	S or SS—skills not transferable	Not disabled
203.25	YI (18–49)	LL	US or N	Not disabled
203.26	YI (18–49)	LL	S or SS—skills not transferable	Not disabled
203.27	YI (18–49)	LL	S or SS—skills transferable	Not disabled
203.28	YI (18–49)	HSG	US or N	Not disabled
203.29	YI (18–49)	HSG—education does not provide for direct entry into skilled work.	S or SS—skills not transferable	Not disabled
203.30	YI (18–49)	HSG—education does not provide for direct entry into skilled work.	S or SS—skills transferable	Not disabled
203.31	YI (18–49)	HSG—education provides for direct entry into skilled work.	S or SS—skills not transferable	Not disabled

How to Use the Medical Listings on Nolo.com

This book comes with PDF files containing the SSA's disability listings that you can download here: **www.nolo.com/back-of-book/QSS.html**

To use the files, your computer must have a PDF reader such as Adobe Acrobat *Reader*, (free software available from Adobe.com.)

List of Files on Nolo.com

To download the following Medical Listings, go to: **www.nolo.com/back-of-book/QSS.html**

Part Name	File Name
Musculoskeletal Disorders and Growth Impairments	Part1.pdf
Vision, Balance, Hearing, and Speech Impairments	Part2.pdf
Breathing Disorders	Part3.pdf
Heart and Blood Vessel Diseases	Part4.pdf
Digestive System Diseases	Part5.pdf
Kidney Disease	Part6.pdf
Blood Diseases	Part7.pdf
Skin Diseases	Part8.pdf
Hormone Disorders	Part9.pdf
Multiple Body System Disorders	Part10.pdf
Nervous System Disorders	Part11.pdf
Mental Disorders	Part12.pdf
Cancer	Part13.pdf
Immune System Disorders	Part14.pdf

Index

A

Ability to work
  at a different job, 172, 174, 199, 228, 229, 233–234, 398–400, 402–408, 411
  appeals decisions and, 228, 299
  assessment in sequential evaluation process, 168–169, 171–172, 192–193
  benefits eligibility and, 2–3, 19–20, 108, 168–169, 171–172
  continuing disability review and, 344, 353, 363–364, 369–370, 372–373
  documenting your disability's impacts on your job, 28, 71
  failure to follow prescribed therapy to restore your ability, 216–220
  the medical improvement review standard (MIRS) and, 365–366, 367, 369–370, 372, 374, 376
  RFC work categories, 175, 177–185
  vocational expert review and testimony (ALJ hearings), 203, 205, 278–279, 283, 285, 288–289
  at your prior job, 171–172, 174, 228, 233, 398–399, 401–402, 412
  See also Functional limitations; Medical-vocational assessments; Returning to work; RFCs; Vocational *entries*
ABLE savings accounts, 17
Acceptable medical sources, 28, 122–123, 153
Activities of daily living (ADLs), 72, 137, 354, 364
  See also Functional limitations
Adaptability and social integration, 189
Address changes
  reporting to SSA, 215, 302–304, 309–310, 314–315
  See also Foreign residents
ADLs. *See* Activities of daily living

Administrative law judges (ALJs), 22, 76, 203, 205, 226, 229, 267–268, 275
  See also ALJ hearings
Adoptions and adopted children, 91, 307, 313, 315
Advanced practice registered nurses (APRNs), 123
Age
  appeal decisions and, 227, 228, 229
  CDR evaluations and, 345, 346, 370
  proof of, 31, 70, 93
  severity of disability and, 21, 166
  Social Security full retirement age, 8, 10
  SSDI dependents' benefits eligibility requirements, 11–12, 90–91, 93
  SSDI eligibility requirements, 8, 10, 93
  as vocational factor, 74, 175, 177, 192, 193–195, 412
  vocational rehabilitation eligibility and, 205
  See also Children's claims and benefits
AIDS/HIV, 108, 110, 117, 118
AIME (average indexed monthly earnings), 297–298
Alcohol use or abuse, 86, 219, 221–222, 312, 318–319
ALJ hearings, 267–287
  attending, 279–281
  attorney advisor proceedings, 274
  authorized representative for, 378
  claims allowed for mild impairments, 371
  consultative examinations, 284, 285
  continuances and posthearing conferences, 287
  continuation of benefits during, 262
  forms for, 268–270
  forwarding forms to SSA, 271
  in-person, 275, 277
  medical expert testimony, 76
  Notice of Disability Review, 271, 272–273

 **NOLO**

More from Nolo

Nolo.com offers a large library of legal solutions and forms, created by Nolo's in-house legal editors. These reliable documents can be prepared in minutes.

Create a Document Online

Incorporation. Incorporate your business in any state.

LLC Formation. Gain asset protection and pass-through tax status in any state.

Will. Nolo has helped people make over 2 million wills. Is it time to make or revise yours?

Living Trust (avoid probate). Plan now to save your family the cost, delays, and hassle of probate.

Download Useful Legal Forms

Nolo.com has hundreds of top quality legal forms available for download:

- bill of sale
- promissory note
- nondisclosure agreement
- LLC operating agreement
- corporate minutes
- commercial lease and sublease
- motor vehicle bill of sale
- consignment agreement
- and many more.

www.nolo.com

 **NOLO**

Save 15% *off your next order*

Register your Nolo purchase, and we'll send you a
coupon for 15% off your next Nolo.com order!

Nolo.com/customer-support/productregistration

On Nolo.com you'll also find:

Books & Software

Nolo publishes hundreds of great books and software programs for consumers and
business owners. Order a copy, or download an ebook version instantly, at Nolo.com.

Online Forms

You can quickly and easily make a will or living trust, form an LLC or corporation,
or make hundreds of other forms—online.

Free Legal Information

Thousands of articles answer common questions about everyday legal issues,
including wills, bankruptcy, small business formation, divorce, patents,
employment, and much more.

Plain-English Legal Dictionary

Stumped by jargon? Look it up in America's most up-to-date source for definitions
of legal terms, free at Nolo.com.

Lawyer Directory

Nolo's consumer-friendly lawyer directory provides in-depth profiles of lawyers all
over America. You'll find information you need to choose the right lawyer.

QSS12